THE SAFFRON WAVE

THE SAFFRON WAVE

DEMOCRACY AND HINDU NATIONALISM IN MODERN INDIA

Thomas Blom Hansen

PRINCETON UNIVERSITY PRESS   PRINCETON, NEW JERSEY

Copyright © 1999 by Princeton University Press
Published by Princeton University Press, 41 William Street,
Princeton, New Jersey 08540
In the United Kingdom: Princeton University Press,
Chichester, West Sussex
All Rights Reserved

Library of Congress Cataloging-in-Publication Data
Hansen, Thomas Blom, 1958–.
The saffron wave : democracy and Hindu nationalism
in modern India / Thomas Blom Hansen.
p. cm.
Includes bibliographical references and index.
ISBN 0-691-00670-9 (alk. paper). — ISBN 0-691-00671-7 (pbk. : alk. paper)
1. Hinduism and politics—India. 2. Nationalism—Religious aspects—
Hinduism. 3. India—Politics and government—1977– I. Title.
BL1215.P65
294.5′5′0954—dc21   98-33355

This book has been composed in Palatino

The paper used in this publication meets the minimum requirements
of ANSI/NISO Z39.48-1992 (R1997) (*Permanence of Paper*)

http://pup.princeton.edu

Printed in the United States of America

10 9 8 7 6 5 4 3 2 1

10 9 8 7 6 5 4 3 2 1
(Pbk.)

Contents

THE SAFFRON WAVE

Introduction

Hindu Nationalism and Democracy in India

WITHIN THE PAST DECADE, the Hindu nationalist movement in India, led by the militant organization Rashtriya Swayamsevak Sangh (RSS), with branches and subsidiaries in many fields of life in contemporary India, has grown into the most powerful cluster of political and cultural organizations in the country. Hindu nationalist agendas, discourses, and institutions have gradually penetrated everyday life and have acquired a growing, if not uncontested, social respectability in contemporary Indian society.

In the general elections in February 1998, the political wing of the Hindu nationalist movement, the Bharatiya Janata Party (BJP), polled more than a quarter of the popular vote in India and emerged as the largest party in the Lok Sabha in Delhi. In late March 1998, the BJP's leader, Atal Behari Vajpayee, became India's prime minister, in charge of a fragile coalition government formed by the BJP and twelve smaller regional parties. Less than two months later, on the 11th and 13th of May, in Pokhran in the Rajasthan desert, five nuclear bombs were tested. This instantaneously put India on the global map as a nuclear power and initiated a new phase in the decade-old arms race between India and Pakistan, and it generated deep worries in western governments and publics. The decision to assert India's place in the world by acquiring nuclear capabilities was met with general approval among political parties in India from left to right. The response from newspapers seemed even more positive, opinion polls indicated overwhelming support to the decision, and the BJP could now appear on the domestic scene in its much-desired role as the most resolute defender of India's national pride and its national interest. When a local RSS organizer in the western state of Gujarat told a journalist, "after the nuclear tests, many other nations have realized that India is not merely a developing nation, but a superpower," he was not merely articulating a Hindu nationalist sentiment.[1] His and the RSS's exhilaration at a newfound national self-respect seemed to resonate with widely held perceptions of nation, cultural pride, and India's place in global hierarchies. Complex questions of how, and why, India's Hindu nationalists could acquire the authority to enunciate this broader quest for recognition and national identity—of how and why they could ensure their popular mandate to govern—arise out of these recent events. One strand of academic work explains the current dominant position of the Hindu nationalists as the result of decades of systematic, painstaking organizational work and imaginative political strategies (Jaffrelot 1996; Basu et al. 1993). Another strand interprets Hindu nationalism in more cultural and historical terms, and argues that the Hindu nationalists could be successful because they were drawing on older reserves of "religious nationalism" that always were central to most forms of Indian nationalism (see for example, van der Veer 1994).

This book is about the processes that moved Hindu nationalism from the margins of Indian society to its center stage. It tries to incorporate both these strands of academic work on Hindu nationalism, and in some ways to go a step further. The book explores some of the broader conditions of possibility in terms of political discourse—forms of governance and political strategies—that made it possible both to enunciate the notion of a "Hindu nation," and to organize it in changing forms up to the present day. I try to understand the history and contemporary articulations of the Hindu nationalist movement in terms of how, in various periods, it was made possible (and impossible) by broader discursive formations of nationalisms; by broader issues of identity, particularly in contemporary urban India; and by continuities and discontinuities between colonial and postcolonial governmentalities, regimes, and genres of political representation.

My main argument is that Hindu nationalism has emerged and taken shape neither in the political system as such nor in the religious field, but in the broader realm of what we may call public culture—the public space in which a society and its constituent individuals and communities imagine, represent, and recognize themselves through political discourse, commercial and cultural expressions, and representations of state and civic organizations. The Hindu nationalists desire to transform Indian public culture into a sovereign, disciplined national culture rooted in what is claimed to be a superior ancient Hindu past, and to impose a corporatist and disciplined social and political organization upon society. According to the movement, the Indian nation can only be reinvigorated when its rightful proprietors, the Hindu majority, resurrect a strong sense of Hindutva (Hinduness). This majoritarian call for Hindutva combines well-established paternalist and xenophobic discourses with democratic and universalist discourses on rights and entitlements, and has successfully articulated desires, anxieties, and fractured subjectivities in both urban and rural India. I argue that Hindu nationalism represents a "conservative revolution," premised upon and yet reacting against a broader democratic transformation of both the political field and the public culture in postcolonial India. The intensification of political mobilization among the lower castes and the minorities has, along with the rise of ambiguous desires of consumerism in everyday life, exposure to global cultural and economic flows, and so on, fractured social imaginings and notions of order and hierarchy, not least within the large middle class and dominant communities in contemporary India. I argue that it was the desire for recognition within an increasingly global horizon, and the simultaneous anxieties of being encroached upon by the Muslims, the plebeians, and the poor that over the last decade have prompted millions of Hindus to respond to the call for Hindutva at the polls and in the streets, and to embrace Hindu nationalist promises of order, discipline, and collective strength.

Hindu Nationalism and Postcolonial Trajectories of Democracy

One of the most remarkable features of the entire phenomenon of Hindu nationalism is the relative ease with which it has fitted into most of the authorized discourses on India and more generally on politics and culture in the postcolonial world, as they circulate inside as well as outside India. The advent of Hindu nationalism, the images of Hindu zealots razing the Babri Masjid in Ayodhya in 1992, and of firebrand orators in front of massive crowds, seem to resonate all to well with dominant perceptions of Indian democracy as somehow incomplete and immature: full of corruption, vulgar manipulators, campaigning film stars, colorful imagery presented to impressionable illiterates not capable of making qualified choices.

We should, however, remind ourselves that Hindu nationalism has emerged out of the longest, most sustained, and most successful trajectory of democracy anywhere in the postcolonial world, at the moment of its most decisive turn toward an unprecedented degree of pluralism, in the wake of the disintegration of Congress's sway over the Indian state and polity. Hindu nationalism's political success does not, in other words, grow out of the deficiencies of democracy but is the product of a series of intensely fought elections over the last decade, and of equally intense battles over religious sites, rituals, and spaces; over the meanings of shared symbols of Indian culture; over the meaning of secularism, history, and so on. However much we may disagree with the objectives and with the pompous and xenophobic style of the Hindu nationalist movement, and without exonerating its frequent

reliance on violence and hate speech, we have to admit that the movement has grown and come to power largely by obeying the procedures
of parliamentary democracy. The authoritarian organization of the
movement and much Hindu nationalist rhetoric leave no doubt that
many Hindu nationalists have only a skin-deep commitment to democratic procedures. Nonetheless, the very fact that this movement has
had to respect the judiciary, the electoral process, and the "rules of the
game" in the political field testifies to how well-entrenched democratic
procedures are in India. At the same time, the success of Hindu nationalism has also revealed how feeble the notions of tolerance, equality,
and rights have become within large groups of the relatively privileged
Indians who form the core of the BJP's constituency.

This opens the larger question of the forms that democratic discourse
and practices have historically taken in India. Was the political culture
of the so-called liberal middle class, which provided the backbone of
the nationalist movement and later the independent nation-state, ever
liberal and democratic? Or was it rather dominated by a paternalist
nationalist discourse within which ordinary Indians merely provided
the necessary but uncomfortable numerical strength? Is Hindu nationalism really revealing the dark side of the middle-class culture and social world of the "educated sections" who have dominated Indian public culture and the Indian state for so long—the authoritarian longings,
the complacency, and the fear of the "underdog," the "masses," and
the Muslims?

The Indian experience of democracy thus challenges several of the
widely held assumptions about the universality of the western trajectory of liberal democracy. It points to the pertinence of Mamdani's ob-
servation that the histories of the postcolonial world cannot be written
through simple analogies, as distorted or "incomplete" rehearsals of
the "western" story line (Mamdani 1996, 9)—in itself, one should add,
a major object of historical fictionalization. One of the tenets of the ideal
"western" story line is that democratic governance, once established
and consolidated, is self-sustaining because it produces a more rational
form of organization of interests, checks the executive agencies of the
state, and produces a democratic culture that provides more tolerance
and more pluralism. The recent Indian experience of Hindu nationalism should remind us that democracy also very often gives birth to
forces, desires, and imaginings of an authoritarian and anti-democratic
nature, or "majoritarian" and moral backlashes against what is seen as
"excessive liberalism" in the public culture.

This is certainly true of both European and North American history
in this century. These same historical experiences, and more recent de-

velopments in the western world, should also remind us that education, literacy, and economic prosperity by no means diminish or
counteract the recurrent constructions of ethnic majoritarianism, intolerance, and desires for strong governance that also develop and proliferate in the heart of developed democracies. On the contrary, historical
experience from most parts of the world points to the fact that educational institutions, literate public spheres, and the social world of the
upward mobile classes, anxious to consolidate their status and gain
recognition from their surroundings, are rather the sites of the production of ethnic intolerance and xenophobias.

Hindu nationalism could not consolidate any major constituency
among the millions of marginalized poor and illiterate Indians. Instead, the xenophobic discourses of Hindu nationalism developed in
the heart of the large and expanding middle class, which political common sense today holds to be the very prerequisite for creation of stable
democracies in the postcolonial world. It was in these mainly urban
environments, rich in education, associational life, and what Putnam
would characterize as "civic engagement" and "social capital" (Putnam 1993, 163–70), that the Hindu nationalist movement has found its
most receptive audiences. To understand and interpret contemporary
Hindu nationalism in India we need, in other words, to map how the
specific trajectory of Indian democracy and the historically changing
governmentalities of the modern Indian state have shaped political
imaginaries and public practices of the Indian middle class.

Political institutions and competitive political mobilization have historically been pivotal in the Indian experience of modernity. The nationalist elite in India was a political elite that developed a rather condescending vision of social uplift of the masses through education and
enfranchisement. They created a form of public culture marked by radical rhetoric and high idealism, but more enduring social structures
such as caste hierarchies, family structures, upper-caste norms of public behavior, and so on, were rarely challenged. In the nationalist movement and in the first decades after independence a peculiar cultural
construction of politics as a "virtuous vocation" emerged. Here upper-
caste notions of selfless duty and purity were inscribed into the construction of the ideal national citizen. Politics and the affairs of state
were constructed as the realm of enlightened men of superior moral
fiber. The process of democratic participation in the postcolonial democracy was seen as a central tool in this civilizing, and essentially
pedagogical, mission, in which the masses under prudent guidance
were to learn how to appreciate their new role as secular citizens of the
nation. This elitist political culture, seeking to mass-produce national

citizens in its own image, could be sustained as long as one dominant party, embodying the nation, could control and envelop both the political processes and the administrative machinery of the state.

Interpreting de Tocqueville's notion of the democratic revolution within a wider field of social practices, Claude Lefort has suggested that one of the most characteristic features of processes of democratization is the often tacit and gradual "dissolution of markers of certainty" pertaining to the solidity of institutions, the credibility of dogmas, and the assumed "naturalness" of a hierarchical social order. Historically, powerful forces have attempted to restrict democracy to a set of strictly procedural routines for governance and legislation, but once in motion, democratic procedures have over time tended to remold the very form in which a society represents and imagines itself, its institutions and its history.

It is my contention that the history of Indian democracy may be fruitfully interpreted in these terms as a gradual and circumscribed questioning of hierarchies and authority, spreading from the political field to other realms in society. As the political field acquired even more prominence due to the weight of the developmental state in all spheres of society in the 1970s, a new political culture marked by "political entrepreneurship" emerged. This gave rise to a new construction of politics as an "amoral vocation," a construction that reflected a widespread discomfort with the proliferating populist techniques of political mobilization and governance, and a disapproval of the new breed of public figures from modest social backgrounds who used their language, manners, and social background to consolidate mass followings. In the face of this "plebeianization" of the political field, sections of the educated urban middle classes and upper-caste groups began to denounce the political vocation, question the legitimacy of the state, and discard the principles of democracy and secularism.

For decades democracy and secularism meant protection and extension of social privileges to the educated Hindu middle classes, and condescending paternalism vis-à-vis lower-caste groups and minorities. However, as it became clear that political democracy was slowly giving birth to this new and unfamiliar form of society, the "softness" of the secular state became the target of the Hindu nationalist critique of a "pseudo secularism" that was "pampering minorities." Antidemocratic attitudes are today widespread in the same urban middle class in India that for years was regarded as the bedrock of political democracy in the country, and the backbone of the nation. Hindu nationalism emerged successfully in the political field in the 1980s as a kind of "conservative populism" that mainly attracted more privileged groups who feared encroachment on their dominant positions, but also "plebeian" and impoverished groups seeking recognition around a majoritarian rhetoric of cultural pride, order, and national strength.

The trajectory of the "saffron wave" in India has, as I have suggested, broader implications for the understanding of democracy in the non-western and postcolonial world. The immense scale, duration, and richness of the experience of democracy in India, a society pervaded by a multitude of hierarchical social forms, allows us to see, first, that the procedures and discourses associated with democracy profoundly modify and transform a society's imagination of itself. Democracy does not merely provide a form of governance but modifies social practices, institutions, and social imaginaries. We must acknowledge that democracy gives rise to a new imagination of society that makes new identities and claims possible, but also makes possible new forms of violent conflict and new fantasies of power and xenophobias. Many of these claims today take a specific cultural form because the objectification and codification of cultural differences and boundaries was one of the paramount governmentalities of the colonial states, to which the postcolonial state in India, like other postcolonial states, are the heirs. The fact that claims of cultural collectivities and identities are dominant forms of political identity in India and in other postcolonial societies does not make them "deformities" in relation to the liberal western political trajectories, but rather results of the specific historiocities and "vernacularization" of democratic discourses and procedures in the postcolonial world.

In the light of this, the success of the Hindu nationalist movement is, second, not the "revenge" of a society where western forms of governance and political discourse—such as democracy—remain unintelligible and alien due to a deep and enduring civilizational incommensurability. Practices of democratic politics are never "the same" all over the world, but are always embedded in historically specific but also changing "cultural constructions of politics" and public culture. Democracy always tends to produce an ever more politicized society in which "undecidability" reigns and expands, that is, where institutions, identities, and social horizons are unstable and always contested. The Hindu nationalist movement is both an expression of this politicization of Indian public culture and a reaction against it. It is, if anything, a "revenge" of colonial governmentality more than any representation of Hindu culture as such.

Third, the democratic experience in India also shows us that although the notion of equality that lies at the heart of democracy has not produced social equality, it has made a certain representation of "the ordinary" of paramount importance in politics. Charles Taylor has argued that the celebration of "ordinary life"—hard work, family life, simple virtues—were central to the construction of modern identity (Taylor 1992, 211–305). The "ordinary" was in the European and American experiences shaped by religious sects and capitalist transformations, whereas democratic politics seems to have been its primary midwife in India. Although the elitist democracy of the first decades after 1947 governed "the masses" as subject of a benevolent state, these "masses" have, through populist leaders, acquired a new assertive visibility in the political field. The Hindu nationalist movement reacts against this perceived encroachment on middle-class society, but it needs, at the same time, to project "the ordinary" onto the ideal national Hindu citizens it seeks to produce.

Hindu Nationalism and the Imaginings of India

The authorized colonial and orientalist knowledge of India as a deeply religious society with self-born, resilient social and cultural institutions is still crucial in academic and political understanding of India. In the western world this form of knowledge could explain recurrent episodes of riots and killings in South Asia as effects of the persistence of premodern religious passions and fanaticism. In India, knowledge of the deeply religious ordinary Indian did for decades imbue many educated Indians with a paternalist sense of being part of a "civilizational mission" of modernity vis-à-vis "the masses." In the hands of the Hindu nationalists, the same knowledge could promote a single reified "Hinduism" as the natural matrix of the true Indian nation. Without transgressing these established tenets of what India "really is" to millions of Indians, the Hindu nationalist movement could stage its bid for remolding the public culture of India and for winning political power in the Indian state as the natural, inevitable, completely unpolitical reaction of ordinary, pious Hindus against a culturally insensitive, westernized, and corrupted state.

Hindu nationalism has indeed successfully recruited and subsumed religious sentiments and public rituals into a larger discourse of national culture (Bharatiya culture) and the Hindu nation, Hindu rashtra. There is little doubt that new social or religious practices, especially in urban India, have made this specific political "packaging" of Hindu symbols intelligible to larger audiences; but the objectives and practices of the Hindu nationalist movement go far beyond religion and ritualized practices. As I hope to show, Hindu nationalist discourse and practices are centrally concerned with notions of national honor and how a vibrant sense of national community can stabilize social identities, governance, and the larger social order, and ultimately extract a much-desired global recognition of India's place among the leading nations in the world. The notion of Hindutva makes sense not primarily because of any religious subtext but because it is made to connect meaningfully with everyday anxieties of security, a sense of disorder, and more generally the ambivalence of modern life.

The emergence of Hindu nationalism in India also seems to fit all too well into the system of essentialized cultural stereotypes and differences of "civilization," the common-sense ordering of the globe to which Samuel Huntington lends some scientific authority. Like Huntington, foreign policy analysts, and most of the religious nationalists across the globe analyzed by Juergensmeyer (1993), Hindu nationalists also understand and order the world through "cultural essentials" of religion, blood, and other practices related to the body—food, marriage, death. According to this view, India was always and will remain fundamentally Hindu in a civilizational sense, just as (it implies) Muslims and other non-Hindus always were alien to India and will remain so forever. The secular Indian nation state is in the Hindu nationalists' view a political fiction that conceals real cultural incommensurabilities, or in their words, a "culturally alien" construction imposed on India by anglicized intellectuals.

My argument is that the notion of a single Hindu culture, incommensurable with Islamic or western epistemes and forms of organization, is the real fiction at work here, imposed by orientalism and painstakingly promulgated, organized, and reformulated by generations of Hindu nationalists and other Indian nationalists for more than a century. I also argue that in order to understand Hindu nationalism we need to analyze carefully the official secularism it opposed. Textbook versions of secularism as the absence of religion from the public sphere, or a more fashionable understanding of secularism as a metonym of scientific rationalism, will not suffice. We need to take a closer and more informed look at the practices and meanings of secularism in the public culture of independent India.

The dominant interpretation of secularism in India did not entail the removal of religion from the political sphere, but rather the belief that religion and culture were elevated to an ostensibly apolitical level, above the profanities of the political. This institutionalized notion of culture and religion as apolitical, and the derived notion of selfless "social work" as ennobling and purifying by virtue of its elevation above politics and money, provided an unassailable moral high ground to a certain genre of "antipolitical activism," conspicuous among social and cultural organizations but also often invoked in agitations and in electoral politics in India. I submit that it was from this discursive field of "antipolitics" and "religious activism" that the Hindu nationalist movement, with great ingenuity, built its campaigns and organizational networks for decades. Like other forms of cultural nationalism, the Hindu nationalist movement always entertained a complex ambivalence vis-à-vis democracy and apprehension toward the "political vocation." The evolution of the movement, its organization, and its political strategies must be understood in the context of a constant negotiation and oscillation across the deep bifurcation in modern Indian political culture between a realm of "sublime" culture and a realm of "profane" competitive politics.

Historically, the contestation of symbols, space, and numbers between Muslim and Hindu organizations was admittedly central to the broader evolution of nationalism and nation-states in the subcontinent. In India, sedimented fears of the abstract and generalized "Muslim" remain today the decisive ideological bedrock of the Hindu nationalist movement, and the most persistent source of its popular and electoral success. There is little doubt that communal subjectivities, especially the fear of Muslims among Hindus, have acquired a certain solidity and "truth" that is independent of social experiences or physical proximities. These subjectivities exists as what Slavoj Žižek calls "ideological fantasies," that is, a kind of knowledge of the other that appears as more true than any appearance or concrete representation, and is thus a construction beyond argument or falsification.

Hindu nationalism is not an antiwestern religious "fundamentalism." What Hindu nationalists desire is recognition of themselves and India by the western powers, but a recognition through assertion of cultural difference and assertion of India's sovereignty and self-determination. The so-called "consumer goods revolution" in India in the 1980s, the spread of satellite TV, and India's entanglement in global economic and cultural flows made the question of India's place in the global order one of crucial importance. Within a decade, these changes transformed the face of many Indian cities, as advertising, fancy shops, new cars, televised soap operas, luxury goods, and a still more visible youth culture proliferated. To sections of the Hindu nationalist movement this "invasion" signifies a national crisis and a surrender of the national pride or, in the suggestive language of a Hindu nationalist activist, "our motherland, bereft of moral fibre and vulnerable to the rape of western capital and consumerism."[2] Other sections of the movement acknowledge the powerful attractions of "western consumerism" and modern technology, and emphasize that India has to develop a strong public morality that could contain hedonistic excesses.

They argue that the prerequisite for developing such a sovereign national modernity is the cultural unity and purity of the Hindu nation. In these ideological fantasies at the heart of the Hindu nationalist movement, the Indian Muslims represent a constitutive defect, an impurity that has to be "cleansed" before India can emerge as a modern self-conscious nation.

I hope to show that the emergence of a mass movement of this magnitude is probably one of the least "natural" processes one can imagine. The Hindu nationalist movement neither expresses essential cultural differences nor merely reflects new social and religious practices in India. It has emerged out of a conjunction of massive and protracted labor of organization and ideological promulgation, the existence of a certain receptivity and disgruntlement in broad social milieus, and the presence of certain strategic conditions of possibility in the political field. I will, in other words, try to understand the precarious and contingent processes through which the dispersed grievances and sentiments in various parts of Indian society were reframed by the Hindu nationalist discourse, organized by its movements and party, and hence aggregated into what appeared to be, and indeed was staged as, a spontaneous surge of social or cultural identity in public arenas.

In this book I try to avoid the language of "cultural aggregation" that dominates much of the discussion of politics and identity in contemporary India. Journalists, social scientists, and political strategists and activists alike seem to buy into a shared paradigm of the primacy of caste in formation of political loyalties, and unreflected assumptions about caste and religion as originary identities prevail. The extensive use of mythico-historical inventories of symbols and narratives in politics and the public culture of India is routinely taken as an index of the existence of the subjectivities and memories they in fact seek to shape.

We need to question such assumptions as, for instance, that public manifestations of the "Hindu community" by the Hindu nationalist movement, or votes cast for the BJP, necessarily reflect deep cultural logics and continuities; or that the language of caste and community always strikes a receptive chord among the Indians, supposedly deeply immersed in their cultural ontology. These phenomena must instead be studied in the context of the specific "economy of stances" in the public arenas in which they seek to intervene. We need to recognize that the field of politics always produces and modifies social or cultural dynamics and identifications in a specific form, that is, in specific discursive modalities and within specific stratagems of the field. To understand the broader "culturalization" of the political field in India, and the surge of Hindu nationalism more specifically, we need to frame it within an anthropology of the political field. We need to analyze the idioms, practices, and stakes that define political practices in their everyday localized forms in mohallas (neighborhoods) and villages, in the constant disjunctures between fractured subjectivities and the pragmatism that political discourse engenders among so-called ordinary people, as well as the ideological fantasies and rationalities at play among the accomplished specialists in political strategy and practice.

In this book, I try to carry out at least parts of this research program, although I probably lapse back into more conventional modes of thinking about, and knowing about, both politics and culture. I hope, nonetheless, to be able to suggest a few modes of inquiry that could contribute to a more differentiated anthropology of the political field in India.

About This Book

This book grows out of an engagement with the phenomenon of Hindu nationalism since 1990. Throughout this period I have tried to make the "saffron wave" in India intelligible within a broader theoretical and historical perspective. But I have also, during longer periods of fieldwork in the state of Maharashtra, tried to understand the specific ways in which Hindu nationalism has been represented and received in the context of social conditions and public contestations in both rural and urban localities in that state. I wanted to know to which extent Hindu nationalist discourse and organizations had been able to reshape and homogenize local grievances into communal subjectivities underpinning the overall Hindu nationalist project. The enormous diversity of India obviously makes it impossible to generalize too heavily from this material. Throughout the following text I only offer a number of brief vignettes presenting ethnographic material collected in Maharashtra between 1991 and 1997, in order to illustrate how existing complexities of power and contestations in neighborhoods and villages decisively shaped the receptivity toward the discourse of Hindu nationalism.

These periods of fieldwork were made possible by a generous grant from the Council for Development Research in Denmark, and I remain grateful to the people who assisted me in various ways during these periods, particularly Professor R. K. Hebsur from the Tata Institute of Social Science in Bombay, Professor Ramesh Babu from Bombay University, Mahesh Gavaskar, Urmila Budhkar, and Prasad Srinivasan.

Over the years I have benefited immensely from comments and suggestions from many scholars of Indian politics and society. Sudipta Kaviraj, Partha Chatterjee, Peter van der Veer, Christophe Jaffrelot, Chris Fuller, Richard Fox, John Martinussen, Bruce Graham, Dipankar Gupta, Zoya Hasan, Bipan Chandra, Paul Brass, Gérard Heuzé, Amiya

Kumar Bagchi, Jonathan Spencer, David Ludden, Jørgen Dige Petersen, Neil Webster, Stig Toft Madsen, and Olle Törnquist have provided insightful comments and criticism of various parts of the material and arguments that went into this book. Without this inspiration, this text could never have been written. Needless to say, the responsibility for flaws and shortcomings in the text remains solely mine.

I also wish to thank my colleagues and friends at International Development Studies, Roskilde University, at the Centre for Development Research in Copenhagen, and in the editorial committee of the Danish journal GRUS for their support and encouragement over the years. The valuable suggestions, the encouragement and the professionalism of Mary Murrell, Margaret Case, Deirdre Mullervy, and anonymous reviewers from Princeton University Press, and of Bela Malik and anonymous reviewers from Oxford University Press, India were indispensable in the final production of this book.

The most important and unfailing support has, however, come from my wife Kirsten, and my children Lærke and Malte, who with understanding and love have tolerated my long periods of physical absence and absentmindedness.

1

Modernity, Nation, and Democracy in India

THROUGH ALL the richness and diversity of public life in contemporary India there traverses one remarkably coherent narrative: declining standards in the realm of politics and public administration. Corruption, declining quality of leadership, shameless display of self-interest by groups and individuals, violence, and lethargy in administration and the judiciary are phenomena routinely explained by the invasion of politics into all spheres of life. The national press debates how the independence of the judiciary and the administrative capacity of the state are threatened by "political interference" in court cases and in administrative routines. In urban neighborhoods, mob violence or demands for ever new "donations" to school boards and building societies are explained as the effect of "someone playing politics." In villages, the routine selection of some farmers rather than others as eligible for new credits, or the stalled construction of an irrigation scheme, is attributed to the machinations of local political entrepreneurs.

Bemoaning the "signs of the times" has probably always been a way of coping with a changing world, just as blaming politicians for virtually any social problem seems to be a regular feature of the very form of democratic representation. Yet we need to note that this critique of "politics" and "the political" in contemporary Indian public life hardly means that political life is ignored. On the contrary, political scandals, conspiracy theories, rumors, and gossip about political leaders constitute an inexhaustible reservoir of fascination and discussion. More importantly, notions of rights and entitlements of groups and individuals vis-à-vis the state proliferate in ever more assertive forms. This is true of the fuzzy zone of clientelist practices and informal organizations through which large numbers of rural poor and slum dwellers are linked with formal institutions of the state, as well as in the realm of more organized "civic," cultural, and political activism. Older notions of "civility," of adherence to procedures and "proper conduct" in electoral politics and in everyday routines of institutions and associations seem to have given way to what appears as a cruder, more direct, and often embarrassingly shameless desire for power, office, money, and recognition.

Within the social worlds of the urban middle classes in India, this apparent erosion of the civility of public culture is routinely attributed to the rise of "unworthy" (read: plebeian) leaders, to contamination of cultural values, to the free reign of material desires in modern urban life, and so on. However, the more brutal languages of politics also flourish at the heart of the middle-class world, for instance when broader anxieties regarding the encroachment of the poor and the plebeians upon so-called "respectable" society are translated into discourses on the "right of the majority," antiminority xenophobia, and fantasies of an authoritarian state and strong leadership. Since the early 1990s, the telephone surveys frequently carried out by various English-language weeklies in India regarding political preferences and attitudes to political issues have shown that the predominantly middle-class respondents (that is, those who own a telephone) have grown increasingly skeptical toward the viability of democracy and more inclined toward stronger and more authoritarian forms of governance.

It is the basic contention of this book that the phenomenal growth and political success of Hindu nationalism in India in the last decade must be understood in the context of this larger disjuncture between democratic mobilization and democratic governance. This is a disjuncture that, needless to say, has deep roots in the structure of colonial and postcolonial governance and in the specific "production of the Indian people," that is, the production of political identities and collectivities in both colonial and independent India. In the following chapters I analyze how Hindu nationalist discourses and organizations emerged in the late colonial period; how they were transformed by new institutional structures and new political imaginaries in independent India; and what conditions of possibilities enabled the Hindu nationalist movement to grow rapidly from the late 1980s. However, such a history of the evolution of political imaginaries in modern India does not offer itself to us in a single line of development, or in its own terms. To write such a history requires a certain theoretical vocabulary and a certain interpretative grid.

The most difficult question is how we can develop an understanding of the social and cultural construction of politics in India that does not reduce it to something else. How can we avoid reducing politics to a mere reflection of the dynamics of the caste system, as much political analysis in India today seems to be doing—assuming, just like earlier forms of class analysis, that the political field is simply a mirror of society, a screen from which the intentions and strategies of elusive "social forces" can be read? How can we avoid the other extreme, the conventional political science interpretation of electoral processes, institutional dynamics of bureaucracy, and strategies of aggregated political actors as if they constituted a world of their own, disentangled from the complex embedding of politics in a wider field of social and cultural practices?

To my mind a promising starting point is a radical reading of de Tocqueville's basic idea that democracy is not merely a set of institutions and procedures for governance but must be understood as the political institution of a process of questioning and subversion of social hierarchies and certitudes that over time produces an altogether different society. Such an interpretation of de Tocqueville entails the view that circulation of democratic discourses, and expansion of practices of democracy, first and foremost reveal the constructed and provisional character of the social world. In this reading, "the political" denotes a generative and destructive process, questioning hierarchies and certitudes, while producing undecidability, as it reveals that every institutionalized and ostensibly naturalized practice is founded on acts of power and decision.[1] To study politics is, in my view, to study how "the political"—the irreducible conflicts and undecidability lying at the heart of the social world—is brought under control and temporarily institutionalized within institutions, procedures, legislation, and so on.

This perspective endorses Foucauldian insights regarding governance as a set of practices of classification and ordering of social practices wider than those directives that flow from the state. At the same time, it tries to combine these insights with a dynamic understanding of how rights, entitlements, and administrative categories are distributed and "inhabited" in surprising and not always governable forms. The problem in a strictly Foucauldian notion of governmentality is, to my mind, that it tends to reify the pervasiveness of the power it depicts, blinding itself to internal inconsistencies and contradictions of governing rationalities and thus relegating resistances and contestations of technocratic rationalities and forms of governance to the margins of society, that is, to more inchoate forms of insubordination and defiance. The entire realm of political passions, of ideologies, of the role of the imaginary elements of politics and the de facto incoherence and impotence of many forms of governance slips out of the picture if we do not take "the political" seriously: the fundamentally undecidable, incomplete, and contested nature of facts and descriptions of society, of categories, of identities, and so on. We need, in other words, to recognize that the very reason why discourses of order and technologies of government try to fix and authorize certain forms of knowledge and certain taxonomies is that these schemes are fundamentally inadequate and impossible. They can never fully create the effects and the order they aim at. Similarly, identity claims and identity strategies have to be constantly reformulated because they never fully produce the categories, groups, or individuals they claim to represent.

Ordinary existence in a modern and democratic society in many ways produces an excess of meaning, a chaotic and amorphous array of phenomena and discrepant experiences that open a large number of interpretative possibilities. This larger society is, in crucial ways, experienced and continuously imagined through its representation in the field of politics—in utterances of leaders, symbols of state and nation, political spectacles, and in the microphysics of institutions. Needless to say, democratic political procedures, constant debates and circulation of competing truths, and open and formalized contest for office and authority present deeply polyvalent and partial re-presentations of the social world. They thus present society to itself in a disenchanted, changeable, and almost profane fashion. At the same time, projects of order, promises of stability, narratives of community and identity are also presented and produced in this world of democratic politics—not uncommonly by presenting themselves as "beyond politics," as justified by technical expert knowledge, "history," or community, and thus appearing as "decidable," fixed, and beyond questioning.

When cultural identities are articulated and mobilized in the realm of democratic politics, as in the case of Hindu nationalism in India, it does not happen as a mere transfer and transmutation of already existing cultural identities into a profane and instrumentalist world of politics. My argument is that the articulation of Hindutva (Hinduness) in politics and in public life is primarily a way of making sense of the social world, a strategy that aims at creating a certain order within the disorderly realm of democratic politics, by imposing a matrix of a natural, eternal, and essentialized "Hindu culture" upon it.

The main argument of this book is that the success of the Hindu nationalist movement in Indian society has to do with the specific ways in which historically produced notions of "Hinduness" were packaged and recirculated at a particular juncture in the development of democracy and modern governance in India. This juncture was also characterized by an intensified democratic revolution, that is, a process of intensified politicization of everyday life, where by many Indians experienced a large gap between a generalized sense of the undecidable character of the social worlds they lived in and an inadequate and even threatening representation of this world in an intensely competitive and pervasive form of mass politics in the country.

In the following, I give a condensed outline of what this "radical" Tocquevillean thesis of the democratic revolution implies for the study of identities, discourse, and more institutionalized politics. Second, I interpret the political history of India since the end of the nineteenth century through this theoretical lens. I do so by exploring how colonial categories of governance shaped cultural-national identities and how the politics of representation in the political institutions of the colonial state conditioned the development of ethnoreligious identities. I then explore the production of national citizens and cultural communities by the postcolonial state and probe into the effects of universal franchise, secular institutions, and the new developmental governmentality of the Indian state.

The Democratic Revolution

In his work on the democracy in America, Alexis de Tocqueville defined the democratic revolution as the process through which all the founding elements of premodern societies—divine legitimization of power, the naturalness of hierarchy, the fatalism of the masses—gradually came to be questioned and undermined by the new revolutionary creed of democracy: the belief in freedom and equality as universal values (de Tocqueville 1966, 49).

With reference to the possible democratization of European societies, de Tocqueville asked: what are the effects on politics, morality, governance, and social cohesion when a society, dominated by multiple relations of inequality, adopts a democratic system of government and universal suffrage? What happens when free institutions, public opinion, and a measure of procedural regularity of decision making develop?

De Tocqueville suggested that democratization produced a society "without foundations," that is, without stable legitimacy and knowledge. In the absence of earlier ontological certainties of divinely authorized knowledge and temporal power, democracy created a range of new ideological forms, such as an abstract civic ethos and national loyalty, both possible and necessary (ibid., 535–47).

De Tocqueville explored the master-slave dialectic to show the new instability that was generated by diffusion of the notion of equality and what we today would call the "nonfoundational" character of democratic society. In principle, democracy dissolved the difference between master and servant. They were both citizens of the country and both human beings. The relation was no longer one of uncontested power on part of the master and unconditional obedience on part of the servant. Old obligations and rules were gone or not adhered to, and new ones had not been fully formed. This undecidable moment, when the old relation was subverted and the new one not yet established, generally characterizes democratic societies: "Obedience, then, loses its moral basis in the eyes of him who obeys; he no longer considers it as some sort of divinely appointed duty, and he does not yet see its purely human aspect; in his eyes it is neither sacred nor just and he submits to it as a degrading though useful fact. . . . There is an unspoken intestinal war between permanently suspicious rival powers. . . . The lines between authority and tyranny, liberty and license and right and might seem to them so jumbled and confused that no one knows exactly what he is, what he can do, and what he should do" (ibid., 554).

This may be read as a parable of modern mass politics premised upon the fundamental split between power and legitimacy. The democratic revolution irreversibly blocked the possibility of power ever being legitimate, as in a premodern age, that is, successfully representing itself as a divinely sanctioned, self-evident general interest embodying the unity of society and defining its boundaries. A new form of secular power now came into being, derived from "the people" which, however, remained abstract and unrepresentable, as observed by Lefort: "The locus of power becomes an empty place. It cannot be occupied—it is such that no individual and no group can be consubstantial with it—and it cannot be represented. Only the mechanisms of exercise of power are visible, or only the men, the mere mortals, who hold political authority" (Lefort 1988, 17). This engendered, in turn, a new imagination of society, no longer based on an uncontested authority but fragmented and traversed by a fundamental undecidability regarding the foundations and legitimacy of power. The paradox of democracy is that although broad legitimacy becomes ever more impossible to achieve in an ever more differentiated and fragmented society, strategies of legitimization of power nevertheless attain paramount importance. Modern political strategies and discourses may all be seen as attempts to bridge this gap between legitimacy and power by invoking discourses on order, security, justice, freedom, and equality.[2]

Nineteenth-century modernity and capitalism in Europe transformed social structures and forms of state. Older hierarchies, orders, and truths collapsed and rendered the domain of "the political"—the undecidable objects of open contestation between antagonistic groups and world views—an ever larger and more central field. This gave, according to Lefort, birth to a distinct "culture of questioning": "In my view the important point is that democracy is instituted and sustained by the dissolution of markers of certainty. . . . [W]ithout the actors being aware of it a process of questioning is implicit in social practice, that no one has the answer to the questions that arise, and that the work of ideology, which is always dedicated to the task of restoring certainty, cannot put an end to this practice" (Lefort 1988, 19). Out of this grew all the central ideological configurations of modernity circling around, and straddling, narratives of loss (of truth, certainty, culture, faith, authenticity), and equally persistent quests for recuperation of the lost in new purified forms.

Social Antagonisms and Politics

One of the sometimes overlooked consequences of the birth and dispersion of this new and abstract discourse on equality, freedom, and sovereignty is that it made a more radical and generalized form of social conflict possible. As Laclau and Mouffe have noted, even the most exploitative form of inequality does not necessarily carry the seed of resistance and conflict within its own logic. There might be what I would call "distributional fights" regarding the relative positions, duties, and obligations within a system of subordination, but something more is needed to construct inequality as the result of malign oppression.[3] Historically this "something more" was exactly what Laclau and Mouffe have termed "the democratic imaginary": "the discursive conditions which made it possible to propose the different forms of inequality as illegitimate and anti-natural, and thus make them *equivalent* as forms of oppression. Here lay the profound subversive power of the democratic discourse, which would allow the spread of equality and liberty into increasingly wider domains and therefore act as a fermenting agent upon the different forms of struggle against subordination" (Laclau and Mouffe 1985, 155).

The entire modern discourse of abstract individuals endowed with equal rights and desires, and the universalized notion of "Man," made it possible to perceive inequality within a radically new horizon, now in terms of an antagonism that constructed the superordinates as preventing the subordinated from fully realizing what they actually were, or ought to become. Social differences, however objectified, cannot in themselves explain why some rather than other identities/differences become loci of organization and political identification. In order to recognize itself, to speak of itself—or to recognize itself when it is spoken for—a collectivity must be defined by what it is not, and why it is not what it desires to become. The formation of political identities does not, in other words, merely take place through the deployment of categories of governance, registration, and classification, but through the contingent inhabitation of these "identity slots" by individuals and collectivities. Needless to say, this inhabitation is precarious and unstable, and always presupposes an active and protracted labor of ideological articulation.

Social antagonism may be thought of in a Lacanian sense as a fundamental ontological principle of undecidability and contingency, a constitutive negativity that prevents the full ordering of the social fields,
and a kind of intrinsic split which is the resistance and limit that any
structure or institution encounters in the process of its making and reproduction (Laclau 1990, 18). Antagonism is thus not simply the sym-
metrical opposite of order or structure—like, for example, ambiguity or
randomness—but something preventing this order, a constant source
of instability and incompleteness.[4]

To my mind, the concept of social antagonism marks a significant
advance in a poststructuralist understanding of "the political" compared with Foucault's more restricted privileging of the epistemological production and authorization of the social world and its governance. To Foucault, "the political" was played out in two ways: either
as intrabureaucratic contestations and strategies involved in selecting
and authorizing certain methods and technologies of government and
production of knowledge; or as dispersed, partial, and uncoordinated
forms of plebeian resistance or defiance on the part of those subjected
to the modern disciplinary regime.[5] Because Foucault largely regarded
scientific discourses as effective, expansive, and encompassing technologies of governance, able to produce a large range of (intended) effects
and capable of technocratic "depoliticizing" of contentious issues, and
because he remained unclear on the issue of strategies (except as an
attribution of "strategies" to certain patterned effects after the fact), he
literally pushed "the political" to the margins of society. Politics became in a sense something external, an outer limit to be overcome, represented as a residue of the not yet fully governed individual or as
fragments of a residual and heroic self—that undefinable residue evad-
ing epistemic domination and governance.[6]

The real merit of the notion of social antagonism is that it reintro-
duces "the political" into the heart of social practices, and points to the
ultimate impossibility of fully functional institutions and fully fledged
identities—not because of any external resistance or resentment, but
because of the flaws inherent in the governing discourses: the inherent
contradictions and destructive character of capitalist production, the
flaws and incompleteness of taxonomic schemes of classification incapable of comprehending the richness of natural or social life, the in-
capacity of any narration of the self and the collective to disclose fully
the identity it purports to portray.

In this reading of the Tocquevillean perspective, discourses of democracy and equality and the political imaginaries they historically
gave birth to were crucial in the shaping of modernity. They not only

shaped the political institutions of modernity and the forms of modern subjectivity but also introduced a radical undecidability in the ontologies of self and society. If this thesis is pushed too far, however, if the dissemination of equality is made into the primary transforming force producing modernity, we may indulge in "explanatory extremism" and obliterate other important forces shaping both western and colonial modernities.[7] We need, in other words, to think about the complex ways in which democracy's "culture of questioning" was made possible by the "creative destruction" of earlier forms of production, social hierarchies, and community formations by capitalism and modern forms of governance, and the very different trajectories of democratization these larger processes followed in different parts of Europe and the Americas, and later in the postcolonial world. If we understand democratization as a complex social process that politicizes widely different societies, we have to abandon teleological ideas of democracy as mere replicas of the political forms institutionalized in western Europe or North America. We also have to understand that democratic political forms are deeply ambiguous, capable of generating emancipatory desires as well as longings for authoritarian order and stability.

Discourse and the Analysis of Politics

To introduce "the political" into the heart of every social practice, and to assert that politics revolves around contestation and hegemonic stabilization of the meaning of certain signifiers, words, gestures, and practices, makes it necessary to restate the specificity of politics as a social practice. Moreover, it also makes it necessary to define what discourse analysis implies for analysis of political phenomena.

The political field may generally be seen as an historically produced realm of institutions and hegemonic discourses, where societal conflicts and dislocations are selected, translated, and tamed into ritualized procedures and practices of politics. The dynamics of change and resilience in political life may become somewhat clearer if we regard the political field as a complex mechanism of three layers of "structuring structures."

The first and most immediately observable layer of the political field includes the debates, struggles, and contestations of policies, political programs, and ideological formations in the public sphere. Such debates are governed by an historically specific "economy of stances," that is, a constant positioning between competing and aligned positions in the political field that assigns to each discursive alteration a specific polemical connotation (Bourdieu 1991, 175).[8]

The field of political discourse is, moreover, governed by antagonistic relations that tend to simplify the discursive space as meanings, symbols, and gestures are perpetually contested and stabilized in "chains of equivalencies and difference"—marking signs of commonality and otherness, respectively, on either side of political front lines (Laclau and Mouffe 1985, 136). Any construction of a "we" depends, therefore, on the coherence of an antagonistic enemy. Identities are basically negative and "empty," haunted by their incompleteness and always dependent upon a joint stabilizing symbol—the nation, the revolution, or the mythical leader—which is what completes and "sutures" them. Political struggles tend to be organized around such elusive metasymbols, or "empty signifiers," which stand in for the absence of the "fullness" around which processes of identification always revolve (Laclau 1996a, 36–46).

This formal understanding of political discourse presupposes, nonetheless, that the precise meaning of discourses only can be found in their localized economy of stances. That leaves us with the question of how the spread and ostensible universalization of discursive elements such as freedom, equality, the people, and the nation can be understood. How do discourses travel in time and space, one may ask.

There is always a tension between localized discursive closures and the multiplicity of meanings inscribed in most ideological constructions. This tension may be expressed as the tension between the conceptual grammar of a discourse and the connotative domain within which it is articulated. Or, more technically, as the tension between metaphorical substitution and metonymic sliding of meaning and signs within discourses.[9] Concepts such as "a nation" or "the people" have, through their historical trajectory, been endowed with conceptual grammars—a certain set of historical referents and infrastructure that I prefer to call "ideological knots"—a kind of historically accumulated closure that they cannot escape without becoming transformed into something different. The conceptual grammar provides a measure of stability, and thus closure, to the range of meanings of a concept and a discourse. An articulation of, say, nationalism without explicit reference to territory, people, and history is perfectly possible, but probably would not have much political mass appeal and thus would be unlikely to occur within contemporary discursive formations. And if it did, the internal infrastructure of people and territory would probably be inferred from the mere deployment of the term "nation."

The connotative domains of a society may, on the other hand, be understood as the historically produced matrices of meanings of words, signs, and symbols—in a local or national political field, for instance. These matrices may vary in stability and degree of openness. The more contested and fragmented a political field and its connotative domain, the more open will discursive elements be to constant "metonymic sliding" and alterations of meaning, whereas a political field marked by a stable hegemony and stable institutional forms is likely to constrict and circumscribe the range of possible connotations of political discourses, say, of a nationalist variety.

The economy of stances governing the political debate in a society is always built upon such connotative domains, and upon the complex transactions through which new discourses and new conceptual grammars are inscribed and domesticated within the political field. This more or less stable coding that prevails in the political field is inscribed into what J. F. Bayart has called "discursive genres of politics," that is, the style and technique of debate and popular oratory, the styles of public political spectacles, the interactions with press and public, and so on.

The second and more durable "structuring structure" in the political field is its mechanism of representation and the ways in which state and governance are organized. Political representation is fundamental to parliamentary democracies, but is also crucial to authoritarian leaders or parties striving to portray themselves as the true representative of the people, the nation, or the "toiling masses." Representation and the institutionalized rituals of representative democracy work as metaphorical and highly codified reenactments of social struggles through which the diversity and opacity of the social world are translated into an orderly, intelligible, and visible matrix for the imagination of society (Bourdieu 1991, 186). Representatives demonstrably embody the groups they seek to represent. At mass rallies the representatives (parties, organizations, and so on) try to "speak the group into existence," and they strive to make the crowd appear to itself as an incarnation of the larger group or community appealed to. Social groups or collective interests emerge in their more objectified and self-conscious forms from such claims to represent a group or community (ibid., 200). Most organizations and parties seek, in other words, to "produce their own cause"—they strive to produce the group, the interest, or the culture for which they claim to be mere vehicles.

In my view, "the state" is a fractured ensemble of institutions whose relative incoherence makes it impossible to "conquer" or control, as militant Jacobinism always dreamt of doing. But it is, at the same time, exactly the dispersion and incoherence of the institutional landscape we call the state that makes it possible for political forces to weld sections of it together in a provisional unity and turn it into a powerful instrument of domination and societal reform. "The state," writes Bob Jessop, " is a specific institutional ensemble with multiple boundaries, no institutional fixity and no pregiven or substantive unity" (Jessop 1990, 267). The unity and coherence of the state is not given a priori but is only provided temporarily by political forces capable of reforming administrative routines, remolding institutions, and redirecting fiscal flows in order to create a specific "state project." Every such project tends to exclude certain propositions, political interests, and social groups from influence, while furthering the political interests, the social vision, and the position of the social groups that the "state project" seeks to represent and consolidate.[10]

As Foucault has pointed out, the most fundamental techniques of governance of the modern state are the knowledge-practices that have historically enabled the state to produce not only technologies of order but also technologies of objectification—statistics, budgetary models, monitoring techniques, registration, models for population and economic prognosis—that embody certain rationalities and produce everexpanding horizons for regulation. The increasing "governmentalization" of the state—the ever more refined tools and knowledges available for government of health, education, delinquency, entrepreneurship, and so on—have historically not been merely constraining political forces. On the contrary, these techniques of government have provided vital inputs to the political imaginations of political parties, pressure groups, and movements concerning possibilities of knowing, monitoring, and regulating new areas of governmental intervention. The historical proliferation of rights claims from formal rights toward social and cultural rights (Bobbio 1996) have been intimately connected with the technological possibilities of implementation, regulation, and securing of such rights by ever more "governmentalized" states (Foucault 1991, 87–105).

Third, hegemonic political forces tend over time to produce relatively durable discourses and forms of state, and durable notions of proper political practice, of legitimate areas of political intervention or questioning—in brief, a political culture organized around what Bourdieu has called "legitimate problematics" (Bourdieu 1991, 72–73). These problematics may be regarded as symptoms of a political culture, that is, as products of a cumulated political history whose multiple layers of references, practices, and meanings provide a sort of structured archive of possible connotations and reconstructions available to the production of political legitimacy. Political cultures are a sort of political common sense or political doxa: a widely dispersed, fuzzy, and yet pervasive and naturalized sense of what politics is about, how it should be properly performed, what a good leader is, what true justice is, and so on. Rather than constituting any national consensus, political culture may be thought of as an "embodied political historicity" that frames political vocabularies, that is, the agreed-upon archive of references and political traditions that inform hegemonic as well as oppositional forms of discourse and organization.

Bayart goes a step further and refers to the "continuity of civilizations" and the enduring "cultural configurations of politics" derived from historical legacies of the state in various parts of the world (Bayart 1991, 56–59). Although I find explorations of specific cultural constructions of politics pertinent, I would argue that the historical archive of courtly rituals and manners, heroic constructions of authority, relations between spiritual and temporal authority all should be regarded as merely resources in the ceaseless and never completed construction of political legitimacy and political culture, rather than as self-evident sources of legitimacy. Bayart rightly points to the longue durée historicity of political vocabularies, but I argue that the importance, or lack of importance, of certain traditions and legacies depends almost entirely on the contingent process of their specific reconstruction in a given political field. Neither history nor culture ever imposes itself as an irresistible force structuring political languages.

To summarize: politics is the name we give to the practices that seek to represent society, to embody and give materiality to a larger political imaginary through certain rites, spectacles, laws, and institutions. What I have suggested here is a brief outline of a nonobjectivist perspective on politics that gives primacy to "the political" as the fundamental undecidability in social life, and that emphasizes the fundamental contingency that is the cause of politics. It is a perspective that makes the political field a concrete and specific field of social activity, and thus available for ethnographic studies of discourse, rituals, and practices of institutions, groups, and individuals at all the three levels outlined above. We may study political discourse as *performance*, that is speech, utterances, and open debating as we encounter them in quotidian discussions, newspapers, political rallies, and interviews. We may study political discourse in a more Foucauldian mode as *objectification* and *authorization*, as we encounter it in administrative archives, legislation, institutional practices, and so on. And we may, finally, study political discourse in its cultural form, as *embodiment* of sedimented and naturalized political practices that have become inscribed in practical and mundane matrices of good and evil, purity and pollution, of the appropriate and inappropriate. This "deep" moment of discourse may be read out of personal narratives, of political practices, ritualizations, and so on.

In the remainder of this book, I try to bring this perspective and these forms of discourse analysis to bear on the broader conditions of possibilities that allowed the Hindu nationalist movement in India to emerge and grow to its present position of national prominence.

Governance and Nationalism in Colonial India

Colonial governance in Asia and Africa aimed at controlling territories and populations through a cadre of local administrators trained and disciplined in the metropoles or in local educational institutions. Anticolonial nationalism emerged among these "bilingual intelligentsias" of the colonial world, as they realized that they were never meant to have full access to the "ethnicized" universalism of the West (Anderson 1991, 113–40).

Indian nationalist discourse was from the outset marked by an ambiguous and painful relation with what were seen as the epitomes of the western world—institutional order, reason, science, and cultural self-assertion—features that were also to be at the heart of the desired new imagined national community. The "nation" was that abstract and highly mobile sign that could enable the emerging native forms of modernity to become both truly modern and, at the same time, deeply authentic and unique.

The varied historical trajectories of western societies had endowed the term "nation" with a complex conceptual grammar and a complex set of connotations. The nation could be located in the political community of national citizens, and thus make the state a supreme national symbol; or the nation could reside in the allegedly perennial cultural *Volksgemeinschaft* prior to, and elevated above, the profanity and contingencies of politics. Nationalism could harbor projects of radical social transformation as well as those of conservative modernization; the nation could signify emancipation from colonialism and yet reify and consolidate existing forms of social domination. The nation could, in other words, be such an effective "empty signifier" only because it was "overfilled," marked by ambiguous and polyvalent closures.

In Europe and the Americas, nationalism was linked to formation of states striving to produce cultural homogenization, authorized histories, unified languages and educational systems, and shared symbols of authority. States attempted to represent the nation as an all-encompassing principle of order and governance, and strove systematically to produce "the people" as an homogenous entity, organizing it around what Balibar calls a "fictive ethnicity." Every nation-state was founded upon a series of exclusions of the "others," and was stabilized through governmentalities inscribing nationality in the most intimate of relations: family life, child rearing, education, public ethos, fears and racist stereotypes of the other, management of female sexuality, and so on. The intention was to install the territorial boundaries of the nation as inner mental boundaries in the minds of its citizens (Balibar 1991, 93–95).

The processes of "nationalization" of states and people in Europe and the Americas were, however, uneven and contingent. We must ask how it was possible for this new nationalist governmentality and this new imagery of emotional links between (equal) citizens and compatriots to replace the constitutive difference between the rulers and subjects. Anderson seems to suggest that if nationalism had not arisen, another cultural system with the same cohesive functions and potentials would have emerged. But can we assume that a society always needs a single hegemonic language and referential frame through which rulers can establish bonds of intelligibility and legitimacy vis-à-vis their subjects? My contention is here that the attempt to hegemonize, to rule through shared values, unification, and consent, was probably an effect of the nationalization of political authority rather than its preexisting imperative.

Similarly, instead of accepting nationalism's claim that it belongs to the realm of culture, as Anderson does, we must ask how the nation became "culturalized." In my view, culture is yesterday's politics stabilized, depoliticized, and authorized as "truth" and "history," and we must scrutinize how governments, intellectuals, and movements made culture and nation coincide, and subsequently made this pair a compelling element of popular identities. In my view the emergence of popular national identities in nineteenth-century Europe was intimately linked to the specific political spaces created by the new forms of governance and the democratic revolutions unfolding in European societies. Hobsbawm observed that "the major political changes which turned a potential receptivity to national appeals into actual reception, were the democratization of politics in a growing number of states, and the creation of modern administrative, citizen-mobilizing and citizen-influencing states" (Hobsbawm 1990, 110). The formation of mass electorates was crucial to the crystallization of national identity in several ways. "The people" could no longer be regarded as an abstract, fascinating object of sentimentality or fear, but appeared now as an amorphous mass waiting at the ballot box to pass its verdict. This introduced a new element of radical undecidability and unpredictability into the social world, and thus also a new desire to control and master this amorphous people through ideological purity. At the same time, the gradual enfranchisement of growing segments of the populations went hand in hand with formation of labor unions, peasant associations, religious movements, and civil associations. This not only changed the imaginings of the social world but also made it possible for ordinary people to inscribe themselves, their lives and localities, into an overall matrix of national space and the collective history of the "nation-people." The state and political and social movements now sought to reach "the masses" in idioms organized around appeals to abstract notions of "people," "rights," "nation," the "citizen," and so on—constructs whose intelligibility presupposed that the state was perceived as a social reality of institutions and authority; that the role of individual citizen had been experienced vis-à-vis the legal system; and that the encounters with an abstract anonymous world of an urban mass society had been frequent enough to make such imagined entities seem meaningful.

My argument is, in brief, that national identities assumed very different modalities in various parts of Europe and the Americas, not necessarily because they reflected cultural differences per se but because they emerged from specific trajectories of modernity, governance, and democratic revolution in each society. The specificities of anticolonial forms of nationalism are therefore not necessarily to be found in a supposedly different civilizational grammar existing in the "Orient" or in Africa. These specificities should, I would argue, be found in the specific ways in which colonial government and modernity shaped the production of cultural differences between colonizers and colonized, and thus rendered certain structured spaces for political contestation of colonial rule.[11]

Colonial Governmentalities

Can colonial government in India be analyzed in a Foucauldian vein as a form of modern technology of scientific government adapted to the peculiar conditions in the tropics, but at the same time completely alien to the colonial subjects? Or should we rather look at the colonial state as an Indian state whose rituals and modes of functioning drew on a cultural archive of political traditions in India? If we combine these interpretative avenues we may understand colonial government as characterized by two sets of not always compatible strategies: on the one hand, the administrative strategies by which the rulers sought to "know" the colonial territory and subject it to bureaucratic systematization; and, on the other hand, the political strategies through which policy objectives, institutional designs, and larger visions of transformation were presented to and negotiatiated with native representatives in designated arenas, in order to retain peace and stability. This perspective allows us to understand not only the strategies and designs of colonial governance but also how this technical governance was unable to fixate and know completely the social world of India. Each new policy was negotiated and provisional; it created new spaces of opposition and provided new potential languages of contention. This double perspective allows us, in other words, to understand the provisional incompleteness at the heart of colonial rule, and it thus allows us to understand the incipient politics of nationalism in colonial India as moments in an uneven democratic revolution.

Colonial governance in India developed slowly. It was not a full-scale violent imposition of a foreign epistemology and domination, but evolved through complex layers of cooptation, complicity, and transformation, not least in and around the urban centers in Madras, Calcutta, and Bombay. The sheer size and sophistication of the emerging educated middle classes, their preponderance in the governmental services, and the general emphasis on pragmatic incorporation of elite segments all over India into the structure of governance meant that colonial rule was organized around a crucial "double discourse." On the one hand there was the huge mass of ordinary people, peasants, artisans, and "coolies"—in brief, subaltern groups that were regarded as irrational, passionate, and traditional and, therefore, in need of firm governance as subjects of the colonial state. On the other hand, were the educated middle classes, the zamindari (agricultural) landlords, the literate elites in provincial towns, and the "natural" leaders of sects, castes, petty kingdoms, and religious communities—a leadership sometimes created by acts of investiture performed by colonial officers—who were considered to be amenable to reasoned persuasion and negotiation. These latter groups were the pillars of colonial rule, entrusted with the local administration below the district level: revenue collection, the management of affairs viewed as internal to communities, and so on. It was also these groups that were accorded certain rights to political representation and rights to organize a diverse range of cultural and civil associations and vernacular public spheres that developed in the latter half of the nineteenth century.

The colonial state in India was, however, never bifurcated, as was the case in parts of Africa. According to Mamdani, the bifurcation of the colonial state in Africa was expressed in a spatial separation between direct rule under colonial law in the urban areas and indirect rule through "native authorities" and customary law in the rural areas (Mamdani 1996, 3–34). In India, the bifurcation was more subtle and negotiable, premised on social rank and on mastery of western conceptual languages rather than on space and "tradition." This flexibility made it a more effective bifurcation between proper "society" and the world of the "masses," and certainly a more enduring construction, as we shall see when we examine the cultural constructions of politics and public representations in postcolonial India. Both the "masses" and the incipient group of partly enfranchised "citizens" were subjected, albeit in different ways, to direct governance in matters pertaining to property, security, and taxation, whereas areas considered sensitive and at the heart of the Orient—religion, community, and family—were expected to be governed by relevant and duly authorized native bodies. The princely states in India were subjected to indirect control, ruled by local notables who were controlled and supervised by the "Resident" (representative) of the British Crown. But even in these states the techniques of governance practiced in the colonial territories were gradually imported and implemented, as Kooiman has shown with respect to the census administration (Kooiman, 1996). I will discuss only two aspects of colonial governance, the imposition of a new legal system and the new system of census operations that made a new form of empirical governance possible.

The colonial legal system was framed around the idea that a common penal code was superior to local customary codes, and around separate bodies of legislation regarding property relations, religion, family law, and so on. The system of legal practices developed unevenly throughout the nineteenth century. In south India, the colonial authorities attempted to turn local customary laws and local panchayats (councils) into effective and more uniform adjudicators of a variety of local disputes. Rules, styles of argumentation, and production of evidence were standardized and anglicized (Appadurai 1981, 68–69), while Brahmin pundits were recruited to provide cogent interpretations of jurisprudence in accordance with ancient Hindu scriptures, and thus provide what was believed to be a more authentic and pure cultural interpretation of legal practices (Washbrook 1981, 653). This process of scripturalization and brahminization of customary law pertained primarily to family matters, marriages, and disputes over inheritance among Hindus. After India came under the direct administration of the Crown in 1858, this legislation was generalized and British interpretations of the *Manusmriti*, the ancient Hindu law code, became the basis for identification of Hindus as a unified legal entity, and major reforms supposed to regulate Hindu marriage practices all over India were introduced (Heimsath 1964).

Although family matters had conventionally been adjudicated by panchayats within endogamous jatis, such caste groups were not, as Galanter remarks, treated as completely on a par with religious communities that had their own rules. They were merely groups before the law and as such, in principle, equal to other groups. The British were reluctant to extend formal legal support or sanction to barriers and inequalities between caste groups, as caste was regarded as a barbaric and undesirable custom. However, direct intervention in the irrational kernel of Indian culture—matters of family and faith—had proved to have adverse effects, for example in the case of the turbulence caused by the Age of Consent Bill introduced among Hindus in western India in the 1880s (Galanter 1984, 18–25). The colonial government refrained henceforth from further direct reforms of Hindu practices in these domains.

The institution and development of separate legal complexes adjudicating personal law for Muslims, Sikhs, and others was intensified and institutionalized in bodies of learned authorities appointed by the colonial government to adjudicate in matters deemed internal to these communities, and to administer religious institutions and property. The outcome was a large body of what one could call "distilled tradition" in the Anglo-Muhammadan law complex (Anderson 1990, 205–23), and a similar though less elaborated legal complex applying to Sikhs evolving in the 1920s, which was from 1925 onward administered by the powerful Shiromani Gurdwara Parbandhak Committee.

In the realm of legal institutions, the colonial double discourse made the issue of legal subjects in India deeply ambiguous. On the one hand, an individual was a person with property rights and an entitlement to due process, liable to conviction and prosecution and so on, under the universal penal code. On the other hand, the same individual was a member of a collective imbued with certain customs, and was assumed to be passionately dedicated to customs pertaining to emotional issues of faith, family, and marriage, all areas that evaded the logic of modern jurisprudence. Clearly, a propertied and educated gentleman of the urban middle class would be expected to identify more with the former concept of legality and would be expected to be capable of rational calculation, whereas the poor and uneducated rural dweller was seen as living almost entirely within the latter more "traditional" concept of legality. The problem seen from the point of view of the colonial state was not merely the irrationality of the masses but rather the undecidable character of the "urban citizen"—the irreducible residue of religion and tradition that prevented the colonial middle classes from being fully modern and fully rational. The solution pursued was to encapsulate these ungovernable religious sentiments in designated institutions, and see to that these potentially explosive sentiments were not made the basis for political mobilizations by "irresponsible" members of the "educated class."

The double discourse of colonial government thus transformed notions of equality before the law and legal codification of rights into an emerging paradigm of equality among castes and religious groups, and into an increasing codification of rights on parts of castes and communities. This process of codification tended to "freeze" Indian society by turning negotiable boundaries of caste and community into timeless, cultural features of a precolonial past (Dirks 1992). Communities were produced as ever more coherent and objectified groups even as they were competing for legal recognition, enfranchisement, preferential schemes, and collective social mobility through education and bureaucratic employment.

The most conspicuous expression of this was the formation of caste associations among higher-caste groups and numerically large peasant jatis from the end of the nineteenth century onward. Caste identities were reified with the help of former census commissioner H. H. Risley's monumental work, *The People of India* (1908). Caste myths were systematized, and the dynamics of vertical bonds of patronage within the caste groups, as well as horizontal solidarities across localities and regions, soon made caste associations into large syndicated regional bodies of growing political importance. In southern and northwestern India, caste associations soon became instrumental in launching educational schemes and demanding government employment for their members (Rudolph and Rudolph 1967, 29–132).

In sum, the imposition and evolution of these bifurcated structures of law and legal procedure in India had two main effects. First, they reified and legally authorized a certain interpretation of Indian society as being made up of discrete and legally incompatible communities and caste groups that were governable only through encapsulation and control of their irrational religious passion. This is a construction that lives on in the postcolonial state, and the inhabitation of the "identity slots" produced by it is still going on. Second, and perhaps more importantly, the introduction of the colonial legal system displaced earlier and more localized notions of arbitration and justice, and introduced into legal practice the two inherently expansive elements of universality and equality, that cut to the heart of the Hindu family, property relations, and so on. This undermined earlier and more distant forms of royal and aristocratic authority based on what Kaviraj has called "majesty and marginality"—grand in their forms but ineffective in their penetration of society (Kaviraj 1997a, 231–33).

The best-known and most conspicuous endeavor toward producing governable objects in India was the census, instituted in the 1870s. In the spirit of positivism, it aimed at establishing all the empirical facts required for modern governance of each district in India. One of the paramount tasks was to map the exact topography of cultural communities in order to establish some sort of systematic intelligibility of that alien world. The north Indian example demonstrates lucidly how the imposition of a colonial governmentality provided a new matrix of intelligibility through which native subjects could come to know themselves as communities, and how this new matrix displaced older hierarchies and produced a social imaginary structured by consolidated— in principle equal—communities in competition.[12]

First, north India had for centuries been marked by rather clear political and military hierarchies governed by a mainly Muslim elite. Religious identities were both visible and subject to political regulation, but were not necessarily important in relation to the distribution and exercise of power, as long social hierarchies and political loyalties remained intact and nonnegotiable.[13] With the intrusion of British colonialism, these political hierarchies were subverted and rendered fluid and negotiable, especially after the rebellion of 1857 and the subsequent curbing of the political power of Muslim rulers all over the subcontinent. The higher-caste Hindu communities that had most effectively utilized and domesticated the new educational and commercial opportunities which emerged within the colonial state gained new power and public visibility as representatives and "natural leaders" of the Hindu community, which was in all respects "fuzzy" and incoherent. Conversely, Muslim elites bereft of both their former aura and their "mandate to rule" and patronage power, were now forced to represent themselves and their authority as representatives and legitimate leaders of the Muslim community as such.[14]

Second, enumeration was also central to the mechanisms through which natives were to be represented in accordance with their numerical weight. From the 1880s on, the Indian Councils overlooking local municipal administration emerged, but the criteria of eligibility was (as in Britain itself) determined by income levels and property, which generally disadvantaged Muslims and the lower classes. This heavily limited the representativeness of the councils in relation to the now-available knowledge of the precise numbers of various communities (however randomly defined).[15] This discrepancy between the size of communities—increasingly thought of as majorities versus minorities—and their relative representation in the political arenas of the state emerged to be among the paramount issues of contention in the remaining part of the colonial period. The nationalist forces exerted pressure for expansion of both franchise and administrative competence but within the characteristically colonial double discourse, demanding more influence for the elite and middle class by claiming that these represented the masses living in discrete communities. The colonial authorities responded in a similar vein, granting franchise according to such ostensibly neutral standards as income and education, while creating separate, though limited, constituencies for Muslims after the Morley-Minto reforms of 1909. In the province of Punjab, Muslims had been granted separate representation at the level of municipalities as far back as 1886–1887 in order to match their numerical weight, as the official argument went (Tuteja and Grewal 1992, 10). The Montagu-Chelmsford reforms in 1919 established separate Hindu and Muslim mass constituencies, in accordance with the Lucknow pact of 1916 between the Congress and the Muslim League. These constituencies, based on the meticulously collected census data of the colonial state, were, however, unable to eradicate all the ambiguities of belonging to communities, and boosted communal mass mobilization in the 1920s and 1930s. This introduction of a quasi-democratic discourse of fair representation, however lopsided, made the colonial enumeration of communities a constant reference in the subsequent struggles over the production of the Indian people.[16]

Third, the notions of equality among communities as well as the knowledge of relative sizes of communities were gradually becoming popular common sense in north India. This added a new twist to the already well established sense of multiple markers of difference separating Hindus and Muslims. Recent historical research has suggested that the sense of exclusionary communities had been articulated and contested in the realm of popular culture in public arenas such as festivals, processions, wrestling pits, religious associations, and networks of dependence and control throughout the nineteenth century (Kumar 1992; Alter 1992). Freitag argues that the riots taking place between communities or against the state in this period were integral parts of this structured expression of communitas (Freitag 1990, 93–94). She argues that communalism in north India emerged because of the increasing disjuncture between state structures of administration and representation, on the one hand, and the public arenas where popular cultures and protests negotiated the terms of domination, so to speak, on the other. In Freitag's perspective, the more politicized versions of

communalism that emerged in the 1920s represented attempts to inte-
grate the two dimensions of the prevalent double discourse on communities, namely, as both popular and irrational idioms of communitas
and as bearers of collective interests with a right to representation in
the sphere of the state. In my view, this perspective tends to reiterate
the conventional view of religion as the "natural" and primary signifier
around which Indian culture is organized, and of Indians as imbued
with an impenetrable spirit of communitas. Freitag seems to suggest
that the masses of north India were incapable of comprehending the
message of modern nationalism unless it was translated into a localized
idiom of community and kinship.[17]

In my view, colonial modernity introduced a novel horizon that crystallized in and around modern institutions and modern forms of
knowledge. This new horizon did not replace older forms of doxa but
dislocated them by introducing a new conceptual grammar into the
meaning of public manifestations and ritual: empirical knowledge-
practices enumerated communities and introduced the notion of numbers and rights to equal representation of abstract, and yet precise,
Hindu and Muslim communities; cultural reform movements strove to
organize and systematize the inner life of communities; and new institutions and practices of community began too impinge on religious
practices, education, festivals, and so forth.

This new conceptual grammar was partly internalized by ordinary
urban dwellers in north India, not because it necessarily corresponded
to historically developed social practices but rather because it was
readily available and authorized by the colonial state as well as the
new elites, in a situation where older principles of intelligibility, such
as the mandate of princely families to rule, had been questioned and
displaced.[18]

The protracted cow protection movement in north India in the last
decades of the nineteenth century was therefore not only an extension
and radicalization of local communitas in public arenas, enlarged by
print capitalism and increased communication. The movement was
successful because it recruited and transformed a range of existing
idioms of community—caste, sect, and locality—into a new and abstract discourse of a cultural community of Hindus, and thus combined
various types of diffuse resentment into a sharper focus organized
around a dense metaphor, the *gau mata* (mother cow) threatened by
the British and the Muslims. This campaign altered and generalized the
symbol of the cow, the meanings of being Hindu, and not least, the
very meaning attributed to communities in local arenas. Communities—especially Hindus and Muslims—could now increasingly be
"talked into existence" within a generalized, supralocal nationalist dis-

course and imagination. The local Muslims or Hindus in a village were no longer merely local; they could also be regarded as anonymous and faceless crystallizations of the larger and ever more systematized social fantasies of the other community.

Colonial governmentalities provided a deeply contradictory matrix for the imagination of society. On the one hand, they fixed, defined, and restricted every unit of the social world with unprecedented clarity, thus defining very precise "identity slots" open for inhabitation. This reified and froze Indian society in several respects. On the other hand, colonial governmentalities also introduced a much higher level of physical mobility, a qualitative leap in communication, and uniform administration and education, creating general subjects of the state. Movement, literacy, and migration were encouraged, and the representation of empire and the colonial state produced essentially supralocal social imaginaries. But mobility was also structured by the colonial double discourse. Apart from going abroad as indentured laborers and being recruited into the colonial army, ordinary people were generally constricted in their movement, tied to labor contracts and land settlements, whereas the colonial middle classes had access to new forms of movement and new forms of supralocal social imagination. As we shall see, this distinction between the bounded, parochial, and therefore innocent masses, and the essentially mobile, knowledgeable, modern, and supposedly responsible national elite remained a cornerstone in dominant social imaginaries of the postcolonial period.

India as a Cultural Nation

The relatively liberal policy of the British government, ostensibly committed to a civilized dialogue with western-educated Indians, generated hope among Indians of achieving more representation and recognition through prudent negotiations. The British did not regard the many organizations and new institutions emerging in the cultural and religious realm in the major cities of India in the nineteenth century as threats to colonial authority, but as natural expressions of the deep commitment to spiritual matters that was the essence of "the oriental" from high to low in society. The endeavors of the religious reform movements were regarded by many colonial officers as laudable attempts to purge Hinduism and Islam of superstition and barbaric practices.

Liberalism and Christian humanism offered to the native colonial elite a vision of recognition through identity and equality, if only the native elite appropriated and mastered the discourses and habits of the

West properly. Early generations of social reformers and intellectuals of South Asia interpreted the messages of liberalism and humanism literally as genuine commitments to universal ideas.[19] These intellectuals strove to retrieve the conceptual grammar of the liberal-democratic discourse from the connotative domain it had developed in the West, and to implant it in a colonial context as a critique of colonialism's incompatibility with true universalism. They constructed public spheres flourishing with newspapers and journals, "learned societies," educational institutions, and associations pushing for social reform legislation, indigenous political representation, and religious reform. The leadership from these associations, and the Indian National Congress formed in 1885, pursued gradual negotiated enfranchisement of the colonial middle class, and supported "enlightened" reforms of a range of social and religious institutions in India (Seal 1968).

In spite of the liberal inclinations of this first generation of nationalist leaders in India, liberalism never evolved into a permanent stream in Indian politics. Although there was a solid commitment in favor of private property rights among early Indian nationalist politicians, a more elaborate rhetoric of individual rights, of the virtues of political competition as a trope of the market, and so on, never developed (Kaviraj 1995a, 96–97). Because the paramount issue governing the political field in colonial India was that of (limited) representation of communities through elite representatives, and because the colonial governmentality had authorized community as the natural oriental form, the discourse of rights and equality was applied almost entirely to collectivities. With the radicalization of nationalist politics around the turn of the century, and mounting mass mobilizations along cultural-religious lines, questions of the right of the nation as such vis-à-vis the colonial power became an ever more dominant problematic. Political competition, mobilization of discrete communities' interests, as well as infighting and factionalism at the local level did proliferate, but were now increasingly denounced as impediments to the greater cause of national independence. Social struggles against indigenous elites had to be curbed and defused in order to build an anticolonial coalition around horizontal alliances among segments of the middle classes and social elites who sought to control their community or locality through vertical ties of dependency.[20]

It was in some ways inevitable that the discourse of cultural difference became dominant in nationalist politics. The discourse of cultural authenticity, which originated in romantic nationalism, constituted a very influential stream within orientalist scholarship. The nationalist philosophy of Herder and Fichte had generated an influential discourse of the nation "beyond politics," residing in the cultural realm of a people as a permanent life force and enunciating "popular truth" in spite of domination and the corruption of elites. This discourse appeared eminently meaningful to large sections of the colonial middle classes in India.

To Herder, nations were fundamental to the natural plan of the world, and "the national soul is the mother of all culture upon earth—all culture is but expressions of national souls" (Herder 1965, 262). This national soul was the fundamental and natural *Geist* (spirit) in the world, a spirit that always resided in its purest form through the ages among the common *Volk*. This spirit, whose true essence Herder argued was inexpressible, encouraged individuals to great deeds and artistic excellence on behalf of their nation. Herder's theories of holism, cultural groups, and nations were most eloquently expressed in his writings that called for a national regeneration of Germany. Here he thundered against the vulgar ways in which French high culture had become the object of snobbery even in the *Volk* he so firmly believed was (or should be) the true bearer of the national spirit. Herder and the group of intellectuals interpreting his work contributed decisively to this political romanticism in Germany and elsewhere in Europe. However, organicist conceptions of societal life and appropriate modes of governance that provided a set of practices closely related to Herder's organicist philosophy had been flourishing both under Prussian absolutism and in many of the princely German states in the eighteenth century.[21]

In J. G. Fichte's famous *Reden and die Deutschen Nation* from 1807 (Fichte 1922/1955) he argued that although cultures were constituted by the nature-given essence of nationality, they could only survive and develop through profound emotional attachment to a state that gave body to the nation. Such a national state, Fichte argued, would be invincible and would surpass other states built on a forcefully subdued population, by virtue of its sheer collective will power and determination. An inner national strength could even make up for inferiority in armament or productive power.[22] To Fichte, cultural nationalism was ultimately dependent on will: the individual's will to loyalty and sacrifice ultimately determined the nation's will to cohesion and organization. Such a forceful national spirit needed to be nurtured and kept vital through education and patriotic enlightenment (Fichte 1922, 83). The ambivalent distinction between state and nation traversed Fichte's work. On the one hand, the state was a necessary vehicle of temporal power, pivotal to the great "pedagogical" effort of producing national citizens; on the other hand, the nation had a more sublime and transcendental quality, existing as a vibrant state of mind and inner bond among patriotic men, elevated above historical contingency and the petty concerns of politics, and therefore providing the very life force of a healthy society (Balibar 1993, 61–86).

This romanticist paradigm remained no mere "German ideology," as Dumont has suggested (Dumont 1994, 17–39), but spread rapidly to the rest of the world. The idea of the nation as popular, cultural, and latent, and yet in need of protection and pedagogical refinement by the state and patriotic citizens, soon became part and parcel of the political imaginary in large parts of Europe. In India, the romanticist vision of recuperation of past glory and latent spirituality of India through employment of modern techniques of scholarship, modern organization, discipline, and collective will in order to overcome the humiliation inflicted by colonial rule struck a receptive chord in parts of the intelligentsia.

Cultural nationalism thus became the most powerful impulse arising out of the late-nineteenth-century public stirrings. Romanticist notions of fullness, spirituality, depth, sensitivity, and authenticity offered a powerful and consistent critique of the flawed universalism of the West; and it offered a critique of instrumental rationality, industrial modernity, and fragmentation of the modern social world without challenging social hierarchies in any radical fashion.

Cultural nationalism in India, in other words, grew not only out of "Indian culture" as such but also out of the specific process through which Indian elites began to inhabit, and make sense of, received romanticist notions of authenticity and deep cultural differences between East and West. This is generally the way in which discursive horizons and conceptual grammars extend themselves in time and space. I therefore find Partha Chatterjee's objection to the notion of historically developed modular forms of nationalisms rendered for pirating in the rest of the world somewhat puzzling. Chatterjee writes: "If nationalisms in the rest of the world have to choose their imagined community from certain 'modular' forms already made available to them by Europe and the Americas, what do they have left to imagine?. . . [E]ven our imaginations must remain forever colonized" (Chatterjee 1993, 5). Chatterjee argues that the colonial world historically was the "radical outside" of modernity, an intransigent web of difference that today also defies western categorization and epistemic dominance, and whose undecidability undermines the entire edifice of a social science with universalizing ambitions.

The question is, however, whether this rule through "colonial difference," the exclusion of Indians from higher office and from cultural recognition on the grounds of their race and alleged barbarism, fully warrants this general conclusion. Were not, and are not, all hegemonic and imperial regimes founded on the differentiation between the ruled and the rulers, on depriving the ruled of their humanity to make it easier and less disturbing to exclude them, imprison them, and exterminate them?

Chatterjee identifies a unique feature of anticolonial resistance in the literate Indian middle classes, namely, its creation of an "inner" spiritual, culturally sovereign realm closed off from the colonial state—while competing along western standards in the "outer" realm of politics and economy—which makes it impossible to talk of any direct emulation of western modular forms of nationalism. But did not the vast majority of European nationalisms also emerge with a similar model inspired by romanticist/cultural nationalism: the cultivation of a national language, history, education, and public sphere outside the purview of imperial or centralized power? This construction of the nation as residing in an "inner" cultural domain, I argue, had to do first and foremost with the structure of domination—the structure of their "othering"—and with the structure of knowledge through which the dominated people came to know themselves as cultures—whether through orientalist celebrations of spirituality and difference, or as inventions of Slavic spiritual mysticism, or of a Celtic golden age in Ireland—rather than through any intrinsic colonial difference.

Like other forms of nationalism, the varieties of nationalism that emerged in India were original, specific, and "different" from the outset. They developed their own connotative domains and vernacularized the ideological forms they imported and had imposed on them. The subsequent production of the Indian people throughout the twentieth century did not take place as a flawed imposition of a western political idiom upon masses living through pristine subaltern or religious ontologies, and thus accessible only through Gandhi's saintly discourse. The Indian masses had always been subjects in their own histories—but never as Indians, and rarely as objectified communities with clear boundaries and identities. The nationalism of the colonial middle classes sought to speak the Indian people into existence for itself through the peculiar modern discourse on the people: on the one hand, imagined as an ignorant, uneducated mass to be dignified and elevated through development and nationhood, while, on the other hand, imagined as a "people-nation" embodying an essential and authentic cultural spirit, but only accessible to that peculiar breed of national citizens who held a genuine and humble understanding of that spirit (Seth 1992). The true people in the latter sense was an "empty signifier," an unrepresentable abstraction that within the horizons of the middle classes remained more true than any of its concrete, always profane, representations. When the actual masses, once in a while, did enter the stage of political conflict during the colonial period they inevitably failed to follow the script prepared by middle-class ideologues. To the nationalist leadership the main challenge appeared to be how the masses and their uncontrollable emotions could be directed and led.

Competing Nationalist Discourses

The 1920s were crucial in the history of Indian nationalism in two respects. First, they marked the point at which "the masses" entered the modern Indian history of political representation. The electoral reforms in 1919 expanded the popular franchise and enlarged the competencies under the purview of the elected bodies at local and provincial levels. This increased the stakes in electoral politics and made the consolidation of popular electoral constituencies—the politics of numbers—a central concern.[23] At the same time, Gandhi's innovative strategies of mass mobilization during the Non-Cooperation campaign and the concomitant participation of the Khilafat agitation, which for the first time mobilized large numbers of ordinary Muslims for political action, meant that the entire Congress organization was enlarged and geared to systematic contact with broader sections of the population in both rural and urban areas.[24] Similar populist strategies were also adopted by other political organizations employing more belligerent idioms than did Congress, such as the Muslim League and the Hindu Mahasabha.

Political activists from urban middle-class backgrounds now became increasingly acquainted with the social worlds of the poor, and public arenas for political assertion moved away from closed sessions and deliberations and into mass rallies in public spaces. Along with this "massification" of the political scene the period saw a steep rise in violent clashes between Hindus and Muslims. The nationalist leadership, the middle classes, and the colonial police often regarded these outbursts of violence as unfortunate effects of the entry of the illiterate masses' irrationality onto the political stage. However, as I shall demonstrate in the following chapters, violence, the manufacturing of demonic others, and fear of the illiterate masses were always crucial to the political imaginaries and the political strategies of the middle class in India.

Second, the 1920s was a period in which the divergent visions of the Indian nation, which since the turn of the century had cohabited under the slogan of "swaraj" (self-rule), now developed into competing nationalist discourses. These competing visions all tried to address the most pertinent question of the day, namely, the relation between cultural communities and the question of which community the Indian nation was going to belong to. Gandhi's radicalization of the anticolonial agenda had pushed this question to the fore. Gandhi had also provided a new answer that combined the older "orientalist mode of production of the people" as discrete entities with a celebration of Indian spirituality consonant with the conservatism of Hindu orthodoxy (*sanatana dharma*) within a new, populist assertion of the overriding antagonism between India and the West.

Although Gandhi's practices were syncretic—he quoted from the Bible, the Qur'an, and the Upanishads at his legendary morning prayers, and promoted the notion of "equal respect for all faiths"—he staged his national vision, his bodily comportment, and his superior will power within an essentially upper-caste Hindu register of cultural practices (van der Veer 1994, 94–99). Gandhi's idea of the nation was cultural in the romanticist sense, that is, an essentially spiritual unity, an ideal state of fullness and harmony that had to be elevated above the petty strife between communities. Gandhi favored tolerance, compassion, and the rule of law, but he was not a liberal democrat. On the contrary, there was a powerful trend of "antipolitical" organicist communitarianism in Gandhi's thought and practices and in his ideal of self-governing, harmonious village communities. Faithful to the teachings of Vivekananda, and inspired by Thoreau and Tolstoy, Gandhi held that the divine resided in the people, and that the pursuit of God was the pursuit of swaraj for the nation, communities, and individuals.[25]

Gandhi's ability to represent and give body to the middle-class social fantasy of the masses as an "empty signifier" of political innocence and religious purity did indeed create a large space for himself within the nationalist movement. To many, he became nothing less than a redeemer who made it possible to transcend the strategic deadlock of the national movement, to abstract from the everyday realities of localized political conflict, and to play down internal differences in favor of the grander cause of independence.

The interpretations of the relation between the greater nation and its constituent communities hence emerged as a continuum. At one pole were the communitarian nationalists in the Hindu Mahasabha and Muslim League, for whom the nation should be a political codification of a single cultural community, Hindu or Muslim. There was Gandhi's syncretic populism that retained the orientalist idea of India as a series of discrete communities united under a larger, spiritual idea of the nation as harmony. Finally, Nehru and many leftists in the 1930s developed the idea of the Indian nation as an abstract, modern (synthetic) ideal that could transcend older identifications with community and caste by relegating them to the realm of the irrational and premodern, and eventually render them irrelevant.

Producing Citizens and Communities in Independent India

The independent Indian nation state that came into being in August 1947 was not a new state. The turmoil around Partition, internal disturbances, and the integration of the many princely states into the Indian Union in the first years after Independence meant that the Congress leadership, in particular Home Minister Vallabhai Patel, was opposed to any major administrative reform (Potter 1986, 121–26). Most of the administrative functions, rules, and technologies of governance of the late colonial administration lived on in the Indian state, not least in the realm of policing, taxation, and the legal machinery. The dominant bureaucratic ethos of an apparatus that for decades had been overwhelmingly recruited from the upper rungs of the caste hierarchies also remained in place. The takeover of the state was, therefore, not any massive process of "deracialization" of the state comparable to the decolonization process in Africa.[26] For decades, the new state carried on the fundamental double discourse that governed middle-class *society* through law and rational procedure, and ruled popular *communities* through rather repressive means and through the long-standing connivance and shared political imaginaries of local social elites and the local representatives of the state.

The other part of the more persistent "political culture" that continued in various forms after Independence was what Kaviraj has called the popular perceptions of the state's "marginality, exteriority, and persistent repressiveness against the lower strata of the people" (Kaviraj 1997a, 233). One of the paradoxes confronting the new nationalist leadership was that it had to reverse its own critique of the practices and governmentalities of the colonial state and make these same, often unreformed, practices and rationalities into an instrument of social transformation. In so doing, the nationalist elite faced a range of popular practices vis-à-vis the state—petty forms of defiance, evasions from control, abstention, and all the other forms of everyday "cunning tactics" that the nationalist movement had encouraged and had occasionally made deft use of as instruments of nonviolent resistance.[27]

What for years had been seen as a welcome nuisance to colonial government, a living proof of the vigor and spirit of the Indian people, was now seen as a problem of order in the nation-state, or rather a problem of indiscipline and lack of "civic sense" on the part of the masses who consistently failed to behave as required by citizens of a nation-state. Myrdal quoted Nehru as saying in 1958: "A country which for a whole generation practiced a certain technique of opposition to the government, when it has its own government, it is not easy to shift over or to make people think differently. . . . [P]eople still have the habit of opposing the government. Secondly, they are apt to adopt that technique, not rightly I think, but some variation of it, just to press on some complaint or something which is sometimes apt to be a nuisance" (Myrdal 1968, 897). The granting of universal franchise to all adult Indians in the new Indian state was a logical corollary of decades of nationalist campaigns for expanded representation of Indians in legislative bodies. The issue of enfranchisement had been subordinated to other concerns, however, such as balanced representation of communities in municipal and provincial bodies. The slogan of "one man–one vote" had never figured prominently during the anticolonial struggle. National independence and national unity were seen as major preconditions for, and safeguards of, the dignity of individuals, the "uplift of the masses," and the other well-known elements of the dominant nationalist discourse of the Congress party.

There was a remarkable shift after Independence in the way social inequality and social and cultural divisions in Indian society were problematized. The anticolonial critique of the injustices of poverty and exploitation ascribed to foreign domination and cruel traditions now gave way to a more practical and more openly paternalist discourse on the "ignorance and superstition" of the masses as obstacles to national development. In the draft for the first Five-Year Plan it was stated, "[Certain] conditions have to be fulfilled before the full flow of the people's energy for the task of the national reconstruction can be assured. The ignorance and apathy of large numbers have to be overcome" (Government of India 1951, 235).

The responsibility of giving political influence to the masses, of reforming social habits, and of gradually civilizing the Indian masses—in brief, to produce the Indian people as a national people through reform and education—now became the task of the institutions of the state, the political elite, and the social world of the middle class they represented. As I noted in the previous section, the language of negative rights defined in opposition to a dominant power were throughout the anticolonial struggle subordinated to a discourse of rights of communities (to representation, separate legislation, recognition, and so on) and of the right to national self-determination. Now the language of rights reappeared, not as negative rights but as positive entitlements to be secured and granted by the state. In the foreword to the first Five-Year Plan it was stated in 1952: "[the objective] is not merely re-channeling economic activity within the existing socio-economic framework; that framework has itself to be remolded so as to enable it to accommodate progressively those fundamental urges which express themselves in the demands for the right to work, the right to adequate income, the right to education and to a measure of insurance against old age, sickness and older disabilities" (Government of India 1952, 8).

Rather than reforming the inherited structure of the state that had been made the central vehicle for promoting economic growth and national cohesion, the Congress governments of the 1950s began under Nehru's leadership to expand the apparatus of the state by adding a range of new developmental functions. The most conspicuous of these was the entire apparatus of economic planning that came into being in the following decade. The planning system, supervised by the apex National Planning Committee, successfully constructed a large and diversified sector of state-owned and managed industries, and quite effectively launched and managed a system of regulation and protection of the considerable private industrial sector through the so-called "license system," which came to be known as the "license raj." The planning system was accompanied by a persistent rhetoric of socialism, committing the state to promoting social equality and to providing a new, more rational and refined scientific form of government that would undermine and displace older forms of local authority, and over time also modernize the Indian countryside.

The desire to attract experts, scientists, and elite bureaucrats to supervise and manage this new apparatus of technocratic planning and development was undoubtedly reinforced by the troubled and slow process of negotiating social reforms through the parliamentary process. As Chatterjee has noted, the enthusiastic support for planning was informed by a certain "scientistic" sense of executing a purely rational strategy, beyond and uncontaminated by the compromises and squabbles of electoral politics (Chatterjee 1993, 200–8). The delay and de facto obstruction by resilient, localized, and dispersed landed interests of the much-diluted policy on redistribution of zamindari land and the introduction of ceilings on landholdings (see, for example, Frankel 1978, 156–201) has become the classical example of the inability of democratic governance to bring about profound structural change.

In the Indian countryside, local notables and rich farmers belonging to dominant caste groups, and the local strongmen of the Congress party, presided over extensive structures of clientelist dominance. Voting at local, state, and national levels was easily incorporated into this system of unequal reciprocity, and gave birth to what political sociology in India termed "vote blocs"—relatively stable configurations of votes controlled by local leaders, who were thus in a position to bargain for the flow of governmental resources to their localities and constituencies.

According to Chatterjee, the subsequent interplay between the ostensible rationality of the planning process and the executive agencies of the state, on the other hand, and the constant obstruction of this rationality and the misappropriation of resources by self-interested political forces, on the other, were part of the larger extension of the hegemony of the Indian state through a "passive revolution." He observes: "The paradox in fact is that it is the very 'irrationality' of the political process which continually works to produce legitimacy for the rational exercise of the planner" (ibid., 219).

This period was admittedly marked by a rather consistent trend of impatient technocratic antipolitics, popular within the bureaucracy and in leftist circles—a trend that in some ways was allowed a free run, with disastrous consequences during the Emergency in 1975–1977.[28]

The Congress government was, however, also committed to social reforms and redistribution, but this commitment was severely restricted by the lack of will to intervene in the social processes unfolding beyond the horizons of the culturally dominant middle-class society— among the masses—and the difficulties involved in doing so by democratic means. Myrdal demonstrated this "middle-class bias" in the so-called Mahalanobis Committee Report investigating the causes behind the obvious ineffectiveness of redistributive policies in the early 1960s. The committee abstained from any systematic inquiry into the question of land distribution affecting the vast majority, and focused almost entirely on the so-called modern sectors, technicalities of taxation, and so on (Myrdal 1968, 758–61). In spite of the enlarged field of intervention of the developmental state that undoubtedly made the rhetoric of equality and social reform a central "legitimate problematic," persisting inequalities in the countryside rarely became a burning political issue.

Universal franchise could not in itself translate the numerical weight of the masses into social reform because, as Kaviraj succinctly puts it, the Nehru regime "created a new arena of public life, which, like our public parks, was used only by the cultivated, leisurely unthreatened elites." What developed was, rather, a "strange inversion in the functioning of India's expanding state apparatus, inscribing it with the mark of indelible bad faith" (Kaviraj 1997a, 235). Accompanied by a high rhetoric of socialism and equality, the Indian state became the main provider of resources, jobs, recognition, and protection for the middle classes of bureaucrats, private entrepreneurs, and wealthy farmers—groups that soon developed a solid interest in the continuation of this style of governance.

Meanwhile, ordinary people encountered the state through local and often corrupt extensions of the state institutions, but also gradually learned to decipher the new developmental schemes and appreciate the strategic importance of the new idioms and entitlement categories of "backward sections," "beneficiaries," various categories of landholders, and so on, according to which resources were distributed. Mass participation in democratic processes mainly took place through local brokers and political entrepreneurs working at a safe distance from the high rhetoric of social reform and equality. But the recurring spectacles of elections, the appeals and promises to voters, the pretenses of respect for the "ordinary man," however passing, and the symbolic transfer of power from voters to elected representatives, over time instilled a sense of a moral entitlement to respect from the local elites, as well as expectations of becoming entitled to benefit from one or another developmental scheme. This incipient and humble quest for recognition and entitlements did not alter the brute fact of continued exploitation and often brutal domination by upper caste/class groups in the Indian villages. It was more like a byproduct, an often unintended social effect of the processes of political democracy and of the specific genre of paternalist political discourse in Indian politics that sought to create social change by moral persuasion of the masses, the good example of patriotic citizens, and so on.

As I argued above, Gandhi and the entire cultural nationalist tradition in India saw the essence of the nation as residing in India's cultural communities, whereas the political realm of the colonial state remained a morally empty space, a set of lifeless procedures and culturally alien institutions that could only be given life and indigenous meaning by a vibrant national community outside the political realm. This construction inaugurated a stream of cultural "antipolitics," that is, a production of culture—religion, tradition, ritual practices—as elevated, sublime signs of the nation. In this perspective, politics was a formalized realm of empty necessity, often of a morally questionable nature, capable of "polluting" cultural communities and thus producing communal sentiments as happened in the 1920s, played out in what Chatterjee has called the "outer" dominated realm of colonial society.

But as colonialism came to a close in the 1940s and in the first decades of the existence of the new Indian state, high politics began to be constructed as a "virtuous vocation," a practice wherein upper-caste notions of proper public conduct merged with the supposedly sublime personal qualities that freedom fighters, according to the dominant nationalist mythology, had acquired through the nationalist struggle. This normative reversal did not, however, apply to the "low politics" played out in local clientelist economies, or to the strongmen (*dadas*) in popular neighborhoods. Here, the entire colonial discourse of the evil of so-called criminal elements, and of the *badmash* (hooligans) residing in popular neighborhoods as emblems of all that threatened society and civilization, was appropriated by the nationalist elite and the middle classes.

Instead of merely dismissing this nationalist construction of a moralizing form of politics as an all-too-obvious substitute for effective change, one needs to recognize that this construction, with all its condescension and social narcissism, was a vital part of the prose of the state and of the political imaginaries of millions of people in India in the 1950s and the following decades. Let me indicate briefly how this construction impinged on the discourse of the "village community," and on the construction of secularism as a legitimate problematic in Indian politics.

The most famous official codification of the subtle inner duality of the governance of the Indian state, distinguishing between a traditional realm of culture and community occupied by the masses and a modern-rational middle-class society, was the Community Development Program gradually implemented in the late 1950s. The program involved two elements. First, there was a comprehensive organization of cooperatives in the villages, the establishment of "self-help organizations" aimed at organizing major development projects in the villages (irrigation, drainage, building of schools), which involved only a modest input from the government. The second element was the formation of the "Panchayati Raj" system of local governance: elected councils at village, blocks, and district levels that would coordinate and manage the entire process of community development (Frankel 1978, 99–106). The program was obviously inspired by the belief that an original harmonious village community remained in place at some level of collective memory and could be dug out and revitalized from beneath the decaying and "derelict collection of mud huts and odd individuals," as Nehru wrote about the current state of village life in India.[29] The idea was basically to organize development along "unpolitical" lines, to utilize the innocent energy of the prepolitical communities in order to prepare them for a later entry, when adequately equipped, into the national-modern world of politics and the tantalizing but corrupting world of consumption, physical mobility, and urban life.

Political parties were not supposed to participate in elections for panchayats, in order not to contaminate and derail the process of supposedly unpolitical development work.[30] Instead, the task of supporting and furthering the cause of community development was left to what were considered neutral government experts, and to a host of Gandhian-inspired development organizations recruiting idealistic middle-class youth and retired bureaucrats for voluntary work in the villages.

These gestures gave birth to a very influential construction of the "ideal national citizen" of modern India: the experienced, educated middle-class citizen, well versed in the wicked ways of the world, who devotes a period of his life, or part of his energy, to immersing himself among the masses, to do "selfless work among the downtrodden," as the well-known rhetoric goes, primarily through exemplary conduct and high ethical standards.[31] Such ostensibly "unpolitical" activism was constructed as ennobling and purifying for the individual, whose selflessness was consolidated and moral standards further elevated by this forgetting of oneself and by sustained contact with the true people. This model became a crucial part of the social imaginary in contemporary India, thriving among voluntary organizations and social movements, and abounds today in the nongovernmental organizations.

In spite of being explicitly "antipolitical," this construction of communities, and of community work as purifying made it possible to construct politics as a virtuous activity. Middle-class politicians from the higher castes could engage in patronizing a host of voluntary schemes and extend help to poor communities, and in this way establish a permanent structure of "purification" that could counterbalance the contamination inflicted upon them by the morally empty, or even degrading, involvement with power and money. Some elements of this construction of a noble and selfless character have also been adopted more recently by upwardly mobile strata of politicians from humble origins, and by local brokers and "fixers" who nowadays refer to their political activities as "social work," as "work for the community," and so on. As I will show in my ethnographic material from Maharashtra in subsequent chapters, the credibility of the model of the "virtuous" politician is, however, very specifically linked to his background in higher-caste communities and in middle-class society. Politicians from humble social origins cannot employ this model with equal credibility. It is broadly assumed, that such "plebeian" individuals simply lack the cultural resources and frame of mind that would enable them to be examples for the masses, and enable them to withstand the base desires for money and power of the political world.

The practices of the secular state in India are in fact intimately linked to this peculiar separation of cultural community from the world of politics. The Indian state has never practiced respectful neutrality or distance from religious communities. State policies have, rather, been marked by active regulation and institutionalization of the practices of religious communities along a principle that Donald Smith called "active non-preference," a principle of equal and balanced treatment of every religious community, mainly inherited from the colonial state (Smith 1963, 381).

However, the Hindu Code Bill, the constitution, and other pieces of legislation from the 1940s and 1950s undoubtedly represented a major encroachment upon the right of Hindus to decide upon their own religious affairs, although Hindus remained an exceedingly heterogeneous community whose boundaries this legislation was unable to define and authorize. By not enforcing a similar legislation on Muslims, the practice of nonpreference of the secular state was violated, Chatterjee argues (Chatterjee 1995). The question, however, is whether the real violation of secular principles in this connection was not the implicit assumption in this legislation that Hindus were the core citizens of India, the "state-community" whose religious doctrines and ritual practices legislators felt entitled to interpret and adapt to what they saw as the requirements of a modern state. This did not apply to the Muslim community.

I would further argue that many endeavors during the first decades of the existence of the independent Indian state may be read as systematic attempts to produce a diversity of cultural communities as so many signs of the nation, and thus to disentangle community practices from their localized or historical context and reinstate them as national monuments, tales and legends in childrens books, historical narratives in school books—as a national-modern aesthetic. In his classic book from 1963, Donald Smith discusses how the Ministry of Scientific Research in 1958 was renamed the Ministry of Scientific Research and Cultural Affairs, and now became busy packaging "Indian culture"—comprising bits of Kathakali dance, Mughal architecture, holy dips in the Ganga, and everything else, precisely as signs of the rich and diverse Indian culture (Smith 1963, 379).

The secular state in India, in other words, not merely produced public spheres full of reason and science, as is sometimes suggested (see for example Inden 1995). On the contrary, the public spheres in secular India remained full of religious signs and practices, packaged and represented as culture, making up a nationalized cultural realm represented as unpolitical, pure, and sublime. Now a Friday prayer, a mosque, or a Hindu procession and temple were no longer manifestations of community and sectarian strength, but picturesque and awesome manifestations of Indian culture and of the Indian nation.

The meaning of secularism was authorized as "equal respect for all religions," and politicians, ministers, and officials would generate and consolidate their nationalist and secular credentials by visiting temples, mosques, and Sikh gurdwaras, and by attending ceremonies and processions of different communities. It was not as if religious manifestations were not allowed in the public sphere. On the contrary, they were encouraged and revered as repositories of the cultural legitimacy that the state, routinely depicted as purely technocratic, could not generate. Similarly, it was not as if public figures were supposed to be atheists in order to prove their secular credentials. On the contrary, deep religious convictions of any persuasion on the part of public persons were revered and regarded as a symbol of moral consistency and national devotion, and thus as the very basis for secular practices.

What was pursued by the secular state was, in other words, a separation of two discursive and strategic realms in the public: one was a political realm wherein the interest of national unity, nonpreference, and the rationalities and naked imperatives of the state compelled political actors to speak and act in certain ways, while at the same time praising the cultural diversity and depth in India; the other was a cultural realm, wherein any community could celebrate itself and its own myths and exclude others. By asserting its own specificity, the community also celebrated and expressed the cultural diversity that was the foundation of the larger nation. In this scheme, the political realm was not supposed to be "contaminated" by the unilateral celebration of one community or the open representation of particularist interests of one confessional group. Conversely, the culture of a community—and by implication the entire nation—would be contaminated if political forces openly interfered with the life of cultural communities, thus injecting partiality and "communal consciousness," which would "poison the hearts and minds of the people," as the well-known rhetoric in India still goes.

In this very elitist vision of politics as a modernizing device, the people remained basically deeply religious, uncontaminated, and good while living within their separate cultural communities. However, if irresponsibly manipulated, this innocent but potentially barbaric people could also perpetrate the most hideous violence. In order to prevent irresponsible manipulation of ordinary people by the criminal badmash, politics should therefore remain in the hands of responsible and virtuous men. Secular tolerance was, in other words, part and parcel of the civilizing mission of the modern state vis-à-vis the masses who, until they were sufficiently educated, had to remain under the paternalist tutelage of the state, and under the supposedly responsible leadership of what in Indian political discourse is known as "educated sections." This discursive structure has also perpetuated the dominant contemporary interpretation of riots and breakdowns of civic order as the handiwork of ubiquitous criminals, land grabbers, and *goondas* (muscle men)—an interpretation which, needless to say, remains hugely useful for the political parties and agencies of state involved in this escalating politics of violence.

These assumptions regarding a deep difference between the masses as communities steeped in "their" culture and the educated sections fit for responsible citizenship can, for example, be read out of Marc Galanter's excellent analysis of Supreme Court cases regarding the criteria for legitimacy and validity of conversions from one religion to another. Galanter shows that there exists a practice according to which the validity of a conversion among the "lower" (uneducated) strata of society may depend on evidence of actually changed ritual practices, because rituals are assumed to be "of utmost importance for people of this class," as a judgment states—and, one must add, because the utterances and self-descriptions from "this class" supposedly cannot be trusted. In the case of educated people the required evidence is merely an unequivocal enunciation of intent: "I am a Muslim and no longer a Hindu." It is noteworthy, however, that in both cases it is not enough to say "I am not a Hindu," or to renounce all Hindu practices. One remains a Hindu, Muslim, and so on until one has proved in practice, or said unequivocally, that one is something else (Galanter 1989, 237–58).

This example not only indicates and affirms the constitutive difference between middle-class citizens of the Indian state and the masses, locked up within their cultural communities. It also demonstrates that the secularism and alleged hyper-rationalism of the Indian state, which nowadays is attributed to the Nehruvian epoch, is largely a myth, shared by the spokesmen of the state itself as well as by its critics from left to right. The fact seems to be that the Nehruvian state never created an effective space for production of secular citizenship, even in legal terms. Governmental and legal practices were always premised upon an ongoing essentialization of the nation's constitutive cultural communities and affirmation of their boundaries.

This purified construction of a composite but unified Indian culture and people above and outside politics added to the proliferation of the older genre of cultural "antipolitics" and allowed for a simultaneous renewed construction of its other: politics as a morally empty, technocratically neutral, or even immoral realm. Not only did Gandhian community activists promote this communitarian antipolitics but also thousands of religious entrepreneurs, reform movements, and social and religious institutions have for decades grown large and powerful, often with active state sponsorship or the goodwill of powerful politicians. Most of the so-called "communal" and revivalist organizations in India have grown and diversified in this peculiar depoliticized space of cultural activism created by the secular state in India. Here, a cultural organization may in principle hold any sectarian view as long as it only claims to be true for its own limited constituency and community. However, if it ventures to move into the realm of public politics, where the nation must be represented within the parameters of the authorized discourse of a single composite culture, sectarian utterances will appear as communal. Obvious examples are religious processions and festivals that celebrate a particular god, mythology, or religious ritual without being perceived as communal. The moment a song, symbol, or imagery employed on such an occasion comments upon political events, or recommends that the particular values of the community be the basis of political decisions, or a religious symbol is displayed and invoked at a political rally, the thin line separating secular and communal politics may be crossed. So what signifies communalism in the political part of the public realm may well pass for culture in another part of the public realm.

This reification of a realm of culture and communities (like so many unpolitical signs of the nation) has been corroborated by the changing cultural construction of politics in India in the last decades. From the late 1960s onward, the public construction of politics has increasingly been transformed toward that of an "immoral vocation," a site of unprincipled pragmatism, corruption, nepotism, and greed—in brief, as the profane antithesis to the sublime qualities of the cultural realm. This transformation reflects the changes in the social backgrounds and cultural habitus of elected representatives and party activists. Middle-class politicians have increasingly been replaced by those drawn from peasant communities and lower-caste groups, and their style, language, and social practices are decidedly more "rustic" and "plebeian" than those of the preceding generation.

To the urban, educated middle class, habituated to think of the nation and of citizenship as a collective entitlement flowing from their status and position, the emergence of these strata in the public sphere—of individuals often cruder and more direct in their handling of the intricate balancing implicit in the practice of secularist nonpreference—has seemed to signify a disintegration of the erstwhile moral fiber in politics. The discourse of a degradation of the political field has often been taken as a sign of a more general decay of society, for example by the influential "J. P. movement" in the 1970s, led by the Gandhian reformer Jayaprakash Narayan. Narayan's call for a "total revolution" of public morality in India left a deep impression on a generation of young people, and remained for more than a decade a moral antidote to the prevailing cynicism of the Congress party. This movement and other similar "antipolitical" trends corroborated and once more recast the antinomy between a profane politics devoid of any morality and a sublime culture that remains the only reservoir of lasting values in a world increasingly politicized.

The bemoaning of the increasing politicization and corruption of the public administration in contemporary India, of education, of the judicial system, and so on, are thus parts of this larger narrative of the decay of the moral fiber of public life. This narrative depicts how the moral emptiness of modernity, the shameless display of self-interest, and the "strategic truths" characterizing competitive politics creep into ever more social realms. According to many a columnist in the Indian dailies, it is a moral void that allows the baser instincts of human beings to thrive, but also a void that throws back the question of regeneration of public morality into the realm of cultural communities, as if they remained reservoirs of values untouched by the larger transformations of Indian society.

Conclusion

Is it meaningful to apply what I initially termed a "radical" Tocquevillean framework to an Indian situation in which the social world is deeply bifurcated, where democracy means competing communities, where the paradigm of rights is translated into community assertion and notions of collective entitlements, and where the state constantly reifies and governs through categories of community and culture?

I believe that it is meaningful, and is even more so in the recent decades. This is not because India represents a replay of the western democratic revolutions or because democracy always tends toward the production of modern individuals and citizenship, as a more conventional Tocquevillean thesis would run. I would argue, quite the contrary, that the idea of a democratic revolution in India makes sense exactly because the trajectory of modernity and democracy in India demonstrates so clearly how democracy makes the political dimensions of society crucial, productive, and deeply problematic. What I have tried to demonstrate is that "the political" in India, as elsewhere, manifests itself as an undecidability and a ubiquitous contingency that necessitates, and yet makes impossible, countless schemes of governance and taxonomy. Historically, these endeavors created categories of caste and community, and an ostensibly orderly range of institutions which, hence, were inhabited, coded, and reemployed by the proliferating range of identitarian mobilizations.

The scale, persistence, and richness of India's democratic experience is in all respects both awesome and fraught with contradictions. Its most interesting aspect is, to my mind, the many consistent attempts to control and limit the logic of democratic politics in India, and the conspicuous failure of virtually all of these attempts. As I have tried to show, democratic politics have almost from the outset a century ago been flanked by two kinds of "antipolitics" aimed at controlling and limiting the play of the political in Indian society. On the one hand, from the utilitarian administrators and scientists of the colonial administrators to the members of the National Planning Committee, there have been consistent attempts to order, administer, and develop India in a rational and orderly fashion. Many of these attempts succeeded in imposing a new categorical order and language on the social world, but they failed in terms of controlling the political uses of the new authorized identities, legal entitlements, and institutions they had created. On the other hand, cultural nationalists, Gandhian communitarianists, and other practicing orientalists sought to claim the "inner" life and spirit of supposedly perennial communities as the prepolitical site of the nation. Just as the imagining of the people derived its strength from its status of an "empty signifier"—as a truth beyond representation and falsification—communities also assumed this function. The communitarian ideal, the rhetoric of a moral revolution led by virtuous men from the upper castes, not only served obvious narcissistic needs but also removed the imagining of society and nation from the almost unbearable profanity of ordinary politics performed by lesser men.

To my mind, the Nehruvian state constructed a crucial marriage between these two antipolitical strategies, and herein lies the mythical material that has made this epoch the "Golden Age" of the Indian nation and democracy, in spite of the fact that democracy at this point was at best a minority affair conducted by middle-class citizens in the midst of a sea of the communities of the masses. It is my general contention that the entire narrative of decay of public life in India derives from the gradual dismantling of this legacy, and from the ever more assertive seizure of the democratic process by genres of political discourse, styles and practices derived from the world of "low" politics. What we see before us is the less than orderly democratization of Indian democracy.

There is a certain irrepressible quality to political life in India, to the incessant transgression of established languages of contention in the political field, the incessant recoding, sliding and reevaluation of virtually every identity and political position. Indian society has become increasingly politicized; it is possibly one of the most politicized societies in the world, but not because its leaders wanted it to be so. It happened because the democratic order they fought for, and ultimately established, released new, assertive, and uncontrollable social identities that over time produced a form of modernity—pluralist, creative, chaotic, and brutal at the same time—that nobody ever envisaged.

2

Imagining the Hindu Nation

NINETEENTH-CENTURY NATIONALISM in India was organized around an "orientalist mode of production of the people." Based upon the colonial objectification and codification of cultural differences, the imagination of an "Indian people" took the form of a series of discrete and well-bounded communities divided primarily by religion, but also by caste and custom. Three processes unfolding in the latter part of the nineteenth century molded this imagination.

The first of these was the governmental objectification and aggregation of existing cultural categories of caste or religion into larger and more abstracted categories, already touched upon in Chapter One. The second was the "inversion of orientalist epistemology" among nineteenth-century Indian reformers, intellectuals, and politicians. These strata interiorized the orientalist construction of the East and the West as essentially different, but reversed the valuation so that the differentiation became a source of recognition of cultural and moral superiority. The third process was that of "semitization" of Hinduism, that is, attempts among reform movements within Hinduism to emulate the features of organization and uniformity that were believed to endow monotheist faiths originating in the Middle East, such as Islam and Christianity, with strength and capacity for concerted action—features lacking in what nationalists saw as a decaying and fragmented Hindu culture. At the same time, the encounter with colonialism also produced Islamic reform movements that in a similar vein sought to "semitize" and "classicize" Islam by purging popular and syncretic practices.

Ideology and the Impossibility of Identities

Before plunging into the complexities of how social imaginaries and identities were produced in colonial and postcolonial India, it may be worth considering in more theoretical terms the intimate links between such imaginaries and processes of identity formation. My contention here is that in order to understand the subtleties involved in the inhabitations of the "identity slots" carved out by authorized discourses and social imaginaries, we need to resurrect and refine the notion of ideology as a crucial dimension of all social practice.[1]

I am not suggesting that ideology constitutes a quasi-autonomous realm of ideas, discourse, or consciousness. Ideology is most effective when inscribed in unconscious predispositions, in sayings, bon mots, dress, and cultural codes, in short doxa lived by human beings in accordance with their habitus, the durably embodied dispositions of human beings that govern their most fundamental sense of appropriateness. The notions of good and evil, the line between the "we" and the "other(s)," and all the other constructions of ideology are, Bourdieu argues, always embodied in a very corporeal sense as bodily hexis: "Bodily hexis is political mythology embodied, turned into a permanent disposition, a durable way of standing, speaking, walking, and thereby of feeling and thinking" (Bourdieu 1990a, 69–70).

But what is it that makes ideological constructions so attractive? Why is there this ostensibly insatiable demand for enemies, boundaries, and clear identifications? To my mind, Lacan's understanding of subjectivation as driven by a desire to overcome a fundamental lack (*manque*), the feeling of never being fully present, never fully identical with oneself, is a fruitful starting point for analysis of ideological effects. Lacan's theory of the subject is organized around the three structural orders of the psyche. First, the imaginary, shaped by the mirror phase in early childhood, a phase in which the child becomes aware of itself through reflection in the mirror and in the gaze of the other (the parents), a process that introduces a constitutive sense of misrecognition. The second structural order is the symbolic, which represents the condensation of language and culture, "the Law" (or *nom-de-pere*, as Lacan often calls it). The symbolic stands for the demand for obedience to rules, the imperative of convention, but also for a powerful source of identification and for projection of desire, not merely sexual in the Freudian sense, but also the more fundamental Hegelian sense of desire as an existential need for recognition by a powerful other, that is, the "desire for the desire of the other."[2] Although the theme of the unrepresentability of subjectivity within language and convention are long-standing themes in philosophy, Lacan's third order, "the real," introduced a highly original instability in the entire construction. To Lacan, "the real" denotes the hard kernel that resists symbolization, a residue that cannot be fitted in but always escapes prevailing epistemologies, and thus prevents the symbolic order and the identities it generates from ever being complete and unfractured. "The real" is contingency, the inevitability of death, the violence at the heart of love, the inhumanity within humans, and so on—something frightening and incomprehensible, and therefore a constant source of fascination and that paradoxical pleasure of transgression which Lacan in his lecture on Sade calls *jouissance*, enjoyment (Lacan 1992, 203). The subject is thus fundamentally split and divided, it is constituted by this "lack," by a constant striving for fullness that will never succeed and therefore will always proceed.

How does this enable one to reflect on the question of why ideological causes make sense? Or on how human beings wear the identities offered by authorized discourses or ideological projects? To my mind, this framework allows us, first, to appreciate the instability and illusory character of disciplinary power and political authority. Power needs to be reproduced and reasserted constantly, through sustained production of subjects, that is, sustained imposition of authorized symbolic configurations of language, images, monuments, tangible benefits, security, and so on. In this perspective the impotence of domination is not a result of more or less resistance by already fully constituted subjects, or by acts of what Foucault termed *parrhesia*, the heroic defiance of power, but more precisely, a result of the impossibility of producing stable subjects.[3]

Second, Lacan's understanding of the subject as a process, as subjectivation, also allows for a more precise understanding of the function of ideology in the formation of subjects, namely, as fantasies vital in the construction of a social reality, and thus vital parts in what one may call a "politics of the unconscious." Ideology misrepresents the social world, not through a smoke screen obscuring the real structures but rather through repression as a principle of construction: "Ideology is not simply a 'false consciousness,' an illusory representation of the world, it is rather this reality itself which is already to be conceived as 'ideological'—*'ideological' is a social reality whose very existence implies the non-knowledge of its participants as to its essence*—that is, the social effectiveness, the very reproduction of which implies that the individuals 'do not know what they are doing'" (Žižek 1989, 21). Repression, or obliteration, is a vital part of what symbolization—that is, ideological practice—involves, because it categorizes, sorts out, and selects. Ideology thus does not obscure, but is inscribed in and enables the very construction of social reality. In Slavoj Žižek's reading of Lacan, ideology acquires this more precise meaning as (social) fantasies whose effectiveness flows from their incorporation and embodiment in social practice, and connectedness with desire and enjoyment (*jouissance*). Žižek argues that ideology can perfectly well coexist with widespread cynicism, jokes, irony, and all the other features normally taken as proof of the impotency of ideology, as long as people act according to the ideological grammar. Whether people believe in commodities or money as real values is less important than that they buy and consume as if they were "commodity fetishists" (ibid., 31). Radicalizing the notion of doxa, Žižek suggests that ideological misrecognition is on the side of practice, rather than on the side of reflexive knowledge:

> what they [subjects] misrecognize is not the reality but the illusion which is structuring their reality. They know very well how things really are, but still they are doing it as if they did not know. The illusion is therefore double: it consists in overlooking the illusion which is structuring our real, effective relationship to reality. And this overlooked unconscious relation is what may be called the *ideological fantasy*. . . . Cynical distance is just one way—of many ways—to blind ourselves to the structuring power of ideological fantasy. Even if we do not take things seriously, even if we keep an ironical distance, *we are still doing them* (ibid., 33, italics in original).

Ideological constructions are vitalized and empowered in two ways. The first and most obvious part of their attraction lies in their ability to convert the experience of amorphous, meaningless contingency into an ostensibly stable symbolic order that promises to close the gap in social existence through construction of a more harmonious social world. Such an "objectivation of belief" often happens as insertions of more or less reflected practices, inclinations, or unconsciously conjured "gut feelings" into a reasoned line of arguments. Social routines and conventions, institutions, and systems of norms compel human beings to conform with practices they often perceive as meaningless, absurd, and repressive. Ideology offers a way to cope with this lack of meaning by repressing the meaningless and by inferring a certain hidden truth, or rationality, behind the ostensible randomness of bureaucratic routines, of social exclusion, of gossip (ibid., 33–40). Ideology thus emerges as an effect of power—as an attempt to conceal and repress the "raw" contingency of the social world.[4]

It is as enjoyment (*jouissance*)[5] that ideology attains its most paradoxical and powerful function in the production of subjects. Identifications are always incomplete, always marred by *manque*—an ineradicable distance between existence and identifications. There is always "something" that escapes symbolization, and this surplus is exactly enjoyment, the fantasies and fascination of "the real." The power of ideological constructions lies, therefore, not so much in their enunciated content as in the subtle ways in which they promise to organize this enjoyment. The power of anti-Semitism derives from the way it posits the Jew as responsible for the fundamental splits in identities and social antagonisms. The Jew thus embodies "the real," as what Lacan called *objet petit à*, the alien element, the impurity, which prevents the ideological fantasy of a unified social order and community from stabilizing itself, and therefore prevents the desired unity between the imaginary and symbolic orders in the subject. Jews therefore become the objects of intense hatred, elaborate mythologies, and deep fascination (ibid., 126–27).[6]

This understanding enables us to see that the generalized ideological enunciations of a "we" versus a range of others is merely the upper layer of a more complex mechanism. The second layer consists of the construction of the self/other difference as an antagonism, blocking the full realization of a collectivity. This construction makes political organization possible, and can, as discussed above, produce extended "equivalential chains" on either side of the front line drawn up by the antagonism. The third layer of the operation of ideology is constituted by what Žižek calls the "objectivation of belief," that is, the way ideology through enactment of repetitive practices, rituals, routines, and institutions offers a framework, a discipline, a direction, and a mechanism for simplification of the social world, which by virtue of its mere form or convention reduces contingency and temporarily "sutures" the fundamental lack in the subject. The fourth and most subtle layer in the operation of ideology is its promise to organize enjoyment, that is, the desire to grasp the innermost kernel of being, the desire to achieve full identity with one's community and self. At this level, the "other" is not merely an outside, but the sign of an inner split, the *objet petit à* marking the impossibility of any full being.

The making and staging of ideological fantasies are always collective endeavors mediated or facilitated by organizations or movements. The "economy of desires" addressed here is played out at the level of individual human beings in their relations with groups, stereotypes, leaders, and larger shared imaginaries. Human beings can only become produced as subjects, as individuals, or as distinct groups through social processes. Freud argued that the individual was always/already a social being: "In the individual's mental life someone else is invariably involved, as a model, as an object, as a helper, as an opponent; and so from the very first individual psychology in this extended but entirely justifiable sense of the words, is at the same time social psychology as well" (Freud 1967, 1). To my mind, any serious engagement with processes of identity formation, with the constitution and reproduction of authority, as well as with the style of production and consumption of cultural and political images and metaphors, needs to analyze, one way or another, the logics of desire and identification at play in such phenomena.

Needless to say, Lacan's three orders are abstract analytical orders, an abstract theoretical claim concerning the structures and logics of this economy of desires, and this claim can never stand alone—even less in studies of political phenomena. We only have access to the effects of ideology—identifications, subjectivity, mass mobilizations, and so on—through utterances, practice, and conflicts in their historical and vernacularized form. In order to interpret and explain such effects one needs to historicize the mediating processes—the structure of the political arenas and the "economy of stances" within which ideological constructions appear, the structure and strategies of the organizations promoting certain ideological causes, and historical and local conditions under which the ideological constructions are made to make sense.

Objectification of Communities

Notions of Hinduism as a unified religion, Hindu culture as a distinct cultural zone, and "Hindu" as a well-bounded cultural category are largely products of scholarly and administrative interventions by orientalist scholars, missionaries, and colonial administrations in the Indian subcontinent since the seventeenth century. Originally used as a territorial term for those living beyond the river Indus, or as a residual term (*Gentoo*) used by early European merchants and colonizers to denote those in the Indian subcontinent who were not Muslims or Christians, the term "Hindoo" slowly emerged as a common denominator for the native culture(s) of the Indian subcontinent. It is, as G. P. Deshpande has noted, "doubtful whether the people talked of themselves as Hindus before the colonial phase of our history" (Deshpande 1985, 25). Early scholars and missionaries took a keen interest in establishing the main tenets and core doctrines of the seemingly amorphous admixture of religious practices, images, and myths they encountered in India. In accordance with the dominant western epistemologies of the time, the brahminical high scriptural traditions that had produced the bulk of Sanskrit texts were regarded as the classical center of the Aryan-Vedic high civilization, sharing a set of fundamental principles and practices regulating social and religious behavior as laid down in the scriptures. This identification and construction of a classical Hinduism, organized around a central high culture, was extended to have a subcontinental dimension, that is, to be a single Hinduism—a religious civilization—with many variations. It was broadly assumed that there existed a common Aryan or brahminical high culture knit together by a common language (Sanskrit), a body of ancient texts assumed to be relatively coherent, and a shared sacred geography marked by centers of pilgrimage all over the subcontinent, as well as shared ritual practices, shared codes of purity and pollution, and so on.

This construction of Hinduism was, to paraphrase Derrida, a truly logocentrist epistemological operation, an attempt to understand and construct the other in one's own image by privileging the scriptures to be an expression of an assumed indispensable center of a Hindu civilization. The problem was, however, that a coherent great tradition was at first sight absent in the subcontinent. Yet "Hinduism" slowly emerged as a metaphysical construct of what should be there in order to make the other intelligible within a system of systematic differences, an idea that made it possible to identify the difference of the East from the West within a single conceptual grammar of civilizational order and hierarchy.

The codification and elevation of brahminical practices into a Hindu tradition took place with the active assistance and help of brahminical western-educated strata, especially in Madras and Bengal, where colonial administration began. Here, educated brahmins and others of "clean" castes became the key informants in comprehensive mappings and registrations of religious practices and communities (Frykenberg 1989, 29–50). The underlying belief that the "Hindoos" were primarily governed by religious sentiments led in Madras to an unprecedented type of detailed state management of temples and religious practices in the first half of the nineteenth century (Appadurai 1981). To brahmins and other upper-caste groups, the keen interest of the colonial power in religious practices provided an opportunity to codify and rigidify existing social and ritual hierarchies, and to consolidate their social position as arbiters of truth and social sanctions. Moreover, the colonial quest for categorical order and cultural mapping also enabled upper-caste groups to get to know themselves in more objectified terms, to construct their own group in accordance with an "ideal" that had not hitherto been so rigorously described.[7]

This construction of a "great tradition" enabled scientists, colonial administrators, and intellectuals to classify and order the vast mélange of cultural differences in the subcontinent into systems of core and periphery, exclusion and inclusion: between the "great" and the "little" traditions, the traditional (*sanatana*) Hinduism versus deviating sects, an ideal type of a hierarchical order found in the scriptures (*varnashramadharma*) versus amorphous and locally differentiated rankings of castes (*jatis*), the classical Gangetic and Aryan civilization versus the various syncretized and depleted forms in which this high culture was assumed to be found in popular religious practices, and syncretic sects, among tribals, in border regions, and so on. This rationalization and centralization of otherwise dispersed religious practices into one civilizational stream, or what Romila Thapar has called "syndicated Hinduism," produced the concept "Hindu" as an synthetic concept that encompassed everything in the subcontinent. Every practice or mode of worship expressed degrees of local, heterodox deviations from a norm—the orthodoxy or the traditional Hinduism—which no single

religious form actually could embody or fully represent, precisely because of its inclusive and diverse character. Modern Hinduism had
thus in epistemological terms been born as a truly "empty place," that
is, as a signifier of the true and full "culture" that made India truly
Indian, thus stabilizing otherwise diverse and alternating ritual and
social hierarchies around an "ideal" core. Yet it was a signifier that no
actual group could claim to control fully.

The attempt to grasp this "true" culture of India became one of the
most contested agendas within Indian nationalism. Most strands in the
nationalist movement agreed that this culture or civilization—mainly
Hindu—provided India with a distinct character in the world. At the
same time, this culture was seen as decaying and defunct and had,
therefore, to be reformed and revived in a new, "synthetic" version. To
most brands of nationalists, regardless of their secular-rational or reli-
gious-national idiom, Hindu culture constituted, paradoxically, both
the impediment (in its old, dispersed forms), and the solution (in its
reformed, nationalized, or synthetic forms) to the final realization of
nationhood.

Inversion of Orientalist Epistemology

A large body of scholarly work has, over the last decade or so, discussed orientalist discourses and their profound structuring of western
as well as Indian knowledge of Indian history and society. The intention here is not to review this debate, but merely to point out how
especially the romanticist branch of orientalism provided interpretations and conceptual grammars that proved central to the anticolonial
and nationalist discourse.[8] Romanticist orientalists were, as Ronald
Inden points out, part of the larger epistemic project of orientalism—
the construction of an effective "other" stabilizing the European "we."
They remained, nonetheless, an opposition to dominant utilitarian and
rationalist imaginations of India (Inden 1990, 90–96). In the romanticist
view, India was an object of fascination, a locus of spirituality, of imagination and mysticism as displayed in ancient Indian philosophy. Most
attractive was the spiritual holism which, according to the German idealist philosopher and linguist Schlegel, was the defining characteristic
of Indian culture.[9] Holism entailed collapsing the spiritual and material
world into oneness, and eradicating the cleavage between the objective
world and individual consciousness through incorporation into an all-
pervasive Spirit. India was Hindu, and classical Hinduism was the
epitome of holistic spiritualism. According to this train of thought, the
Hindu aptitudes for imagination, sensuality, and mysticism were superior to those of the West. This, the romanticists argued, was the real

contribution of Hindu culture to the world. Hegel endorsed the view that India was essentially Hindu, understood as pure spirit, but spirit of the imaginative (soft, feminine) sort, thus of a lower logical order than the rational (masculine) spirit of the West. To Hegel, this predominance of imagination precluded the emergence of reason, which explained the feeble sociopolitical structure of the Indian states. In the absence of reason, India could only produce dispersed communities and people, never a viable state (Hegel 1956, 160–61).

Orientalist scholarship, in Germany already informed by the nationalist quest for difference vis-à-vis France and Britain, produced an image of India as ontologically different from the West that became crucial to generations of Indian nationalists. One of the most influential contributions to this orientalist construction was Max Müller's translation of the *Ṛg Veda*, believed to be the oldest and thus the most authentic self-born and founding text in the larger body of Hindu philosophy. Among parts of the European public, India thus became a locus of pure essences, of immobility, of high spirituality, and an embodiment of an organic, unfragmented community whose very existence represented a critique of the West, and therefore an important repository for radical dreams of pristine existence and the whole and healed self. There was, in other words, a European tradition for criticism of utilitarian rationality and crude universalism, with India in the role as the spiritual heroine, which was ready to be acquired and reoccupied by a nationalist discourse in India.

The notion of a spiritual India versus a materialist western world emerged from this transmission of conceptual grammar, evident even in writings of a self-declared secular rationalist like Nehru. In his *Discovery of India*, Nehru quotes liberally from Max Müller's eulogies of Indian spirituality, Schopenhauer's praise of the Upanishads, Romain Rolland's treatise on the intimate relations between Hindu culture and Hellenic-Christian culture, and so on (Nehru 1980, 84–100). To Nehru, India was spirituality and a concomitant plurality and tolerance—which had eroded and degenerated from a golden Upanishadic Age to contemporary disarray—versus a materialist, individualized West. India versus the West was posited as culture versus politics, or femininity versus masculinity.

This construction clearly informed the Bengali novelist Bankimchandra Chattopadhyay's authorship. In his analysis of Bankim's writings, Partha Chatterjee points to the crucial relation Bankim established between power and culture: the West was seen as victorious because of its strong, organized, and autonomous culture, whereas Indian culture—seen as spiritually superior to that of the West (and much older)—was weak, unorganized, and passive. In Bankim's vision, national glory could only be regained through national regeneration of culture; a strong national, organized religion; comprehensive and popular education of the masses; and an enlightened leadership provided by his own class, the Bengali *bhadralok* (Chatterjee 1986, 67–91). Chatterjee identifies two tensions in Bankim's vision of a national life. One was the painful marriage between his rationalist, scientific mode of cognition and reasoning, and his critique of colonialism, which gradually compelled him to embrace the orientalist discourse on India as "spirit, culture and antiquity."[10] The other was the importance Bankim ascribed to the recruitment of the broad masses in a reconstruction of the nation. In Bankim's vision, the role of the masses was not conceived through the eulogies of simplicity and cultural essence that one finds in Gandhi decades later, but rather through a paternalistic project of education and recruitment of the masses to give body to the national regeneration defined and led by the literate elite. This nationalist vision was distinctly Hindu, however, and was informed by a strong anti-Muslim undercurrent (Sarkar 1996).

The recruitment of Indian culture as spirituality into nationalist ideology became fully articulated in the writings of Swami Vivekananda. Here romanticist notions of fullness, the superiority of imagination over practical reason, and the spiritual superiority of Hinduism over all other philosophical systems were posited as the very basis of Indianness constructed against the alleged poverty and profanity of western civilization: "Politics, power and even intellect form a secondary consideration here. Religion, therefore, is the one consideration in India" (Vivekananda 1960, 3: 204). To Vivekananda, the West had become intoxicated and degenerate by virtue of its own success in the economic, political, and military fields. The greatness of India lay in its spiritual superiority, and he exhorted: "Up, India, and conquer the world with your spirituality. Spirituality must conquer the West. Slowly they are finding out that what they want is spirituality to preserve them as nations. . . . Heroic workers are wanted to go abroad and help to disseminate the great truths of the Vedanta . . . the only condition of national life, of awakened and vigorous national life, is the conquest of the world by Indian thought" (Vivekananda 1960, 3: 277).

Vivekananda believed that the real living spirituality which would reinvigorate the nation was to be found in the masses. He believed in education of the common man in order to make the masses realize their own potentials—not as a subversive political force, but as a self-confident cultural expression, the realization of the Indian spirit that ultimately would render politics and power obsolete. Vivekananda developed Bankim's paternalism in a populist direction, and provided a basis for later interpretations of both Gandhian and militant Hindu nationalist varieties. Vivekananda's philosophy and practice thus represented a step toward the transformation of Hinduism from a signifier of religious faith to one of nationalist ideology.[11] To Vivekananda, one should see "man as God," and true worship consisted in work for social ends. One found here a preoccupation with spirit as the basis for a national community of culture, that is, a mediated version of Herderian axioms. One also finds the notion of a world mission, the idea of the creation of a "complete man," an individual infused by the Indian spirit, educated, culturally awakened and carrier of the "national will," that is, a vernacularized version of Fichte's national citizen.

Vivekananda's eulogy of the inherent tolerance and syncretism of popular traditions was fed by a certain animosity toward Islam. Tolerance and inclusiveness was largely portrayed as the essence of true Hinduism as opposed to Islam, which Vivekananda saw as doctrinal and intolerant. Only because popular Islam was immersed in the "soft sponge" of Hindu culture had it become equally tolerant and flexible. The narrative of Hindu tolerance and inclusiveness, which in this century became part of common knowledge of Hinduism in India as well as the rest of the world, emerged from this particular inversion of romanticist orientalism. As Bipin Chandra Pal and other political radicals began to depict the nation as a popular essence, the evils, tensions, and contradictions in and between communities were ascribed to manipulation by elites, particularly the Muslim and the colonial elite. The Muslim elite was seen as particularly dangerous—clinging to religious doctrines, writing in Persian and Urdu, and holding on to other "un-Indian" ways. The Muslim masses, however, were seen as good, speaking in the vernaculars and sharing many of the rituals of their Hindu neighbors, being converts and not of alien origin, and so on.[12] It was thus possible to reduce the problem of communal tension to the manipulation by self-seeking, alien elites. In this crucial ideological maneuver, the innocence and purity of the "Indian people" was saved, while the popular ethos was defined as basically Hindu.

This idea of holism and encompassing harmony in Hinduism became central to the more politicized ideology of nascent Hindu nationalism as it was expressed by the prominent Bengali "extremist" leader Bipin Chandra Pal: "Nationality has been defined by Joseph Mazzini as "the individuality of a people" . . . but Mazzini failed to fully reach out to that higher philosophy of Nationalism, which could offer a true and effective antidote against the isolating and disrupting tendencies of the popular European gospel of Equality and Freedom. . . . Hindu culture, however, is able to present an ideal of nationhood much superior to the European view of it" (Pal 1958, 69–70).

To Pal, the main problem in European thought and social practice was social fragmentation and excessive individualism. Against this,

Hindu political philosophy emphasized the gradual development of the self to higher levels of consciousness, freeing itself from the obligations of social life. The sannyasi renouncing the world is, argued Pal, a representation of the universal in every aspect of life. A sannyasi has become a law onto himself. To reach the clarity of the sannaysi and become "laws onto themselves" should be the objective of all nations (ibid., 72–73). From this, Pal derived his "integralist" view of the nation as a realization of individual freedom through full integration with "the whole." The realized nation would entail "cancellation of all conflicts and absolute settlement of all disputes. . . . [For the Indian nationalist] politics is part of his larger religion; it is a department of the science or philosophy of salvation" (Pal 1910, 47–48). This was cultural nationalism at its purest, a form of antipolitics that envisaged the Hindu nation as the point of realization of full social harmony, a sort of collective state of world renunciation (*sannyasa*), canceling all "lacks" and voids in identities and social life.

Semitization of Hinduism

Rammohun Roy and the Brahmo Samaj in nineteenth-century Bengal were inspired by Unitarian theologies within Protestantism, and promoted individualism, equality, and rationalism. Roy initiated translation of Vedantic literature into vernaculars in order to make the sacred texts available to a wider audience, and he initiated campaigns against sati, child marriages, and other practices he regarded as "archaic." Decades later in western India, M. G. Ranade expressed a similar quest for reform in his Prarthana Samaj, a religious society promoting rationalization of Hindu practices on egalitarian and unitarian grounds. Ranade saw equivalencies between the bhakti (ecstatic devotional) saints of Maharashtra and protestant reformers in Europe, in what he saw as an attempt to create a devotional religious practice that emphasized personal faith rather than ritual, and equality among believers rather than a dominant clergy.[13]

The largest, most influential, but also most conservative of the movements emerging in the nineteenth century, aiming at reform and reinvention of Hindu practices, was the Arya Samaj, founded in 1875 in Punjab by Dayananda Saraswati, a Sanskrit scholar. Opposed to aspects of the caste system, idolatry, and popular ritual traditions, the Arya Samaj was strongly revivalist and proselytizing. The movement opposed Christian proselytization and English education, as well as Muslim influence in education, language, and social life. Swami Dayananda admired many elements of western culture, especially the capacity for organization and discipline, virtues that in the swami's

view had made the West powerful but had vanished from Hindu culture.[14] The anti-Muslim component in the Arya Samaj became ever
more central due to the fierce symbolic competition between Hindus,
Muslims, and Sikhs in Punjab. At this juncture in Punjab, its three
main religious communities were becoming more clearly bounded and
more organized; temples, mosques, and gurdwaras were constructed
as symbolic markers of community space and loci of congregation.[15]
Newspapers published in Hindi (written in Devanagari script) addressed a Hindu public, whereas Urdu newspapers catered to a public
capable of reading the Arabic script, and newspapers in Punjabi written in the sacred Sikh script, Gurumukhi, catered to a Sikh public (Dixit
1986, 126; Fox 1985; Jones 1976).

Dayananda wished to save what he saw as a weak and disorganized
Hinduism from Islamic and western challenges, by organizing it
around a canonization of what orientalism had presented as the oldest, most original, and hence most authentic bodies of text, the Vedas.
Dayananda believed, as did Bankim, that a national-popular religion
was a precondition for national regeneration. If Hindus were imbued
with the ideals depicted in the Vedas, the Hindu community would
become self-conscious and strong, and national liberation would grow
into an irresistible demand: "The four Vedas, the repository of knowledge and religious truth are the words of God. I regard them as infalli-
ble and of prime authority. They are authority in themselves and do
not depend on other books for their authoritativeness. Just as the sun or
a lamp is self-luminous as well as the lightgiver of the earth, so are the
four Vedas" (quoted in Purohit 1986, 57). A reformed Hinduism should
be organized around the notion of Aryans as the chosen people, egalitarian access to religious knowledge, and visible institutional structures. A crucial instrument to this end was the shuddhi movement, a
movement for "purification" of the faith, and a front organization that
from the 1880s onward attempted to stop conversions of lower-caste
Hindus to Islam and Christianity, and worked to reconvert Christians
and Muslims to Hinduism (Ghai 1990).

In line with the strong pedagogical trend within cultural nationalism
in Europe and elsewhere, the Arya Samaj also assigned primary importance to education and to molding a new national culture and a new
generation of nationalist individuals. From the 1880s on, the Arya
Samaj established a system of educational institutions all over north
India: the Dayananda Anglo-Vedic (DAV) colleges, in which English
was the medium of instruction, and gurukuls (schools re-inventing
the older guru-student relation), in order to instill in the young generation a sense of national culture, history, and religious-cultural self-
consciousness.

Another basic tenet of cultural nationalism, a common national language—Sanskrit and a sanskritized, "pure" Hindi—was promoted by the Arya Samaj in educational work, in publishing books, magazines, translations to Hindi and Sanskrit, and so on (Pandey 1972). Swami Dayananda was convinced of the necessity of promoting and transforming Hindustani from a spoken popular language into a "high vernacular" in Devanagari script in order to replace written Persian and Urdu as the dominant vernacular languages of administration, education, and public discourse. At around the turn of the century the first regular Hindi magazines appeared, college curricula in Hindi were drafted, and Madan Mohan Malaviya, provoked by the founding of Aligarh Muslim University in 1898, initiated the protracted campaign for a Hindu university with Hindi as the sole medium of instruction. In 1915 Benares Hindu University was founded and became the central institution in the movement for establishment of Hindi as a national language.

The relationship between Urdu and Hindi had historically been that of two modes of writing the same language, Hindustani, encompassing a number of distinct regional dialects. In the last decades of the nineteenth century the differentiation between the two grew sharper and more distinct as they became related to the emerging definition of Muslim and Hindu nationalism, respectively. A Muslim speaker of Hindustani now spoke Urdu and wrote it in Arabic script, while a Hindu speaker of the virtually same language spoke Hindi and wrote in the Devanagari script. The 1920s saw systematic efforts to construct a distinct literary Hindi tradition and canon, wherein the essential criterion became the community of the author and the themes rather than the language of writing, which for centuries had been predominantly Persian and Urdu (Kumar 1992, 4–26). A similar authorization of Urdu as the canonical medium in a constructed literary tradition of Indian Muslims, and the preferred medium in a fast-growing "Muslim public sphere" in north India, had taken place a bit earlier than in the case of Hindi.[16]

Like most cultural nationalist movements, the Arya Samaj was preoccupied with physical strength and youth. The ailing Hindu culture should be given new life through bodily purification and control of sexuality by ideological means. In the network of gurukul schools physical training, mountain climbing, cold-water baths, and similar physical exercises were given high priority in order to strengthen the manliness and purity of the "Aryan nation."

The Arya Samaj promoted an eradication of traditional caste identities defined by birth, and suggested a caste system based on virtue and merit, which in principle would be open to all. If an untouchable became a virtuous, learned, and pious person he should be granted the status of a brahmin (Pandey 1972, 72–112).

In spite of such radical postures, the Arya Samaj project remained largely conservative in its implications. The critique of caste was aimed only at the immobility of the system and at brahminical orthodoxy and its exclusion of lower-caste groups; but neither the hierarchical logic of caste nor the essential virtues and character ascribed to each varna (category) and jati (caste) were questioned.[17]

Predictably, the rise of the Arya Samaj in Punjab and north India also produced countercurrents among more orthodox Hindus—especially brahmins—who formed a large number of *sanatana dharma* associations and educational institutions promoting and inventing a glorious, unified Hindu tradition. The sanatanists were on the whole no less anti-Muslim than the Arya Samajists and supporters of the movement for Hindi.[18] Decades later, Hindu nationalist movements and parties, such as the Hindu Mahasabha and RSS, seem to receive considerable support from both sanatania and Arya Samaj environments. Gandhi appealed directly to the influential sanatana tendency and called himself a sanatana Hindu to signal respect for tradition, and to mark a certain distance to the more belligerent and rationalist reformers of the Arya Samaj and affiliated organizations.

It is probably difficult to overestimate the impact of the Arya Samaj in the subsequent development of culture and politics in north India, especially within the upper-caste literate section of the Hindu population. The entire network of DAV colleges, the Hindi press, Benares Hindu University, and other institutions produced generations of young well-educated men from the upper castes militantly devoted to the cause of the Hindu community. A large number of leaders and activists of the RSS and Hindu Mahasabha were to emerge from these milieus, just as the Arya Samaj's vision of a strong Hindi-speaking India, mainly Hindu in spirit and complexion, found many takers within the Congress movement.

From Hindu Community to "Hindu Nation"

Nationalist politics in the first decades of the twentieth century was marked by two fissures. One was the disagreement over political strategy toward the colonial power. Moderate Congress leaders, led by Gokhale, believed in constitutional, gradual, and negotiated change in close collaboration with the "enlightened sections" of the British colonial administration and liberal politicians in Britain. Reason, arguments, and demonstration of the political and administrative capabilities of the Indian elite would eventually, this group believed, earn Indians the right to self-rule.

A minority of younger, militant elements, especially in Bengal and Bombay Presidency, mistrusted the benevolence of the British and advocated a militant strategy of armed destabilization of the British colonial administration. The intellectual father figure of this group became Bal Gangadhar Tilak, who was strongly opposed to what he saw as a naive trust in the good intentions and enlightenment of the colonial regime. Tilak's politics and public utterances in his famous Marathi newspaper *Kesari* and his English-language *Mahratta* turned still more radical, denouncing colonial rule as illegitimate, unjust, and as impeding any cultural or economic development in India. Influenced by the cultural nationalism of Mazzini, he believed that the most important feature of a vibrant nationalism was the shared and collective sense of a common spirit, history, and culture. Tilak also learned from the cow protection movement in north India that popular religious festivals and symbols could be recruited as very powerful symbols in such an effort to "nationalize the masses." His prime inventions, the Ganpati Utsav (festival honoring Ganesh) and the annual celebration of the birth of the Maratha king Shivaji (Shivaji Jyanti), contributed significantly to an assertion and creation of Hindu identities in western India (Cashman 1975, 70–76; Inamdar 1986, 116). The figure of Shivaji was also invoked in north India. The militant Congress leader in Punjab, Lala Lajpat Rai, soon emérged as a prominent spokesman of "Hindu sangathan"—the organization of the Hindu community. In his 1896 treatise in Urdu entitled *Shivaji the Great Patriot*, he regretted that his countrymen "had no taste for the study of history" and that they were more interested in "getting degrees after the study of Shakespeare, Milton and Huxley . . . they don't turn their minds to the great men produced by our nation."[19] To Lajpat Rai, Shivaji was a great martial figure who demonstrated that there was no contradiction between India's great spiritual tradition and the existence of "a warrior ethos" (ibid., 10).

The other fissure concerned the definition of the Indian nation. Whereas Gokhale and the liberal reformers endorsed most of the reform legislation of the British and condemned "the evils of traditional Hindu-society," the caste system, the position of women, and so on, Tilak insisted on the ability of Hindu society to reform itself. Inspired more by the sanatana movement in north India rather than by Swami Dayananda and the Arya Samaj, Tilak glorified the deeds of Vedic civilization. In books and articles, Tilak rejected the right of foreigners to criticize and judge the qualities of the Hindu civilization. The antiquity of Hindu civilization, its resilience, its profound philosophy, and scientific character were proof of its viability and its coherence. Echoing orientalist romanticism, Tilak claimed the Vedic civilization to be the oldest in the world, the most refined, and the mother of all civilizations (Wolpert 1961, 62–65).

Around the turn of the century, Tilak emerged along with Lala Lajpat Rai in Punjab and Bipin Chandra Pal in Calcutta as important spokesmen for a radical populist mobilization of the Hindu community on themes of cultural, economic, and political self-reliance and self-determination. Yet none of these leaders advocated an exclusively Hindu nation. They envisioned an Indian nation as a balanced alliance between distinct and self-conscious cultural communities, and remained committed, in spite of their shared belief in the primacy of the Hindu culture in India, to cooperation with the Muslim organizations.[20] Tilak was instrumental in forging the Lucknow pact of 1916, which stipulated the terms of collaboration between Congress and the Muslim League in what Tilak, encouraged by Britain's weakening during World War I, envisaged as a new anticolonial coalition.[21]

The Congress leadership attempted in the following period to steer a course between an open commitment to a Hindu community/nation that could generate considerable popular support but also endless violence, and continued cooperation with a Muslim leadership that remained skeptical toward the intentions of Congress. In the most politically active centers in India, communal clashes and antagonisms were on the rise, and most nationalist leaders feared that the wave of popular resentment against the colonial power after the war would be deflected and derailed by mounting violence between Hindus and Muslims. The inverted colonial construction of India as consisting of numerous equal communities, which nationalist politics had been popularizing since the 1880s, had increasingly produced a sort of "communal common sense" that turned out to be a major stumbling block in the development of a joint anticolonial strategy.[22]

This dilemma was particularly evident in Punjab, where the idea of a "Hindu nation" in the contact of stiff intercommunal competition had first acquired a formal political dimension with the formation of the Punjab Hindu Sabha in 1907, and subsequently the formation of the Hindu Mahasabha in 1915. The driving forces behind these attempts to galvanize the Hindu community into an operational political unit capable of representing "Hindu interests" were figures prominent in the Arya Samaj and in the promotion of Hindi, such as Madan Mohan Malaviya and prominent Congressmen such as Lala Lajpat Rai. Although Malaviya was unequivocally committed to the promotion of the formula "Hindi, Hindu, Hindustan" and the assertion of Hindu culture, Lajpat Rai attempted to unite the Hindu perspective with a larger pan-Indian one. He gave voice to a significant number of political activists in northern India who believed that swaraj (independence) could best be secured if each of the constituent communities promoted its own interests and self-consciousness. According to Lajpat Rai and other leaders behind the Hindu Mahasabha, the lack of organization and cohesion in the Hindu community necessitated a systematic organizational effort (*sangathan*) if it was not to be overwhelmed by Muslims and Sikhs (Tuteja and Grewal 1992, 15).

The Hindu Mahasabha was in its early years mainly a provincial organization in northern India drawing support from the Arya Samaj network in Punjab and the Hindu sanatana networks the United Provinces and Bihar (Gordon 1975), but soon its significance reached far beyond the complexities of north Indian politics. The Hindu Mahasabha, conceived as an articulation of Hindu assertiveness and strength in reaction to Muslim communitarian organization, presented to Muslim organizations a living proof and justification of their program of separate constituencies. At this juncture, the quest for Hindu assertiveness and manliness, and the fears of Muslim aggression and corporate strength, were given an eloquent formulation by V. D. Savarkar.

Hindutva and the "Lack" in the Hindus

V. D. Savarkar addressed the "lack" in the Hindu directly, and tried to identify a remedy: the discovery and construction of Hindutva, a "Hinduness" shared by all Hindus. Savarkar was arrested several times on charges of terrorism and illegal activities in connection with the secret society Abhinav Bharat (Modern India) he founded in 1904, and he spent many years in colonial prisons. The writings of Giuseppe Mazzini, with which he became acquainted during his four years in Britain from 1906 to 1910, made a profound impression on Savarkar.[23] In Mazzini, Savarkar found an ideological framework and a political philosophy that combined cultural pride and national self-assertion with a modernist outlook and a vision of a strong, culturally homogenous nation embodied by a unitary state—the vision of the making of a modern Italian nation-state that Mazzini had developed under the influence of Herder and Fichte. In the opening chapter of *Hindutva*, Savarkar stated: "Hindutva is not a word but a history. Not only the spiritual or religious history of our people as at times it is mistaken to be by being confounded with the other cognate term, Hinduism. Hinduism is only a derivative, a fraction, a part of Hindutva. . . . Hindutva embraces all the departments of thought and activity of the whole being of our Hindu race" (Savarkar 1969, 3–4).

Savarkar's main concern was to define the two main coordinates of the Indian nation, its territoriality and its culture, and most importantly to demonstrate their congruence. The term "Hindu," he argued, is basically a territorial denomination of the civilization developed through millennia on the eastern side of the river Indus, "Sindhu," which gradually became known as "Hindu." Savarkar refused to accept the theory of Aryan invasion of the subcontinent, and stated that the ancient land of "Sindhu" comprised the entire subcontinent. He argued that the sense of nationality was already present four thousand years ago in the "Vedic Nation" as a cultural self-consciousness that took root through the development and refinement of a common language, Sanskrit, and a common body of philosophy and ritual practices (ibid., 10–44).[24]

Let me briefly dwell on Savarkar's concept of Hindutva in the light of the classical tenets of cultural nationalism as they had been transmitted explicitly through Mazzini's writings, and as they had been "naturalized" implicitly as common-sense knowledge both among previous generations of Indian nationalists and within colonial knowledge-practices.

Savarkar rehearsed a number of these tenets. First was the primacy of territory in forming a nationality and praise of the unique and supreme qualities of each nation. Second, there was the notion of the antiquity and common emotional attachment to the name of the nation. Savarkar claimed that "Hindusthan" had been the preferred name for India through millennia (ibid., 82). The third tenant was the coherence and unity of language as the central carrier of cultural essence and feeling—that is, first the unity of a shared Sanskrit and later, of modern Hindi. The fourth tenent involved the holistic concept of culture as a corporate whole held together by shared blood and race. Savarkar praised caste endogamy as a mechanism keeping the blood of the nation pure. Being unable to argue for any intrinsic racial unity, Savarkar resorted to the notion of a common will suffusing the entire Hindu nation: "We feel we are a jati, a race bound together by the dearest ties of blood and therefore it must be so" (ibid., 89).

Another striking feature of Savarkar's thought was the simultaneous influence of Fichte's idea of the "internal border," that is, the internalized individualization of nationhood. Hindutva is essentially a question of subjective feelings, loyalty, individual patriotism, a "will to nationhood." The tension in Savarkar's argument between given, objective criteria of nationhood and chosen criteria of emotional attachment becomes crystal clear in his final chapter, "Who Is a Hindu?" in which he tried to operationalize his definitions and apply them to the political reality of India at his time.

Savarkar argued that the ultimate criterion for being a Hindu was the definition of a "holy land" (pitrubhoomi), which is the geographical location of the sacred shrines and myths of one's religion. "Hindu" denoted all those whose religion has grown "out of the soil of India"—Buddhists, Jains, Sikhs, and the multiple Hindu sects, the Hindu Dharma. It was equally clear, however, that Aryan/Vedic Hinduism remained the real core of the Hindu nation: "Thus Hindu Dharma being etymologically as well as actually and in its religious aspects only (for Dharma is not merely religion) the religion of the Hindus, it necessarily partakes of all the essentials that characterize a Hindu" (ibid., 110). To what extent it made sense to Buddhists or Sikhs to be called Hindus or to have India as a "holy land" seemed of little importance to the thrust of the argument, which sought to define Hindus by excluding those from nationhood who actually or potentially could pose a political or cultural threat to Hindu culture. Christians and Muslims had potentially "extraterritorial loyalties," as their "holy lands" were outside the territory of India, and they could not be counted as Hindus. These communities could have patriotic feelings for their country, or even have Hindu blood in their veins (though it remained unclear how blood would change in the wake of conversion) and observe most of the Hindu festivals. Still, they could not be true Hindus, as they never would devote themselves fully to India because they had chosen to have another "holy land." If, on the other hand, they gave up their "alien" belief they could be admitted back in the Hindu fold as true Hindus (ibid., 115).

With Savarkar, and the simultaneous advent of Gandhi as a national leader, there emerged two distinct political interpretations of the idea of a modern Indian nation based on Hindu values. Savarkar's cultural nationalism was communal, masculine, and aggressively anti-Muslim, but also rationalist and in favor of rapid modernization. In his later work on Shivaji, Savarkar stated his belief in the nation as a "higher form" in explicitly social Darwinist terms: "men, groups and races [are] in the process of consolidation under the stern law of nature, to get forged into that larger existence on the anvil of war through struggle and sacrifice. Those alone who can stand this fierce ordeal will prove their fitness, not only the moral but even the physical fitness that entitles races and types to survive in this world" (Savarkar 1925, xii).

Gandhi shared the glorification of the Golden Age of Hindu culture and the celebration of spirituality with both the sanatanists and the Hindu nationalists, but his cultural nationalism was populist, syncretic, and distinctly anti-Western. Whereas Gandhi tried to define India as the antidote to the West, as the spiritual fullness that would supplement the "lacks" in the West, Savarkar's relation to the West was more ambiguous. Savarkar found it difficult to construct the West as the "other" of Hindu culture. On the contrary, "like a good sportsman we admire the skill and might" of the British nation that, according to

Sarvakar's social Darwinist reasoning, entitled them to form an empire. In the eyes of Savarkar, Muslims were the main threat to Hindus, not only because of the ongoing struggles over the cultural complexion of the nationalist movement but also because their ostensible self-confidence and corporate strength constantly reproduced what Savarkar saw as self-destructive weakness and lack of confidence among Hindus.

The Nation as Fullness and Purity: M. S. Golwalkar

The militant Hindu nationalist discourse was further developed by M. S. Golwalkar, whose writings revolved around the question of construction of a cultural holism and national strength to negotiate and control the fragmenting impulses of modernity. Golwalkar was the longstanding leader and the most prominent ideologue of the Rashtriya Swayamsevak Sangh (RSS), which from the 1940s on became the most powerful and important Hindu nationalist organization in the country (see chapter 3 for an analysis of the RSS). In his writings, Golwalkar expressed the anxieties produced by modernity, democratization, and mass society in the classical elitist tale of loss and declining standards leading toward an "abyss of degeneration." "[We live in] strange times indeed, when we do not live but merely exist. Strange and altered. Words which for centuries conveyed to us certain definite ideas have changed meaning. . . . Nobility is at a sad discount. . . . Sterling merit is discouraged. In fine we are rolling down at a terrific speed into the bottomless abyss of degeneration" (Golwalkar 1947, 6).

The sources of Golwalkar's inspiration are not as directly discernible as Savarkar's admiration for Mazzini, but Golwalkar was operating within the same connotative domain created by cultural nationalism of the late nineteenth and early twentieth century in India. In Golwalkar's first book, *We, Our Nationhood Defined* (1939), which became infamous for its obvious admiration for what Golwalkar called "the German Race-spirit," it was obvious that Golwalkar was drawing his basic concepts from western history and scholarship: "We must also see what the idea [of] nation should denote to us in our struggle for national regeneration, by applying the universal concept to our case" (Golwalkar 1947, 7).

In the book, Golwalkar went through a number of academic definitions of nationality, and identified what he called the five "unities" defining nationhood: geographical unity, racial unity, religious unity, cultural unity, and linguistic unity.[25] From a discussion of European nations, Turkey, Russia, and America, Golwalkar tried to show that cultural unity is a precondition for the viability of a state. That was true of India as well, and in the remainder of the book Golwalkar tried to prove in quasi-scientific language that Hindus constituted the racial, religious, and linguistic backbone of Bharat. Golwalkar adopted the draconian view that those who did not comply with the standards and culture of the Hindu nation "fall out of the pale of National Life" (ibid., 52). They "deserve no privileges, far less any preferential treatment— not even citizen rights" (ibid., 56).

In the 1940s, and especially after the first ban on the RSS in 1948 to 1950, Golwalkar abandoned this hard-nosed nationalist rhetoric in favor of a more "orientalist" emphasis on spirituality and culture in the building of the nation. This change was obviously related to Golwalkar's apprehensions regarding the ambiguities of democratic politics, and was a tactical move to comply with the changed political conditions after the killing of Gandhi and the traumas of Partition.

In a collection of essays and articles entitled *Bunch of Thoughts*, Golwalkar embarked on a classical orientalist trail as he portrayed Hindu civilization as the "first thought-givers to the world. . . . [L]ong before the so-called modern age the seers and savants of this land had delved deep into the vital questions" (Golwalkar 1966, 2). Consistent with Vivekananda, Gandhi, and many others, Golwalkar asserts that the materialist West has failed in providing human happiness because of an excessive emphasis on strife, conflict, competition, and individual enjoyment and hedonism. The strength of Hinduism and the spiritual correction offered by the Hindu mode of thought lies in holistic thinking—the understanding of the tiniest thing, organism, or being as an integral part of a larger whole (ibid., 2–22). In a truly romanticist vein, Golwalkar asserts that individual originality and genius only can flourish within a true and lasting community of other human beings, insofar as this community unfolds its own innermost being, its national culture (ibid., 33).

In India, he wrote, culture is intimately connected to spirituality and to an all-encompassing conception of "Divinity." The essence of the divine is exactly its "inexpressibility," and Hinduness is "too fine to be defined": "We feel it, though we cannot define it. . . . [O]ur sentiments, ideals and aspirations have a reality of their own and have a very vital role in our life though they cannot be expressed in terms of definitions and mathematical equations. In fact it is such subtle factors that form the real human personality rather than such gross things as can be measured and defined" (ibid., 46).

A more succinct statement of romanticist ontology is difficult to imagine. In Golwalkar's rendition, the secret of the Hindu community is that it cannot be defined, only felt. It is empty and inexpressible, a community of "lack," but it is exactly this "subtlety" that ennobles it.

Throughout Golwalkar's writings the features of Hinduness, Hindu nation, and Hindu patriotism are all defined as in a state of "becoming." The ideal state of nationhood can only be realized through cultivation of strength, physical and spiritual: "The first thing is invincible physical strength. We have to be so strong that no one in the whole world will be able to overawe and subdue us. For that we require strong and healthy bodies. [But] character is more important. Strength without character will only make a brute of man. Purity of character as well as the national standpoint is the real life-breath of national glory and greatness" (ibid., 65–66). Golwalkar draws here on the Fichtean notion of will and the character of individuals as the building blocks of the nation, but he also promotes physical strength as a path to national regeneration to counter colonial notions of the "effeminate Hindu," so deeply internalized in the quest for Hindu sangathan (organization). The axiom of "national will," however, is in Golwalkar rendered as an orientalist spirituality that prevails over the physical manliness of Hindus. This comes out clearly in his jingoistic commentary on the deeds of Indian soldiers in the war with Pakistan in 1965, under the headline "Potent Men versus Patton tanks." Here is a double expunction at work, both the erasure of the myth of Hindu effeminity, and the erasure of the Pakistanis by liking them to machines, that is, to signify the mechanical and inhuman element in human beings.

> It has once again given glowing evidence for the irresistible valor and virility of the children born and bred in the bosom of our great Motherland: The way our *jawans* [soldiers] crushed scores of Patton-tanks—considered invincible—as so many empty match-boxes and reduced the much-vaunted armoured divisions of the enemy to shambles has made many, even its Western masters, sit up and ponder. . . . But they have ignored the fact that it is the "man" and not the "machine" that counts. Our superior "man" has proved to be far superior to the "machine" of the enemy. . . . Our jawans have in these few days smashed the myth assiduously built up by the British, and believed by the world and by many of our countrymen, that we are a meek and weak lot who have always been at the mercy of any and every freebooter who chose to trample on us" (ibid., 414–15).

The national spirit is a latent and intrinsic part of Hindu culture, but to make it flourish and become manifest, education is required, Golwalkar asserts. Once again the classical cultural nationalist axioms of the education, will, and cultivation of nationalist individuals are projected as a perennial and unique Indian tradition for "selfless" individual perfection and the unique position of the guru, the teacher, in the Hindu tradition. The essence of this strategy for national reawakening is to keep a spirit of devotion and brotherhood vibrant and never to rely on "institutionalization," formalism, or brute power. In the national regeneration, the RSS volunteer, the swayamsevak, must be the relentless missionary of the national spirit, as the survival of the nation entirely rests on the daily and constant emotional attachment to the nation. This, Golwalkar asserts, is the only way to serve the nation, the Mother. Under the headline "Mother Wants." Golwalkar activates the oedipal connotations of the concept of "Motherland," and challenges Indian men to rid themselves of fear: "Let us shake off the present-day emasculating notions and become real living men, bubbling with national pride, living and breathing the grand ideas of service, self-reliance and dedication in the cause of our dear and sacred motherland. . . . Today more than anything else, mother needs such men—young, intelligent, dedicated and more than all virile and masculine. And such are the men who make history—men with capital 'M'" (ibid., 587–88). The vision of Golwalkar and the RSS was obviously a political vision, understood as an organized and conscious effort to change the social, cultural, and political life of a society. Yet, according to Golwalkar, this vision was not political but mainly cultural, gradual, and long-term—to be effectuated through gradual injection and assertion of a true national spirit in all spheres of social life.

Golwalkar's "antipolitical" stance reflected his fear of the impurity of politics, and was a logical derivative of his romanticist nationalism and the orientalist theory of Hindu society as constituted by culture rather than any strong or viable state. To Golwalkar, power in its manifest political sense was corrupting the high moral standards necessary for national regeneration; it was incapable of changing the character of individuals and the spirit of society. State power, therefore, had to be restrained and limited in order to permit the nation to flourish (ibid., 99). This rejection of "politics" and "power," however, also points to a deeper feature of closed organizations like the RSS, namely, the fear of the profane and ordinary. Systematic engagement with internal democratic procedures would have made it clear that the RSS, like any other movement, was founded on power and was seeking power and its various gratifications. It would thus also have revealed the circular logic sustaining all brotherhoods, sects, and secret societies: that the "spirit" of the movement only flows from effacing all traces of the power that enacts it. Their innermost secret, namely, that "there is no secret," only profanity, must, hence, be carefully guarded. It is, after all, precisely this ritualized guarding, this objectification of belief, that generates the illusion that there is a secret in the first place!

Political power understood as sovereignty and national strength was, nonetheless, always crucial to Golwalkar's vision of a Hindu nation. In the 1950s Golwalkar advocated a strong "Unitary State" and opposed the reorganization of the Indian state into linguistic units, which he believed would weaken the cohesion of Hindu society and set in motion centrifugal forces. Instead, the country should move toward "One Country, One State, One Legislature and One Executive" (ibid., 299) in order to strengthen itself and be able to counter foreign aggression. Golwalkar was also in favor of a strong defense, in favor of a final, if necessary large-scale, war against Pakistan and China, and so forth.

Like Herder and Fichte, who wished to recruit culture and nation on a unique German road to modernity, Golwalkar wished to recruit Indian spirituality and culture in order to arrive at modernity as a strong, unitary, and coherent society. Nationalism, as we saw from Vivekananda onward, had represented a strategy of acculturation of modernity by what Blumenberg would term "reoccupations" of older "positions" within a new secularized horizon (Blumenberg 1983, 47–65), thus modifying and reinventing both the old and the new: dharma turning into national culture or race spirit; the notion of social harmony of the caste hierarchy into commitment to the corporate nation; the practices of sannyasa into the activism of devoted, selfless patriots; moksha (spiritual liberation) into national fullness, and so on.

The many parallels between European nineteenth-century cultural nationalism and cultural nationalism in India may at one level be explained through such things as influence of Mazzini on Savarkar, of Tolstoy and Thoreau on Gandhi, the impact of orientalist scholarship, and Golwalkar's readings of European political scientists.[26] Seen as discursive formations distributing themselves in time and space, however, the similarities also testify to the relevance of exploring the historically accumulated conceptual grammar of nationalist discourse itself, how it mutates and yet reproduces central notions of territory, culture, race, gender, and so on. The journey of conceptual grammar from Herder to Golwalkar reflects no simple process of dissemination, but is an example of a process of changing discursive forms and references as the notion of "India" developed, as well as of several continuities both in contents and style.[27]

In the Gandhian Garb: Deendayal Upadhyaya and "Integral Humanism"

Deendayal Upadhyaya was a full-time organizer of the RSS, commissioned to work as an organizer in the Hindu nationalist party Bharatiya Jana Sangh from its inception in 1951. He developed a set of concepts that, under the name of "Integral Humanism," was adopted by the Jana Sangh in 1965 as its official doctrine. Integral Humanism did not depart much from Golwalkar's organicist thought but supplemented it by appropriating significant elements of the Gandhian discourse, and articulated these in a version of Hindu nationalism that aimed at erasing the communal image of the Jana Sangh in favor of a softer, spiritual, nonaggressive image stressing social equality, "Indianization," and social harmony. This creation of a new discourse suited specifically to the legitimate problematics and dominant discourses of the political field of the 1960s and 1970s in India also reflected an attempt to adjust the party and the larger Hindu nationalist movement to a new high profile on the right fringe of the political mainstream, with a considerable following in the urban middle classes in north India after the 1967 general elections. One of the most significant changes in relation to Golwalkar's writings was the use of the term "Bharatiya," which Richard Fox has aptly translated "Hindian," a mixture of "Hindu" and "Indian" (Fox 1990: 64). The use of the term "Bharatiya" thus signified an adaptation to the political realities of official secularism, which had made explicit references to "Hindu" impossible and illegitimate outside the religious field.

Drafted as a political program, Integral Humanism contained certain concrete visions organized around two themes: morality in politics, and swadeshi (Indian manufacture and consumption) and small-scale industrialization in economies—all Gandhian in their general thematic but distinctly Hindu nationalist in the characteristic style of "integralism." That is, these notions revolve around the same basic themes of harmony, primacy of cultural-national values, discipline, and so on. According to Upadhyaya, the paramount concern in India must be to develop an indigenous economic model that puts the human being at center stage, and that differs sharply in this respect from both capitalism and communism. Swadeshi and decentralization should become cornerstones in economic development, but without being embedded in a cultural ethos of materialism and technical fetishism, Upadhyaya argued in his characteristically imprecise style (Upadhyaya 1991, 58).

Integral Humanism was mainly Gandhian at an idiomatic level, using concepts such as swadeshi and sarvodaya (welfare for all), while the more radical ideals of Gandhian thought—the idea of swaraj, understood as autonomy, at all levels, the skepticism toward state institutions, and the commitment to equality—were subsumed within a framework that assigned undisputed subservience of individuals and groups to the nation as a corporate whole. Fox calls this operation an "ideological hijacking" and a "transplant" solely designed to appropriate the authority of the Gandhian idiom (Fox 1990, 69–70). The adoption of Integral Humanism as a political doctrine and the Jana Sangh's new openness toward other forces in opposition did in important ways pave the way for the first major public breakthrough for the Hindu nationalist movement: the alliance with the powerful Gandhian Sarvodaya movement led by J. P. Narayan in north India in the early 1970s (see Chapter 3).

Constructing the "Founding Myth"

These strategies, aimed at appropriating a Gandhian idiom, fit into the RSS's larger ideological endeavor to represent itself as the sole and true inheritor of Indian nationalism and the only legitimate guardian of Hindu society, which throughout its history has fought against foreign domination in order to "become itself."

A founding myth provides a movement with a sort of condensation of the effervescence of its "nascent state," in which the basic objectives, the ethical standards, and the major grievances that gave birth to the movement all are concentrated. Although movements organized around charismatic leaders often construct a narrative around the life and ordeal of the leader, more ideological movements often organize such accounts around symbolically significant events (Alberoni 1984, 152–55). Tales of conflict and heroism under adverse circumstances— such as the accounts of selfless heroism emerging from the history of successive bans on the RSS by the Indian state—make it possible to restage, and renarrate, its founding myth and favorite tale of representing the inconspicuous "Hindu society" against a hostile or arrogant state.

All publications of the RSS are written in an unmistakable flowery and passionate language. One finds devoted hagiographies of the founder Dr. Hedgewar, of his successor Golwalkar, and an unmediated praise of the virtues of swayamsevaks, (volunteers) their deeds and virtues, and of the might and size of the organization. K. R. Malkani's account of the foundation of the RSS, *The RSS-story*, sets the favorite tone of the RSS family of organizations (Sangh parivar)—the unspectacular, silent, devoted work of thousands of swayamsevaks that marks the greatness of the organization: "There were no press reporters or photographers around to record the event. The new organization not only had no constitution; it was not even given a name. No office bearers were proposed or elected. And yet a great event had taken place. The Rashtriya Swayamsevak Sangha had been born" (Malkani 1980, 1). What follows is a loving account of the life, vision, and work of Dr. Hedgewar, sprinkled with small anecdotes and parables that demonstrate his selfless and exemplary character as founder of the RSS. The official RSS biography of Hedgewar, *Dr. Hedgewar, The Epoch-*

maker (Seshadri 1981) is even more passionate, and depicts Dr. Hedge-war as one of the most significant personalities of the twentieth century, whose historical significance is rivaled only by Gandhi.

The setting in which the RSS emerged is depicted as one of frustration and desperation on the part of truly patriotic men. In Nagpur, Dr. Hedgewar's hometown, Muslims had rioted and killed Hindus, and it was felt—so the myth goes—that Hindu men had to come together and train physically to be able to defend themselves and foster a patriotic feeling. The RSS achieved its first public breakthrough when RSS swayamsevaks effectively, over three days, beat up Muslim rioters. This sudden determination on part of the Hindus deterred the aggressive Muslims and brought the communal clashes to an immediate halt. (Seshadri 1981, 93–97).

Malkani's loving portrait of *Guruji* Golwalkar, the chief ideologue and architect of the RSS, emphasizes his wisdom and selflessness, and he is presented to the readers as the ideal RSS man. The accounts of both founders are sprinkled throughout with anecdotes of "historical meetings" with Gandhi, of talks with India's first home minister, Sardar Patel, and other important persons, in each case emphasizing the profound impact and admiration such encounters with the "spirit and excellence of the RSS" had on these important persons.

Accounts of the RSS's work are in similar ways supported by sympathetic and admiring comments and praise from well-known and important persons. In 1992, Malkani edited an entire volume entitled *How Others Look at the RSS* (Malkani 1992). The volume is filled with accounts and praise of the RSS from a range of politicians and intellectuals on the Indian scene, most of them known for their affiliation with Congress or other leading forces. This peculiar publication, which seeks to represent the RSS as respectable, moderate, and mainstream, betrays the impact of the many years of relatively stigmatized isolation in which the RSS found itself until the late 1970s. It indicates the pertinence of the RSS's quest for recognition—by the Indian elite, the West and others—which remains a driving force among the provincial, vernacular-speaking intellectuals who have always provided the backbone of the movement.

The construction of Indian history as an unbroken teleological drive for realization of the national spirit, as well as the construction of its other(s), are brought out succinctly by Malkani in the final chapter of *The RSS-story*. The history of India is the philosophy of India, Malkani states, and he goes on to argue against the theory of Aryan invasion in the subcontinent. Referring to Toynbee, Malkani argues that Indian culture has developed in so much depth because it has been constantly, for millennia under outside pressure—from the Greeks, Buddhism,

Islam, Christianity, and lately communism. India always survived by turning inward and absorbing all invaders in its superior and accommodating culture (Malkani 1980, 191).

This realization of Hindu nationhood is not only natural, says Malkani, it is also irresistible, because Hinduism and the Hindu concept (here Malkani quotes Toynbee again) "is at once more natural, more human and more scientific" than other religions. In one sentence Hindu culture is recognized by a famous Western historian as surpassing the West in the fields of naturalism, humanism, and scientific rationalism.[28]

Conclusion: Hindu Nationalism and Democratic Revolution

Organized and militant Hindu nationalism as it appeared in the 1920s with the Hindu Mahasabha and the RSS, whose histories we shall follow in the next chapter, was neither an accidental deformation of nationalism into bigoted communalism nor an inevitable outcome of the recruitment of religious symbols in the nationalist mobilization. It was, as I have tried to show, one of several contingent outcomes of a protracted struggle over the definition of Indian nationhood. From the middle of the nineteenth century, this struggle had involved sustained efforts to construct and consolidate a Hindu community and a "great tradition" of Hinduism, on the basis of received orientalist categories, colonial objectifications, and the domesticated conceptual grammar of cultural nationalism. These efforts must be seen as elements in an incipient process of democratic revolution that dislocated older hierarchies and social orders, and enabled new classes, new institutions, and new public arenas to emerge, wherein modern ideological idioms of equality and sovereignty produced a powerful language of rights, which in India remained captive to the orientalist imagination and thus were articulated as both inherently collective and based on communities—rights to culture, to community, to representation, and to self-determination. This democratic revolution had around 1920 prepared the ground for articulation of a range of competing nationalist discourses—from communitarian nationalism over Gandhian syncretic populism to a liberal and modernist vision of a "synthetic" nation elevated above communities and tradition.

The competing nationalist visions of the 1920s must, in other words, be seen as both structured and contingent. They were structured by a process that mobilized social groups around quests for equality among communities and new social identities at many levels, but also contingent upon their positioning and contestation in the complex strategic web of institutions, possibilities, and compulsions in the political field.

Historical processes are inevitably judged in the light of the events and institutions they produce. The dominance of Gandhian and secular interpretations of Indian society and culture in the nationalist movement in India is often seen as a proof of their intelligibility to the vast majority in colonial and postcolonial India. Similarly, the lack of political fortune for militant Hindu nationalism from the 1920s onward is often taken as a proof of a lack of correspondence between the Hindu nationalist discourse and broader popular practices and cultural idioms.

As I have tried to indicate, however, matters were never that simple. There were wide areas of conceptual overlap between the competing nationalist visions, and neither the Gandhian nor the militant Hindu nationalist discourse was a logical offspring of structural forces, pre-existing interests, or worldviews. They were contingent articulations in an intensely contested arena of emerging mass politics, and their later political fortunes were by no means prefigured in the 1920s. Their respective success or failure should, therefore, not merely be sought in their fit, or lack of fit, with existing notions of culture and community. The fortunes of these competing visions must, rather, be found in the strategies through which their proponents sought to construct such notions within the field of strategic possibilities available at the time, and within the historically produced connotative domain of nationalism in India. It is to such strategies of mobilization and organization on part of the Hindu nationalist movement that I turn in the next chapter.

3

Organizing the Hindu Nation

LIKE OTHER FORMS of cultural nationalism that hold the nation to be a single unifying thread that always/already unites "the people," Hindu nationalism is marked by a fundamental ambivalence vis-à-vis modernity and its release of desires and social fragmentation. Cultural nationalisms are generally projects of ideological control, which seek to shape and control the always unfamiliar and unpredictable social forms generated by capitalist modernities. The corollary of such a project of control is an emphasis on discipline and a tight corporate structure that seeks to realize the ideological utopia within the microcosm of the organization. Another corollary is an emphasis on physical strength and self-control: the ability to control one's desires and libido in order to sublimate these urges to unconditional dedication and service to the cause. Historically, these organizational forms have been present in various ways from Turnvater Jahn's gymnasiums in nineteenth-century Germany, to Mazzini's Young Italy and patriotic uniformed corps all over Europe and elsewhere in the twentieth century.

Most strongly disciplined movements are constructed and reproduced through what Alberoni has termed "unanimity through symbolic integration" (Alberoni 1984, 152–55). In such movements, it is the ability to make assurances of certainty and truth—"we are on the right path"—and to reaffirm identity—"we are the true people" or "we are the authentic nation"—that bestows power and authority on a leadership. The invention and perpetuation of a founding myth is therefore essential for a strategy of unanimity. The founding myth outlines the basic dilemma or conflict that the movement addresses, and invents a certain "fundamental experience" through which a new vision has been formed—most often portrayed as an encounter with and revelation of the true nature of the other. In political movements it may be the formulation of a vision or a "cause"—constructing a collective subject such as the "toiling masses," a class, the oppressed people, and so on—on whose behalf the movement acts.

The purpose of the founding myth is twofold: first, to demonstrate to the followers as well as to potential supporters that the movement is still as effervescent and vital as at its inception; and second, to realize perpetually and practice the vision inside the movement, and thus create a sort of counterculture, a counterlanguage, a counterinterpretation of history. The movement thus presents itself as a microcosmos of what is going to come when the vision of the movement is eventually generalized in society as such. The movement must be meticulously organized and disciplined in order to keep this idea of the actual realization alive internally, and in order to present itself to the surrounding environment as a living laboratory striving to realize its vision in a pure form.

Followers subjected to harsh discipline, however, can only reexperience the atmosphere in which the movement was formed through the gestures of its leadership. In Lacanian terms, the leader(ship) comes to represent a sort of condensation of the cause, or a new symbolic order, a new "name-of-the-father," an internalized authority, experienced by subjects as being "more in themselves than themselves," bestowing both a sense of certainty as well as fear and fascination on the followers.

What is expounded in this ideological construction is a paradoxical dual teleology. On the one hand, history is invoked to justify the movement and its objectives. The movement is but a realization of inevitable historical development, and individuals in the movement are merely inconsequential actors in a great, unfolding historical drama. This is true not only of the communist movement, but also of many anticolonial movements, religious movements, the labor movement in the West, and social movements in many parts of the world. On the other hand, the founding myth almost always revolves around a notion of self-birth and self-celebration, depicting the founding of the movement in an extraordinary situation by farsighted individuals who, through extraordinary difficulties, succeeded in creating the present movement. Due to their intervention the course of history will be altered as the movement will gradually realize its vision.

The dual teleology produces an irreconcilable tension between determinism and radical voluntarism, especially in radical and millenarian movements that transgress mundane norms of behavior as they address the question of guilt vis-à-vis the surrounding society and the constant fear of treason by the insiders. It is tolerable to be a persecuted, marginalized outsider as long as one is convinced that history, and the people in the abstract, are on one's side. Historical teleology and determinism may, in other words, mitigate guilt vis-à-vis the societal conventions that were violated when individual members joined the movement. The fear of treason can be controlled, on the other hand, if one is convinced that the movement is unique and path-breaking, and its members courageous individuals. Posteriority will, it is therefore believed, hail the movement and its individual members as heroes, and thus render contemporary society's condemnation of the movement hollow, false, and shortsighted. This hope of a future recognition contains doubts and incipient fragmentations within the movement itself.[1]

In India, uniformed corps became common from around the turn of the century onward. The Arya Samaj had a certain dress code, and after 1920 uniforms, drills, and paramilitary schemes began to proliferate. The Hindu Mahasabha gradually started to use uniforms. The Muslim paramilitary khaskars were uniformed, and so were the Congress volunteers in the front organization Rashtriya Seva Dal. The use of uniforms and paramilitary outfits expanded in the 1940s in conjunction with the world war and the mounting communal tensions and confrontations, up until Partition in 1947. Nationalist control projects did not necessarily put on a uniform, however. Gandhi's entire project of sarvodhya, of self-reliance, of "truth-force" (*satyagraha*), of ascetic control of desires and libido, may also be read as a project of control premised on the same ambivalence vis-à-vis the modern world, which he, like the RSS, inherited from nineteenth-century reform movements.

Culture versus Politics

Although operating within the same organicist paradigm, Savarkar and Golwalkar developed two rather different strategies for the realization of Hindu rashtra. Savarkar focused on politics, agitation, and political mass mobilization, whereas Golwalkar focused on more introverted cultural activism and "character building." The crystallization of these two positions in the late 1930s marked, in a sense, a restaging of the double-stringed strategy of gradual cultural change and public political articulation, which emerged in Punjab around the turn of the century, when Arya Samaj activists began to articulate their grievances vis-à-vis the Muslim community through the Hindu sabhas of that area. Although the Hindu Mahasabha initially functioned as one of several interest groups inside Congress, promoting what were perceived as specific "Hindu interests," it gradually became an independent force during the 1920s. In this period there evolved in north India a symbiotic relation between the Arya Samaj and the Hindu Mahasabha, with double membership and an emerging ideological unity.[2] This became particularly evident in the still more aggressive shuddhi campaigns conducted in Punjab, where the political atmosphere was marked by high levels of political and communal competition. As the communal logic escalated, Muslims "retaliated" by launching tanzim (organization) and tabligh (propagation) movements to reassert the hold of Islam, particularly among poorer groups (Minault 1982, 167–208).

The founder of the RSS, Dr. Hedgewar, envisaged a synthesis of Arya Samaj elitism and sanghathan methodology: the creation of a numerically small but devoted and efficient organization of patriotic men who could provide leadership for a progressive organization of the entire Hindu community. The methodology of the RSS refashioned a number of existing practices, notably the akhara institution—the long-standing popular tradition of young men meeting at wrestling pits, and doing physical exercises—as well as the institutional form of a religious sect gathered around a spiritual authority.[3] Although the akharas had traditionally been popular among both Hindu and Muslim artisans and peasant castes, the religious sects had traditionally attracted members of the higher castes. In a move that in many ways encapsulates the entire Hindu nationalist endeavor, the RSS tried to bring these two traditions together by giving the akharas an ideological/spiritual content, and by imparting a martial, masculine accent to the spiritual tradition. The central tool was the shakha, where boys and young men would meet one hour every day for physical exercise, drill, inculcation of ideals and norms of good and virtuous behavior (samskars), and ideological training (baudhik). The shakhas thus worked as what Jaffrelot calls "ideological akharas" (Jaffrelot 1996, 34–35). The guiding idea was to inculcate a national spirit as the ultimate and supreme loyalty and to build up a strong fraternal bond between the volunteers, the swayamsevaks. Hedgewar wished to create a "new man"—patriotic selfless individuals, loyal to the Hindu nation and the RSS—physically well trained, "manly," courageous, self-disciplined, and capable of organization. The RSS swayamsevak was to be the kshatriyaized antithesis to Gandhi's nonviolent, "effeminate" bhakti-inspired Hindu. The ideal swayamsevak was supposed to be a selfless activist dedicated to lifelong service of the nation, but not only preoccupied with a search for truth and perfection of the soul, as were the traditional yogis.[4]

In the 1930s, the organization gradually spread out from its heartland around Nagpur to western Maharashtra, where Pune became a major center, and to northern and western India, where the rapid deterioration of relations between Hindus and Muslims created a political climate hospitable to militant Hindu organizations.

Hedgewar carefully avoided any involvement of the RSS in political agitations in order not to jeopardize the relatively good standing the organization initially had among Congress men. The spread into communally very tense areas did, however, push the organization in a

more overtly militant direction. The RSS had at an early point in its
history established its own military department in charge of supervising and implementing military discipline and full-scale infantry
training, minus weapons (but with swords and lathis—metal-tipped
bamboo staffs) in the shakhas. Ideological training was also considered
important, just as the gradual weaving of close fraternal bonds among
young men in their most formative years under guidance of older
swayamsevaks played a crucial role.

Throughout the 1930s, the RSS maintained close relations with the
Hindu Mahasabha, which provided profound inspiration for the ideology and organization of the RSS.[5] The links between the RSS and the
Hindu Mahasabha and with the Savarkar brothers, legendary in Maharashtra, served to introduce the RSS into militant circles, especially in
Maharashtra, Punjab, and north India, where Savarkar enjoyed considerable popularity.[6] Hedgewar, however, seemed to be convinced that
the RSS should play a silent, inconspicuous role in the formation of a
Hindu nation, by quietly recruiting and training boys and men, and by
leaving the political field to Congress.

The disjuncture between the RSS and the Hindu Mahasabha evolved
more clearly after Savarkar was elected president of the Hindu Mahasabha in 1937. Savarkar set out to strengthen and expand the organization of the Hindu Mahasabha by sharpening radical anti-Muslim postures and downplaying the critique of the British. The RSS tried to stay
outside political campaigns and refused to support a major Hindu Mahasabha campaign in 1938–1993, which among other things aimed at
projecting the Hindu Mahasabha as a full-fledged political party. In
1939, the gap widened even more and the Hindu Mahasabha established its own uniformed youth corps, the Ram sena (Ram's army). The
breaking point occurred in the early 1940s, when Golwalkar became
sarsanghachalak (supreme leader) after Hedgewar, and the world war
had created a new strategic situation in India.

While the Hindu Mahasabha openly supported the British war effort
and especially encouraged Maharashtrians to join the British Army, in
order to acquire the martial skills and military prowess needed in the
army of independent India,[7] the RSS remained detached from the debate over the war and its implications for India. This created serious
conflicts within the RSS, where many younger men wanted to follow
the Quit India campaign conducted by Congress in 1942.[8]

Golwalkar changed the orientation and complexion of the RSS away
from its paramilitary and militant profile toward a more "brahminical"
strategy of creating an RSS culture, a Bharat Mata in miniature, which
by its example and high moral stature would gradually transform
norms and habits of the larger society (Andersen and Damle 1987, 43).

At this point in the evolution of organized Hindu nationalism, the tension between culture and politics as strategic fields of intervention became fully articulated as two different programs of rejuvenation and organization of the Hindu community.

As the RSS took the "cultural path" and terminated many of the public, high-profile activities, considerable internal tension arose. Two camps evolved in the organization—as tendencies rather than factions—one consisting of "traditionalists," the older generation, mainly Maharashtrians, favoring character building; and "activists," the younger generation, mainly north Indians, favoring agitation and mass action. (Andersen and Damle 1987, 108–9).

The activist wing held that the RSS, with its good organization and firm base, could replace the Hindu Mahasabha as a dominant representative of the "interests" of Hindus. In the sharpened communal climate preceding Partition, and during the chaotic and bloody communal carnage and exodus that followed, the RSS swung into action in the communal conflict. In this process, many units of the RSS discarded the caution favored by the supreme leadership of Golwalkar and his closest lieutenants. At this crucial juncture, where communal front lines overdetermined all other differences and former alliances, RSS activists found themselves in a situation corresponding to their preferred ideological fantasies. The Muslim enemy was clear and threatening, front lines were drawn, communal loyalty became a matter of life and death, and there was ample scope for demonstrating the image of dedication, sacrifice, and organizational capacity the RSS had built. During the de facto breakdown of the administrative machinery in these weeks and months, the RSS organized large-scale relief work and extended help to the Hindu refugees from Punjab and Sindh, who in this situation proved a most receptive audience for RSS ideology. RSS activists were also very active in communal violence, though this was never officially sanctioned by the leadership. Yet in the logic of RSS ideology this was "just" violence, acts of self-defense against the cruel Muslim enemy.

To RSS workers, Partition was a result of a mistaken soft line toward the Muslims, and only served to confirm the innate moral weakness and corruptibility of politicians. The RSS view was (and remains) that all those who believed in the good will of Muslims (including Gandhi), were dangerously naive and therefore responsible for the mass killings and the expulsion of millions of people. From my interviews with older RSS men, it became clear that the communal carnage of Partition was seen as a kind of patriotic baptism, an initiation through blood and sacrifice to the nationalist cause, for the individuals involved as well as for the corporate RSS body. These events were referred to with the greatest enthusiasm. This reflected the fact that the role of the RSS during Partition has become an essential element in the mythology of the RSS, to the extent that many RSS men argued that Hindus would have been absolutely defenseless, starving, and at the mercy of well-organized Muslim marauders had it not been for the mild, well-mannered and yet superbly trained and brave swayamsevaks. The significance of Partition in the RSS mythology also confirms that nationalist movements have their "optimal habitat" in situations where contradictions are clear and so are, antagonisms, and the struggle is one of life and death. Fuzziness, shifting stands, and overlapping complex loyalties—typical of democratic politics—may be lethal to the cohesion of such movements bent on ideological cohesion.

Around Partition, the strategic pendulum within the RSS thus swung from character building toward activism such as relief work, propaganda, and paramilitary intervention in communal violence. There is little doubt that the RSS earned itself a certain reputation in north India, particularly among the refugees from Punjab and Sindh, and others affected by the communal carnage and displacement, but also in Congress circles. Soon after Partition, however, the organization was banned due to an alleged involvement in the murder of Gandhi.[9] Although Naturam Godse's inspiration came from Savarkar rather than Golwalkar, the RSS was banned and 20,000 swayamsevaks were arrested during the next months, while the Hindu Mahasabha remained legal but effectively stigmatized, especially in Maharashtra. The Chitpavan brahmins (Godse's community) were attacked in a collective retaliation against a community whose Hindu nationalist leanings were well known, and whose claims to past glory and historical dominance in the area were a contentious issue in Maharashtra.[10]

The Sangh Parivar

After the ban was lifted in 1949, the RSS was forced to develop a new "respectable" image in order to overcome its public stigma. The most important instrument became diversification. Semi-autonomous affiliates of the RSS, run by deputed organizers and RSS volunteers as the core activists in many fields, were gradually started. As in the communist movements, an elitist and clandestine philosophy of professional revolutionaries, leading and educating the masses, informed the evolving network of full-time organizers (pracharaks), who in the RSS were dressed like ascetic sannyasis and spoke like brahminical teachers, but acted like professional organizers, as Hindu nationalist karma yogis.

The mass organizations emerging in the following decades were in both organizational and ideological terms subsidiaries of the RSS.[11] Financially and in terms of public representation they were, however, formally independent of the RSS, which had no de jure responsibility for their actions. The primary cohesive factor between the RSS (often referred to as the "mother organization") and the affiliates (the "sons") was and remains to this day the network of full-time organizers, pracharaks, circulating in and out of the RSS and the various affiliates, as they are deputed or appointed by the senior leaders in their region and sector. The local RSS pracharak in a city or region will always be consulted and will act as arbiting authority when major decisions within the affiliates are to be made. The formal organizational hierarchies within the affiliates themselves are, in other words, secondary to the informal hierarchies at various levels across the organizations. These tacit, informal hierarchies always place the RSS at the helm of the decision-making process, in spite of what at a formal level may appear as a parallel structure.

The first subsidiary of the RSS was the women's wing, Rashtriya Sevika Samiti, organized as a structure parallel to the exclusively male RSS. According to the "founding myth" of the Sevika Samiti, two women, both wives of leading RSS men, felt disturbed by the general unrest in the country, particularly the assertiveness of the Muslims, and the inability of Hindu men to defend Hindu women. The myth revolves around a single incident in which a young newlywed Bengali bride was raped by bandits in a train right in front of her husband, who, like the other passengers, did not dare to resist the bandits. Given this weakness of the Hindu men (or "Hindu society" as it is euphemistically referred to in the Sevika Samiti discourse) in the face of Muslim aggression and British domination, women had to learn how to defend themselves physically and morally. The story continues that the founder, Mrs. Kelkar, after receiving only lofty rhetoric from Gandhi, had to turn to the RSS to get assistance in organizing. Women, however, could not be included in the RSS, as "the different physical capabilities and different locations in social life of men and women would only create confusion," as a founding member of the Samiti put it.[12]

Besides creating practical problems of etiquette and appropriate conduct in various situations, the mixing of men and women would have violated one of the fundamental themes of RSS ideology: the creation of a brotherhood held together by affection for peers and superiors, and psychologically based on the sublimation of sexual energy to patriotic devotion and work. The Sevika Samiti was therefore organized as a parallel organization to the RSS, as a character-building organization for women. It comprised wives, daughters, and relatives of RSS men and through informal networks maintained intimate relations with the RSS. The activities were similar to those of the RSS: physical training, including martial exercises at shakhas separate from those of the men; samskars—moral teachings of the duties and obligations of women— especially emphasizing their role as mothers and caretakers of the family; and baudhik sessions inculcating Hindu nationalist ideology in the volunteers, the rashtrasevikas. Paola Bachetta observes that this term leaves out the *swayam* (self) of the male swayamsevak because unlike the men of the RSS, who are seen as unitary, mono-gendered selves capable of heroic deeds, female selves are constructed as relational, bi-gendered in the sense of always being inscribed in societal forms on which they depend (family, kin, culture) and yet capable of action (Bachetta 1996, 130). This is, however, a construction fraught with contradictions, in that the Samiti was also a necessary producer of the ideal unambiguously female "Hindu nationalist women," complementing the overall endeavor of the Sangh parivar toward expunging sexual ambiguities in the cultural constructions of the Hindu male and constructing an equally unambiguously masculine Hindu man (ibid., 149).

The symbolic language of the Samiti leans heavily on RSS ritual, using the bhagwa dhwaj (the saffron flag), celebrating the same festivals, and following routines similar to those of the RSS, although it attaches slightly different signified contents, referring to female heroes and to goddesses rather than to heroes and gods. It is quite clear that the Sevika Samiti has, more than anything else, worked as an auxiliary force to the RSS, consolidating the incipient sangathanist subculture— an embryonic creation of the Hindu nation to be revived in its entirety.

Forgetting oneself, discovering the pleasure of giving and serving rather than receiving, cultivating the virtues of forgiveness and compassion, and putting the service of the nation above anything else are some of the themes that in a rather sentimental language and style, assumed to conform with and confirm the likings and self-images of its female audiences, still runs through contemporary publications from the Sevika Samiti. The recruitment of motherhood for the nationalist cause, or "patriotic motherhood," remains a manifest and visible part of the Sevika Samiti discourse, especially in its publications and public gestures, still dominated by an older generation of higher-caste women.[13] It is readily admitted, however, that the Sevika Samiti faces difficulties in attracting sufficient backing from younger women, who, insofar as they are drawn to the Sangh parivar, seem more attracted to the activist style within the BJP and the VHP. In accordance with the general strategy of the RSS, the conventional policy on mobilizing women may be summarized as an attempt at "controlled emancipation," which allows for visibility and mobility of women mainly within the institutional confines of the larger RSS networks.[14]

SEVIKAS IN THANE CITY

The regional headquarters of the Rashtriya Sevika Samiti in Konkan is situated in Thane city. The headquarters is a three-story building constructed in 1970 by the Jijamata Trust, which was set up by the Sevika Samiti to receive locally collected funds. The local sevikas take pride in the fact that the architect was a women, funds were collected by women, and the daily management of the building is in the hands of Sevika Samiti members. The building consists of a nursery school run by a Sevika; a hostel for single working women, mainly from Sangh parivar-affiliated families; a library; a marriage hall that is given at concessional rates to sevikas and to underprivileged families; a meeting hall for Sevika Samiti activities; and rooms available for full-time Sevika Samiti workers passing through the Bombay region. The Sevika Samiti also runs a small bank in the city that gives cheap loans to poor women, enabling them to start a small business, pay medical bills, and improve their houses.

In 1992 the Sevika Samiti had around five hundred members in Thane city. Approximately one hundred young girls attended the five daily shakhas in the city. The remaining members were mainly women from families with traditional affiliations with the Sangh parivar.

The main problem faced by the Thane city branch of the Sevika Samiti is recruitment of young girls. There is a problem in keeping the girls attached to the organization when they reach adolescence and start higher education. Although many children are attracted to the Samiti, only those who come from RSS families remain attached to the organization when they reach their teens. Others go into the student organization, the Akhil Bharatiya Vidyarti Parishad (ABVP), or into the political party, the BJP, but the impact of the "Bombay culture" is difficult to cope with:

> Although Samiti members or sympathizers bring their daughters to the organization it is difficult to keep them attached if their friends attend other clubs. Our society has become lethargic and the people do not want any discipline. Our camps are always held on holidays and nobody wants to get up early to attend these camps. Nobody wants to take any hardship

and discipline. . . . Now we have to adjust our timings according to the TV programs. We have started to hold shakha from four to six in the evening so that the girls can go back in time for their favorite program (Sevika Samiti activist in Thane, 16 November 1992).

The steep rise in real estate prices in Bombay's metropolitan economy has affected the Samiti's work among women in various ways. The expensive apartments make joint family systems increasingly difficult, and only a few families can afford bigger apartments. More and more young families live on their own, and more and more women have jobs. This gives women little time to leave the house after work, the sevikas explain. Some of the older sevikas also complain that the breakdown of joint families prevents the older generation from inculcating good values and traditions in their grandchildren. They also find that their children are not very keen on looking after their parents. Those living with their son and daughter-in-law find it increasingly difficult to get along, "as emotional attachments in families are getting weaker." Interestingly, the younger working women in the organization did not regard these transformations of the family structure as a major problem.[15]

Alhough the Sevika Samiti in Thane city is fairly well organized, the bulk of the activists are middle-aged and older women with a conservative social outlook, nurturing a traditionalist version of the Sangh parivar ideology. As in the case of the RSS, the Samiti attempts to transgress its middle-class "cocoon" and mobilize poor and lower-caste women through social welfare work. The assertiveness among lower-caste groups in slums and low-income areas has, however, made this "maternalism" of the Sevika Samiti rather ineffective, at least in Thane and elsewhere in the Bombay region.

Durga Vahini (Durga's Battalion) is a women's militant organization founded by the RSS in 1990, which imparts training in martial arts, self-defense, and nationalist ideology to young women mainly from the lower castes. There are only two subunits in Thane, with around thirty members. Durga Vahini aims at organizing young girls from poorer and lower-caste families from outside the orbit of the Sangh parivar but, like the equivalent organization for young men, the Bajrang Dal, the organization is build around a core group of activists drawn from families with long-standing affiliations with the RSS and Sevika Samiti. Mrs. Bapat described the strategy of the Durga Vahini as nonreligious and, rather, part of a therapeutic strategy for keeping the nation healthy and strong: "The main motive behind Durga Vahini is physical training. Only if we have strength can we have a say in society. . . . These organizations [Bajrang Dal and Durga Vahini], were started when the VHP [an organization within the Sangh parivar; see just below] decided to solve the Ram-janmabhoomi issue [the conflict in Ayodhya over Ram's reputed birthplace]. The motive behind this was to strengthen Hindu society and not religious awakening. . . . These organizations are also important to keep the younger generation occupied and to prevent them from falling prey to narcotics" (Mrs. R. Bapat, interview in Thane, 17 November 1992).

According to the activists, the response among lower-caste groups not previously acquainted with the Sangh parivar, is better than among middle-class families, who care little for patriotic issues and are more interested in entertainment and pursuing careers. Lower-caste people are simply more spontaneously patriotic than educated groups, it was said. In line with the generally paternalistic spirit of the Sangh parivar, the organizers are completely convinced that the attraction of lower-caste families to the Durga Vahini stems from the inculcation of cultural values in the girls, the revelation of important national issues, and the feeling that even the families of the young girls gain good values and high culture from the encounter with the Sangh parivar.[16] This strategy betrays a feeling that the sanctity and protection of the female body from public exposure and physical danger is regarded as less important in the case of lower-caste women. Whereas the middle-class, higher-caste women should be controlled primarily through morality and ideology, the lower-caste women can be controlled and disciplined primarily through physical exercises.

One of the most important branches of the Sangh parivar, the Vishwa Hindu Parishad (VHP) led a relatively low-profile existence until the late 1970s. Founded in 1964, it was intended to provide a bridge between the religious establishment and the RSS. Its objectives were formulated at the outset: to consolidate "Hindu society," to spread the Hindu values of life, to establish a network comprising all Hindus living outside India, and "to welcome back all who had gone out of the Hindu fold and to rehabilitate them as part and parcel of the Universal Hindu Society," as a VHP pamphlet puts it.[17] The VHP represented a continuation of the efforts in the 1920s to produce the "Hindu nation" through establishment of rashtra mandirs and an all-encompassing catholic national Hinduism overriding divisions of sect and caste. As in the 1920s, it was sadhus and sants (holy men) drawn from dissenting branches of the religious establishment who propagated the idea of creating a public platform that would enable religious authorities to acquire an authoritative voice in larger societal and national questions. Several of the leading gurus recruited by the RSS on the VHP platform in the 1960s were so-called "modern gurus," that is, modern godmen whose discourse on spirituality as a road to individual perfection and social and material success catered to the modern urban middle classes.[18] These modern gurus are often politically active as spiritual advisors to high-ranking politicians, and often comment upon current events and recommend certain proper "ethical" views.[19] Others have a background in the Arya Samaj, the Hindu Mahasabha, the Rama-krishna Mission, and other organizations sponsoring a "nationalized" modern Hinduism and practicing a high-profile public and populist style of appearance and discourse, far removed from the strictly inter-personal relation between guru and disciples in more traditional sects (Jaffrelot 1994, 187–92).

The development of a national Hinduism—"adapted to the modern age"—remains one of the very significant activities of the VHP, which started as early as 1966 with the first International Hindu Conference in Allahabad. The idea was to develop a simplified, easily comprehen-sible, and commonly accessible Hinduism, understood as a catholic set of common symbolic denominators acceptable across sects and castes. The aim was to disseminate a common code of conduct for all Hindus—allegedly in consonance with "the Spirit of Hinduism and the Hindu Nation," and to disseminate the VHP's version of Hinduism as the standard, mainstream Hinduism.[20]

The syncretic strategy has been pursued with great energy, with the aim of bringing together representatives of various sects (including Jains and Sikhs) under a canopy provided by the VHP at national Sam-melans (conferences) several times each year, as well as at congrega-tions at the local level, in order to arrive at a mutual understanding of views and practices and to extract certain common denominators.[21] This entire endeavor intends to position the VHP in an elevated ar-biting and coordinating position in and around religious institutions. It also intends to inject an articulate nationalist reference into religious identifications, as the common ground for a national Hinduism. The far-reaching significance of this subtle strategy was demonstrated in the late 1980s, when it became evident that this and similar forms of catholic discourse of modern Hinduism were evolving as a common locus of "knowledge" of Hinduism in many parts of the country. This made the symbolic inventory of modern Hinduism an ideological tool in the RSS's and VHP's Ramjanmabhoomi agitation, whose power and efficiency surprised even its most ardent supporters.

The other part of the strategy of standardization and homogeniza-tion of Hinduism has been a less well-publicized effort to extract a com-mon code of conduct in the religious as well as nonreligious sphere from diverse scriptures and practices. At a conference of religious experts conducted by the VHP in 1967, six minimum requirements for being a good Hindu (of any kind) were agreed upon. They include regular visits to temples, regular pujas (worship) in the home, basic knowledge of the sacred geography of Bharat and of the mythical epics and, in a nationalist vein, basic loyalty to India and the Hindu culture (Vishwa Hindu Parishad 1981, 8). Another interesting modification made by the VHP was a certain "rationalization" of ritual practices, recommending that the many different samskaras (rituals) be reduced to three main forms performed around birth (*namkaran*), marriage (*vivah*), and death (*anteshi*). Part of the rationale behind this simplification-and-standardization was to make Hinduism more accessible to the tribals, who the organization tried to wean away from Christianity.

A broader activist line was adopted in the early 1970s, when the VHP more systematically entered the field of social welfare work, starting schools, medical centers, and hostels all over the country. A lot of this work is today carried out locally—as in the Christian tradition—by converting temples into centers of social work and relief. Existing trusts and networks of devotees are activated and reorganized in order to carry out active social work in their vicinity, particularly in slums and rural areas. Another important and widespread activity carried out under the auspices of the VHP is the so-called Vanvasi Kalyan Ashram (Tribal Development Centers) set up in 1966 as a combined social work and (re-)conversion organization. The organization runs a large number of ashrams, centers of education, medical facilities, and vocational training, as well as hostels and scholarship programs for tribals. The aim, as put by one organizer, is "to galvanize Hindu society by consolidating its soft and vulnerable flanks." A pamphlet stated its aim as that of preventing "the apprehensions amongst the have-nots [from leading] to a storm of hatred which will destroy the whole structure of society." The concluding sentence in the pamphlet, which seeks financial assistance for the work done in a tribal district, read: "Millions of semi-clad and semi-starved tribals living at your doorstep, so to say, are waiting to offer millions of thanks to you."[22] This mixture of fear of the underdogs, paternalism, and social vanity, appealing to the narcissistic desire of the urban middle classes to indulge in philanthropy and the expected gratitude it is supposed to generate, pervades most of the literature and discourse from the Vanvasi Kalyan Ashram. As stated by other VHP publications, the objective of the work among tribals is also to "produce nationalistic leadership among them[!], bringing them more and more to the mainstream of national life."

In one publication the cow is promoted as an object of worship, a symbol of Mother India, and a useful device in agriculture and nutrition, and thus—the argument goes—an important vehicle for the development of the country in ways not producing cultural alienation. The cultural narcissism that runs through the tribal missionary activities comes out in this revealing passage from a pamphlet from the Bombay unit of the VHP: "Since a very long time the tribals spread in these areas were not aware of cow. Never knew they anything about milk or the usefulness of cowdung!. . . . Slowly and gradually they were told about cow. . . . Hindu religion, cow milk and cow dung. They were given cow milk to drink for which they were not ready to have it. They were convinced, explained and, at last, they believed in all this and also started to have faith."

HINDU MISSIONARIES AT THE FRONTIER

The most elaborate attempt to transgress the middle-class "cocoon" of the Sangh parivar in Thane district was the network of educational ashrams run like boarding schools, hostels, and associations built in the tribal areas in the northern talukas in Thane district since the late 1960s. The motive was initially to counter the increasing Christian influence in these areas, where missionary schools, hospitals, and social-welfare schemes had for decades resulted in a large number of conversions of tribals to Christianity. The efforts of the VHP have been particularly successful in Mokhada and Jawahar talukas, to the extent that the BJP has become a dominant political party in many villages there. The president of the BJP in Thane district, Chintaman Wangar, who was elected as MP in 1996, is a tribal from this area educated through the system of ashrams, hostels, and educational grants created by the VHP. The VHP's attempt to proselytize and gain influence in tribal areas has been multifaceted, involving primary and secondary boarding schools, hostels in the cities for tribal students going for higher education, small projects in tribal villages, and more general political mobilization, especially of young tribals. The students of the ashrams are encouraged to go back to their villages "to make them Hindu again," as an activist put it, by organizing Ganpati festivals and other Hindu festivals. The brightest and most motivated students are recruited for the RSS, and many former students are active in the BJP in villages and in small towns in the area. In line with the general RSS methodology, the VHP's strategy is to create a lifelong attachment of the students to the Sangh parivar, and to create networks of local leaders who owe their education and position to the Sangh parivar.

In the third taluka with a large tribal population, Talasari, the Communist Party of India (Marxist) (CPI-M) and many independent nongovernmental organizations have been active for decades and have a solid backing due to their social work and their organization of the tribal population against Bombay-based timber merchants and landlords, on whom most of the tribals depend as wage laborers. Here left-wing organizers and Christian missionaries have for decades been competing over the loyalty of the tribal population. Madharao Kane, long-standing RSS man and president of the Kalyan Municipal Council for the Jana Sangh in the 1960s, started the Vanvasi Kalyan Ashram in Talasari—one of the largest and most controversial of the VHP's projects in the area—precisely to intervene to combat this "disease" creeping into the political and cultural loyalties of tribals: "Both these groups [Christians and communists], could be said to do antinational work, and hence I thought that the part that was diseased should be treated first. Therefore I started the work here" (M. Kane, interview in Talasari on 27 November 1992).

The ashram has 180 boys and 65 girls, recruited from all over the taluka. The daily schedule is a disciplined routine of education, Sanskrit prayers, "patriotic" training, and practical work in the attached gardens, workshops, and cowshed. The older boys participate in regular RSS shakhas, and the ashram also works as a local community center with weekly dispensaries, public functions, and arrangements for the local villagers and the families of the children. The overall objective of the ashram is, according to Kane, to "stop the leakage of tribals who were converting to other religions." The method is to impart education, culture, and Hindu civilization, which would enable the tribals to cope with all the evils of modern world. The paternalist discourse of the RSS pervades the depiction of tribal society and the civilizing progress that the ashram has brought about: "Previously they stayed in the forest, they lived a carefree life and did not feel a need to work hard. They never struggled for life and were quite independent. Immediately after marriage the young couple would set up a hut and live independently. This concept was similar to the animal kingdom that after attaining strength to sustain oneself, one lives independently" (ibid.).

After initial difficulties in persuading the parents to send their children to the ashram, the recruitment of students was smoother as the results of education and "inculcation of values" impressed parents and the outside world. As a result of the success of the civilizing mission of VHP, most of the traits of tribal culture were erased from the students' minds and conduct: "People saw that there was more

cleanliness with the students and because of the Sanskrit prayers that
are recited, their language and pronunciation improved and they
spoke more clearly. And they stand out from the rest. The difference
is such that no one would realize that they originally are tribals"
(ibid.). Most of the students came from very poor families, small-
holders with a few acres of land and large families, entirely dependent on low-paid and irregular wage labor jobs for landlords or timber companies. The education at the ashram was free of cost, and the
VHP also offered free hostels to those who wished to study in colleges in nearby cities. Most of the students expressed gratitude to the
VHP in general, and to "Sir" (Madhavrao Kane) in particular, and
had clearly internalized the strategy of social mobility through "acculturation" which the VHP's ideology of "integration into the national mainstream," that is, sanskritized Hindu culture, opened for
them. Most of the students I met in a VHP-run hostel in the nearby
town of Dahanu wished to become teachers or clerks in the cities,
and only a small part of them expressed any wish to go back to their
villages again. The VHP's strategy of "cultural uplift" had also
clearly left lasting marks on the identity of the students. One student
of the ashram expressed the result of his successful "civilization" in
comparison to his crude and primitive tribal fellow tribesmen thus:
"People generally recognize us by the way we talk to others and
present ourselves to others. They feel that we are more polished and
refined than the others, and that we speak and address elders with
respect, unlike others. Our language and pronunciation is more polished, unlike our native language which is Warli, and there are so
many dialects with that language. We stand out among the rest"
(student at Vanvasi Kalyan Ashram, Talasari, Thane district, 28 November 1992).

The *ashram* in Talasari, which Kane clearly regards as the "frontier" of Hindu culture in the wilderness of savages (tribals) and hostile manipulators (left-wing activists), has in recent years been the
locus of political clashes between communists and Hindu nationalists. In spite of all the rhetoric of social work and a civilizing mission
whose discourse and practice seems to have taken over the entire
inventory of colonial paternalism, the long-term objective of the
Sangh parivar in the area remains political and social dominance in
a constituency that is regarded as particularly susceptible to molding by projects of social reform. After years of minor skirmishes, the
situation escalated in 1991, when the ashram was assaulted by what
the VHP people claimed were "communist activists," who beat up
the staff and destroyed some property. According to the VHP, the
CPI-M and other left forces still dominate in the area. Or, as Kane

admitted, "there is a great deal of political awareness around here, and our progress in the area has been slow compared to other talukas" (ibid.).

The VHP is probably the affiliate of the RSS in which a strategy of "nationalist sanskritization" within the Sangh parivar is most clearly articulated. The syncretic platform, the recruitment of the religious establishment, and the paternalistic reconversion strategies all point to the equation of a brahminical "great tradition," seeking to heal up and cover over the many disparate, contradictory, and fragmented "little traditions" of dispersed Hindu practices under a simplified, "thin" national Hinduism, largely defined in terms of sanskritized practices. In this sense the VHP is broadening and reinterpreting the Arya Samaj strategy of nationalization through "classicization"—going back to the Vedas and Sanskrit. The sanskritization strategy is clearly articulated in VHP publications that report the teaching of Sanskrit to poor and backward people, whose aptitude and receptivity of the "sacred language" is unsurpassed, allegedly because they were never "contaminated by foreign ideologies."[23]

Since the late 1970s, the VHP has more systematically pursued a strategy of constructing a catholic Hinduism along more populist lines. Today, the VHP strategy of building a national Hinduism revolves around a program of organization, syncretism, and nationalization of existing practices. This search for a common ritual and symbolic denominator has tilted the VHP's version of national Hinduism in a decisively kshatriyaized direction—emphasizing, for instance, Ram's martial deeds and giving VHP's Hinduism a more aggressive, belligerent, and overtly political incarnation than the Arya Samaj ever articulated.

Cohesion, Leadership, and Control in the Sangh Parivar

Formation of militant groups often take place in the conjunction of two circumstances: when a group or already formed community experiences a pronounced sense of loss of meaning and identity, of humiliation in the wake of dislocations (war, urbanization, migration, or rapid modernization); and when a leadership or ideological virtuosos are able to transform this experience into a positive, however desperate, projection of affection onto a leader and an ideological cause that can produce a collective "grandiose self," that is, a community organized around enjoyment (*jouissance*) of a shared secret, an inexpressible core or spirit. The power of the charismatic leader and the symbolic rituals of the movement stem from the fact that they embody this "secret" without revealing it.[24]

Such a construction of a "grandiose self" is always threatened and undermined by the ambitions and "theft of enjoyment" by other groups or authorities. This constant threat—the enemy, the other—consolidates, even constitutes the group's cohesion. Militant groups need strong and demonized others in order to construct themselves as a strong and cohesive force.[25]

The Sangh parivar is an excellent example of such a subculture, concealing humiliation and loss of self-esteem by a vision of a "grandiose self" (the Hindu culture or the Sangh parivar) organized around a central, inexpressible secret (the Hindu spirit, the brotherhood of the sangha), providing a strong and demonized other (the Muslims and to some extent the West); and continuously absolving its members from guilt and fear (of hedonist fantasies of giving in to "lust and desire") by enforcing a strict discipline of a masculine community, which sublimates libido from sexual desire to devotion to the patriotic cause.

The RSS works through multiple layers of symbolic integration, with each symbol given a specific valorization by its ideological construction. The most important are the bhagwa dhwaj, the saffron flag, which is considered an age-old symbol. The flag is revered enthusiastically, for instance, by Golwalkar: "It embodies the color of the holy sacrificial fire that gives the message of self-immolation in the fire of idealism and the glorious orange hue of the rising sun that dispels darkness and sheds light all around" (quoted from Andersen and Damle 1987, 61). The question of its status vis-à-vis the national flag of India, wherein the coexistence of several communities in India is symbolized, was one of the thorny issues when the RSS was forced by the government to adopt a written constitution in 1949. Today, the saffron flag and the saffron color—though used widely in religious rituals and processions—has in the political field been appropriated by the Hindu nationalist movement. During riots, the saffron flag is often employed to mark Hindu areas, and it is planted upon Muslim dargahs (tombs) and masjids (mosques) to mark Hindu superiority.

Another important symbol is the celebration of six specific festivals during the year by the RSS and its affiliates.[26] The celebration of these festivals serves to strengthen the inner bonds of the organization and to portray the RSS and its leaders as the greatest men India ever produced, the leading nationalists in the country, and so on. Another function is to introduce new "patriotic" practices, based on Hedgewar's philosophy of organic growth of the RSS to become congruent with Hindu society. An important aspect of this strategy of "invention" of cultural nationalist practices in a quasi-religious language is the projection of Maratha king Shivaji to a status of demigod. The "nationaliza-tion" of Shivaji started in the late nineteenth century, and Shivaji has become a popular and clear-cut martial figure, brave, masculine and daring. As a popular metaphor for the lost strength of the Hindus, Shivaji has proved extraordinarily useful to Hindu nationalist forces.

Another important symbol is the language and idiomatic style used in the Sangh parivar. The RSS promotes Sanskrit as a national symbol, and the daily prayer of the RSS shakhas is performed in Sanskrit. The use of Sanskrit signifies a brahminical style, which is even more evi-dent in the special phraseology and discursive style employed by RSS workers. Any organization produces a set of key phrases and concepts employed widely by its grass-roots workers. The RSS idiom constantly refers to harmony, culture, Dharma, self-perfection through selfless service to society, and the "sterling character of men," while ridiculing average politicians in metaphors that are woven around the notion of "plebeian," vulgar, power-hungry, and self-seeking individuals. As I indicated in Chapter 1, this is a discursive ground shared to a very large extent with Gandhians and many other critics of modernity and contemporary political culture in India. Older RSS cadres committed to the strategy of character building exemplify this bloated self-percep-tion of dislocated brahminical strata when employing a paternalist dis-course regarding the RSS as imparting "good conduct" and "self-disci-pline," "the influence of cultured people," "education of the masses," and so on. The discursive style of the RSS is packed with phrases and words that seek to transmit deep emotion and affection toward the nation and the RSS: "devotion," "love," "attachment," "commitment," and "service" are frequent phrases that give RSS rhetoric an unmistak-able flavor of pathos and solemnity.

Summarizing what the RSS stands for, a pracharak demonstrated this pompous style:

> Serve the country as your Motherland. My homeland, your homeland. My forefathers, your forefathers. Just as I am economically exploited so are you. You are brother of our blood, son of this soil—no more, no less. This is what the RSS propagates. . . . only when Hindus become strong, virile, organized, vibrant is Hindu-Muslim and Hindu-Christian unity possible. . . . I shall col-lect people who share my dream, who are ready to go to any ends of sacrifice for this goal, who will give priority to this work. Then they will be ready to work, suffer for the purpose of this work. Attachment, commitment, readi-ness to sacrifice are the basic qualities of a patriot. The RSS is interested in creating this basic quality among people in this country.[27]

The RSS prayer is recited collectively in Sanskrit by the swayamsevaks standing in rows with their hands stretched in front of their chests, before a map of Akhand Bharat (undivided India, that is, colonial India including present-day Pakistan, Burma, Sri Lanka, and soon), the bhagwa dhwaj (saffron flag), and statues of Shivaji and the founder, Dr. Hedgewar. It runs in the same pompous style as the overall RSS rhetoric, and refers to "sacrifice," "spiritual bliss," and the "stern heroism" of the endeavor of the RSS:

> Forever I bow to Thee, O loving Motherland! O Motherland of us Hindus, Thou hast brought me up in happiness. May my life, O great and blessed Holy land, be laid down in Thy cause. I bow to Thee, again and again.
>
> We, the children of the Hindu Nation, bow to thee in reverence, O Almighty God. We have girded up our loins to carry on Thy work. Give us Thy holy blessings for its fulfillment. O Lord! Grant us such might that no power on earth can ever challenge, such purity of character as would command the respect of the whole world, and such knowledge as would make easy the thorny path that we have voluntarily chosen.
>
> May we be inspired with the spirit of stern heroism, which is the sole and ultimate means of attaining the highest spiritual bliss with the greatest temporal prosperity. May intense and everlasting devotion to our Ideal ever inspire our hearts. May our victorious organized power of action, by Thy Grace, fully protect our Dharma and lead this Nation of ours to the highest pinnacle of glory.

VICTORY TO MOTHER INDIA

In the central passage one finds the central creed of the RSS, its secret, namely, the quest for respect: "Grant us such might that no power on earth can ever challenge" and second, "such purity of character as would command the respect of the whole world." The last sentence prays for the nation to reach the "the highest pinnacle of glory."

This is the pompous rhetoric of a cultural nationalist "grandiose self"—a phantasmagoric construction of abiding strength feared and respected by the whole world. It also marks an ideological fantasy of recognition originally created by a displaced and declassed stratum of brahmins in Maharashtra and central India.

The style of conduct promoted in the RSS is modest, ostensibly self-effacing and inconspicuous, expressing an underlying self-confidence and self-assuredness. RSS men of the older generations are soft-spoken, mild, and gentle in their manners and never in a hurry to get their message across. They take their time, listen patiently, speak in a paternal, mildly lecturing manner, and convey an image of "having arrived" at a consummate level of cognition of the world and the self. This is a carefully nurtured style, easily discernible and recognizable, especially at pracharak level and above. The concept of "good behavior," of "cultured language and manners," of modesty and self-effacing asceticism obviously draw on brahminical ideals and values. There are many signs, however, that this pattern is gradually changing. With the rapid expansion of the RSS and affiliates the long-time "molding of character" has given way to more emphasis on mass-contact programs. Loyalty and discipline in the shakha are today more imposed from above and symbolically represented than internalized over long periods of time by every swayamsevak. The question of proper conduct, or the lack of it, especially among young supporters of the BJP and VHP, has become a matter of great concern among old cadres. They fear that the massification of the Sangh parivar—the inclusion of what often is called "all these new people without a proper RSS culture"—will deplete the RSS's "sterling qualities."

Discipline remains the most central symbolic construction within the Sangh parivar. The discipline and orderly conduct vis-à-vis elders and women, and the nurturing of a certain civic sense, are objects of inordinate pride in the organization. This discipline serves to project every individual swayamsevak as unique and special in relation to others. Its most important function is, of course, to consolidate the commitment of the members by reassuring them of the unquestionable truth and grandiosity of their collective pursuit. Harsh discipline seems to invest in a cause and a mode of functioning a corresponding sense of urgency, strength, and a certain fear on part of its surroundings, flowing from fascination with the supposed extraordinary secret protected by such stringent discipline. For the activist-members the many forms of discipline—shakha, prayer, uniformed parades, endless rehearsals of the same doctrines—contribute in multiple ways to "mind the gap," that is, to create a sense of fullness and sublime unity with the corporate body of the organization.

But discipline also acts as an "objectivation of belief," a symbolic enactment or ritualization of an ideological cause whose literal meaning remains unclear or opaque. This is not merely a sign of "empty" routinization but also a source of strength and continuity, as the discipline works as a support structure for the ideological construction. When activists or leaders begin to see glimpses of "the real" in the cause—the cynicism of the leadership, the self-righteous hypocrisy of dedication, the naked tussles over power and influence—the routines of the organizational discipline can help to erase, efface, or conceal such rifts. In this Žižekian sense, ideology existing as objectivation of belief is more durable than the literal beliefs, because it leaves room for cynicism. The ideological construction and the secret of the RSS are reproduced both outwardly in public and internally in the organization, to keep up appearances, so to speak; and as long as these rituals are exercised, prayers are recited, and so on, the "secret" persists.

Another crucial dimension of ritualization in the RSS is physical self-discipline and worship of strength. The sublimation of sexual energy is one aspect of the cult of masculinity and strength, through which the RSS tries to "semitize" itself, to overcome the "effeminate" Hindu man, and to emulate the demonized enemy—the allegedly strong, aggressive, potent, and masculine Muslim.

The Hindu nation is seen as having been historically produced as a feminine object, an object of worship, reverence, and protection, expressed in Bankim Chattopadhyay's image of Bharat Mata, the Motherland.[28] The metaphoric feminization of the nation was popularized during the cow protection agitations between 1880 and 1920, in which the worship of the gau mata, the mother cow, acquired new layers of meaning as a symbol of the Hindu nation condensed in a symbol of popular, everyday ritual significance (van der Veer 1994, 86–94). Simultaneously, Hindu nationalists embarked on a strategy of partial imitation of the features of Islam and Christianity to create a modern, masculinized Hindu culture, capable of protecting Bharat Mata. The construction of motherhood in this discourse emerged as an articulation of the conventional worship of mother goddesses (mata), embodying the fundamental creative power (shakti), protecting their human flock, and converging with the construction of the "Indian woman" in the emerging nationalist middle-class cultures in colonial India as a supreme sign of the nation, of the inner spiritual realm marked by devotion and purity in which the woman was both mother and goddess (Chatterjee 1993, 114–34). The Hindu nationalist construction of the nation as mother, subtly structured by Victorian ideology, sought to elevate the woman to mother, and thus downplay and control the sexual and aggressive sides of womanliness, as articulated for instance by the goddess Kali, the destructive goddess worshiped especially in eastern parts of India, or as they are expressed in the language and practices of "plebeian," lower-caste women.

The RSS strategy of managing Hindu male sexuality thus seeks to exclude women—as concrete sexual beings—from the cause, and to place men in a purified, masculine space undisturbed by sexual drives, while it encourages a systematic sublimation of sexual energy into service to the abstract, generalized mother—the nation. In Golwalkar's discourse this operation took place with great passion, in a language of almost oedipal qualities. The conquest of India by Muslim invaders is in the RSS idiom portrayed as "rape of the Motherland" by a potent and dangerous enemy. Only if the "sons of Bharat," the RSS cadre, organize themselves as men along military lines can they win this oedipal battle, and become true males worthy of the love of the mother nation.[29]

Another source of discipline is the peer-group pressure exercised among the youngsters in the shakhas, and by the shakha leader (*mukhuya shikshak*). This is a fundamental mechanism in the reproduction of brotherhood within the RSS. The shakha members know each others' families, and a swayamsevak cannot easily leave the organization. If he does, his peers will visit him, talk to his parents, and try to persuade him to rejoin the RSS. Although this strategy is often successful, a lot of young men do leave the organization when they start to work or establish families. But many men continue in a lifelong attachment to the organization, and introduce their sons and family into the organization as well. Certain neighborhoods and caste communities are entirely pervaded by RSS culture, the most prominent example being the Chitpavan brahmins of Maharashtra.

The selection of leaders of shakhas as heads of local areas (*nagars*), of cities, and up to district level where full-time pracharaks are the organizing forces, takes place on the basis of loyalty, of organizational capabilities displayed, and not least of personal relations and informal contacts with leaders higher up the hierarchy. These relations are often established in the course of daily work, but also at the various camps held by the RSS. Those selected for organizational work attend "Officer Training Camps" every summer over three years, where they receive ideological and physical training and have an opportunity to meet leading figures of the RSS.

The batches from these camps form part of the basis for informal networks that govern the loyalty as well as the possibilities of ascendancy in the organizational hierarchy. The dominant method of exercising power in the RSS and between the RSS and its affiliates is "rule by proxy" in appointments. Those RSS workers who are trusted by the senior pracharaks are appointed and allocated to various posts, and others are removed and relocated. This method is generally considered legitimate among the rank and file as the pracharaks, assumed to be intimately connected with central leaders, are expected to act prudently and to have good reasons, however inscrutable to those of lower rank, for their actions. Here, an element of what Žižek calls "fetishism" is at work, in that the rank and file ascribe a higher rationality even to obvious cases of nepotism and abuse, only to prevent their own ideological horizon from cracking up.

The other dominant method of exercising power is the so-called informal consultation, where RSS leaders at various levels meet their counterparts from the affiliates for discussions on urgent matters or long-term planning. Here the RSS workers—even if formally on a par with the leaders of the affiliates—always command the ultimate authority. RSS pracharaks are like the "commissars supervising the commissars" in the communist movement, superintendents whose authority flows from their direct access to higher leadership in the RSS, and from their supposedly superior moral standards due to their full-time service to the cause and their austere lifestyle.

This leads us to the final aspect of the authority, the construction of leadership. Hierarchies in the RSS are not only accepted, they are also revered and fetishised—not only hierarchies of rank within the organization but also hierarchies of age, education, and social position whose naturalness and legitimacy seem even less questioned among the rank and file than in the surrounding society. Ultimate power within the RSS lies with the sarsanghachalak and the general secretary, representing the entire central leadership.[30] Movements like the RSS are, however, not dependent on the personal qualities of one or a few charismatic leaders who have a lot of room for maneuvering and a certain elevation above standard norms of behavior.

The RSS depends, as I have argued, on symbolic integration and on a high degree of "objectified" and ritualized beliefs. Each person in the RSS hierarchy is replaceable, and although the successive sarsanghachalaks have had their individual styles and strategies, the basic function and legitimacy of that position has not been challenged. The RSS is almost a textbook example of a movement in which the shared secret is generated from a founding myth, carried by a whole network of full-time workers who earn their right to a share of the "mystery of ministry" by demonstrating loyalty and contacts upward, and full command over the symbolic devices and codes of the RSS downward. The lack of transparency of flows of power in the Sangh parivar, the informal character of the exercise of power, of consultations, and so on, only add to the mythic qualities ascribed by the rank and file to the central leadership and its many secret and hidden resources—like an inverted version of the demonized fantasy of the secret of the Muslim community.

Although the RSS does not officially promote individuals as such, some of the leading figures of the front organizations are projected for mass consumption as "larger than life" figures endowed with extraordinary qualities. Charisma projected onto a personality is considered to be more suited for mass consumption than the "secret" of an ideological cause or collective myth. The increased public construction of BJP leaders such as Vajpayee and Advani as charismatic personalities, and the VHP's promotion of charismatic speakers and performers like

Sadhvi Ritambra in the late 1980s, are intimately connected to the mass-mobilizing strategies of this period.

In sum, the images of the power and wisdom of the leadership of the RSS reflect a complex interaction between the structural logics operating in a closed, hierarchical organization, the systematic creation of a heroic mythology inside the organization, and the psychological need among rank-and-file RSS workers to believe in the all-pervasive wisdom and foresight of their leaders.

Constituencies and Strategies of the Sangh Parivar

The original constituency from which the RSS emerged in the 1920s and 1930s were Maharashtrian brahmins, especially the Chitpavan brahmins, from whom most of the leaders of the RSS were drawn. Chitpavan and other Maharashtrian brahmins still constitute a considerable portion of senior leaders, and remain today a stable source of recruitment for the RSS. The popularity of Hindu nationalism and revivalism in general among these communities can be ascribed to the relative isolation of the brahmins in Maharashtra due to the strong antibrahmin movements in the state, as well as to the legacy of Tilak, who effectively mobilized and politicized the once-powerful and ruling caste of western India on a socially conservative program. In north India, the RSS acquired a large following in the affluent Hindu community in Punjab, characterized by a "beleaguered mentality" in the tough communal atmosphere in that area. Later the Hindu refugees from Pakistan proved to be another hospitable environment for RSS, as did the urban areas in U.P. and Madhya Pradesh.

Judging from the Jana Sangh electoral performance in the three first general elections, its program and strategy evoked a certain response in the urban areas in Hindi-speaking states, and primarily among higher castes and the urban middle classes, traders, landlords, and the rich peasantry.[31] After the relative success in the 1967 general election, when the Jana Sangh attracted broader sections of the electorate, and throughout the 1970s, when the RSS and its affiliates attracted new groups to its fold with a new emphasis on populist activism, it became possible for the Sangh parivar to break out of its relative social isolation in terms of audience and backing. The high-caste bias in recruitment until the 1970s is readily admitted by RSS workers, who characteristically use the euphemism "educated sections" for their early constituency. Similarly, it is evident, that the "RSS culture," the strategy of character building, the emphasis on virtue and conduct, and the

cautious attitude to the impurity of electoral politics and mass mobilization all bear the mark of brahminical practices. The following account of the dense RSS networks in Pune points to the environment of
social narcissism and claustrophobia in which the Sangh parivar was
born and later consolidated.

———————

THE "SANGHA" CITADEL IN PUNE

From the early 1930s, Pune became an important center for RSS activities and a center for the Hindu Mahasabha and other radical
Hindu nationalist organizations. The RSS headquarters in Moti
Baug, located in the Shaniwar Peth area five minutes' walk from the
old Peshwa palace, is a large complex with rooms and apartments for
full-time pracharaks, several meeting halls, offices, and a book shop.
The VHP has its zonal headquarters for Maharashtra, Gujarat, and
Goa in Pune. The RSS newspaper *Tarun Bharat* (Young India) was
published and printed in Pune until it succumbed to financial con-
straints and was ousted from the market by Shiv Sena's more aggressive *Saamna* in 1991. The well-knit Sangh parivar network in the city
has on several occasions hosted large RSS camps, VHP sammelans,
and other large arrangements. In spite of the indisputable organizational strength of the Sangh parivar in the city, its dominant position
in the many educational trusts and college boards, and its many organizations, it was not until 1991 that the BJP managed to wrest the
parliamentary seat away from Congress and get Anna Joshi elected
to the Lok Sabha from Pune. But the BJP has not been able to sustain
its position here. Most of the MLAs elected for the state legislative
assembly from Pune in 1995 belonged to Congress. One of the important reasons for the relative political weakness of the BJP—both parliamentary and in the Municipal Corporation, where the party in the
1992 election only secured 24 out of 111 seats—is the relative concen-
tration of its networks and constituencies in the Marathi-speaking
middle-class parts of the old city, the traditional center of Maharashtrian high culture for centuries.

The backbone of the Sangh parivar network in Pune is the rather
dense network of RSS shakhas spread over most of the city. The esti-
mate by RSS functionaries as well as more independent sources is
that there are more than two-hundred shakhas with more than four
thousand active swayamsevaks, mainly concentrated in the old city
and the affluent Deccan area, but scattered less densely in the Cantonment area (Camp)—the commercial heart of Pune inhabited by a

"cosmopolitan" mix of migrants from all over India. Here, mainly Sindhis (Hindus from the province of Sindh in present-day Pakistan) form the backbone of the organization. To this figure must be added thousands of occasional activists and passive supporters, as well as a vast network of more loosely affiliated men who have been swayamsevaks for years, but due to work and social obligations are unable to attend shakhas. Many of the swayamsevaks are also active in other RSS-related organizations. The Sangh parivar in Pune almost constitutes an "alternative civil society," with separate schools, its own banks, dominance in a large number of colleges, its own associations for youth, students, women, children, social organizations working in the slum, informal networks, frequent marriages between RSS-affiliated families and, of course, its own informal communication channels and structures of authority, both vitally reproduced on a daily basis in the shakhas. The considerable strength of the RSS in Pune is paraded at various large arrangements during the year, such as the annual meeting inside the premises of the Peshwa palace.

One of the most important functions of the RSS is to coordinate the entire parivar, or rather to extend ideological and political guidance to the specialized subsidiaries. Besides the rather effective informal hierarchy within the pracharak networks, this function is also formalized in many cities and districts in coordination committees, mahanagar samanvaya. In a closely knit RSS network such as the one in Pune, the regular meetings of the city committee mainly function as a channel of information and monitoring for the RSS, and as a vehicle that can be activated when joint agitations or organizational activities are launched.

The backbone of RSS activists in Pune are Maharashtrian brahmins and Marwaris (members of a wealthy north Indian trading community). In many cases their association with the RSS goes back several generations and is entirely interwoven with family tradition and family practices. The typical RSS family sends its young boys to shakha at the age of six, and in conjunction with the domestic atmosphere, the so-called "Sangha culture" becomes effectively ingrained in the identity of these individuals as a culture marked by unsurpassed moral stature, honesty, hard work, decency, cleanliness, respectability, and devotion. The favorite self-image of the RSS workers is of themselves as part of a "unique experience—never seen before in the world," as an activist put it to me. The RSS constructs its own horizon as a self-referencing group whose greatness, unsurpassed patriotism, incomparable contribution to the nation, secret power, and organizational genius have never been duly recognized by the larger environment but always suppressed by the government and anti-Hindu forces. Every act of misrecognition, ridicule and banning have been transformed to confirm and strengthen the organizational fiber, the commitment of the members, and the conviction that everyone fears the might of the RSS. As expressed by a group of RSS activists—just returned from and still enthusiastic over the kar seva and mosque demolition in Ayodhya in December 1992—the ban just imposed on the RSS at this juncture grew out of fear of the RSS:

> Sangha is such a power that they will do their work without any expectations. They are the ones who first help those in need. Congress have realized this power and the capacity of the Sangha. They know that whichever party the Sangha supports will come into power. That is why this ban has been imposed. . . . But nobody can ban Hindu thought. The Hindus are in majority, so nobody can stop their thinking process. . . . [The power of the Sangha comes] because the volunteers are taught a certain discipline right from their childhood and they are taught to love and work for their country.
>
>   In Ayodhya the excitement was tremendous. *Everybody felt this is the foundation of the Hindu nation.* It happened because what was happening to Hindus had to be washed off. So many of our leaders had been insulted and so much wrong had been done to us. It had to stop somewhere. Whatever has been done [in Ayodhya] was to bring together the Hindus and show them how outsiders are violating them and their country. Once the Hindu power is established . . . the Muslims will be shown their place (interview with a group of RSS swayamsevaks, Bhavani Peth, Pune, 17 December 1992); italics added).

Although numerically and culturally strong in Pune, the RSS workers here display a characteristic oscillation between imaginations of omnipotence (toward other Hindus of lesser moral stature and character) and fears of impotence (vis-à-vis the Muslims and the state apparatus). The entire RSS subculture in Pune seems to be fundamentally haunted by fears of exclusion and misrecognition from the powerful, rich Anglo-Indian establishment and the intellectual elite, physically located in the Cantonment area or in and around the many national institutions in the city. The vengeance of the conservative upper-caste establishment in Pune, declassed and stigmatized especially after Independence by a Congress party that strategically occupied the popular, rural, nonbrahmin and Maratha pole in the overriding ideological polarity, especially in western Maharashtra (Hansen 1996c, 177–85), has become transformed to the present-day "hyperpatriotism" of the Sangh parivar. This is patriotism that, through an independent organizational structure, constantly engages in internal hierarchization and consolidation while drawing clear external boundaries. It seeks acceptance and respect from the powerful elite through expansion and proselytization, and seeks to dominate its own environment and control its own experience of modernity. It also seeks to conceal the fact that it is a partial and incomplete representation of "respectable society" of the upper-caste social world, wherein Congress and other parties still enjoy considerable support, and an even more partial representation of a "Hindu community," given the relatively marginal support the RSS enjoys among nonbrahmins and lower castes in the city.

The "significant other" of the RSS's alternative civil society in Pune remains, nonetheless, the anglicized establishment from which it has been excluded, while the immediate cause of fear and object of hatred, as always, is the Muslim community—not necessarily local Muslims in Pune but the "abstract Muslim," who stands in as an *objet petit à* for the more immediate experiences of "lower castes" encroaching upon the once-secure world of the upper castes.

For this "besieged" mentality that in so many ways informs the atmosphere in the Sangh parivar in Pune, the events in Ayodhya served to assert the misrecognized power of the RSS, to shatter and humiliate the government, to unite the Hindus, and to scare the Muslims. The entire upbeat post-demolition atmosphere in the Sangh parivar subculture in Pune was pervaded by a vengeful, though mostly implicit, feeling of that justice was finally being done, that is, that the Sangh parivar was finally was recognized as large and powerful. The triumphant feeling after December 6 that "our time has finally come" was clearly not addressed to Muslims—whose protests the police dealt with in the most brutal manner—but was addressed to the English-language press, the Congress, the anglicized intellectuals, and the self-confident social elite that for so long either had banned or derided the RSS.

The indisputable fact that the RSS emerged from an urban upper-caste environment has led both scholars and political opponents to view the RSS as a manifestation of an alliance between brahmins and banias (merchants, businessmen), determined to reassert the supremacy of the twice-born castes in the face of mounting lower-caste political assertiveness. Golwalkar and other RSS ideologues have on many occasions defended the varna system, and the RSS strategy of "controlling modernity" may well be interpreted as an attempt to control and envelop the tide of rising assertiveness among the lower castes (Basu et al. 1993, 16–17). The question remains, however, whether these features of RSS's discourse and "constituency effects" disclose any essential nature or "original design" of the RSS.

The assumption underlying the search for the social base of a movement seems to be that this reveals the character of the (preexisting) social interests it represents. The assumption seems to be that regardless of the ideological intentions and program of the movement in question, its constituency will over time force the movement to act according to their class or caste interests in order to keep this base intact. This further presupposes that supporters, in the long run, will act rationally to optimize their class and status positions by supporting the party or movement that caters to this interest. According to this line of reasoning, the level of articulated discourse, albeit distorted by manipulations, ultimately expresses the underlying always/already existing configuration of socioeconomic and cultural groups in a given society.

The brahmin-bania thesis has been substantiated empirically by Bruce Graham in a meticulous and detailed study of which social interests the Jana Sangh appealed to and catered to from 1951 to 1967 (Graham 1990, 158–95). Prudently, Graham does not conclude that catering to these interests expressed the essential class nature of the Jana Sangh and RSS, but concludes that the limited success of the Jana Sangh may be ascribed to its narrow socioeconomic appeal in that period (ibid., 195). The Jana Sangh's turn in a more populist direction in 1967 and the 1970s was, in fact, an attempt to break out of the brahmin-bania constituency and win a somewhat broader political base.

Like other opposition forces, the Sangh parivar successfully carved out a large and socially mixed constituency during the years of Congress weakness in the late 1960s, but lost this constituency again after 1971, when Congress recouped political strength and the moral high ground of patriotism after the Bangladesh war. However, unlike Congress and other actors based on aggregation of vote blocks and political elites in the political field, and who are rather penetrable for various interests, the Jana Sangh and the RSS were not penetrated by their new mass constituencies. Cadre-based parties are not very susceptible to pressures from organized interest or local elites, due to their autonomous organization and the importance they assign to ideological cohesion. The social base of such parties, in other words, cannot necessarily be taken as evidence of their role as carriers of certain social interests, but seems rather to be the contingent effect of their discourse, organization, and strategy. Such an effect might be intended or unexpected, and often reveals interesting disjunctures between the intentions and the effects of mobilizing strategies, as Graham has shown in the case of the Jana Sangh's early history.

The Sangh parivar's constituency and its strategies to acquire and consolidate a mass base must be seen in the light of its overall commitment to an ideological project. The RSS is committed to a culturally conservative vision of a rejuvenated nation, and to a somewhat reformist project of social reform and uplift of the weakest sections, not on the grounds of equality per se but, like many Gandhians and conservative forces in the Congress party, in order to promote social integration and a vision of a patriotic "swadeshi capitalism." This vision does not entail any subversion of hierarchies but is, on the contrary, founded on hierarchies and will, if implemented, undoubtedly be more beneficial to the upper castes and the middle classes than to the poorer sections of the population.

The strategic tension between culture and politics is in this context merely a difference of opinion as to how the RSS can best expand its influence and power. Mass mobilization of the electorate is a necessary part of this process, but the possibility of particular social interests forcing the RSS in new policy directions has so far been limited. The main constituency of the Sangh parivar has always been itself, its own ideological vision, its cadres, and the subculture it is building all over the country.

The ambiguous discourse on caste within the Sangh parivar is particularly revealing in this respect. Although untouchability and "casteism" have officially been condemned by the RSS from the outset (inspired by the Arya Samaj), and the caste system has been denounced as a perversion forced upon Hindu society in order to encapsulate itself in the face of Muslim aggression, hierarchies of all kinds are cultivated in the Sangh parivar itself. The strategy seems to be that coexistence and integration of different communities and castes under one common formula of nationalism and one abiding hierarchy will eventually render caste obsolete. Although systematic recruitment of Dalits (untouchables) and tribals has been pursued for years, the approach remains a condescending view of "sanskritization" of the "uncultured." As in the case of the VHP's drive to halt conversions among tribals, the recruitment of the lower castes is regarded as a consolidation of the flanks of Hindu society rather than a reformist project committed to equality. The RSS discourse tries systematically to conceal caste, to treat it as a nonissue that might divide the organization by questioning the predominant values of purity, strength, devotion, and austerity, mainly derived from an upper-caste inventory of values. A parable related to this author by a group of old RSS workers at the headquarters in Pune is particularly revealing in terms of the "classical" view of caste within the Sangh parivar:

> If you draw two lines on a piece of paper, one short, the other a little longer you have a difference in length. How can you diminish the difference between these two lines, without altering or interfering with any of them? The answer is: by drawing a much larger line above them. In comparison with the difference between the small lines and the big line, the internal difference between the small lines has been diminished. Thus, the small lines are castes and the big line is the Hindu nation. Instead of focusing on the small lines and their internal differences, one should look at the big line, the Nation, and forget about internal differences. This is how we in the Sangha look at caste in our society.

This is not brahminical revivalism but rather conservatism, reluctant—as in the case of the public role of women—to question prevailing hierarchies and purity/impurity paradigms. This unwillingness stems from a fear of fragmentation, internal strife, and Hindu disunity, and from a belief in the ability of a strong national loyalty to override other differences. The RSS is committed to create such an unfragmented, "integrated," that is, controlled modernity through the making of a strong, united nation. Caste divisions are, like other divisions and hierarchies, undesirable insofar as they hamper national unity and integration, but acceptable insofar as they provide a community feeling compatible with that of the nation and that of the RSS. All the prejudices, anxieties, and stereotypes that sustain and reproduce caste distinctions are nevertheless active and present in the social environments in which the Sangh parivar thrives, and inform in multiple ways the style in which the Sangh parivar attempts to reach out to lower-caste communities, as the following example from Pune demonstrates.

LOWER CASTES FOR A HIGHER CAUSE

A rather different articulation of Hindu nationalism is found in the high-profile militant youth organization Patit Pawan (literally "the purification of the fallen"—a label given by Savarkar to his social reform activities in the coastal Konkan region), which is fairly large in Pune and in smaller provincial cities in western and northern Maharashtra, but is an organization confined to, and unique to, Maharashtra. Patit Pawan was started in 1967 as a street-fighter organization by some RSS pracharaks in the city. The organization initially called itself Hindu Jajvalaya Sanghatana (the Hindu Attack Organization) and was formed in order to fight the Youth Congress and the perceived Muslim threat in the mixed neighborhoods of Pune:

> Up to 1972 there were several riots between the two communities. During riots the Muslims are always united. Our Hindu community will never unite at a moment's notice, but the Muslims can do so. Thus the Muslims can attack and do whatever they like. . . . Our founding members realized that we too must have some unity, not in order to attack them but to protect our community, our house. Now they know what can happen if anything is started (interview, Dhananjay Lele, Patit Pawan leader in Pune, 20 October 1992).

In 1971 the organization, whose leaders and activists had several criminal cases pending against them for stabbing and violence, was renamed and reframed, and gradually turned to more systematic organization of young Hindus. The organization went into student politics and engaged itself in "social work," that is, involving itself in local conflicts and disputes on behalf of what is broadly defined as Hindu society. The activities ranged from assistance to local areas in providing civic amenities, campaigns against various criminal rackets (liquor, gambling, false examination papers at colleges, and so on), and campaigns against corrupt politicians, bureaucrats, and police officers, to more direct political and symbolic actions such as assaults on "anti-Hindu" politicians and media persons, and participation in the agitational campaigns of the Sangh parivar.

Up to the mid-eighties, Patit Pawan established itself in many districts, and in Pune the organization acquired an almost mythic status because of its agitational radicalism and efficiency. Today it has more than eighty local branches all over the city, units in thirty colleges, and claims to have ten thousand members and sympathizers in Pune alone. The organization regards itself as a sort of a "rapid task force" of the Hindu community—a militant organization entirely geared to agitations, street fighting, and prompt action on small and big issues. It sees itself as an organization that provides justice for those Hindus who are otherwise deprived of it in a hostile establishment. The organization claims that at any time in Pune, within a few hours, it can gather five thousand young men ready for action.

Ideologically, Patit Pawan claims to be inspired by Savarkar and the militant and confrontational style of the Hindu Mahasabha prior to Independence. It is also loosely associated with another Hindu nationalist organization, Hindu Ekta Andolan, which in the early 1980s was particularly active in southern Maharashtra. The independence of Patit Pawan is, however, mainly formal and tactical. The leadership and many activists of Patit Pawan—especially in middle-class areas—are RSS swayamsevaks, or are active in the BJP, or at least acquainted with the work of the Sangh parivar. Patit Pawan has for years attempted to draw nonbrahmin groups into the Sangh parivar. The present BJP leader of the opposition in the legislative assembly, Gopinath Munde, started his career in Patit Pawan, and so did a considerable number of the nonbrahmin leaders in the BJP. The Patit Pawan leadership is in constant touch with the RSS leadership, which includes Patit Pawan in its planning and execution of agitations, while it always keeps a safe distance from the more radical actions of the organization.

The majority of the activists are nonbrahmins, mainly from poor and middle-class families and from slum areas. Dhananjay Lele (Chitpavan brahmin) explains the strategy in the following terms, which betray his paternalist contempt for what he calls the "vagabond style of Marathas," and vividly demonstrates how caste distinctions are reproduced on an everyday level by circulation of "petty stereotypes," continuously translated into metaphors of blood and kin. "From when the RSS first was established and till today the working style of the organization was like a brahmin—silent work, no attack, goal achievers. This is typical brahmin style. If anyone attacks, agitates, demonstrates, then this is vagabond style typical of the Marathas. People identify the RSS with brahmins because of the working style. Patit Pawan is not identified with brahmins because our style is the other one—the Maratha" (ibid.). The working style of Patit Pawan is in several ways similar to that of Shiv Sena. Both organizations cultivate a militant, activist style, appeal to young nonbrahmin men, and propagate a very simple and highly communal version of Hindutva. One of the bon mots of Shiv Sena has even been taken over by Patit Pawan: "If Patit Pawan takes up an issue, half the problem is solved"—because of the reputation of the organization for action and violence. In spite of its militant postures, Patit Pawan is rather moderate and permeated by a craving for middle-class respectability, compared to the more "plebeian" atmosphere cultivated by Shiv Sena.

The working style and strategies of Patit Pawan can be illustrated by an incident of communal symbolic contestation that took place in a low-income area, Dattawadi, mainly inhabited by Maratha and OBC (Other Backward Castes) communities near the old city in Pune. The area, which has approximately fifteen thousand inhabitants, also comprises a small Muslim pocket with around four hundred people. In May 1987 a Patit Pawan branch was started in the area by a handful of college boys. On that occasion one of the city's Patit Pawan leaders put a task before the boys: they should start agitations to prevent the construction of a small masjid in the area. On a particular spot in the area there was a grave that the local Muslim community held was the tomb of a local Sufi saint. A few yards from it were a few small stones and an old tree, worshiped by some of the Hindus in the area as a site for the forest god. The Muslim tomb had for decades been surrounded by a few tin plates, while the Hindu deity had just been marked by some saffron and red paint on the stones. In 1987 the Muslims in Dattawadi had received some funds to construct a small masjid on the spot, and the Patit Pawan boys started to agitate against the construction, which they claimed would desecrate and hide the Hindu deity. The Patit Pawan boys started to mobilize the neighborhood on the issue and started two mitra mandals (friends' associations) in the area, which for the first time organized local Ganpati festivals. The boys claimed subsequently that the Ganesh idols were broken and burned during the festival in 1988.

> Our Ganesh idols had been defiled by them and that is why it was we who started a riot here. . . . We actually terrorized them and they could not fight us [they were in a minority]. We burned their houses and broke them down. We did not get enough time because the police came immediately. Whatever time we had, we did our best. Eleven of our members were arrested. . . . Pune is more peaceful because they are in minority and are always beaten up. This year they unfurled the national flag on their masjid here, and a Muslim came during Shivjayanti and garlanded Shivaji' s portrait (interview with Patit Pawan members in Dattawadi, 30 January 1993).

After the riot in 1988, the police intervened in the area, and the masjid was completed. The Patit Pawan boys then collected money for a temple, which a few years later was constructed less than one foot from the masjid. Because of the intervention of Patit Pawan and their mitra mandals in the area, this temple has become a focal point for every religious festival in the area. These incidents have made Patit Pawan well known in the area, and the unit has swelled to more than fifty activists. Many of them went to Ayodhya both in 1990 and in 1992, and the Dattawadi area has now become known as a "communally sensitive area." The police regularly make so-called preventive arrests of some of the activists in the area prior to major campaigns, political events, and so on.

As I argued elsewhere (Hansen 1996c), this type of communalization through symbolic contestation of local sacred space was a regular and widespread instrument in the spread of Hindutva in urban as well as rural areas. Further, the adoption of religion as the preferred idiom for popular mobilization was illustrated by the example of

Patit Pawan: assuming that the "people," more than the so-called "cultured sections," was steeped in deep religious emotions, supposed violations of religious sentiments were identified, direct anti-Muslim rhetoric aimed at communal escalation of conflicts was employed, and a violent, actionist, supposedly Maratha style of agitation was applied.

The Pune setting displays with great clarity the historical dilemma of the Sangh parivar in Maharashtra, namely, its isolation in an urban middle-class, upper-caste environment, politically trapped at the brahminical pole of the brahmin-Maratha antagonism that continues to structure Maharashtrian politics and culture. With the "saffron wave" from the mid-1980s, the Sangh parivar in Pune was able to transgress many of the social and cultural boundaries of its constituencies and establish shakhas and political support in lower-caste and low-income neighborhoods in the city. However, most of the organizational backbone of the Sangh parivar is drawn from the large group of middle-class brahmins who wield decisive power and provide the dominant cultural outlook within the RSS and affiliates in Pune. The new support from nonbrahmin groups to the BJP, the RSS, and Patit Pawan is constructed and conceived within this dominant worldview, depicted in a condescending language of "uplift," of "their" acceptance of "our cultured habits." In this cultural narcissist worldview, the Sangh parivar remains structured by a pole of ideological and spiritual mastery (and purity) among the higher and central echelons in the parivar living in a world of "cultured habits" in the old city, on one end, and a pole of physical prowess, aggressiveness, and street-fighting courage (impurity) among the specialized branches of the parivar that recruit and save the lower castes who live in worlds of ignorance, "vagabond culture," and dirt on the outskirts of the old city, on the other end. Within this worldview, the "Hindu nation" is the vision that may tie these otherwise disparate worlds together, a construction by which lower castes can ennoble themselves, learn "cultured habits," and become integrated into the "great tradition" of Hindu culture.

The Sangh Parivar in the Political Field

Competitive electoral politics had from the inception of the RSS been regarded with profound skepticism by leading circles in the organization. The ban on the RSS in 1948–1949 shocked Golwalkar and the RSS leadership, and their lack of preparation for this situation demonstrated the lack of political instinct characterizing the RSS leadership up to the 1960s. After the ban, there was strong pressure from younger activists in the RSS to fill the gap left open by the demise of the Hindu Mahasabha as a force to reckon with.[32] There seemed to be a constituency for Hindu nationalism awaiting a political voice. The formation of the Jana Sangh in 1951 took place as a compromise between two clusters of disparate interests. On the one hand, there was a group of experienced politicians and leaders rooted in the Hindu Mahasabha and Arya Samaj. On the other hand, there was the RSS leadership, generally hostile to the entire democratic notion of fighting out social differences in public arenas. The motivation on the part of the RSS for entering the political sphere seems to have been the chance to acquire a public voice, and public legitimacy and, ultimately, to extend the influence of the organization through its political affiliate.

The first election manifesto was thus a carefully worked-out document outlining the common ideological positions of the disparate groups in the new party: India should be viewed as an indivisible organic unit, based on a common culture with ancient roots in history. The manifesto underlined the need for cultural rejuvenation but also the need for a strong state, and liberties and rights for its (Hindu) citizens without concessions to minorities (Graham 1990, 48–51; Baxter 1969, 27).

It soon became clear, however, that the main conflict over the building of the party emerged in the field of organization. Mookherjee and his cadre favored an open party structure with formal and competitive elections of leaders, whereas the RSS preferred to control the party through informal networks and strictly regulated debates. These internal differences in the Jana Sangh evolved into a full-blown contradiction during the crisis following Mookherjee's sudden death in 1953. Deendayal Upadhyaya had at that time acquired the post of general secretary in the party (responsible for organizational matters), and he stood in a very strong position by commanding the loyalty of most of the organizers and activists as well as the support of the RSS hierarchy. After a protracted battle between the two camps, an RSS loyalist was elected party president, and the general secretary, Deendayal Upadhyaya, emerged as the central person in the party until his death in 1968.

Within a period of four years, the RSS had succeeded in building a party structure and establishing its dominance at all levels in the internal apparatus. The relation between the public front figures, the elected members of parliament, the president, and the background group of full-time organizers became more or less modeled on the relation between the public leader of the RSS in a region (the sanghachalak), and the real network of power resting with the professional organizers, the

pracharaks. With the dominance of the RSS, the Jana Sangh's orientation gradually shifted from appeals to the liberal, educated middle
class in the big cities toward appeals to the lower middle classes in
north Indian small and provincial cities. There was a shift from English
to Hindi in the language of the party, and the method of mobilization
changed from rapid electoral mobilization toward gradual organizational expansion, often in close conjunction with other members of the
emergent Sangh parivar (Graham 1990, 67–68; Jaffrelot 1996, 129–57).

This transformation of the party coincided with a policy orientation
of the Jana Sangh that emphasized campaigns on issues of national
unity or anti-Muslim sentiments: the campaign for liberation of Goa
(1955); the campaign against division of Punjab on linguistic/confes-
sional lines (1955–1957); the campaign against the use of Urau in northern India (1954–1961), producing communal tension and riots in Uttar
Pradesh; the campaign for Hindi as the national language (1958–1965);
and the anti-cow-slaughter campaign from the late 1950s onward.[33] Although some of these campaigns consolidated the Jana Sangh's local
networks, they also reinforced the image of the Jana Sangh as a sectarian party outside the mainstream of politics as defined by Congress
and the moderate Left. This was also reflected in the electoral fortunes
of the Jana Sangh. The party's share of the popular vote grew at a slow
pace throughout the fifties and early sixties (1957, 3.8 percent; 1962,
6.07 percent) and it was were still confined largely to Madhya Pradesh,
parts of Uttar Pradesh, Delhi, Rajasthan, and Punjab. The appeals of the
party were limited to upper-caste segments of the middle class and
among culturally conservative strata in the former princely states.

A decisive reorientation of the Jana Sangh in a more populist direction took place from 1965 onward. Within a few years it adopted a new
program based on Upadhyaya's "Integral Humanism." It ceased to
isolate itself in the right corner of the political field and started to explore possible alliances with other opposition forces. This reorientation
was prompted by the opening of the political field for alternatives to
Congress in the wake of Nehru's death and the subsequent weakening
of the ideological hegemony of the Congress party.

This new direction was welcomed by those local leaders and activists
of the Jana Sangh who had adapted themselves to the rules of the game
in the political field and who had apprehensions regarding the high
moral postures of the deputed RSS pracharaks. Under the leadership of
Balraj Madhok, an RSS heretic who contrary to the general RSS line was
in favor of a more confrontationist and "political" line, the Jana Sangh
did well in the 1967 election. The party ranks swelled as many new
activists were recruited outside the closed ranks of the RSS, and the
party was able to exploit the unprecedented weakness of the Congress

and secure thirty-five seats in the Lok Sabha and more than 9 percent of the total vote (Graham 1990, 262; see also Madhok 1986, 60).

After the electoral success in several states, mainly in northern India, the Jana Sangh joined United Front governments with socialists and the Akali Dal in Punjab.[34] These coalition governments broke down within a few months, and in the following midterm elections the Jana Sangh lost much of the popular vote again. The deep-running differences concerning strategies in the political field now erupted in a revealing conflict. Balraj Madhok worked to make the Jana Sangh a conservative-liberal rallying point, open to mass membership, to wrest the party from the tight hold of the RSS, and to make it an initiator of a concerted anti-Congress and antisocialist strategy. Madhok wanted a more robust direct strategy of liberal capitalist development, much in line with the program offered by the conservative Swatantra party from the early 1960s onward, and he worked for a merger of the Jana Sangh and Swatantra in the following years.

Deendayal Upadhyaya and his lieutenants, A. B. Vajpayee and L. K. Advani, envisaged the party as a populist platform for many groups, but under the control of the RSS, rather than as a clearly profiled vehicle for conservative and private-enterprise interests that could challenge the authority of the RSS. Vajpayee, the leader of the parliamentary wing of the Jana Sangh, became especially identified with what Jaffrelot has aptly termed "sanghathanist populism" (Jaffrelot 1996, 233). Madhok lost the power struggle and Upadhyaya, after one and a half decades as an efficient general secretary unknown in the public, moved into the limelight as president of the party. After his sudden and mysterious death in 1968, Vajpayee took over as president and served along with L. K. Advani as leader of the party. Under this leadership, Madhok and his conservatives were isolated and excluded from the party, and the entire strategy was drawn in a populist direction. The sweeping victory of Indira Gandhi—banking on the victory in the Bangladesh war and the slogan of "garib hatao" (remove poverty)— added further credibility to the idea of adopting a similar mass appeal to the "common man" and to abandon the older stigma of being a narrow brahmin-bania party.[35] The fact that the Union government seriously considered banning the RSS and imposed a temporary ban on RSS shakhas in Delhi in 1970 was probably another significant reason behind the Jana Sangh's rather dramatic shift toward what in the contemporary economy of stances in the political field was a "centrist" position (Jaffrelot 1996, 239).

Moving along with their reading of the popular mood and the hegemonic terms of discourse and "legitimate problematics" in the political field, as they once again had been laid down by Congress (socialism, antipoverty, a stronger role for the state in the economy, nationalization, and soon), the party decided to focus on socioeconomic issues, to project itself as an alternative to Congress, in brief to adopt what Jaffrelot calls a "legimitate opposition" (Jaffrelot 1993, 369). In 1973, Advani suggested strict control of foreign investment, with large industrial houses, an efficient re-distributive taxation system, and cuts in imports in general. This policy was both in consonance with the swadeshi philosophy inherited from the nationalist movement and re-formulated by Upadhyaya, and struck a familiar chord among opposition parties at this juncture.

This "populist" strategy became even more prominent when the Sangh parivar decided to support the J. P. movement from 1973–1974 onward. The general polarization of political discourse and the mounting protests against Mrs. Gandhi provided fertile ground for Jayaprakash (J. P.) Narayan's call for a "Total Revolution" of Indian society, and J. P. Narayan became the indispensable center of the opposition to Congress—a reborn Mahatma—to whose spiritual leadership inordinately high expectations were attached. The RSS had become deeply involved in the J. P. movement from an early stage through its student wing (ABVP), which had provided manpower and organization to J. P. Narayan in Bihar from early 1973 (Jaffrelot 1993, 300–1).

One of the results of this anti-Congress wave was the formation of the Lok Sangarsh Samiti in 1974, a body coordinating several parties and movements, all supporting J. P. Narayan's Sarvodhya movement. In an unprecedented move, the RSS issued a public statement supporting J. P. Narayan, who was hailed as a sannyasi comparable to Gandhi, Bhave, and Golwalkar(!), elevated above the greed and chaos of petty politics. J. P. Narayan in turn endowed the RSS with a new public legitimacy by calling members of the organization "true patriots," "revolutionaries," and so on.[36] These scattered statements by J. P.—the most recent saint of national stature in the political history of India—are still extensively quoted by the RSS in its pamphlets, along with similarly sympathetic statements from Gandhi. This eager embracing of any authoritative recognition, combined with an extremely autocentric principle of organization, demonstrated the central paradox in the Sangh parivar's encounters with the political field: striving for public recognition and legitimacy while, at the same time, internally consolidating its symbolic cohesion through reaction to the pressures and threats of marginalization exerted by the stigma attached to it.

The concerted and coordinated pressure on Mrs. Gandhi resulted in imposition of the Emergency in 1975 and a subsequent ban on the opposition, including the RSS, which was identified as one of the main forces in the anti-Congress front. The preceding activist strategy of the

Sangh parivar in general and the Jana Sangh in particular had, however, allowed the RSS complex to establish itself firmly in most parts of
India. The Jana Sangh's support base was still largely found in northern India, but the larger network of the Sangh parivar made the ban far
more difficult to enforce in 1975 than in 1948. The ban also had the
unintended effect of positioning both the Jana Sangh and the RSS in an
unprecedented position from which they could claim to be champions
of democracy and freedom—willing to undergo imprisonment and
persecution to sustain democracy.

The Janata Experiment

The Janata party, formed few months before the general election of
1977, was a direct result of years of cooperation between the Jana
Sangh and other non-Congress forces in the Lok Sangarsh Samiti. The
party consisted of defectors from Congress, Congress (O) headed by
former Congress leader and old-style Gandhian Morarji Desai, the Socialist party, the Bharatiya Lok Dal headed by the north Indian peasant
leader Charan Singh, and the Jana Sangh. All the constituent parties
gave up their separate identities and merged in the new party on a
common platform which, in spite of vague common programmatic
statements, was held together primarily by a common determination to
defeat Indira Gandhi. The role of the Jana Sangh cadres and of the
Sangh parivar in securing an electoral victory for the Janata party was
significant. Out of 298 seats secured in the Lok Sabha by the Janata
party, 93 were won by Jana Sangh candidates, especially in the old
core areas in Uttar Pradesh, Madhya Pradesh, Himachal Pradesh, and
Rajasthan.

The coalition of political interests behind the Janata party was amorphous and contradictory. The largest influence was beyond any doubt
exercised by Morarji Desai, whose vision of restoring the political order
of the Nehruvian "Golden Age" of the 1950s exercised considerable
influence on the entire political discourse of this period (Graham 1987a,
6). His somewhat saintly style and charisma inherited from his association with Gandhi, as well as the blessings J. P. Narayan had given his
leadership, made him popular with the RSS and the activists rooted in
the Jana Sangh. The RSS accepted his political leadership, in spite of the
fact that the Jana Sangh formed the single largest contingent of MPs in
the Lok Sabha. Further, after the state legislative assembly elections in
the northern states in 1977, Jana Sangh candidates became the decisive
bloc in most legislative assemblies in the Hindi belt, and three former
Jana Sangh leaders became chief ministers in various northern states.

The Jana Sangh settled for two significant posts in the central cabinet: Vajpayee as foreign secretary and Advani as minister for information and broadcasting.

Seen from the point of view of the RSS, the Janata experiment brought about a few significant policy changes in the direction favored by the organization, such as more emphasis on small-scale industry and agriculturally related industries. The long-standing RSS demand for withdrawal of standard historical works promoting a secular interpretation of Indian history, and a rewriting of history books in accordance with a Hindu nationalist interpretation was launched by MPs of the Jana Sangh. This initiative caused a lot of public protest from leading historians, and eroded the relations between former Jana Sangh members and especially the leftist contingent in the Janata party (Rudolph 1984).

The thorniest issue encountered by the former Jana Sangh members of the Janata party was the so-called "dual membership controversy." The RSS had expected to work closely with the new government, not as a political body but as a distanced moral voice, exercising moral pressures and "guidance." It soon dawned on the RSS that the other forces in the Janata party would allow the RSS to play only a rather circumscribed role. There was considerable pressure on the various RSS affiliates for a merger with other organizations in the student and labor field in order to consolidate the support base of the Janata party in general. However, the RSS refused to provide manpower to a party not fully controlled by itself. This reluctance reactivated long-standing suspicions regarding the longer-term objectives of the Sangh parivar, which in a few years had experienced a rapid growth due to its newfound respectability and visibility. Charan Singh and the socialists, in a bid to weaken the position of Morarji Desai, demanded that the former Jana Sangh members should give up their membership in the RSS in order to continue as fully-fledged members of the Janata party.

This issue sparked off an intense debate on the "fascism" of the Sangh parivar, which further boosted the factional struggles within the Janata party. It also provided a welcome stepping stone for a well-staged comeback of Congress as the only true protector of secularism in India. In 1979 the second Janata party cabinet, led by Charan Singh, collapsed and elections were scheduled for 1980. The Janata party, decimated by defections and disagreements, did very poorly in the elections, and Mrs. Gandhi won a convincing victory all over the country. The RSS and the Jana Sangh group remained loyal to Morarji Desai, although RSS men at local levels, angry with what was seen as "backstabbing" by their former allies, supported Mrs. Gandhi rather than their former partners in the Janata party.

The defeat of the Janata party and the disenchantment within the RSS with the Janata experiment resulted in the formation of a new political affiliate of the RSS, the Bharatiya Janata Party (BJP) in April 1980. This party, led by Vajpayee and his populist wing, claimed to be the true inheritor of the "spirit" of the Janata Party. It aimed at retaining a substantial part of the popular goodwill and the newly acquired respectability in the public realm that the Sangh parivar had earned during the Janata years.

Ambiguities of Politics

The collapse of the Janata experiment once more activated the tension between culture and politics as strategic areas of activism within the Sangh parivar, albeit in yet a new form. The experience of large-scale activism, mass mobilization, and the systematic effort to "go public" had pushed the attitude of RSS workers in a more activist direction than it had been just a decade earlier. It had become widely accepted that political influence and visibility through various affiliates could yield rich dividends. However, the Janata experiment had also confirmed the deep-running skepticism, especially among older RSS men, regarding the "corrupting" impact of electoral politics on the Sangh parivar. A substantial portion of RSS activists also had apprehensions about the "populism" of the late Jana Sangh and the Janata party, which they saw as an accommodation of political coalition partners and a depletion of fundamental Hindu nationalist principles. The admission of a few Muslims and other "minority leaders" into the newly formed BJP in order to consolidate its secular credentials, as well as the adoption of "Gandhian socialism" as an official policy of the new BJP, further alienated substantial sections of the more conservative and militant sections of the Sangh parivar.

The "cultural" tendency within the RSS now began to advocate a delinking of the RSS from electoral politics. Advocates of this policy pushed for a purer ideological line in social work and religious matters, more consistent with the traditional RSS ideology, more autonomous, and less dependent on changing electoral fortunes in the political field. On the other hand, the leaders and activists in the newly formed BJP wanted to consolidate the gains of political respectability and public profile made possible by the Janata experiment. They believed that the BJP could become a dominant party within the political mainstream, if it was able to reformulate and reactivate the disenchantment with Congress. As we shall see, these two strategies were pursued rather independently throughout most of the 1980s.

4

Democracy, Populism, and Governance in India in the 1980s

IT IS TEMPTING to view the "saffron wave" from the late 1980s onward as a logical outcome of decades of disciplined, well-planned organizational and ideological expansion of the Sangh parivar (see, for example, Basu et al. 1993, 6). This interpretation tends, however, to reproduce the RSS's narrative of its own history as an unbroken, consistent, and thus irresistible effort to "organize Hindu society" and to "awaken the Hindu." Such an interpretation excludes from view the specificity of the political space created by the broader societal transformations in the 1980s, which the Hindu nationalist movement and a multitude of other forces sought to occupy.

As I will explore in more detail in the following chapter, the "saffron wave" certainly had much to do with new and bold public strategies, including effective appeals to widely disseminated communal mythologies. Nonetheless, the successes of the RSS, the BJP, and other affiliated organizations in winning broad support in new areas and within new social groups remained crucially dependent on processes beyond the control of its organized effort. The central argument here is that the "saffron wave" was made possible by the conditions of possibility offered in the political field: the emergence of a "majoritarian democracy," new forms of "populist governmentality," and proliferation of new demands and new identity claims in a process of "intensified democratic revolution." I argue that the success of the Hindu nationalist movement was far from inevitable, but it was able to expand and change the political common sense in India because it drew on already existing discursive registers, because it voiced broad-based if imprecise disgruntlements and anxieties, and because in large parts of India it could occupy the political space that opened up as the Congress party gradually disintegrated.

Populism and the Transformation of Governance

Congress returned to power in 1980 and began to reconstitute its political power on the basis of huge electoral majorities in the elections in the following decade. It soon became clear, however, that the edifice of the "Congress Raj," as it had evolved in the course of the first three decades after Independence, had changed irreversibly. The political upheavals of the 1970s had mobilized larger sections of the electorate than ever before, and had further spread a language of rights and a sense of entitlements vis-à-vis the state among still larger groups in Indian society. The Congress organization had been fatally weakened by Indira Gandhi's consistent attempts to deinstitutionalize the party, and her reliance on populist electoral techniques. At the same time, a still more self-confident, if heterogeneous, range of opposition parties had built constituencies in north India and in such states as West Bengal, Tamil Nadu, and Karnataka.

The classical Congress structure of the Nehruvian period was an intricate institutional mechanism negotiating power, resources, and mandates among districts and between the states and the center, distributing fiscal resources and arbiting social and political conflicts. Its resilience was premised on the inclusion of most important elite groups within a structure of negotiation, bargaining, and aggregation of the discrete powers and constituencies of local elites upward to the center (Kothari 1970; Weiner 1967).

After the split of Congress in 1969, Indira Gandhi set out to consolidate her own weak position by creating a new parallel system of authority in the party based on loyalty to her personal leadership. The formal structures in the party were bypassed, internal elections were continuously postponed and stalled, and large groups of ambitious but inexperienced politicians made fast careers in the political apparatus by virtue of their unconditional loyalty to the central leadership. The other instrument was the institution of "electoral populism" and the search for unassailable majorities. This method combined effective slogans and centrally organized lavish campaigning at rapidly increasing cost with recruitment of "winners" at the local level on Congress tickets. Locally influential businessmen and wealthy peasants who could finance a campaign and secure a seat would get Congress support. Prominent persons believed to be able to deliver electoral support from their specific community would also get on the ticket. The distribution of places on the ticket became commercialized and engineered from above, often bypassing the local party organization. This generated considerable instability within the Congress party and within state governments, where factionalism was regularly encouraged by the central leadership in order to prevent state-level politicians from building large independent followings.[1]

By increasing the potential gains in terms of money and power in politics, the clientelist structures within Congress further accelerated the articulation of conflicts and the mobilization of new groups.[2] To prop up the electoral base of a still more deinstitutionalized Congress

party, candidates from poor and marginalized communities such as
Muslims, tribals, scheduled castes, and other lower-caste groups were
promoted, along with flimsy promises of benefits and protection from
a distant but benevolent state. These populist campaigns often depicted the Congress as the ally and protector of all depressed groups in
their conflicts with local elites and upper-caste groups.

The Janata party's tenure in power had in some ways broken the
spell and self-evidence of Congress's mandate to rule. But more importantly, the Janata party represented a configuration of political and social forces in the old heartlands of Congress in north India that gravitated around large communities of upwardly mobile peasants. In the
face of these challenges, Congress produced in the 1980s a new configuration of electoral and mobilizational strategies, as well as a new system of political bargaining, which has been characterized as "majoritarian democracy" (Mitra 1992). This new configuration was marked,
above all, by a proliferation of agitation and popular mobilization
based on symbols of community or on single issues. Such manifestations were no longer confined to election periods but became more permanent strategic devices deployed in conjunction with institutional
bargaining and in connection with launching new high-profile policy
initiatives or development schemes.

The very large majorities secured by Congress in the general elections of 1980 and 1984, and in many states during this period, however,
could neither cancel nor coopt the growing demands from a still more
assertive opposition and from active movements and interest groups.
Effectively banished from institutional politics at the national level as
well as from general elections organized around a few overriding emotional issues, these proliferating demands were instead staged by social
movements, in concerted campaigns and agitations, and in many cases
also through the growing range of regional parties.

The practices of competitive populist mobilizations have been interpreted as effects of the ongoing institutional decay of the Indian state.
This decay has rendered more and more people available for a host of
extra-parliamentary agitations and political mass demands, and has
further strained the crumbling capacity of the overloaded Indian state
to deliver development results to groups outside the established networks of patronage presided over by the ruling elite coalitions. According to this influential analysis, clientelistic forms of distribution of
resources and populist forms of political mobilization stand in a mutually contradictory position.[3]

This argument seems, however, to underestimate the extent to which
clientelist practices, factional competition, and the institutionalization
of brokerage (*dalal*) have become naturalized elements in the political

culture in modern India, and have acquired widespread legitimacy in what we may term quotidian forms of political common sense. The expectation that elected representatives will look after and favor their constituency, their faction, and their caste or community, and only incidentally work according to more universalist standards, is probably one of the most common de facto "legitimate problematics" in Indian politics. Politicians may be criticized for this type of "favoritism," for corruption, and so on, but ordinary voters do, at the same time, expect a local elected representative to be efficient as a broker, available for local complaints, and able to provide services to the constituency or group regardless of the strictures of formal rules. Obedience or submission to formal rules is not uncommonly interpreted as a sign of weakness.

Populist mobilization, as it is exercised by virtually all parties in Indian politics, revolves around expansion of clientelistic networks by consolidating the position of the party, or a faction, in legislative bodies and government institutions, thus enabling it to accumulate more resources and control larger flows of resources.[4] Access to large resources is, hence, employed to conquer larger constituencies through expensive election campaigns and, through its promise of patronage, attract local "big men" and community leaders. Contemporary Indian politics is undoubtedly marked by such an expansive logic of competing "clientelist populisms."

I wish to argue, moreover, that the majoritarian and plebiscitary democracy instituted and administered by Congress in most of the 1980s in fact created new forms of governmentality, that is, new forms of governmental technologies as well as new forms of rationalities informing governmental interventions. New modes of high-profile framing and implementation of centralized programs were introduced, aimed at direct distribution of benefits and bypassing intermediate governmental structures, or at liberalizing access to foreign technology and capital for the numerous upcoming groups of parvenu entrepreneurs. These new techniques suspended a major part of the intricate but flexible institutional bargaining that had characterized the older Congress system, in favor of manipulative and covert strategies of undermining adversaries. It also produced populist techniques of representation and overt manipulation of central symbols and "legitimate problematics" in the political field, such as secularism and national unity. Congress deployed these new techniques of government and representation to contain the many new forces and contentious issues unleashed by the intensified democratic revolution in the 1980s.

The first years of Rajiv Gandhi's tenure as prime minister were marked by a initially successful staging of him and his group of young,

"cosmopolitan" advisors as "modern," in the sense both of being westernized and of being dynamic, self-reliant, and self-confident. Rajiv
Gandhi blamed the degeneration of the party for having caused a general decline in popular faith in politics and politicians, and he promised
to cleanse the body politic of these vices. However, neither internal
elections in the party nor the long-overdue panchayat elections scheduled to be held all over the country in 1989 were ever implemented.[5]
Instead, the populist governmentality was further developed. Centralization of institutions and policy making continued, and the framing of
policies seemed still more to be informed by short-term electoral rationales—consolidating constituencies as well as weakening potential
adversaries—rather than by the pursuit of any consistent administrative practice aimed at producing more general effects.

The enthusiasm for advanced technology within the party leadership produced a peculiar technocratic mode of governance through
communities. The party headquarters's extensive, centralized computerized mapping of the caste and confessional composition of every
district and taluka in the entire country became an indispensable tool
in selecting and fielding party candidates at all levels, but also in framing policies, special programs, symblic gestures, and so on. This governmentality rested on a rather unveiled arrogance vis-à-vis democratic processes, as well as a peculiar computerized version of the
objectified (colonial) knowledge of the electorate as a series of culturally defined communities that could be reached and mobilized through
effective engineering of their respective symbols of community.

Within the agricultural sector, the Union government ignored the
discretion of state governments in this area and launched a number of
large and high-profile schemes such as the "Prime Minister's Massive
Program," waiving loans and extending new credits through the district administrations without involving the state level. A series of em-
ployment-guarantee schemes launched by Rajiv Gandhi to commemo-
rate his grandfather Jawaharlal Nehru bypassed state governments
and was designed to maintain the dynastic aura of the Nehru family,
and to prove the patronage power of the party. The fact that in several
states this program actually did ameliorate the lot of landless poor and
raise rural wage levels somewhat was one of the few substantial successes of Rajiv Gandhi's administrative strategies.

Throughout the 1980s Rajiv Gandhi developed TV coverage of his
day-to-day activities to an extent that he, in the popular wit, had more
screen presence than even the leading film stars. The national television station, Doordarshan, also launched major TV serials that were
presented as beneficial to national integration, such as a semi-drama-
tized version of Nehru's *Discovery of India* and the more controversial

but hugely popular serialization of the *Mahabharata* and *Ramayana* epics.[6]

Circulation of newsreels, video machines, and satellite TV quickly went beyond the larger cities and the English-language audience, and spread to rural areas and provincial towns as well.[7] This opened new opportunities and mass audiences to critical journalism and provided unprecedented opportunities for articulation of opposition, just as the introduction of regular TV coverage of parliamentary sessions deprived the parliamentarians in the ruling party of a good deal of their earlier aura. During the general election in 1989, electronic media were massively introduced in electoral campaigns with wide circulation of election propaganda on videocassettes, and video raths—trucks with huge screens and video equipment—were taken from village to village. Although the effects of this escalation of media technology in election campaigns seemed of limited significance in terms of the electoral results (Rudolph 1992, 86), video circulation and heavily media-borne campaigns now became regular elements in the inventories of the electoral machines of all political parties in India.

Introduction of advanced technology in the industry, the administration, and the media, and an incipient liberalization of the economy that made importation of technology, technical cooperation, and joint ventures with foreign firms easier, were favorite themes of the Rajiv Gandhi administration. The much-publicized dismantling of the "License Raj" was, however, gradually played down in the face of resistance from parts of the large-scale sector, the public sector, and agrarian groups. The impact of the liberalization policies was limited to the expanding consumer goods sector which, aided by numerous joint ventures with Japanese and western firms, poured a host of new products into the market. Cars, electronic gadgets, computers, and a range of modern household items appeared and made the consumer goods sector expand rapidly. The urban middle classes reaped most of the benefits of the results of the liberalization and modernization programs as they entered the brave new world of computers, electronics, and emulation of western consumption patterns and taste. But this "consumer goods revolution" also spread very fast to the rural areas and to minor towns. Soon, many of the symbols of urban modernity—two wheelers, electronic devices, VCRs, refrigerators, sunglasses—became available to the more affluent sections in many villages.[8]

The designs and quality of a lot of the new products manufactured in India on a joint venture basis also exposed the poor quality and technological backwardness of many consumer products from the licensed industry in the country. In the automobile sector, the difference between the modern Maruti car and the traditional Ambassador or

Premier cars reflected a technological gap of three decades. The incipient liberalization in the 1980s gradually generated a widespread "foreign technology fetishism"—an obsession with the stereotyped symbols of modernity: Japanese efficiency, American ingenuity, German solidity, French sophistication, Italian taste—as these qualities were believed to be embedded in commodities. Commercial advertising underlined the nationality of the foreign technology behind the particular product. It showed rather interestingly that "commodity fetishism" in the age of globalization is linked not only to certain global styles of consumption but also to the imagined location of one's culture and nation in a global hierarchy.

Not surprisingly, the "foreign technology fetishism" generated a feeling of displacement of the Indian nation, especially vis-à-vis the economically successful Asian countries. The success of China and the East Asian economies attracted considerable attention among educated groups in India, and produced a feeling of being somewhat left behind a dynamic economic development in neighboring areas. The exposure to new technologies and global media flows deepened the sense of India's gradual "sliding" downward in the global hierarchy of nations. This imprecise but powerful frustration in the middle classes further depleted the credentials of the Congress party in its erstwhile core constituency. A more coherent policy of economic liberalization was, however, not implemented until 1991, when the Government of India, in the face of a rapidly growing foreign debt and an acute deterioration of Reserve Bank deposits, agreed to implement a comprehensive liberalization and reform package negotiated with the International Monetary Fund.[9]

Competing Populisms

From the late 1970s on, the peasantry of north India began to emerge as a significant constituency in national politics. In these years, Delhi experienced for the first time hundreds of thousands of north Indian farmers staging rallies to express their support of the Janata party. Peasants in Karnataka, Gujarat, Tamil Nadu, and other states were organized by independent leaders not directly connected to the political parties. The common features of these rallies and agitations were their straightforward staging of economic demands toward the government, their social base that stretched across various categories of peasants but gravitated around a core of "middle peasants." They employed innovative tactics and agitational methods, such as rasta rokos (road blocks), preventing transport of food to the cities; gavbands, sealing off the villages from outsiders such as politicians and officials; and disciplined dharnas (sit-in actions).

The primary problem facing this large and amorphous group, whose production and economic strategies were fully integrated into monetized systems of credit and trade, was profitability of production in the face of state regulation of prices, infrastructural facilities, and inputs. Compared to earlier peasant organizations that were often closely related to political parties, this "new agrarianism" represented, Dhanagare argues, a form of "apolitical populism" seeking direct influence on the formation and implementation of government policies (Dhanagare 1988.

The movements revealed that a language of rights and entitlements—the right to articulate protest, the right to assert oneself, but also the entitlement to be heard and to be accommodated by government schemes—had become naturalized in rural India as processes of commercialization had transformed structures of class and status (Lenneberg 1988). The gradual deinstitutionalization of Congress and the marginal influence of opposition parties had closed the conventional channels of negotiation and accommodation within the political field. Instead, farmers led by people like Tikait and Sharad Joshi took to the streets and staged large rallies in Delhi, Bombay, Bangalore, and many other cities in the first half of the 1980s. (Omvedt 1988).

Paradoxically, the techniques of agitation employed by the movements led to an elaboration of the populist governmentality they opposed. The movements actually caused a modification of agrarian policies in many states, and many of their demands soon became part of official political rhetoric. They demonstrated, in other words, that extra-parliamentary campaigns on simple agendas were able to produce results, as the Congress party found it relatively less complicated to accommodate such precise demands than to deal with larger issues of structural reform.

The Rise of the Other Backward Classes as a Political Identity

Whereas the 1970s were marked by a gradual political mobilization of the cultivating castes in northern and western India, and a rising assertiveness of cultivating and landowning nonbrahmin groups in southern India, the lower castes—squeezed between the scheduled castes and the dominant landowning groups—became politically mobilized in the 1980s.[10] These groups were initially targets of Indira Gandhi's "garibi hatao" strategy, and a number of leaders from these hitherto politically docile groups were promoted by Congress as part of its endeavor to reconstitute its popular base after the split in the party in 1969.

The term "Other Backward Classes" (OBC) had been coined as a residual administrative category as early as in 1950, but it was only after the Mandal Commission in 1980 recommended the reservation of 27 percent of all educational seats and governmental jobs for this social category that the OBC denomination gradually acquired political potency as a rallying point for a range of upward mobile groups falling within these categories.[11]

In northern India the rather condensed congruence between socioeconomic status, political power, and ritual rank made the OBC formula a potent instrument in the hands of opposition parties. The Janata Dal sought to forge an alliance between dominant landowning castes such as Jats and Yadavs and a multitude of OBC groups on a platform of agrarian populism. The successful mobilization of middle farmers by the farmers' movements was simultaneously drawing support from the same moderately prosperous, socially ambitious, politically assertive, impatient, and politically highly "available" group in north India.

The growing social ambitions and life expectations of the cultivating middle farmers were directly related to the effects of agrarian commercialization and the general growth of the middle classes in the 1980s. The political articulation of this amorphous grouping as a distinct political identity through the employment of the Mandal Commission's categories were, however, largely conditioned by two powerful logics governing the "majoritarian democracy" of the 1980s. One logic was the search for stable electoral majorities. The tantalizing promise of a potential 52 percent share of the electorate made appeals to the OBC categories a central element in Janata Dal's vaguely socialist, antiestablishment rhetoric. Another powerful logic was that reservations of government jobs and education opportunities had developed into a widely used clientelistic device for securing electoral support from disadvantaged groups. In the southern states the reservation providing for a host of nonbrahmin groups had since the 1960s grown to cover more than half of all admissions to higher education. The strength of nonbrahmin sentiment in the southern states had made this gradual development possible without attracting much political conflict. Gujarat was one of the first states in the northern and western parts of India to be affected by open conflicts over rising ratios of reserved seats and jobs. The reservation issue created serious disturbances in that state from the early 1980s onward, as an alliance of lower and scheduled castes emerged as a stable political constituency.[12]

What today has become known as "Mandalization" of the political field in the late 1980s has often been interpreted as a watershed in Indian politics, as the beginning of a new phase in which the poor and lower-caste majority began to assert its rights against centuries of tyranny by the upper castes (see for instance Omvedt 1991). The entire issue of caste-based reservations seemed, however, neither to upset nor challenge the logics of the majoritarian democracy. The promises of social uplift enshrined in the "Mandal formula" were in many ways premised on the populist governmentality developed by Congress policy making and implementation bent on high-profile symbolic action rather than structural reforms.

In fact, the expectations engendered by the Mandal agitations bore very little resemblance, or reference, to the realities of existing schemes of reservation and to the very limited number of jobs that could become available.[13] The reservation of 27 percent of all seats and jobs for OBCs as recommended by the Mandal Commission would in many states have only a marginal effect on the prospects for OBCs as well as for higher-caste groups. What the Mandal formula provided was, rather, a focal point for diverse identifications, a label invented by a statistician that could provide a common ground for expressing and condensing multiple subtle exclusions experienced by ever more assertive and self-conscious groups of upwardly mobile peasants and others outside the social world of the upper-caste Hindus.

The methodology used by the commission gave economic criteria a very limited weightage in the overall evaluation of the backwardness of a person or community.[14] In keeping with the prevalent ranking of status, the most important criterion was whether a community was "considered backward by others." Other decisive criteria were high frequency of manual labor, low age of marriage, and above-average percentage of working women. The criteria were perfectly suited for identification of culturally conservative peasant castes. The importance of status parameters over economic parameters in fact extended the OBC denomination to the significant number of dominant castes such as Jats, Yadavs, Lingayats, and Rajputs who rapidly emerged as the leading forces in this numerically strong vertical alliance of backward castes encompassing wealthy peasants and businessmen as well as marginalized landless laborers.

The Mandal Commission scrutinized communities and not individuals. It was assumed that in spite of singular examples of successful social mobility, the overwhelming majority of "backwards" shared modest living conditions and bleak prospects of life improvement, and lived, in the words of the commission, in "a climate of extreme social and cultural deprivation." The community approach reflected the widespread paternalist assumption entertained in the urban middle class world that "backwards" and rural people simply live in their caste world, and that individual assessments of educational and cultural needs was therefore superfluous and not applicable. Besides, the community approach further entrenched and codified the long-standing knowledge-practice in the political field of representation, imagination, and self-objectivation of lower-caste groups.

The commission thus codified the historical mode of production of the Indian people, and codified the prevailing political practices of democracy and accommodation between cultural groups—be they caste, linguistic, religious, or ethnic—objectified by the state and continuously reproduced by self-proclaimed representatives. The endeavor toward objectivation of essential caste cultures, the trust in a symbolic enfranchisement and populist governmentality, and the belief in a "natural" solidarity among lower-caste groups were expressed in strikingly naive terms in the recommendations of the commission. Here it was clearly stated that the objective of reservations was to give OBCs "a feeling of participation in the governance of this country," while admitting that the effect would mainly be "a psychological spin off." It was even anticipated that future OBC officers might be "a shade less competent" but that this would be outweighed by their "first-hand knowledge of the sufferings of the backward sections of society."[15] Needless to say, this peculiar style of representation in the political field of the "backward community" had little resemblance to the widely dispersed and contradictory social, economic, and cultural practices within each of the categories depicted in the commission's report.

The emerging OBC identity thus gave voice and stage to an "intensified democratic revolution," as the 1980s became dominated by competing populist agitations—farmers, OBCs, regional formations—within the overall framework of "majoritarian democracy." The Mandal issue also played a crucial role in providing a distinct focus to the mounting resentment among upper-caste and middle-class groups (rural as well as urban) against the growing assertiveness of lower-caste and less well-educated communities.[16] As I argued in Chapter 1, the urban middle classes (predominantly Hindu) had historically provided the backbone in Congress's construction of the Indian nation state. For decades these groups had been confident that the future belonged to them as a socially, culturally, and economically dominant group, and only a fragment of this group had until the 1980s proved to be a receptive audience for communalist discourse. The growing responsiveness within these groups to Hindu nationalist discourses revolving around themes of the endangered nation was conditioned by what was felt as a sense of encroachment on their social world by ascending groups of peasants, traders, and entrepreneurs. The feeling of encroachment had partly to do with sharpened competition over jobs and education because of the entry of newly mobile social groups. But it was also linked to a sense of "depurification of values" accompanying the increased visibility of lower-caste groups in the public realm, in institutions, government offices, and so on. This effect of social transformation and democratic revolution—belated in north India compared to the rest of the country—in turn challenged the sense of security, status, and competence in the middle classes, already shattered by the gradual retreat of the Indian state from the economic and regulative model of which it had been the main beneficiary. The anti-Mandal agitations and self-immolations of upper-caste students in north India in 1990 must be understood against this background of an established middle class, haunted by fears of what was seen as a "plebeian" threat to its hitherto complacent way of life and social position.

CASTE AND THE IMPURITIES OF POLITICS

To most of the families I met and interviewed in Pune, the political imaginaries and the imagination of the mechanisms of the political field were marked by deep ambivalences. On the one hand, politics was seen as corrupt and politicians generally denounced as dishonest and semi-criminal. The political field was depicted as an area marked by erosion of moral principles and proper behavior in favor of commercialized and criminalized behavior. In this upper-caste environment, the "decay" of the world of politics was unequivocally ascribed to the rising assertiveness of lower-caste politicians— depicted as "goonda types" or "uncultured types." Similarly, the ostensible decline in the quality of public administration was attributed to the influx of ever more officers from the lower castes.

Almost all the families denied that caste was an active factor in the community. The official discourse of caste as a thing of the past has become integrated into everyday language, not least in upper-caste educated families. But other discourses on caste did frequently break through these narratives, as remarks in passing on the essential character of certain other caste groups, on cleanliness, on the "atmosphere" of an area, and so on. The parameters of caste were in a sense extended and transformed into an idiom of civic conduct and order: private purity was extended into public hygiene; brahminical values

into societal discipline, education, and culture; the notion of a brahmin caste spirit into "modern mentality"; and erosion of caste
boundaries became translated into erosion of morality and civic
sense, wherein pollution became disorder (dangerous to women),
noise, and dirt in public places.

These changes seem to me to constitute genuine transformations,
and not mere translations of perennial hierarchies into the idioms of
urban modernity. One might say that the conceptual grammar of
caste seems to continue as the reproduction of logics of differentiation and hierarchical separation (see also Gupta 1991). The political
organization of caste obviously contributes in numerous ways to the
consolidation and simplification of castes into states of "sociological
solidity." Confronted with the problematics of urban modernity, a
competitive labor market, competitive electoral mobilization, the al-
phabet—or signification—of caste is constantly sliding. The meanings of certain practices, boundaries, and caste myths have within
the last few decades increasingly become inscribed into changing
surfaces of democratic competition between groups and communities, and of competitive access to jobs, business, and education. As
the signification of caste has changed, the signified—the hierarchy of
differences—has also been transformed and extended from ritual purity toward civic conduct, Oxford degrees, or NRI (nonresident Indian) status. It seems, nonetheless, that important dimensions of the
conceptual grammar of caste—separation and hierarchy—tend to be
reproduced again and again.

To the middle-class professionals living in Pune and aspiring to
become as "modern" as those in the Camp area, caste identities appear obsolete in their older forms. Instead this logic of discreteness
and hierarchization is reproduced in notions of the advanced stage
of their own sophistication (as modern liberals) and as the natural
physical and cultural distance of their community from other, less
advanced groups. In the old city the brahminical ethos is transformed and displaced into a sense of superior ability to capture and
utilize the instrumental rationality of modern knowledge and to in-
ternalize the utility of civic order, without losing the ancient cultural
heritage and the cultural groundedness one requires in the turmoil of
urban modernity. Communities placed lower in the hierarchy do not
possess this shield of cultural sophistication, many brahmins here
argue. When exposed to the perils and temptations of urban life they
become rootless, vulgar, dirty, and greedy for money and power.

Most of the upper-caste people from these environments who dismissed politics as immoral were also intensely interested and en-

gaged in politics, captured by the *jouissance* derived from the constant display of the "scandalous secret" of politics—corruption and naked power—that was an obvious drive for most of these persons. But it was also broadly realized that without political connections and political brokerage it was next to impossible to conduct a business, to pursue a career, to see that one's children get a good education and a job, or to get proper housing, civic amenities, and so on. As if to disentangle those necessary practices from the "immoral" sphere of politics, both the "buyers" and "sellers" of dalal employed a rather depoliticized businesslike vocabulary to depict this sphere of life—"to get work done," "a small job," "everyday business," and so on.

Most traits that the families saw as repulsive in politics—corruption, dishonesty, and vote catching—were at the same time ethically neutralized as necessities in politics for "our party" to win, or necessary for "our work to be done." There was, especially among BJP supporters, an additional dimension to the *jouissance*, namely, fascination with and enthusiasm for the adroit management and maneuvering by "our people" in the immoral web of intrigues and games in the political field.

A tale of loss and declining ethics marked most of the narratives of politics among the middle-class families I interviewed in Pune. Bemoaning the loss of the "original effervescence" of independent India in the (golden) era of Nehru and lamenting the declining standards of politicians often seemed to serve as metaphors for a fuzzier sense of loss of community, security, predictability, justice, and meaning and direction of society. These narratives are, to my mind, intrinsic to modern political imaginaries and "symptoms" of the unfolding of the democratic revolution. Lack of order, lack of development, and the bemoaning of an immoral modernity threatened by "uncultured people" are all seen as results of a faulty and corrupt polity producing an excessively liberal, fragmented, and immoral society. A brahmin clerk said: "We don't need these silly corporators whoever they are, they are useless. . . . There should be a single person to decide. With a thousand persons thinking in all directions nothing will work out. Nowadays democracy only means 'by the political people, for the political people.'" A wealthy Marwari businessman stated: "Self-discipline is the core of democracy. We need a clean and tidy house—in elections the candidate must be learned, be able to think of a democratic way of functioning. I believe in the background of a person because education and culture must form the thinking of a person."

The narrative of loss of order and democratic ethics applies mainly to the realm of electoral politics. In the realm of everyday local issues, the rights to citizenship seem to be interpreted in more mundane terms as the entitlement to school admissions, "to get work done," to be looked after by the corporators—members of the Municipal Corporation. Also in this sense, the primary parameters of public justice seem to be equal entitlements and endowments of various castes and cultural groups. The ostensible disorder and the loss of a civic equality (which only, if ever, has been extended to privileged groups) experienced by the upper-caste families in Pune was mainly attributed to a rising assertiveness and a growing will among hitherto excluded and marginal groups to use whatever channel is available— democratic or not—to get access to resources and entitlements. Although the rise of more resolute "plebeian" modes of politics among lower-caste communities is often framed as a way of winning social respectability, influence, and recognition, middle-class residents in Pune seem increasingly to dream of "a clean sweep," an imposition of an authoritarian moral order that would privilege those in possession of culture and status.

Religious Symbols in the Political Field

The increasing prominence of religious symbolism in Indian politics in the 1980s was in many ways initiated by the somewhat paranoid strategies pursued by Indira Gandhi and her sons in order to secure and consolidate a perpetual Congress majority in national electoral politics. The political manipulations in Punjab in the 1980s and the subsequent creation of a "Sikh menace" paid off in the massive victory of Congress in 1984 due to the wave of sympathy and national rage in the wake of the assassination of Indira Gandhi.[17] To counter the growing assertiveness of the Janata Dal and regional parties in the 1980s, the Congress leadership embarked in the following years on a rather clumsy communal arithmethic, practicing a shifting accommodation of both Hindu and Muslim communal forces.

In April 1985 the Supreme Court in Delhi delivered an historic verdict granting a divorced Muslim women (Shah Bano) maintenance from her former husband by applying a section under the general Criminal Penal Code to the case. The decision broke with the legal precedents of treating matters of family dispute under the special provisions stipulated in the Muslim Personal Law Application Act, which was interpreted by the members of the ulama appointed to the Muslim Personal Law Board (MPLB).[18] Muslim leaders influenced by conservative and fundamentalist currents in the Islamic world regarded the verdict as an infringement on the cultural autonomy of Indian Muslims and called for public protests. The agitation started as a cautious protest call during the Friday prayer, but quickly developed into a mass movement all over the country, to the surprise of both Muslim and non-Muslim leaders. Coordinated as a "shariʿa protection week" by the newly formed All India Muslim Personal Law Board (AIMPLB), hundreds of thousands of Muslims gathered in October 1985 at rallies against the Shah Bano verdict and for upholding the status of Muslim personal law. The size and spontaneity of the mass rallies—such as the 300,000 people who gathered in Bombay on a call by a handful of relatively unknown Urdu journalists on 20 November 1985—indicated that frustration and a sense of insecurity had been fermenting for a long time among the Indian Muslims, especially in the major cities.

The Shah Bano agitations provided an escape valve for this accumulated frustration, while at the same time it also propelled a new and more communally minded Muslim leadership into national prominence. In an attempt to align Congress with the most conservative elements of the Muslim leadership, which appeared to have a grip on the Muslim community during the 1985 agitations, a bill annulling the Shah Bano verdict was passed haphazardly in May 1986, in spite of massive protests from most quarters of political life.[19] Seen from an electoral point of view, the strategy never worked properly for Congress. Since the mid-1980s, the Janata Dal and the Samajwadi party in Uttar Pradesh emerged as major political rallying points for Muslims in northern India. Both these parties tried to articulate the interests of the large numbers of small farmers in the Gangetic area, among them many Muslims. Both parties also took a firm pro-Muslim stand against Hindu nationalist claims to the site of the Babri Masjid, the disputed mosque in the town of Ayodhya in eastern Uttar Pradesh.

The site of the Babri Masjid had been legally contested by Hindu and Muslim organizations since the nineteenth century, and had been sealed off for decades by the colonial authorities. The core of the dispute was a small platform (chabutra), inside the mosque, allegedly constructed on the site of Ram's birth, and worshiped by Hindus. In 1949, militant Hindus—probably militants from the Hindu Mahasabha—installed sacred Ramlila idols inside the mosque. Shortly afterward the masjid was again sealed off for worship, and a title suit was filed by local Muslims, demanding the removal of the idols and reopening of the masjid for worship. These had been left pending at the local court in Faizabad since 1950.

The Vishwa Hindu Parishad began its agitation in 1985 by filing a writ petition in the local court in Faizabad requesting a reopening of the "disputed structure" for Hindu worship. To everybody's surprise, a court order reopening the premises was issued within a week. There is little doubt that this swift action was promoted by the Congress leadership in another transparent attempt to accommodate the rapidly growing constituency for militant Hindu nationalism. The Congress strategy in 1985–1986 thus displayed the shortsighted rationality of populist governmentality, now aimed at heightening communal tension, while hoping to reap the electoral benefits of the ensuing sense of insecurity among Hindus as well as the minority communities.

In keeping with previous opportunistic election strategies, Rajiv Gandhi openly appealed to communal sentiments among Hindu voters.[20] He started his electoral campaign in 1989 in Faizabad—the constituency in which the town of Ayodhya is located—with promises of creating a Ram Rajya ("rule of Ram") using language in several ways resembling that adopted by the BJP. This strategy also failed, and in 1989 Congress was for the second time in independent India voted out of power at the hands of Janata Dal's anticorruption slogans, and by the Hindu communal campaign of the BJP deriding the "pseudo secularism" of the Congress.

There is little doubt that these transparent maneuvers in the realm of symbolic manipulation aggravated tensions between Muslims and Hindus in north India in the 1980s.[21] Congress's most decisive contribution to this process of "communalization," however, was its de facto authorization of a majoritarian discourse on democracy and a culturalist discourse on political loyalties. Furthermore, the continued depletion of the capacity, skills, and legitimacy of the party, especially at the local level, created important conditions for the subsequent emergence of communal politics at center stage of Indian politics in the late 1980s.

Muslim Minoritization

Economic growth in the urban sectors and the steady commercialization of agriculture in large parts of India in the 1980s had relatively few beneficiaries among Muslims in India. The burgeoning urban and rural middle classes were overwhelmingly Hindu, whereas Muslims generally remained stuck in such economically marginal positions as self-employed artisans, traders, and marginal farmers. Although a middle class of Muslim traders, and professionals was emerging in the urban centers of western and northern India, the consistently lower rate of literacy and the lower attendance in formal education among Muslims

as compared to Hindus testified to the continued economic marginalization of this very large minority in the Indian state.[22]

The virulent anti-Muslim rhetoric disseminated by the VHP and the
RSS in the wake of the conversions to Islam of approximately one thousand scheduled-caste people in Meenakshipuram in Tamil Nadu in
early 1981 (Jaffrelot 1993, 407–9), made it clear that the Hindu nationalist forces were allowed a relatively free hand in public, whereas the
Muslim community stood without powerful public leaders. In this vac-
uum, disparate leaders such as the populist Syed Shahabuddin who
advocated cultural equality, and the conservative Imam Bukhari of the
Jama Masjid in Delhi—previously Indira Gandhi's informal contact
to the religious establishment—emerged as Muslim leaders on an out-
spoken and culturally conservative platform.

A brief glance at some of the transformations of this rather bleak
horizon of many Muslims may, however, shed some light on the out-
burst of what appeared as "conservative radicalism" in the community. From the late 1970s onward, an increasing number of Indian Muslims (and Hindus) had gone to the Gulf countries to work as skilled
workers, technicians, and domestics. They brought back money and
status to their otherwise deprived communities, such as the Muslim
Moplahs in northern Kerala.[23] The apparent might and affluence in the
Arab world strengthened the Muslim identity of many Indian migrant
workers, though not without ambiguities born out of the generally brutal treatment of migrant labor in places like Saudi Arabia.[24]

Simultaneously, the radical antiwestern and assertive rhetoric of Islamic radicalism in Iran and the Middle East impressed a new urgency
of articulation and assertion of a distinct Muslim identity upon groups
of younger intellectuals and journalists, as well as parts of the more
conservative clerical Muslim establishment in India.

The strong assertions of a Muslim identity in connection with the
Shah Bano agitations in Bombay, Gujarat, and Kerala were undoubtedly informed by the newfound pride and the quest for recognition
produced by this new flow of wealth and religious discourse. However, the development of ties between Indian Muslims and the Gulf
countries and the conservative postures of Muslim leaders seemed
to confirm all the run-of-the-mill stereotypes about inherently "anti-
national" Muslims. This contributed in no small measure to making the
Indian Muslims a perfect and demonized other in the Sangh parivar's
subsequent mass production of communal stereotypes.

A brief, but unexceptional, quote from an 1991 editorial in Shahabuddin's monthly magazine *Muslim India*, whose title signals the proposed hierarchy of loyalties of the Muslim community in India, certainly seems to indicate that the Muslim identity propagated here

tended toward the same essentialist and totalizing construction of cultural and religious identities as those of the Hindu nationalists.[25]

> For a Muslim, at the personal level, his religious identity is supreme, rising above race, language, geography or political jurisdiction. Indeed he is not prepared to trade his religious identity at any price—bread, profession, vocation, political ideology or national identity. . . . By Islamic doctrine, the Muslim family code, to the extent it is based on his scriptures, the Holy Koran and the Traditions of the Holy Prophet, is universal sacrosanct and immutable, valid for all times and for all societies. No one has the authority to change it. . . . In short, for the Muslim, Personal Law is Religion. . . . Even a welfare state in a developing society, with an expanding role, cannot be permitted to change the Shariat, or to replace it with a man-made code in the name of unity or progress.[26]

The growing Hindu nationalist visibility in the religious and political field made Shahabuddin's audience ever larger in the 1980s. The Sangh parivar's sustained anti-Muslim campaign and the rapidly escalating communal violence in many parts of the country, in which Muslims in most cases were targeted and attacked, produced anger and incipient radicalism among sections of young urban Muslims.[27] A disturbing trend was that the long-term trend toward dispersion and "normalization" of the Muslim vote, that is, its distribution over a number of political parties according to social position and ideological inclination, was abruptly reversed in the 1989 and 1991 elections as Muslims in large numbers chose to vote en bloc against the BJP, or against Congress (Graf 1992).

A Hegemonial Crisis

An effective hegemony in the Gramscian sense presupposes an effective historical bloc—a strategic alliance between dominant social interests—and a moral and political leadership capable of modifying institutions and reproducing societal cohesion through the governance of the state and by virtue of control over "civil society." In spite of the continuation of the historical bifurcation between a middle-class society and the uneducated communities of the "masses," the Congress party was in all these senses a truly hegemonic force in the first decades after Independence. In the late 1980s the economic basis of this hegemony, the "License Raj," gave way to various attempts to liberalize the economy; governmental institutions crumbled under the weight of corruption and were transformed to ad hoc instruments in a new populist governmentality; the security apparatuses were unable, and unwilling, to retain law and order effectively; the political system of institutional bargaining gave way to competing populist projects; and the moral and ideological leadership of the secular state disintegrated as the dominant Hindu middle classes drifted toward Hindu nationalism.

Faced by these challenges, the chaos and the "plebeian" assertiveness thrown up by the democratic revolution in the 1980s, the majoritarian and populist interpretation of state and society promoted by the Hindu nationalists began to appear as a more effective guarantee of stability and continued privilege among dominant strata in Indian society.

5

The Saffron Wave

Toward a National Hinduism

The Sangh parivar emerged stronger than ever from the upheavals of the 1970s. The movement was entrenched in an expanded network of shakhas and subsidiaries all over the country, and was more self-confident than ever regarding its ability to shape and organize Indian society. The RSS now devoted most of its energy to relaunching the original project of Hindu nationalism, Hindu sangathan, the organization of Hindu society. With the Ekamata ("one mother") Yatra campaign in 1982–1983 in south India, the Vishwa Hindu Parishad (VHP) became the main vehicle of this strategy. One of the significant ritual innovations in this campaign was the incorporation of the image of Bharat Mata[1] along with other deities in the three large yatras, processions that in 1983 meandered from north to south and east to west in India to symbolize the congruity between the national and the sacred geography.[2] The yatras as well as a number of large religious conferences organized in Tamil Nadu, Karnataka, and Kerala were conceived and organized by the VHP and successfully attracted support from numerous sects.[3] Though inclusive and syncretic in its design—the Ekamata was represented as a spontaneous surge of Hindus irrespective of caste, class, gender and sect—the entire campaign had a clear anti-Muslim undercurrent, and derived vital energy from apprehensions vis-à-vis Muslims and other non-Hindu minorities who were depicted as "encroaching" upon Hindu culture through conversion. The yatras and the many smaller upayatras feeding into them were thus, as is often the case with public, organized manifestations of religious community, also assertions in space claiming the public space and ultimately the imagined national space for the Hindu community. This bid to dominate the public space with symbolic manifestations of religious community in order to give material body, concrete crystallization, and emotional affiliation to the imaginary national space, became something of a trademark in most of the campaigns conducted by the VHP and the Sangh parivar in the years to come.

The Vishwa Hindu Parishad was reorganized and expanded in the course of these campaigns. A permanent local infrastructure, parallel to though distinct from that of the RSS, was established in large parts of the country. For the first time, the VHP and the Sangh parivar as such acquired a network in the entire south Indian region, which marked a significant step toward an actual "nationalization" of the movement. The local units emerged in the course of the 1980s as more than indispensable local wheels in the larger agitational machinery of the VHP. In connection with local temples, the VHP formed committees that initiated renovation and expansion of temples, collected funds among local traders, and organized social work in the localities, such as distribution of food and free meals, education of women along patriotic lines, construction of latrines and sewage systems, and childcare courses in adjacent slum areas. The local units of the VHP were also active during the festival season in organizing religious mandals (committees), and in bringing various sects together on common platforms. At the level of city, region, and state, the VHP also worked to bring influential industrialists, politicians, and leaders of religious sects together on platforms of Hindu unity, or as honorary supporters or benefactors of large religious congregations, rallies, or conferences.[4]

A new emphasis was also put on the literal representation of religious unity when the VHP organized a series of local margdarshak mandals (councils of spiritual guides) in several regions and a central mandal for the entire country in 1981. In 1984 this representational structure was expanded and formalized in a regular body of sadhus, the Dharma Sansad, which from 1984 began to organize nationwide congregations (sadhu sammelans) in various parts of the country in order to deliberate and discuss "vital spiritual problems."[5]

In the same year, the Shri Ramjanmabhoomi Mukti Yagna Samiti (the committee for sacrifice for the liberation of Lord Ram's birthplace) was formed, and in September 1985 a series of processions and marches to Ayodhya was launched from twenty-five places in north India. In February 1986 the campaign yielded its first results when the Faizabad District Court decided to open the Babri Masjid for Hindu worship. This was celebrated by the VHP as a major step toward the Hindu nation (Noorani 1991). Though attendance at this yatra was limited, it succeeded in putting the Ayodhya problematic on the political map of India. The VHP's ambitions, however, went much further. In the summer of 1984, Vinay Katiya, an RSS pracharak, formed the Bajrang Dal in Uttar Pradesh as a militant youth wing of the VHP, with the intention of recruiting young underemployed men from the lower castes for militant and daring action in conjunction with the ensuing battle for the Hindu nation that the VHP envisaged. By the late 1980s, Bajrang Dal had an estimated membership of 100,000 young men mainly in north India (Jaffrelot 1993, 205). In the late 1980s, the VHP also started a similar militant outfit for young women, Durga Vahini (Durga's battalion), which in many places was put directly under the guidance of the Sevika Samiti.

Simultaneously, the VHP's effort to reach out to the large and prosperous Indian emigrant communities in Africa, Europe, the Caribbean, Southeast Asia, and North America was expanded and strengthened. A series of Hindu world conferences was held in the 1980s in Europe and North America, where the VHP catered to conventional orientalist forms of knowledge of India prevailing in the western world and represented Hinduism (and itself) as a great tradition clustered around an essential religious core, consisting of peaceful contemplation, tolerance, and spiritual development of the self.[6] The primary targets of this strategy were no doubt the Indian migrant communities, whose disentanglement from local religious complexities and politics in India made them receptive audiences and generous sources of funding for the VHPs version of a syncretic, nationalized Hinduism. The same removal from the localized complexities of rural and popular religious practices, and the embrace of a modernized "spiritual Hinduism" preaching personal development, success, and this-worldly ethics, applied in many ways to the growing urban middle class in India itself, which was a main target of the VHP's campaigns in the 1980s. As van der Veer has pointed out, the prominence of a modern "spiritualist guru" like Chinmayananda in the VHP, the proximity between the VHP and the preachings of the Ramakrishna Mission, as well as the increasing use of the language of "spiritual Hinduism" by such learned authorities as the shankaracharyas (heads of prominent Hindu religious institutions), indicates that the success of the VHP's syncretism and nationalized Hinduism in the 1980s was made possible by a broader transformation of the religious practices and imaginations of the middle classes in India.[7] This transformation was also connected to a broader transformation of public representations of nation and community in the majoritarian democracy where, for instance, television came to play a new and prominent role in modifying the style in which society, state, and nation were imagined in India. The production and broadcasting of the epic *Ramayana* and *Mahabharata* from 1987 onward, the enormous attention and interest they attracted all over India among all kinds of communities, including Muslims, and the multiple ways they produced images and narratives that fertilized the ground for the subsequent Ramjanmabhoomi campaign from 1989 onward, have been widely discussed.[8] Though far from ideologically innocent, these serials were, however, not merely the communal representations they are sometimes made out to be. They were parts of a qualitatively new style of national imagination and were actually followed by serializations of Nehru's *Discovery of India*; they were also, in keeping with the official governmentality of "communal balancing," followed by a number of episodes from the Bible.

In sum, one could argue that the Sangh parivar's strategy of generating a nationalized Hinduism through production of a new sense of a religious community imagined around the national geography and sites like Ayodhya proved to be an apt reading of the conditions of possibility for ideological intervention provided by the majoritarian democracy of the 1980s. In the field of political discourse, majoritarian and communal themes were becoming ever more accepted and legitimate; the nation had been "massified" in a rather concrete spatial sense, as urbanization and proliferation of relatively inexpensive means of transport enabled ever more Indians to live and experience the nation-space through migration, cross-regional family ties, travel, and tourism. Various religious minorities and hitherto docile lower-caste groups had become more vocal and mobile than before, and all these processes had become visible in shared televised representations. The majoritarian notion of the "rights" of Hindus was gradually becoming a "legitimate problematic," as the dominant interpretation of secularism as a permanent balance between various communities—in many ways the central political episteme in the postcolonial democracy—had settled among broad groups as a fundamental principle of intelligibility of the social world. The label of "pseudo secularism" for any policy or measure that did not benefit Hindus as a majority was surely a BJP invention, but its enormous popularity and vernacularization in local languages reflected the fact that one of the effects of the deep enfranchisement of the population through democratic processes was the "naturalization" of Hindus as majority and as "proprietors" of the nation. When Hindu communalists today refuse to recognize majority assertion as communalism, but insist that it is tantamount to "natural justice" and "democracy," they do not address the vocabulary of the political elite but widely held "folk" understandings of what secularism and democracy mean.

BJP as a New Beginning

In the early 1980s the idiomatic differentiation between the various branches of the Sangh parivar turned from a division of labor into two rather disjunctive strategies. In the political field the BJP attempted to recover and save the moral and secular legacy of the Janata party, while the RSS and especially the VHP promptly responded to the new majoritarian, pro-Hindu signals from Congress, as well as to the signs of increasing cultural assertiveness of various minority groups.[9]

The BJP's attempt to display secular tolerance by attracting a number of Muslim personalities and candidates for state and general elections, and by encouraging candidates to participate in Muslim festivals and so on, engendered widespread dissatisfaction among RSS cadres at the ground level, and a considerable debate arose within the Sangh parivar on this issue (Jaffrelot 1993, 389–93). In 1984, leading RSS figures openly called upon the RSS cadres to support Congress, rather than the BJP.[10] Not only had the sheer force of Congress at this juncture rendered opposition parties weak and fragmented but the party was also playing the majoritarian and communal cards with far greater force and efficiency than the BJP was capable of, or willing to, under Vajpayee's leadership (Graham 1987a, 15).

At the first national convention of the BJP, its president Atal Behari Vajpayee justified the break with the Jana Sangh legacy by referring to two advances made during the years of the Janata party. First, almost 2.5 million members, many of whom had never associated with the Jana Sangh, had joined the BJP in its first nine months. Second, the legacy of J. P. Narayan's Gandhian "value-based politics" had far from exhausted its potential as a mass-mobilizing device.[11] The new central party document, entitled *Our Five Commitments*, enshrined both a basic commitment to the Nehruvian development model of strong state intervention, planning, and large-scale industry, and a commitment to small-scale and village-based industry, which the Jana Sangh had made its trademark.[12] The program and strategies of the BJP in the period between 1980 and 1986–1987 was in many ways based on the imagined restoration of the broken Janata party: a moderate Hindu nationalist ideology combined with a cautious moral critique of Congress management of the state, and guided by an overriding "logic of opposition"—that is, a sustained effort to create a measure of unity among the disparate forces opposing Congress.

Although the party did relatively well in the state assembly elections in 1980 in states such as Madhya Pradesh, Rajasthan, and Gujarat—all places where the RSS network was fairly strong and where the Jana Sangh once had good support—the party incurred heavy losses in the "cow belt" in Uttar Pradesh and Bihar.[13] The BJP participated with other opposition parties in loosely co-ordinated attacks on Congress on a variety of issues—Punjab, center-state relations, economic policy—without much effect. At the 1984 Lok Sabha election, Congress won its biggest victory ever (403 out of 513 seats), due to the wave of sympathy generated after the murder of Indira Gandhi, as well as the disarray of the opposition parties.

Evaluating the reasons for the dismal performance in the elections, where the BJP only won four seats, Vajpayee admitted the failure of his centrist politics of loyal opposition to Congress, his personal responsibility for this, and the deep crisis of the party.[14] Vajpayee's mainstream opposition line had proven fruitless at a time when Congress was ex-traordinarily powerful, aggressive, and majoritarian, and when the RSS proved reluctant to support the party.

The National Executive of the BJP decided to form a working group to scrutinize the organization, funding, ideology, and political strategy of the party. The report of the working group, based on a large survey of attitudes and performance among four thousand party workers, re-viewed most of the strengths and weaknesses of the BJP.[15] From these intense and protracted deliberations over strategy and organization emerged a set of new compromises between the contradictory pulls and compulsions within the Sangh parivar. On internal matters, de-cisive concessions were given to a more "purist" line emphasizing the BJP's profile as the defender of "Hindu society," in order to win back the support of the local RSS cadres. Coalitional politics were scrapped and a solitary strategy more in line with the self-images of RSS cadres was adopted. However, broader populist themes were also strengthened: expansion among the poor sections was given priority, agitational politics was emphasized, electoral strategies professional-ized, and public relations functions upgraded—all indicating a some-what belated adaptation to the strategic imperatives of majoritarian democracy.

Communalizing the Political Field

It has become part of conventional political wisdom in India to attrib-ute the gradual turn of the BJP toward a clear-cut communal strategy from 1986 onward to L. K. Advani's election as party president in 1986. A closer look at the chain of events reveals, however, that this turn grew out of events in the political field from 1986 onward that could not have been fully anticipated. As we saw in Chapter Three, a radical anti-Muslim discourse had coexisted with political pragmatism within the Sangh parivar and within the older sangathanist tradition for al-most a century. What was new in the 1980s was, in other words, not so much the employment of the idiom of Hindu communalism per se, but rather the ingenuity and scale with which this idiom was differen-tiated and disseminated through an array of new technologies of mass mobilization.

There was, indeed, a clear change of accent from Vajpayee's tem-pered condemnation of the Shah Bano agitations and defense of the principle of a uniform civil code in January 1986 in the name of mo-dernity and equality,[16] to the rather belligerent proposals regarding control of "Pakistani infiltration" only one year later.[17] The illegal immigration to India of thousands of impoverished job seekers from

Bangladesh and Pakistan every year was portrayed by the BJP as an organized Muslim invasion and infiltration into India. This argument became in the following years a standard element in the building of the specter of a threatening Muslim menace of destabilization, job snatching, and exploitation of "goodhearted Hindus," which other parts of the Sangh parivar had been building up for years.

In 1989, the communal rhetoric was gradually built up again in a continuous stream of press releases, resolutions, and statements from the BJP, which in these years appeared as the most professionally managed, well organized, and public-relations conscious of all the Indian political parties.[18] During this period, the BJP took the lead in Indian political discourse and mass produced the simple slogans and concepts alluding to the weakness and effeminization of Congress in the face of determined Muslims that became so widely used in the years to follow: "pseudo secularism," "pampering of minorities," "appeasement of Muslims," "foreign infiltration."

The Ramjanmabhoomi/Babri Masjid issue, for long staged and fermented by the VHP and RSS, only became part of the official ideological inventory of the BJP from July 1989 onward, however, not as a front issue in the first place, but quoted as one of several examples of Congress's lingering weakness and subservience to Muslim pressure.[19] In spite of the communal tension that had been built up in north India over the dispute, and the violence it had produced, the dominant theme of the 1989 election became primarily related to high-level corruption in Congress, which was also a main target of the BJPs manifesto.[20]

The Congress counteroffensive to ward off and preempt the campaigns of the opposition once again revealed the populist governmentality that had developed throughout the decade. To combat the BJP, the Rajiv Gandhi administration attempted rather openly to buy into the momentum of Hindu communalism building up in north India. In September 1989, the government allowed the VHP to undertake the Ram Shila Puja, a nationwide procession of consecrated bricks collected from all over the country for the construction of a large Ram Mandir in Ayodhya. The government also declared the plot adjacent to the Babri Masjid to be "undisputed land," which amounted to a thinly veiled invitation to the VHP to begin construction of a Ram temple on this plot. Six days later the government attempted to accommodate Muslim protests by ordering the VHP to stop the construction work.[21]

The launching of the Ram shila pujan in 1989 marked the beginning of a new series of closely coordinated campaigns of the Sangh parivar in the years to come. Leading BJP figures were appointed to the Kendra

Karyakari Mandal, the central working committee of the RSS, and high-level coordination between the BJP and RSS leadership was now fully formalized.[22] Like the Ekamata yatras, the design of the Ram shila puja aimed at giving materiality and concreteness to the spatial imagi-nation of a Hindu rashtra. Several hundred thousand bricks were taken to villages, towns, and residential areas all over the country by VHP and RSS activists. Village elders or local brahmin pujaris (priests) con-secrated the bricks in ceremonies prepared by the activists, and funds for construction of a Ram temple in Ayodhya were collected. The bricks were then wrapped in saffron cloth, worshiped for several days, and often carried in processions through adjacent localities. Finally, the bricks were collected in larger arterial streams heading for Ayodhya. Before and after the puja campaign, VHP and RSS activists arranged mahayagnas in the localities—meetings and propaganda that espe-cially targeted women, who were assumed to be the most receptive audiences to religious appeals, and young men, assumed to be most receptive to inciting communal rhetoric.[23]

Due to its simple but effective symbolic language and its superb or-ganization, the campaign proved to be a major success for the Sangh parivar, and became a decisive breakthrough for the Ramjanmabhoomi agitation at the national level. According to the VHP's own estimates, almost 300,000 pujas were performed and more than 100 million peo-ple attended the processions.[24] It remains doubtful, however, whether one can establish any straightforward causal relationships between the mass attendance at these ceremonies, that is, watching the spectacle of consecration, and the subsequent increase in votes for the BJP and the increased propensity for violent assaults on local Muslims. The rela-tionship seems rather to be at the level of indirect transformation of the entire "public atmosphere." The campaign enabled the Sangh parivar to disseminate its discourse of Ram as a national hero and Ayodhya as the symbolic center of the Hindu nation to very large, and rural, audi-ences. As an example from Aurangabad district indicates, the pujas were primarily organized as spectacles with limited participation, aim-ing at strengthening the Sangh parivar networks in the villages in the district.

PATRIOTIC BRICKS

As in other provincial cities, the VHP network in Aurangabad devel-oped primarily within middle-class localities where the RSS had some presence. Activists in the VHP were overwhelmingly drawn from middle-class families with prior ties to the Sangh parivar. In the villages in adjacent districts, RSS shakhas were rather scattered and rarely organized with regular drills and ideological teaching. Most village shakhas were organized around a single individual who had come in touch with the RSS during his education in Aurangabad, and who gathered a few young people around him for play, sports, "storytelling," and so on, and worked as a local contact for the RSS or VHP in the village. The VHP gained a larger audience in the rural areas in the district with the Ram shila puja in 1989, especially in the villages in Paithan and Aurangabad talukas, which were covered intensely and where many hundreds of bricks were collected. The subsequent mobilization of kar sevaks (volunteers for temple construction) in October 1990 gathered more than two hundred activists from the entire district, while the local units of the VHP claim to have sent more than one thousand kar sevaks to Ayodhya in December 1992, mainly from the rural parts of the district, and including a substantial number of women.

According to a VHP activist in Paithan, a cloth merchant and a correspondent of the RSS newspaper *Tarun Bharat*, the success of this brick consecration ceremony had to do with its simplicity and its speed:

> Premanufactured bricks were given to us by the Vishwa Hindu Parishad in Aurangabad. Then we took the bricks in jeeps to the villages. Say ten-fifteen bricks to each village. There the sarpanch [village headman], the police patil [commander], or some elderly respected person was asked to perform the *puja*: to apply turmeric paste, put flowers, and burn incense sticks. Then the bricks were carried around in the village, a small meeting was held with a speech or two, and we then took the bricks by the jeep back to Aurangabad, and from there by rail to Ayodhya.... I think we covered some one hundred and seventy villages that way (Vasant Rao, VHP activist in Paithan, interviewed on 3 October 1992).

VHP activists admitted that they were received more enthusiastically in villages with a substantial Muslim population and a recent history of enmity between Hindus and the substantial groups of Muslims in this former part of Hyderabad state. Many of these villages had seen the revitalization of communal antagonisms promoted and encouraged by Shiv Sena, a Maharashtrian organization that in the 1980s turned to rabid Hindu communal rhetoric and expanded from Mumbai into the interior of the state.[25]

The brick campaign was followed by widespread communal tensions and violent incidents all over the country. A massacre in Bhagalpur in Bihar in November 1989, where hundreds of Muslims were killed, was one of the largest since Partition and took place in the tense and communally surcharged atmosphere created by the sustained Ramjanmabhoomi agitation.[26]

The systematic promotion of VHP and Bajrang Dal leaders as candidates for the BJP in the 1989 elections, vigorously supported in their campaigns by VHP activists and VHP sadhus, testified to a careful electoral utilization of the communal mobilization hitherto mainly promoted by the Sangh parivar's specialized branches in cultural mobilization. This division of labor enabled the top BJP leadership to remain relatively moderate in its public statements on the Ayodhya dispute, on Muslims, and so on, and thus remain largely within the dominant parameters of political discourse. The official party discourse, addressed to a middle-class audience, could focus on the critique of Congress governance.[27] Open enunciation of communal hatred could be left to local-level cadres, and could be reserved for occasions when more popular segments of the electorate were addressed.

The results of the 1989 election marked a decisive breakthrough for the BJP, which now emerged as the third largest party in the country. The increase in votes (from 7.4 percent in 1984 to 11.4 percent in 1989) yielded as many as 89 seats in the Lok Sabha because of seat adjustments with the left and center coalition, the National Front. The seats were won in two types of constituencies. They were partly in older core constituencies, where a strong and well-extended Sangh parivar organization provided an effective campaign machinery, and where BJP candidates had a certain reputation for being less corrupt than the average Congress politician; and partly in constituencies where the party capitalized on a heightened communal tension and complex patterns of caste mobilization that had fragmented former strongholds of Congress.

The 1989 election results also seemed to indicate a close correlation between the routes of the Ram shila puja, the subsequent communal violence in September-October 1989, and at least 47 out of the seats won by the BJP in the states of Gujarat, Madhya Pradesh, Bihar, Rajasthan and, in a less clear-cut manner, Uttar Pradesh (Chiriyankandath 1992b, 68).[28]

Following the anti-Congress logic of the Indian opposition parties, the BJP entered, hesitantly, into a precarious position as support party, along with the Left parties, for V. P. Singh's National Front cabinet formed by the end of 1989. The party now found itself aligned with such MPs as Syed Shahabuddhin of the Babri Masjid Action Committee, and it constantly found itself in disagreement with the government on vital issues on national unity and the Ayodhya dispute. Many leading forces in the BJP feared that the party would soon jeopardize its credibility and thus its new-found mass constituency.

These difficulties were exacerbated at the state legislative assembly elections in March 1990, where the BJP won a majority and formed governments in Madhya Pradesh, Rajasthan, and Himachal Pradesh, and won a large number of seats in Gujarat and Maharashtra. Even more than in the 1989 elections, hard-hitting communal rhetoric dominated the campaign of the BJP, and as in 1989 the party reaped significant electoral benefits from the heightened communal tensions in all the affected states.

The tensions between the National Front and the BJP reached a breaking point with V. P. Singh's announcement in September 1990 that his government intended to implement the Mandal Commission's recommendation of 27 percent reservation of educational seats and government jobs for OBC ("backward") communities. Within the Sangh parivar and its upper-caste constituencies there were widespread apprehensions regarding the Mandal formula, which was opposed on the pretext of its inclusion of certain Muslim communities in the OBC category. At the same time, it was obvious that a flat rejection of the Mandal formula would jeopardize the party's protracted drive to attract support from lower-caste groups. Encouraged by strong forces in the RSS and VHP, the BJP decided to break with its position as serious and "loyal opposition," to dissociate itself from V. P. Singh, and to embark even more strongly than before on the platform of Hindutva and the Ramjanmabhoomi agitation, in order to oppose what was seen as the "dangerously divisive effects" of the Mandal formula on a prospective Hindu majority nation.

In September 1990, Advani launched the Rath yatra—a procession in a rath (chariot)—from the rebuilt Somnath temple in Gujarat, winding some 10,000 kilometers through western and northern India, and scheduled to conclude in Ayodhya. The idea was, once more, to represent the national space as sacred space, and this time the full-scale involvement of a large political party made the publicity enormous. The rath was a modern Toyota van decorated like the chariot used by the warrior Arjuna in the widely popular televised serial *Mahabharata*, but also with the RSS symbol (the bhagwa dwaj, saffron flag) and the BJP lotus symbol. On the van, loudspeakers played music from the televised *Ramayana* and *Mahabharata* serials, while militant slogans calling for the building of a Ram mandir (temple) in Ayodhya, and for the cause of Hindutva, were repeated again and again. Widely reported in the news, the yatra—which the RSS forthrightly called a dharma yuddha (holy war), an expression borrowed from Savarkar's writings—received an enthusiastic response in many places. The popular response, often organized and encouraged by local Sangh parivar activists, was a mixture of traditional pious worship, political militancy, and muscular kshatriya traditions, which had become the trademark of the Hindutva campaign. Women brought coconuts, incense sticks, and sandalwood paste, and worshiped the motorized rath in traditional ways. Youngsters met the Rath yatra armed with bows and arrows, swords and trishuls (tridents), sadhus applied tilaks of blood on Advani and other "holy warriors," and the BJP/RSS organizers organized rallies and welcome parties in towns and villages along the route.[29] Prior to the passing through of the yatra, VHP and Bajrang Dal activists prepared the route with decorations, and saffron colors, and incited communal propaganda and a series of minor but effective campaigns such as the Ram jyoti: a torch lit in Ayodhya was multiplied and carried to even remote villages, where local people were encouraged to light their Diwali lamps with this "consecrated fire" emanating from Ayodhya.[30] On the whole, the Rath yatra was designed, however, primarily as a drama which, through careful facilitation of extensive media coverage, was staged on the national arena, rather than the multiple extensions of local networks that characterized the brick-consecration campaign in 1989 as well as the Ekmata yatra in 1983.[31]

As in the case of the Ram shila puja, the Rath yatra sparked serious communal tensions and violence. It left hundreds of minor and major incidents of anti-Muslim pogroms in its trail. The events took a dramatic turn when Advani was arrested by the Janata Dal administration in Bihar in late October, and the BJP used this as a pretext for withdrawing its support of V. P. Singh's government. On October 30 a small group of kar sevaks attempted to storm the heavily guarded Babri Masjid in Ayodhya, and they managed to place a saffron flag on top of the structure. Thereafter, a confrontation between the local police and thousands of kar sevaks escalated and resulted in the death of more than fifty persons in police firings. Thousands of kar sevaks were arrested, and traffic and trains were stopped in an attempt to defuse and prevent the yatra from igniting the very combustible communal situation in Uttar Pradesh. This direct confrontation with the state government, headed by what the BJP called a "pro-Muslim pseudo secularist" (Mulayam Singh), created a heroic legend of kar seva martyrdom in Ayodhya and provided the optimal habitat of confrontation and clear frontiers in the ensuing campaigns of the Sangh parivar.[32]

Contingencies of Electoral Politics

When fresh elections were announced in early 1991, the BJP's election machinery embarked unrestrainedly on the theme of Hindutva. The areas where the Ramjanmabhoomi agitation had evoked the most active response were targeted in an intensive election campaign marked by an unprecedented number of candidates affiliated with the VHP (Chiriyankandath 1992b, 71). The swelling VHP-organized "religious parliament," Dharma Sansad, was this time involved in the campaign—at least officially—as an "advisory board" representing these intimate connections between the party and the VHP-styled religious authority as a kind of spiritual authorization of the BJP. The party also began to attract support from certain intellectuals, journalists, and public figures in the influential English-speaking public sphere. Party ideologues launched direct attacks on what they called "Left intellectual mandarins," deriding them as "sarkari intellectuals" (puppets of the government) and as fellow travelers of the lost cause of communism. At the level of popular campaigning, saffron-clad sadhus and scores of young men armed with trishuls, swords, and other weapons became a regular feature of many election rallies, where the VHP and BJP staged fiery speakers such as the female orators Uma Bharati and Sadhvi Ritambra. These speakers became known for their inciting oratory and direct attack on Muslims, not merely as "pampered minorities," as the BJP official rhetoric had it, but as enemies of the nation, and dirty, lustful killers—evil incarnated that had to the "cleansed" from the national body so the Hindus could rise from their state of weakness and lack of self-confidence.

The 1991 election campaign became the most expensive, the most violent, and the most brutal election campaign in the history of independent India. The parties used modern electronic media—videos, cassette tapes, video raths (trucks with large videoscreens), and public relations material as never before, along with an enormous variety of posters, stickers, photo booklets, and leaflets of all kinds. The campaign was marked by an unprecedentedly sharp and communal tone, and on numerous occasions election rallies sparked off episodes of communal violence that sometimes escalated into full-scale riots, even in places that had not previously experienced communal rioting.[33]

The assassination of Rajiv Gandhi in Tamil Nadu changed the entire tone and focus of the campaign, and elections were postponed for a month. In the new round of campaigning, BJP tried to occupy Congress's position as the natural locus of national unity and the guarantee of stable and responsible governance, now rendered vacant by the demise of the Nehru dynasty from the political scene. Congress succeeded, in turn, in extracting a considerable "sympathy effect," but could not prevent the BJP from emerging as the second largest party in the country, with 119 seats in the Lok Sabha, expanding its share of the total vote from 11.4 percent in 1989 to 19.9 percent in 1991.

Polls suggested that the large constituency won by the BJP was generally fairly young, predominantly male, urban, and upper-caste, though the party also gained a considerable rural constituency, particularly among upper-caste communities in the north, whereas the party's voter profile was somewhat more broadly based in parts of Gujarat and Maharashtra.[34] Although the election results did not meet the high expectations of the BJP workers, the party managed to break out of its north Indian heartland and expand to the east and south, and to make itself a "respectable" choice in the fast-growing middle class in the many provincial cities. It was able to attract large funds from the business community and from many non-resident Indians, who increasingly saw it as the party of the future. Finally, the BJP became widely popular among retired army personnel and inside the armed forces and the police, where the promises of a stronger army, nuclear armament, strong-arm policies in Kashmir and Punjab, and the general celebration of national strength, honor, and a martial stance found a receptive audience.[35]

The BJP was also able to win a majority in the simultaneous state legislative assembly elections in Uttar Pradesh, after a thoroughly communalized election campaign that divided the electorate deeply along community and caste lines (Hasan 1996).[36]

In spite of its astounding success, the 1991 elections also revealed some of the BJP's limitations in terms of retaining its electoral support beyond the enthusiasm generated by electoral campaigns. On the one hand, although the party was successfully riding the emotional wave generated by the Ramjanmabhoomi agitation, the enthusiasm and emotions this generated were unstable and could not always be converted into votes for the BJP. Voters could well support the construction of a Ram mandir and share the communal agenda but still cast their vote for Congress. At the levels of state and district, on the other hand, the political machine of Congress and the political culture of clientelism it had nurtured for so long remained superior to the BJP's capacity in this field. However, Congress's resort to majoritarian electoral populism had undoubtedly opened a new set of strategic possibilities for the BJP and the Sangh parivar in the late 1980s, which was utilized to the hilt with a host of innovative technologies. The BJP had only recently begun to practice institutional politics on a larger scale, and to grapple with the patronage structures and flows of money pervading this field. The resulting "amateurism" of the BJP in institutional politics and governance resulted in a mixture of paralysis, inflexibility, and cases of blatant abuse of office that contributed to the subsequent defeat of the BJP in several state elections in 1993.

Opening Other Fronts

After the 1991 election, the Sangh parivar sought to diversify its strategies. The Kashmir problem had already been the target of a campaign by RSS's student wing, ABVP, in 1990. The climax of the campaign was a march of 10,000 students determined to perform satyagraha ("truth force") in Srinagar and unfold the national flag in the central square, Lal Chowk, where Kashmiri militants had repeatedly burned the Indian flag. The ABVP activists were wearing blouses with such slogans as "I am ready to kill Bhutto"; thousands of letters pleading for firmer action, all signed in human blood, were sent to the president of India; and shastrapujas, that is, worship of arms symbolically meant for the liberation of Kashmir, were performed during the campaign.[37]

In early December 1991, BJP president Murli Manohar Joshi commenced an ambitiously designed Ekta yatra (procession for unity) from Kanya Kumari on the southern tip of the Indian peninsula, winding through fourteen states, and scheduled to reach Srinagar, the curfewed capital of Kashmir, in order to hoist the national flag on Republic Day. The yatra was designed to project the BJP as more devoted to patriotism than any other political party.[38] Along the route of the yatra, Kashmiri Hindus narrated their stories of displacement, and video films of Hindu refugee camps in Jammu and destroyed temples in Kashmir were shown. In each state and major city the yatra was joined by a number of local yatras in the area, and as in all the previous yatras, public rallies were held along the route. The BJP claimed to have organized a kesaria vahini, half a million young volunteers determined to sneak into the curfewed state of Kashmir and appear in Srinagar on for the Republic Day celebrations, which Kashmiri militants had successfully prevented for some years.

The response to the yatra was generally lukewarm, except in BJP strongholds such as Bangalore, Indore, and cities in Rajasthan and Gujarat where the BJP's organizational machinery displayed its considerable efficiency in organizing rallies as "popular welcomes." As the yatra approached Delhi and proceeded northward, it took on critical political dimensions. The BJP had made the arrival of the yatra in Delhi a conspicuous event. After a large rally in Delhi, where more than 100,000 party workers from all over the country had gathered to see the yatra off to its last and dangerous phase, the mood of the participants in the rally was militant and upbeat.[39]

The yatra entered Punjab under heavy security arrangements. This could not prevent attacks on the convoy. Four BJP workers were killed, and they were immediately projected as national martyrs in the almost epic atmosphere of sacrifice and honor that the BJP propaganda machinery worked hard to generate. This staging of martyrdom, widely covered by national and international media, transformed the hitherto "sober" line of the party leadership into belligerent jingoism. The demands for nuclear armament, for a heavy hand in dealing with what the party called "insurgency" in Kashmir and Punjab, and for a heavily armed "security zone" along the Pakistani border were advocated in still more militant forms.

For security reasons the yatra, with an estimated 100,000 participants, was stopped before entering Jammu. After prolonged negotiations, the BJP leadership—visibly loosing courage when faced with the actual sites of combat—agreed to cut down the contingent supposed to reach Srinagar to a few hundred persons. The diminished BJP yatra proceeded by military helicopter to Srinagar, where Joshi, in a very brief and pathetic ceremony under tight military security, hoisted the national flag at the central Lal Chowk in Srinagar and hastened back to the military headquarters, only to leave the state of Kashmir a few hours later by military helicopter.[40]

The Ekta yatra, like the Rath yatra, was designed to acquire nationwide dimensions through extensive press coverage, and was clearly targeting a middle-class audience supposed to be concerned with matters of national unity rather than religion. Narendra Modi, chief BJP organizer from Gujarat and organizer of the Ekta yatra, stated: "All those liberal sophisticated people who could not associate with us through the Rath yatra are now able to come out openly in support of the Ekta yatra."[41] However, the political gains from the yatra were modest. Unlike the draconian measures that made heroes out of the kar sevaks when entering Uttar Pradesh and that made it possible to project Mulayam Singh as the incarnation of all Muslim evils, the accommodating tactics of the government vis-à-vis the Ekta yatra deprived the BJP of any such clear villain.

The following example from Maharashtra indicates the compulsions and risks involved in relying on high-profile media-borne political campaigns, and reveals that the Sangh parivar was far from having developed any stable, unassailable constituency or even audience for its nationalist discourse.

ROADSIDE PATRIOTISM

In Maharashtra, the BJP staged a upa yatra, a kind of local yatra that would join the larger Ekta yatra once it reached Aurangabad. To the

BJP it was important to demonstrate its standing among the nonbrahmin communities, and the upa yatra was consequently led by a young Dalit, Sandesh Kondwilkar, state secretary of the BJP, and a Maratha, Vijay Kalke, municipal corporator from Pune. In a bid to rid itself of the brahmin stigma still attached to the party in Maharashtra, and in order to challenge the Congress power in the state, the yatra moved through the sugar districts in western Maharashtra, the traditional stronghold of Congress in the state. The yatra was launched at the so-called "Holy Pass" where a famous warrior of the Shivaji period was killed, and ended in Aurangabad (or Sambhajinagar in the parlance of Shiv Sena and the BJP) six days later. The yatra carried saffron-colored urns with holy water and soil gathered along the route, played patriotic film songs, and displayed most of the public rituals that had become associated with the peculiar genre of what Richard Davis has called "Sangh Hinduism" (Davis, 1996: 51). Nonetheless, it had limited success in terms of evoking the mass response it aspired to. The lack of a developed infrastructure of the Sangh parivar in the affluent sugar belt of western Maharashtra, the historical center of Maratha power, made the yatra a rather unsuccessful undertaking. The only well-attended mass meeting was in Aurangabad, where both the BJP and Shiv Sena had considerable backing and were able to mobilize a few thousand activists. The Ekta yatra also failed to attract public attention or arouse nationalist feelings in the predominantly rural districts of Marathwada and Vidarbha it passed through in early January 1992. Villagers in a roadside village on the highway to Aurangabad recalled: "We had heard rumors of a new yatra coming through our village. We heard the music long before it arrived and we ran to the roadside. There were thirty to forty cars and trucks. But they didn't stop or anything. They just rushed through and went straight to Aurangabad. We didn't even see Joshi."

A leading BJP man in the state attributed the failure of the yatra to the fact that there "had been no major opposition to the yatra in the state," and that there had been "insufficient press coverage, even from the Marathi press." Although the official self-image of the Sangh parivar emphasizes hard and systematic work as the key to success, the adoption of new political technologies revolving around public rituals meant for mass consumption had made the BJP crucially dependent on sustained media coverage and on the incessant production and public staging of "political events."

After the new economic policy, including liberalization, deregulation, and privatization of the public sector, had been proclaimed by the gov-

ernment in 1991, the RSS embarked on a campaign for a swadeshi
approach to economic development. The RSS published a pamphlet
listing the brand names of 326 consumer products manufactured by
multinationals and mentioned an Indian-produced alternative to each
product. The pamphlet called for a popular movement against multinationals, and called upon its members and supporters to divert their
consumption away from the products of "exploitative multinational
companies" and toward Indian-produced goods. In a central passage
in the pamphlet it was stated: "Every morning we begin the job of
cleansing our body with the help of products manufactured by these
filthy companies which have a history of exploiting poor countries of
the world."[42]

The rhetoric of swadeshi and the call for nationalist consumption
had deep resonances in modern Indian nationalism. The critique of
multinational investments and the notion of swavalambhan (self-
reliance) were borrowed from the Left and from Gandhian discourse.
RSS sarsanghachalak Deoras compared multinationals to the East India
Company, and claimed that swadeshi was but the natural continuation
of the anticolonial struggle; he called upon "patriots to shun everything foreign and prize everything swadeshi."[43] Throughout, the pamphlet employed metaphors of purity and pollution to allude to the
depurification of culture and values brought about by "modern consumerism." The pamphlet thus tried to make itself resonate with
broader historical themes of nationalist discourse and attempted to
draft the Sangh parivar's desire to control (capitalist) modernity—here
equated with economic globalization—as the natural desire of every
true patriot. The swadeshi campaign of the RSS did, however, bring
BJP into a somewhat awkward position. The party had initially welcomed the economic reforms of the Congress government, a move that
had caused disgruntlement among older RSS leaders. In the RSS fortnightly Organiser, a series of articles hammered on the Congress government as "bonded to the Worldbank" (8 March 1992); one described
multinational corporations as "imperialist designs, subjugating and en-
slaving the developing countries" (15 March 1992). At the same time,
there were fears in the BJP that the new liberal policy of Congress now
would make inroads and create sympathy in the erstwhile backbone of
the Sangh parivar constituency, the small traders and the small industrialists. (Organiser, 15 March 1992).

The BJP soon modified its pro-liberalization line in the face of pressure from the RSS to adopt a more swadeshi-oriented line. The revised
economic policy statement referred to the marginalization of India in
the global context: "India is today at the bottom of the international
pile ... an abject basket case that has to beg regularly for alms from

International agencies that treat it with disdain."[44] Likewise, the increasing gap in technology, productive power, and standard of living between India and most other Asian countries served as background for the quest for a new model. The answer to the new challenges was to develop an "Indian model," in nurturing "self-confidence and capability in consonance with our cultural mores and ethos," and in a "swadeshi of a self-confident, hardworking modern nation that can deal with the world on terms of equality."

A remarkable contradiction ran through the entire document. On the one hand, it expressed a desire to achieve national strength as fast as possible through a strong, high-tech type of capitalist growth while, on the other hand, it was woven around an equally powerful desire to control and check the consequences of such a development within a vision that elevated "cultural harmony" to be the main component of the economic strategy. Throughout the policy document this contradiction appeared as series of attacks on the regulative policies of the Congress in all fields, followed by suggestions that mainly recommended a slightly trimmed version of these same policies.

The launching of the new economic strategy of the BJP and the Sangh parivar revealed a new displacement and recasting of the older antinomy between culture and politics as strategic fields of operation. On one side stood the older generations of RSS pracharaks—highly critical toward liberalization and the prospect of India getting further entangled in global currents of trade, investment, and cultural products. On the other side stood a growing section of leaders and activists, especially in the BJP—many of them involved in private enterprises—who welcomed the break with decades of semi-planned economy, and who regarded liberalization and integration in the world market as the only viable course.

Ayodhya and Organized Communalism

The political potential of the Ramjanmabhoomi agitation and its many derivatives lay primarily in the multiple ways it engaged with the dominant discursive formations created by the postcolonial democratic revolution in India: the Nehruvian state as the embodiment of modern rational governance of the "masses" by the "educated sections"; secularism as the condensed signifier of tolerance and "communal balancing"; Indian society as dominated by an inherently tolerant Hindu culture; the moral high ground and purity of religious idioms vis-à-vis the "polluted" character of pragmatic politics; communalism as sectarian and antinational sentiments among minorities; and the continuous production and reification of communities through extension of quasi-collective rights and benefits to cultural communities through legislation, to mention but a few.

The power of the Ramjanmabhoomi agitation also resided in the intricate economy between metaphor and metonymy in its many discursive modalities. Ayodhya was made the central and highly mobile metaphor of a "lack" among the Hindus, and the Babri Masjid was made a sign of this traumatic wound in the nation and in Hindu civilization—a "lack" that could be healed through removal of Babri Masjid and construction of a Ram mandir in Ayodhya.[45] The metaphor of "lack" and its possible overcoming by the Hindu nation was imposed on an array of connotative fields—law and politics, history, religious devotion, and nationalism and gender, in order to halt the incessant sliding, differentiation, and relativization of the signification of the sacred, of political rights, of culture, of Hinduism, of national pride, and so on. In various discursive modalities, the construction of a Babri Masjid-Ramjanmabhoomi couplet—as a sign of an "original lack" (in Hindu society) and a prospective "fullness" (of the Hindu nation)—sought temporarily to reorganize the entire discursive formation of Indian society and politics.

First, Babri Masjid signified the violated rights of the Hindu majority within a paradigm of "equal rights of communities" that remains at the heart of the notion of secularism authorized by the postcolonial state. Articulated around slogans like "pseudo secularism," "pampering of minorities," and "minority appeasement," this discursive modality emerged as an important anti-Congress and anti-establishment idiom within the BJP. In this majoritarian idiom, the democratic principle of the superiority of decisions made by ad hoc majorities became displaced to be an a priori right of a pre-given majority. In a political field organized as majoritarian democracy it was easy for this discourse to become "political common sense"—as self-evident truisms about the character of power, state, and politics—not least in the urban middle classes. This majoritarian discourse was organized around metaphors that sought to infuse a sense of radical rupture: of the awakening of the dormant, hitherto silent Hindu majority, rejuvenation of the Indian nation, and the beginning of an epochal change from the old humiliating order to a new, proud, and bright future. The notion of epochal change was related to the breakdown of the Nehruvian model of planned economy, to the worldwide retreat of socialist-egalitarian rhetoric, to corrupt Congress practices favoring minorities; to stalled and slow economic development; to alliances with the communist bloc, and so on. The collapse of communism and the collapse of "Nehruism" in India at the hands of the Ramjanmabhoomi movement were thus claimed to be connected with manifestations of popular resistance elsewhere in the world to arrogant, oppressive political elites who in the name of equality and progress had perverted their societies. By ruling through "foreign ideologies" such as communism and Islam, these elites had prevented their societies from finding their true and essential cultural identity.

Hindutva, it was claimed, was the only possible road to a new, strong, developmental, and competitive Indian state, respected by the rest of the world because it was "true to itself," in Lacanian terms enjoying an (impossible) "fullness."[46] An influential producer of this discursive modality of Hindutva underlined during the 1991 election campaign that middle-class support for Hindutva stemmed less from devotion to Ram than from a persistent disgruntlement with corruption and disillusionment with Congress, and from a desire for modernity and equality with other nations in the world.[47] In this discourse designed for the political field, Ram was openly depicted as an agitational device mobilizing the masses on religious and emotional grounds, while it enabled the allegedly rational middle classes to restore the moral fiber and pride of Hindus in their own nation and culture—a pride that had allegedly been suppressed and ridiculed by Congress. BJP leaders, among them Advani, publicly announced that they were irreligious and never went to temples. They posed for the educated urban middle classes as "political Hindus" in a modern, secularized (but not secular) and nationalist sense of the term.[48]

Second, Ram was made into a metaphor of the essential Hinduness of Indian culture—a Hinduness claiming to encompass the authenticity and tolerance espoused by Gandhians as well as militant and martial traditions. Although the Ramjanmabhoomi agitation in the political field was staged as a break and a rupture in the politics of modern India, the RSS discourse on "Hindu culture" emphasized the foundational significance of Ram to the Hindu nation. The Ramjanmabhoomi agitation was staged as a modern manifestation of an ancient, irresistible cultural stream, a corporate Hindu culture. To subdue and destroy this perennial Hindu culture, Muslim invaders had to destroy the supreme symbol of national pride, the ancient mandir claimed to have existed in Ayodhya, and erect a masjid on the spot. This created

> an eternal blot on the secular face of India. . . . Hindus over the centuries have been subjected to aggression, tyranny, and indignities. Thousands of temples have been destroyed. . . . This sordid tale is too deep for tears. But Hindus don't talk of revenge or destruction of Holy places of others. We Hindus are magnimonious [sic] people—docile, gentle, godfearing, considerate for others. . . . Well, Muslims did beat Hindus time and again, not

because Hindus lacked bravery or sacrifice, but just for one reason—
Disunity.... After centuries of humiliation the Hindu's Atma [soul] has
arisen like Phoenix from the ashes. Hindus want to possess what is theirs
(Daljit Singh, columnist, *Organiser*, Deepavali Special, October 1990).

In this discursive modality, Ram was a national symbol, Hindutva signified national pride, and the removal of Babri Masjid and construction
of a Ram mandir in Ayodhya was the great symbolic purifier of "the
Hindu psyche," which would remove the "eternal blot" of humiliation
and prove the existence of a common Hindu national will. The RSS
always worked to produce this "abstract Hindu" as a united culture-as-
nationality, as a "Volk," and Ram was fielded as a superb unifying
figure in the cultural work of reconstruction on the part of the RSS. The
materiality of a "magnificent Ram mandir"—portrayed in widely circulated posters and miniature cardboard models—was meant to be a
tangible touchstone for national grandeur. But the blossoming of this
grandeur was prevented by an even more tangible and material representation of a negativity—the Babri Masjid—a negativity radicalized
by its alleged construction on the rubble of an older temple for Ram.
This now long-abandoned and "dilapidated structures," as it was
called in official discourse—as if to diminish its significance and assert
that it belonged to a bygone age of humiliation—represented the traumatic historical kernel of Hindu disunity and effeminacy that had to be
removed to produce a Hindu Volk. At the same time, the presence of
this radical negativity was the indispensable condition of possibility for
this Volk ever to exist.

It was exactly because of the significance of Babri Masjid as radical
negativity that it was of paramount importance to the Sangh parivar to
establish the historical facticity of an older temple structure beneath the
mosque.[49] This would not only lend scientific credibility to the Hindu
nationalist claim of the systematic destruction of Hindu places of worship but would also lend scientific positivity to the VHP's claim that
Ram had always been a paramount god in the Hindu pantheon, a
mythical figure symbolizing the entire Bharat. Yet this act of symbolization could neither be fully supported by "facts" nor recognized by
historical circumstances, just as the VHP's attempt to insert Babri
Masjid in a narrative of Hindu subjugation was constantly questioned
and undermined by counterarguments from the All India Babri Masjid
Action Committee (AIBMAC), from the Left, and from independent
experts. This undecidability of the Babri Masjid, in spite of its materiality, provided in turn an even stronger argument for its removal. Interestingly, whenever the VHP or BJP was challenged on the flimsy
factual evidence supporting their claims, they displaced the entire

question of the historical veracity of the preexisting Ram mandir into a question of faith and thus beyond the reach of the "rational discourse" of science, which otherwise played such a vital part in the entire attempt to rewrite history from the point of view of majoritarian communalism.

Third, Ram was employed as a metaphor for the catholicity of traditional Hindu forms of devotion and piety, depicted as a tolerance and pluralism intrinsic to Hindu culture. This discourse was mainly articulated by the Vishwa Hindu Parishad, which in partial contradiction to the BJPs "political Hindu," appealed to prospective kar sevaks on the following note:

> Shri Ram is not a political idea. It is not a historical idea. Shri Ram is the very existence of every Bharatiya. . . . As a Bharatiya you are a descendant of Shri Ram. For crores of Hindus Shri Ram is a God, an article of faith, and more real than living human beings. . . . The common man understands Ram instinctively and responds to Him positively, e.g. in the TV serial *Ramayana*. . . . The reconstruction of Shri Ram Mandir at the birth place of Lord Ram at Ayodhya is an issue of religious faith for crores of Hindus. 350,000 Shilas [bricks] were consecrated and worshipped from as many places in India now awaiting the construction of the dream Mandir. These religious feelings and fervour of millions of people, rich and poor, with different regional, lingual, caste and class-distinctions is a supreme example of unity of religious feelings amongst Hindus. . . . Such unanimity amongst the sects of Hindus and their acharyas [religious teachers] is a unique event in the history of Hindus (VHP, *Facts and Our Duty*, Bombay, n.d.).

Hindu culture, always inclusive, tolerant, and syncretic but also always lacking a clear center, a clear-cut identity, unity, and sense of cohesion, has finally come into itself, as a nation, through the Ram janmabhoomi movement, the VHP rhetoric went. Through the collective worship of Ram, posed as a latent nationalist practice, the Hindus have come together on a common platform and have made the Hindu nation manifest, not as a series of "lacks" as in the orientalist renditions but as a positivity.

With this discursive operation, the VHP tried to transgress both the classical problem of identifying a positive "core" in Hinduism and to transgress the semitizing strategies of the Hindu reform movements. The greatness of Hindu culture, according to the VHP, was exactly its antiquity, its continuity, its catholicity, and its doctrinal breadth. Hinduism is a culture, a "way of life," and not a religion organized as an institution or a set of doctrines with all the intolerance and fanaticism that implies, the VHP argument went. The Ramjanmabhoomi agitation asserted the greatness and unity of Hindu culture in the form of the multiplicity of traditions within Hinduism—its inherent "secularism," as a popular argument went. With the discourse on Ram as the paramount god in the Hindu pantheon, the VHP sought to derive, reconstruct, and superimpose a symbolic center—Ram in Ayodhya—on a large and diverse field of ritual practices. It thus sought to transform the worship of Ram from a localized and heterogeneous set of religious practices to be a symbolic expression of a supposed syncretic and inherent "unity in heterogeneity" of Hindu culture.[50] By charging Ram with national significance, the VHP could claim that even the simplest, most inconspicuous popular form of worship of local varieties, or derivations, of Ram, essentially amounted to daily affirmations of adherence to Hindu culture as such. However, unlike Renan's concept of the nation as a "daily plebiscite," VHP's cultural determinism left no room for dissent. This sliding, or reconfiguration, of the signification of ritual practices away from the sacred and onto a larger field of objectified, national culture was a crucial innovation in the politicization of Hindu symbols, which had precedents in Gandhi's notion of Ram Rajya, but indeed transformed the practices of devotion to Ram in a more militant and martial direction.[51]

In sum, this "religious" modality of the VHP's discourse was aimed at popularizing the idea of Hindus as a "people-nation" engaged in perennial conflict with alien and intolerant semitic faiths. The struggle of Ram against Ravana in the *Ramayana* epic was displaced into a struggle between Ram and the Mughal emperor Babur, the Muslim invader. The VHP's "national Hinduism" was rendered as a martial kshatriya Hinduism, depicting Ram as a warrior, a "Rambo," with bow and arrows and in heroic postures with a bare, muscular chest.[52] This was an imagery in keeping with the overall sliding in the representations of Hindus from being peaceful believers toward being assertive and aggressive men, which was always a trademark of Hindu nationalist representations. With the Ramjanmabhoomi agitation this imagery found a receptive audience among peasant castes and the masses of young uneducated and semi-educated men in cities, small towns, and villages in northern and western India.

The final layer in the Ramjanmabhoomi agitation was the discourse on the danger and demonic character of the Muslim other, both as a geographical other (Pakistan and the Muslim world), and an internal other, the Indian Muslims with extraterritorial loyalties. The sharpest edge of the entire Ram agitation, which sought to create a collective Hindu subjectivity as it spoke, lay exactly in the constant drawing of the external boundaries of the "Hindu-community-becoming-nation."

It was the Muslim otherness that by its threat(s) engendered a Hindu positivity as a self-conscious culture, blocked by the permanent "insult" of the Babri Masjid in Ayodhya; as a territorial bounded state, threatened by Pakistani aggression; as a cohesive state unity, threatened by Kashmiri separatism; as a continuous historical entity, mutilated by Muslim invasions; as an inclusive, syncretic culture, threatened by Muslim exclusiveness and proselytization; and as a modern, homogenous nation, threatened by Muslim resistance to a uniform civil legislation.

Just as it was imperative almost to fetishize the materiality of the Babri Masjid, it was imperative to essentialize the Muslim other. In this energetic and hateful modality in the Ramjanmabhoomi agitation, Muslims were depicted as essentially intolerant and unfit to live under the conditions of democracy: "Democratic and secular India has gone soft in the face of Islamic subversion. They [Muslims] use the secular pretext to strike at India's very cultural roots. . . . Muslim society here has failed to imbibe the Indian spirit. Thus secularism for their leaders is only a one way traffic, a system to promote separatism and secessionism so that they can destroy the very system ultimately" (V. P. Bhatia, *Organiser*, Republic Day Special, 1993).

Islam, this discourse suggested, was always and essentially expansive, aggressive, intolerant, and a latent threat to Hindu culture. By virtue of faith, any Muslim embodies the doctrinal inflexibility and fanaticism associated with Islam. Any Muslim, therefore, always has a capacity and propensity for violence, secrecy, and dominance. As in the writings of the older Hindutva ideologues, the tight-knit, corporate, and secretive Muslim community was assumed to be an always/already existing entity, more immediately threatening than the equally essentialized "Christian West." Alluding to the orientalist depictions of the "primitivity" of the Muslim invaders conquering the refined and peaceful agrarian Hindu civilization, the alleged resistance among Muslims to both birth control and a uniform civil code (extended to family legislation) was ascribed to the "backward," "feudal," "male-dominated" nature of the Muslim community in India. There were also more subtle allusions here to racist myths of the superior procreative powers of "primitive peoples" (Muslims), as a compensation for their lack of civilization, as against the more feeble physical frame of the more advanced and modern people (Hindus); this echoed colonial myths of the excessive sexuality and masculinity of Muslims—as against the effeminacy of Hindu men—and seemed to energize these many varieties of anti-Muslim discourse.

The demonic power of the Muslim community not only threatened, it also disorganized and divided other nations; its very existence prevented the jouissance of the Hindu nation, as it "stole the national enjoyment" and weakened Hindu identity by the fear, envy, and "perverse attraction" (*jouissance*) it engendered. The centrality of this "perverse attraction" came out earlier in the twentieth century and before as the drive to semitize and organize Hinduism. A similar trend was articulated in the obsession with the strength and determination of modern Islamic fundamentalism. "The only answer to Muslim fundamentalism is Hindu unity" (D. Singh, ibid.); "in a nutshell, Hindus and Muslims are two ideological groups and the supreme Islamic mission is to convert the Hindus, one and all. It is the ideological struggle for Hindustan, and it has grim lessons for the easygoing Hindu. As long as the Hindus do not believe in conversion it will be a oneway traffic. That only underlines the importance of a powerful Hindu resurgent movement ("A Missionary's Manifesto," ibid., Republic Day, 1990).

The obsession with fantasies about the brutality and evil ingrained in Muslims reached a rhetorical crescendo in the speeches of Sadhvi Ritambra, a young woman who from 1986 on gained a position as one of the most effective crowd pullers in the VHP, and Uma Bharati, another young woman with a meteoric rise through the VHP to the leadership of the BJP. Ritambra took the vow of sannyasa and posed as a sadvi (feminine form of sadhu) who sublimates her femininity in an immensely passionate rhetorical style in the service of the Hindu cause. Tapes with her speeches were widely circulated throughout the country, and they represented one of the clearest examples of how the discourse of Hindutva and Ram for mass consumption effectively recruited a variety of fantasies of violent Muslim threats against the everyday existence of the equally phantasmagoric notion of the "ordinary peaceful Hindu." It was Ritambra's position as an "abstract Hindu woman," yet protected by her sublimation of sexuality, that enabled her to provoke and mobilize the hurt and deprived masculinity—the lack of status, power, and access to women—of her predominantly male audience for the cause of Hindutva. Her speech was dramatic, high-pitched, intense, and without breaks. She was able to speak continuously for hours, rhythmically, in verses and rhymes navigating in a sea of mythical metaphors that all were given a strongly communal twist. While speaking she gasped, moaned, and worked herself up to what sounded like almost orgiastic climaxes at strategic points.

The favorite theme of Sadhvi Ritambra's speeches was the Muslim menace, destruction, bloodthirstiness, and brutality—epitomized in Partition, which she depicted as a "vivisection of Bharat . . . now a country without arms." Muslims were the cause of the sense of inferiority and the ridicule of the Hindu culture, the cause of latent fear of violence, of anxieties and imbalances in a broader sense. However, Ritambra went much further into connotations that referred to Muslim rape of India and Hindu women: "In Kashmir, the Hindu was a minority and was hounded out of the valley. Slogans of "Long live Pakistan" were carved with red-hot iron rods on the thighs of our Hindu daughters. . . . The state tells us Hindus to have only two or three children. After a while, they will say do not have even one. But what about those who have six wives, 30–35 children and breed like mosquitoes and flies?"[53]

One of the main attractions of Ritambra's oratory undoubtedly lay in the call for action—collective action—to overcome the weakness, impotency, and fear of the demonic, stereotyped lustful Muslim. Here was a woman—an abstract woman, that is—who challenged the Hindu man to protect Mother India and the Hindu woman, and who offered a ready-made vehicle for action, the Vishwa Hindu Parishad.

Uma Bharati, who took the sannyasa vow after rumors of a secret love affair with a leading pracharak of the BJP, was projected as an OBC leader and, as part of her public staging, adopted an even more direct, rabid, and supposedly "plebeian" anti-Muslim style than that of Ritambra. As her rhetoric goes in one of the widely circulated tapes:

> Declare without hesitation that this is a Hindu rashtra, a nation of Hindus. We have come to strengthen the immense Hindu shakti [force] into a fist. Do not display any love for your enemies. . . . The Qur'an teaches them to lie in wait for idol worshipers, to skin them alive, to stuff them in animal skins and torture them until they ask for forgiveness. . . . [We] could not teach them with words, now let us teach them with kicks. . . . Tie up your religiosity and kindness in a bundle and throw it in the Jamuna. . . . [A]ny non-Hindu who lives here does so at our mercy (Uma Bharati, election-speech, 1991).

This type of militant rhetoric coming from young women presented a double subversion of the hegemonic image of peaceful and tolerant Hindus rendered by orientalist knowledge and official ideology. One part of the message was that the "silent majority" of otherwise peaceful Hindus had lost patience with the essentially violent Muslims, and that Hindus now would show that they can fight. The other subversion was the demonstration that now even women, conventionally depicted— within the Sangh parivar as well—as more religious, tolerant, and forgiving, as quintessential mothers and Hindus, would take to a more aggressive course. The staging of Uma Bharati as a young, angry, and impatient OBC woman also played subtly on the upper-caste fear of and fascination with stereotypes of lower-caste aggressiveness. The message was that if Hindus were provoked further, the cultivation and restraint of upper-caste Hindu culture could no longer hold back and control the anger and wrath of the lower-caste Hindus vis-à-vis the Muslims.

These four discursive modalities of the Ramjanmabhoomi agitation were intermingled in various combinations, adapted to their audience and circumstances, but all revolved around the narrative of "lack" and the "exorcising" of Muslims in order to create the Hindu nation. Like other effective ideological discourses, the strength of this discourse was neither its sophistication nor its correspondence with any "social reality," but its ability to recruit widely held myths and ideological fantasies around a construction of an antagonistic and "radical evil." The power of the discourse of Hindutva also had to do with its capacity for bifurcating political and societal space, that is, building "chains of equivalence," recruiting and fixing still new differences, or floating elements, as signs of either Hinduness or a reified otherness on either side of the antagonism. The discursive power of Hindutva rested, therefore, on the perpetual extension of the political fronts it produced to encompass still new arenas and problematics. The example of the hateful campaign against the intellectual "mandarins" in Delhi showed how the inferiority complexes of the vernacular intelligentsia, along with a broader populist anti-intellectualism, were brought to bear on the Hindu-Muslim antagonism. The secular intellectuals were denounced as alienated pseudo secularists full of contempt for true Hindu culture, in stark contrast to the "organic" intellectuals supporting the Sangh parivar, allegedly in touch with an authentic, popular Hinduism. This extension of political fronts into various fields did not displace and deplete this "original" antagonism. As an adept producer of ideological forms, the Sangh parivar succeeded throughout a decade to re-impose the common symbolic center, the Ramjanmabhoomi/Babri Masjid couplet on multiple discursive forms and thus reproduce the grammar of inclusion and exclusion, of holism versus fragmentation, of "us" versus "them" in new situations, with still new ideological material.

The Demolition of Babri Masjid and After

When the BJP government came to power in Uttar Pradesh in 1991, Chief Minister Kalyan Singh said that it had come to power through a "referendum on *Mandir*," a mandate from one-third of the voters to go ahead with the construction of a Ram mandir in Ayodhya. Once in office, the BJP government became entangled in the web of legal and bureaucratic intricacies that the issue had produced, and faced the prospect of dismissal if the court orders directing a stay on any construction activity at the site were violated. Meanwhile, the VHP and the Dharma Sansad wished to push the agitation further and go ahead with the construction of the temple regardless of resistance from the BJP.

The problem for the BJP was to work its way out of a mounting dilemma between a somewhat forced compliance with the Congress central government, whose evasion of any confrontation presented a tactical problem; and on the other side the still heavier pressure from the VHP and the RSS to step up the Ramjanmabhoomi agitation. This strategic impasse in the BJP was complicated by increasing cleavages within the party between a relatively pragmatic wing represented by Advani and Vajpayee, who sought a broad constituency for Hindutva by demonstrating "clean" and competent governance in the states ruled by the BJP; and a wing led by Murli Manohar Joshi who, after his failed attempt to match Advani's stature in the party, had aligned himself still more with the ideological hardliners of agitational politics in the VHP and RSS, and the many upper-caste BJP leaders who regarded the systematic inclusion of individuals from OBC communities into the apparatus of the party as a depletion of the RSS ethos. The former group had adopted the dominant rationale and parameters of the political field in order to win political power through a mixing of agitation with a communal bent, electoral arithmethic, and selective populist governance; meanwhile, the latter group dreamt of accumulating a large mass backing through cultural transformation, which would enable it to take over the "rules of the game" in the political field altogether and impose the discourses and rationales of the Hindu nationalist movement upon it.

In a bid to conceal the internal squabbles in the larger Hindu nationalist movement, the RSS embarked in June-July 1992 on an intensive campaign for kar seva and temple construction. However, the ensuing kar seva proved disappointing to the RSS and the VHP both in size and nerve, and the RSS opted instead for a settlement with the central government, now carried out directly between VHP sadhus and the prime minister, with the RSS, personified by Rajendra Singh, the powerful RSS coordinator in north India who in 1944 became *sarsanghachalak* of the RSS, in the role of mediator.

In the following three months, the BJP kept a very low profile on the entire Ayodhya issue, gave few comments on the matter in interviews, and passed no resolutions. In October 1992 the VHP embarked on what was supposed to be a replay of the grand success of the Ram shila puja, this time as a nationwide Paduka puja, worship of thousands of copies of Ram's sandals and a collection of donations for the construction of the Ram mandir. The campaign attracted much less attention than the previous ones had, and betrayed a certain "Ayodhya fatigue" among activists.[54] It was amply clear that the Ramjanmabhoomi agitation could not go on forever, and that more tangible results had to be produced at the site in Ayodhya to keep up the momentum and political potential of the issue.

On the date when the agreed period for deliberation of the issue expired, six thousand sants and sadhu (holy men) were assembled by the VHP in Delhi in a sammelan called by the "Religious Parliament," Dharma Sansad, to discuss the Ayodhya problem. As expected, the VHP announced unilaterally that it would start kar seva on December 6 in Ayodhya, and would not stop until the temple was completed.

As the negotiations stalled in November, the BJP entered the field once again and recommended performance of a symbolic kar seva consisting of the singing of bhajans and kirtans (devotional songs and prayers) at the place where the temple construction had initially been allowed to start by Rajiv Gandhi in November 1989. The response of the Union government was hesitant, but eventually a symbolic kar seva was allowed; thousands of paramilitary troops were sent to the area to prevent the kar sevaks from physically attacking the Babri Masjid.

Seen in retrospect, it was clear that the Congress leadership had overestimated the extent to which moderate elements in BJP could influence the Sangh parivar, just as it had underestimated the inner compulsions of the Ayodhya agitation, and the determination and zeal of the VHP and RSS leadership. For the leadership of the RSS, the Ramjanmabhoomi agitation had to be concluded once and for all. The staging of an almost epic final countdown between "true Hindus" and "pseudo secularists"—as the RSS jargon had it—would also sanitize and force the "politically infested" (read: moderate) elements of the Sangh parivar back under the hegemonic control of the RSS. All over the country, activists from various branches of the Sangh parivar were now mobilized in large numbers, and some of the most able organizers were selected to be in charge of the activists in Ayodhya, in what promised to become a protracted and delicate clash of strategic rationales between the RSS and the central government. Kar sevaks were pouring into Ayodhya from all over India, while BJP leaders tried to hang on to the imbroglio by staging small yatras, starting from the famous (and disputed) temples at Kashi (Varanasi) and Mathura and headed for Ayodhya. On December 6 more than 200,000 people had assembled, ready to perform symbolic kar seva.

In the afternoon a small group of well-prepared kar sevaks started systematically to attack and demolish the Babri Masjid, guarded only by a handful of police officers under the command of the BJP state government. Some RSS and BJP leaders did for some time call upon the kar sevaks not to attack the mosque, and groups of RSS workers tried to prevent more people from entering the area. Shortly afterward, the BJP leadership left for Delhi while the firebrand orators of the VHP and the local BJP took charge of the situation. Throughout the afternoon they shouted slogans from the stage and encouraged the massive congregation of kar sevaks to go on with the demolition. As if to conceal the act and prevent documentation, journalists and photographers covering the event were chased and beaten up, and cameras and films were smashed and destroyed.[55]

The BJP cabinet in Uttar Pradesh resigned on the same afternoon, and in the evening paramilitary troops started to clear the area. The kar sevaks quickly dispersed, leaving the entire country in a state of shock. In the following days events moved very fast. BJP leaders of a more liberal mold, such as Vajpayee, appeared repentant in the press, and Advani resigned as leader of the Opposition in the Lok Sabha in response to what was widely seen as his public humiliation. Large-scale riots broke out in cities all over India. On December 8, Advani, Joshi, Ashok Singhal, and several other VHP leaders were arrested and on December 11, the RSS, VHP, and the Bajrang Dal were banned. Less than a week later, the BJP-run state governments in Madhya Pradesh, Himachal Pradesh, and Rajasthan were dismissed on the grounds that they were unable to maintain law and order and prevent riots from raging.

This sudden change in government strategy from soft accommodation to legal repression worked as an almost instant energizer of the BJP and the Sangh parivar. The RSS had clearly sensed that in spite of the government actions against the movement, the demolition of Babri Masjid had created a sort of "Hindutva wave," a wave of untrammeled pride in Hindu strength, a wave of revenge vis-à-vis the Muslim community, and a new jingoist self-confidence among broad sections of the Hindus—middle and lower classes, rural and urban. The triumphalism came out in frequent comments in this period about "teaching the minorities a lesson," "do not take on the Hindu wrath." These fragments of Hindu nationalist discourse gained enormous popularity and ubiquity, fueled by the fear of violent Muslim reactions, and a sort of collective *jouissance* organized around transgressing the norms of public utterances, around saying the "unsayable"—sensing "the real" of communal hatred and fascination floating freely. If not before, the idea of Hindu rashtra—as a sense of common "flow" of Hindu *communitas*—

lived transiently in these short days and weeks when "Ayodhya" became the common symbolic locus of the political field, before the multiple complexities of the political field again splintered the political imaginaries into their normal state of fragmentation.

The ban imposed on the RSS and VHP was unusually light compared to earlier bans. Most arrested leaders were quickly out on bail and swung back in action, giving interviews and issuing statements. In spite of the closing down of offices and financial accounts—which had been declared days before its implementation and had offered ample scope for preparation for the ban[56]—and the termination of certain public activities, such as daily shakhas, the Sangh parivar seemed almost unaffected by the very soft, almost token ban. After some initial preparations for a *jail bharo* (fill the prisons) action, and identification of "safe havens" for the RSS leadership as in 1975, it became clear that in keeping with the populist governmentality of the Congress administration this was merely a "political ban," a symbolic action to affirm the secular and democratic commitments of the Congress party.

The Disjunction of Agitational and Electoral Politics

The preceding analysis allows us to see that neither a conspirational master plan nor mere political tactics can account for the emergence of the "saffron wave." It grew out of a complex interplay between the inner tensions and logics in the Sangh parivar and the strategies these had engendered, the strategic impasse in the ruling party, and the presence of large "available" audiences in the broader political field, which made the mobilizations of various agencies of the Sangh parivar both possible and successful. The main objective of the entire Ramjanmabhoomi agitation had been to build up and expand the Sangh parivar, but not necessarily to demolish the Babri Masjid. The gradual exhaustion of the energy of the agitation in 1992 compelled the RSS to make a decisive move, and the carefully planned "spontaneous action" in Ayodhya was probably decided and planned from some time in November, when it became clear that the negotiations were stuck and that the popular mobilizations no longer produced sufficient enthusiasm.

To the VHP, the objective was to construct a powerful symbolic center in Ayodhya for its own brand of syncretic "nationalized Hinduism," but certainly also to survive as a large agitational movement. To the RSS, it was a compulsion to consolidate its growing mythical authority in the public, as well as to "cleanse" the larger movement of the pragmatism creeping in, and to reunite the movement for a greater and loftier cause by plunging it into its preferred habitat, that of agitational confrontation. For this purpose, the state governments run by the BJP and some of Advani's personal prestige had to be sacrificed.

To the BJP leaders and to the Congress government, the entire Ayodhya imbroglio was part of a tactical game of winning the upper hand in the press, in the legal battles, and in the elusive sphere of asserting leadership, credibility, and political cunning. In that game, Advani and his lieutenants were fine-tuning a host of strategies and discursive modalities—negotiations one day, radical agitational postures the next, legal intricacies the third—in order to humiliate the Congress and further expand the BJP. This methodology was, at least temporarily, defeated by the "antipolitics" of the RSS in these tense and confused months.

The demolition suddenly opened up an articulation of the mass communalism that the Sangh parivar offensive had been building up for years. This brief and intense articulation showed that elements of the Hindu nationalist discourse had filtered down and connected with a more common-sense skepticism vis-à-vis politics and politicians. The question before the BJP and the rest of the Hindu nationalist movement was at that juncture to capture this moment of ideological domination and convert it into the changes in the "the rules of the game" in the political field it desired—changes that had rarely been specified beyond the lofty declarations of *janpad*, government by the people.

An indication of the BJP's difficulties with even articulating such a new political culture was revealed during the nationwide campaign of the former chief minister of Uttar Pradesh, Kalyan Singh, who in a series of rallies in early 1993 was staged as "the hero of Ayodhya," as the man who protected the kar sevaks and resigned "voluntarily" from the "murkiness" of politics in the service of a greater cause. Interestingly, the main content of Kalyan Singh's discourse in the meetings was a long and detailed narration of the law-abiding actions of the Uttar Pradesh state government, and the injustice done toward Hindus by taking an article of faith to court. Singh did not fill in the role cast for him as a triumphant, saintly victor of noble battle elevated above the nitty gritty of politics, but appeared precisely as a politician justifying his own acts and denouncing adversaries within the larger discourse of rights and legality of government, which remains a crucial "legitimate problematic" in Indian politics.[57]

The crux of the problem seemed to be that although the BJP and the Sangh parivar had introduced a host of innovations and new idioms into the practices of agitational politics, and had set up a finespun network of committed activists all over the country, their lack of a more concrete societal vision beyond the fuzzy rhetoric of social harmony and general social conservatism also meant a lack of an alternative vision of what political practice in government and at the local level could be like. In this field, the BJP remained largely a captive of the dominant political culture of populist governmentality developed by Congress, and only added notions of the high quality of moral "character" and decency that political representatives ideally should possess, but rarely did.

The Sangh parivar had certainly changed the "economy of stances" in the political field and had also challenged several fundamental "legitimate problematics" in the political field, such as the official definition of secularism and the secular state. But this challenge only rejected secularism in its strictest sense as the separation of politics and religion, while de facto it endorsed the prevailing practice of secularism as a system of communal balancing and separation of a profane sphere of politics from a sublime sphere of culture. The edge of its majoritarian critique of "pseudo secularism" was the lack of balance in this distribution, giving undue advantages to minorities while neglecting the majority who deserved the major share of political space, rights, and resources, according to this logic. This critique obviously presupposed official secularism as it was practiced through the dominant populist governmentality of the Indian state—as selective distribution of representation, spoils, and benefits between cultural groups—and as it had settled as a dominant political episteme wherein secularism figured as a "nodal point," a condensed signifier of the (inherent) multiplicity, tolerance, and democratic character of Indian (Hindu) society, enacted through the constant symbolic representation of cultural groups. The Sangh parivar's challenge to the secular state in the 1980s was therefore, as pointed out above, founded upon a majoritarianism that Congress had already made dominant in the political field. The entire Ramjanmabhoomi agitation did not actually demolish secularism as a "legitimate problematic" but recoded it to signify in "high" political discourse what it already meant in political practice: the competitive mobilization of more or less intersecting majorities and minorities in the political sphere, combined with a certain measure of everyday coexistence along increasingly non-negotiable community boundaries.

The "saffron wave" obviously did not undermine the stability of Indian democracy to the extent that was believed in the heated climate after 6 December 1992. But it irreversibly challenged the optimistic belief that democracy in the long run harbors the growth of tolerance and humanization, and reduces the likelihood of intergroup rivalries and enmities. The intensified democratic revolution, that is, the consistent social displacements as well as upward social mobility of large social and cultural groups, and their political mobilization in the course of the 1980s, provided crucial conditions of possibility for the "saffron wave."

This intensified mobilization provided manpower and energy for the communal and xenophobic projects of Hindu nationalism—both from within the upper-caste groups who feared social displacements and from within the upwardly mobile lower-caste groups—but also for social assertion around the "Mandal formula" and the rising assertion of scheduled castes all over India. Less than a year after the euphoria following the demolition of the Babri Masjid, a part of the energy of "plebeian" assertion proliferating throughout the political field began to turn against the Hindu nationalist movement itself in the legislative assembly elections in several states in 1993.

In a somewhat larger perspective, the "saffron wave" undermined elitist forms of knowledge of a peaceful and tolerant democracy evolving under the Congress hegemony. What had emerged for all to see were the much less tantalizing contours of an immensely dynamic system of competing populisms, and Hindutva as a millenarian discourse which, at least temporarily, had been "normalized" by the structural compulsions of this larger system to become a more flexible, but no less sinister, "communal populism," oscillating between pragmatic electoral politics and high-pitched anti-Muslim agitations.

The complex ways in which the BJP's networks were involved in, and dependent upon, local configurations of power and strategic possibilities, and the various ways in which its discourse spiraled in and out of everyday practices of community and politics may be exemplified by the following account of the BJP's development and environment in Kalwa, a Mumbai suburb.

HINDUTVA AND RESPECTABILITY

Kalwa is a densely populated satellite town adjacent to Thane city, forty kilometres north of the center of Mumbai. The area was a fishing village on the brink of Thane creek inhabited by the agris—a large, landowning caste community in the coastal zone in Thane district. From the 1960s on, the area developed fast and became connected to Thane city with a bridge, and a suburban train station was built. The agris developed and sold their land, and as in other parts of Thane city they emerged as a very affluent and influential community. The first RSS shakha was opened in Kalwa in the early 1950s, and a small unit of the Jana Sangh was started a few years later by an RSS man, Shriram Kunthe, who also started a local school, Dnyana Prasarani. The shakha and the school mainly attracted children from trading and upper-caste families, whereas few agris or other communities attended the shakha. As the development of Kalwa accelerated after the early 1970s, Shiv Sena also opened one of their shakhas and attracted many young agris, and soon Shiv Sena emerged as a strong contender for power in the area. From 1981 on, the BJP started systematic work in the area, and in 1982 Datta Kamat ran for the Municipal Corporation for the first time, though unsuccessfully. The BJP's work was gradually built up throughout the 1980s. A regular office was opened, the party took up many of the urgent civic problems, such as lighting, drainage and roads, pollution from the nearby industrial area, enlargement of the narrow bridge to Thane city, and so on.

The fast and haphazard development of Kalwa in the 1960s and 1970s left the area without proper infrastructure and there was a general feeling of neglect in the area. It was felt that the considerable funds at the disposal of the wealthy Thane Municipal Corporation were either stolen by corrupt politicians or spent on huge prestigious projects in the city.

Datta Kamat has made a name for himself as a good provider of municipal funds to the area, and as a competent and uncorrupted local troubleshooter. He has provided an active environment around the BJP office, which in the evenings has become a regular meeting place for the more than fifty activists in his own municipal ward. Kamat has also started a local Ganpati mandal, Namaskar Mitra Mandal, which has become one of the largest and most active mandals in Kalwa, and another popular meeting place for young people and activists.[58] Kamat's successful projection of the BJP as a dynamic and uncorrupted force, representing and taking care of the somewhat overlooked and peripheral Kalwa vis-à-vis the Municipal Corporation, has given the party considerable goodwill in the area. Unlike central Thane, where the support for the BJP is connected to the general image and cultural activities of the Sangh parivar, the base in Kalwa is not equally dependent on the RSS. There is still only one shakha in the area, which along with the Dnyana Prasarani provides the core group of activists, but the BJP is the primary Hindu nationalist force in Kalwa.

Thane city was one of the Bombay suburbs where in the late 1960s Shiv Sena quickly developed strong support and significant representation in the Municipal Council. The organization built a network of local branches (shakhas), which provided social services, ambulance services, and a meeting place for young men in slums and middle-class areas. Shiv Sena borrowed the term *shakha* from the RSS, but although in the RSS the shakhas are sites for daily exercise and other routines, a Shiv Sena shakha is a building—often decorated as a fortress from the time of the seventeenth-century Maratha king Shivaji—that functions as a meeting hall and office for the local leaders of Shiv Sena. The organization used to be very strong in Kalwa, and there are still many activists attached to the large shakha at the central square in the area, but in the late 1980s the Shiv Sena was displaced as the dynamic organization capable of attracting young activists. This used to be one of Shiv Sena's "safest" municipal wards, but new legislation reserved it for female candidates. This created difficulties in Shiv Sena, and the political significance of the area was hence lowered somewhat in the distinctly macho atmosphere of the party.

In spite of its high-profile activism, the BJP remains marginal to the powerful patronage structures controlled and operated by the agri elite in Kalwa, through banks, real estate development, various educational and social welfare trusts, school admission boards, and so on. Due to their positions as brokers of accommodation, credit, and civic amenities, the local elite—overwhelmingly organized in Congress—has repeatedly been able to get their candidates elected for the Municipal Corporation in several of the four municipal wards in the area.

The BJP in Kalwa has been able to attract support from some lower-caste voters and a sizable chunk of the middle-class vote, disgruntled with the corruption in Congress, and uneasy with what is widely regarded as "criminalization" of Shiv Sena. The advances made by the BJP in Kalwa also reflected the gradual demographic transformations in the area. In the 1980s the number of high-rise apartment blocks expanded significantly and attracted still more upwardly mobile lower-middle-class families from the entire Mumbai region in search of a "respectable" neighborhood at an affordable cost. The BJP's brand of "respectable Hindutva" appealed more to the desired lifestyle and self-representations within this large group of newcomers than did the strong-man style of politics practiced by Shiv Sena.

The changing patterns of political loyalties in Kalwa in the early 1990s thus represented a scenario that many BJP leaders in the Mumbai region hoped would develop on a larger scale. The BJP, due to its image of middle-class respectability and a consistent and disciplined grassroots-level work, would get access to middle-class groups and constituencies previously attracted to Shiv Sena. More generally, the party hoped that it would reap the electoral benefits of the communal seed sown and nurtured by Shiv Sena. The attraction of this scenario was that it would provide a certain mass base to the BJP's cultural "cocoon" and still allow a division of labor between the two parties, which rendered the mobilization of low-income, "plebeian" groups to Shiv Sena. The cultural codes and social world of these groups still remained alien and frightening to most of the BJP activists and leaders.

POLITICAL IMAGINARIES IN SUBURBIA

As in the other areas I studied, I was interested in the interpenetration between organized political discourses and local grievances and imaginings. I tried to explore to what extent the conceptual grids generalized in the political field provided "knowledge," frames, and conceptual tools through which local conflicts were interpreted, and to what extent the local dynamics had their own logic and conceptual frames. I interviewed a cross-section of families in Kalwa with different political views, from a range of caste communities and class locations. During our conversations, I tried to probe into how these people perceived their locality and its configuration of communities; how their political imaginaries were structured; and how they felt about Hindutva, other communities, and communal stereotypes.

According to most of the families I interviewed, Kalwa was not really thought to be an integral part of Thane city, but a place of its own. Three main features, not entirely consistent, seemed to appear in most representations of Kalwa. First, it was a place dominated by agris, who owned the land and controlled business in the area. Second, Kalwa still was like a village—divided into caste hamlets, with agris as the village elite, with lower-caste slums, Muslim pockets, and so on. Third, Kalwa was mainly a middle-class area with "a cultured atmosphere," as higher-caste residents put it.

A prosperous accountant whose wife was active in Congress said: "The agris are dominant here. By money but also in politics—they are specifically in the Congress party. Manohar Sahir, Rajaram Sahir, they are brothers [in charge of the dominant bank in Kalwa], and Janardhan Gawli are all important Agri Sena leaders. . . . Gopinath Patil, another agri, is powerful here and he is involved in a bank, a consumers' society, a library, in Janata Dal, and so on. . . . Politics in Kalwa is like in a village."

A retired brahmin schoolteacher regarded the rise of the agris as a "sign of the times"—the declining value of earlier standards, loss of respect for the authority of the higher castes, and the rule of money rather than culture and education. "In terms of numbers agris are not more in numbers than other communities, but they have money—

they buy votes and people vote for them. . . . Most of the land and the buildings are owned by agris and they are in the Congress party. Some of them are intelligent and some have come up because of goondaism. Real wisdom and education has no value any more, and what really counts is the money one has."

The imagination of numbers and sizes of other communities depended on the configurations of power and status these communities were entangled in. Most of the upper-caste people and supporters of the BJP, whom I met in Kalwa believed that the agris made up more than a third of the population in Kalwa although, according to a survey I made in the area, they hardly constituted one-fifth. Similarly, the minuscule Muslim population in Kalwa (less than 5 percent according to my survey) was considered by many to be one-fourth of the population or more. Similarly, it was commonly assumed that the relatively limited share of the people in Kalwa living in *zopadpattis* (slums)—less than 20 percent—was so large that elections were decided solely on the basis of purchase of votes in these slum areas.

These inflated assessments reflected, as we saw above in Pune, the deep-running sense of insecurity vis-à-vis lower-caste communities, and the social world of the zopapattis prevailing in the middle class in larger urban areas. There was a sense of being beleaguered by these unknown, uncultured, and violent agris, who were intoxicated by their (undeserved) success, and by dirty slum dwellers. BJP supporters saw themselves as threatened by Congress's unholy alliance of the vulgar economic interests (agris), aligning themselves with the anti-national, and numerous, Muslims, jointly buying support in the slums.

The uneasiness with the questioning of caste hierarchies was, as in Pune, expressed in the transposition of brahminical notions of spirituality and culture into notions of education and modernity. A brahmin clerk who had abandoned the Sangh parivar because of its "lack of real thinking and reflection" held that brahmin leadership was "natural." "People know that you are a brahmin, and still, to be frank, an honest man would consider a brahmin to be a person to be followed—for his intelligence, his good habits and all that." To a family of kayasta prabhus, in which four brothers were retired civil servants, the assertiveness of the lower castes had meant loss of status. Their sons were rickshaw drivers and manual laborers, and the social derailment of the family was blamed on the reservation system:

Promotions are given to people who cannot read and write; in spite of the fact that I was to get promotions, I did not because another man who was junior to me and belonged to a weaker section was promoted. I lost three chances because of such a policy. [Another brother:] I can speak English fluently, but today even a graduate cannot speak English. The teachers are taken from the lower class, who do not even speak their own language properly, so how can they teach the subjects to students. . . . The government is not paying attention to the middle class. They are just trying to get votes from laborers and other uncivilized and uncultured people.

The sense of threat from an uncontrollable social world—governed by a distant, powerful elite aligned with the underworld, the lower classes, and the minorities—was a powerful feeling, which was crucial to the receptivity of BJP and RSS notions of a "controlled modernity" in the middle classes who are in search of security and respectability, anxious to defend their haven of "order and cleanliness." It was indicative of the more radical nature of the urbanization process in a rapidly expanding suburb like Kalwa that the perceived threats to the social order were experienced as acute and ubiquitous. Families from many different communities were settled in the same block, and the habitation patterns had not evolved around caste clusters, as in villages or older urban areas. Notions of class, caste, and education were collapsed into an imagined middle-class world of order, striving to expunge every trace of the "plebeian" from this world by projecting broader anxieties onto an imagined threat from slum dwellers and other "uncultured" people.

As elsewhere, one found in Kalwa general apprehension regarding the corruption of political life and a never-ending *jouissance* derived from revealing the secrets of the political world. This ostensible cynicism regarding politics actually seemed to conceal a widespread longing for some sort of belief in "dedicated leaders," "a moral force," and "men of moral stature," which would enable one to forget, and efface, the profane truth of politics. A retired civil servant expressed this peculiar *jouissance* when he recounted the widespread narrative of loss and decline that also was pronounced in Pune. "For many years there were dedicated workers in Congress, who had fought for Independence. We may have given them bad names once in a while, but morally they were far superior. . . . Today a person is selected as candidate on the basis of money and muscle power. That means that the person who is more likely to be elected will get the ticket. This is something radically wrong—even in the BJP."

The widespread image of Datta Kamat as an honest and sincere person was intimately connected to his work in the locality—work conceived as "community work" and therefore uncontaminated by politics. Kamat's greatest asset, according to many informants, including Congress supporters, was his "culture and education." But, according to an older RSS sympathiser, there was little hope of finding these in democratic politics, where governance is based on "illiterates." "Many people from the lower classes are backing the Congress, and the BJP people are a few educated people. In this country the illiterates are more and the educated the few, and that is the reason why BJP will never sweep the polls." His son believed that Hindutva could provide a regeneration of politics, because even lower-class people "have some feelings." Once the enlightened sections of the Hindus, the only true Hindus according to many of the BJP supporters, awaken the "lower class," everything will change. "Congress wins the polls because of lower-class people, but even they have some feelings—and when their suppressed feelings come out they will vote for the BJP. As Hindus their blood will boil and they will vote for the BJP."

A group of enthusiastic young BJP workers also had high hopes tht the BJP would reform and "cleanse" the "dirty" political field by introducing a "good and clean alternative." The recurrent use of metaphors circling around cleanliness in the discourse of BJP supporters obviously referred to a wider field of connotations, all vital to the "cultural narcissism" prevailing among many upper-caste and middle-class groups.

> Now people enter politics to make money and politics has a touch of gang war, and hence people get disturbed. But their approach toward the BJP is much better, and when we make people realize that they have to exercise their right to vote and elect the right person, only then politics will be smooth. . . . As a remedy for this the BJP has introduced good and clean workers to show the people that the BJP can provide a good and clean alternative. The BJP workers who were left aside by the dirty politics will be reintroduced into the national mainstream and given some position in the party.

The BJP discourse of representing the clean, the educated, and the cultured connected effectively with the generalized feeling of betrayal, and the loss of respect and order prevalent in these strata. At the same time, the paternalism inherent in this discourse, which was aimed at reconstructing the self-respect and security of the middle class by extending "values," "culture," and arousing "emotions" in the lower castes, once more testified to the limitations inherent in the BJP's strategy, and the compulsions within the party to use the only "popular idiom" it had mastered, that of communalism.

Nowhere in my field work did I find any indications that Hindutva meant anything but assertion of an extremely fuzzy Hinduness vis-à-vis a phantasmagoric construction of a Muslim threat. Although the desire to assert a larger identity obviously flowed from the complexities and pressures of a "depurified" and chaotic everyday life in the turbulence of metropolitan Mumbai, the communal consciousness, the fear of Muslims, seemed to have two main sources. First, fragments of the communal discourse of the BJP and Shiv Sena had clearly settled as stable elements of the common-sense knowledge of Muslims—especially the notion of Muslims as a "pampered minority," which had gained a popular currency and credibility reaching far beyond the actual supporters of the BJP and Shiv Sena. Second, a certain fear based on older myths of the inherent aggressiveness and power of the Muslim community seemed to prevail in a place like Kalwa. It was a fear reproduced by the actual physical and social intimacy of the two communities, combined with a virtual lack of knowledge of each other, a lack of communication, and a general lack of friendships and personal relations across the community boundaries. This situation, which resembled what one finds between caste communities in many places, tended to reproduce a sort of mythical knowledge that in itself prevented its adherents from encountering differences and complexities within the Muslim community, even where the Muslims lived virtually next door.

The "knowledge" of "pampering" was cautiously articulated by a moderate Congress man from the Jain community: "The facilities that are enjoyed by the minorities are given by the government because of its interest in them. From the beginning there was a feeling that the minorities were enjoying more facilities than they deserved. . . . Hindutva is more like a reaction among Hindus that Muslims are getting more benefits and that the government has a soft corner for them. The conversion to Islam was also noted, and the permission granted to loudspeakers for *namaz* [call to prayer]. There was a distinct feeling among Hindus that they were being dominated." The same argument was put forward, more crudely, by a retired civil servant: "The government is trying to accommodate all communities and giving several facilities to all other religions except Hindus. Why is this so ? Why should not the Hindus live with honor? We are in the majority. . . . We have given their part to them as Pakistan, and according to me they should not live here, except with the consent of Hindus."

Another construction boosting communal consciousness was the BJP's demand for a common civil code, and the dismantling of the Muslim personal law. This had been effectively combined with the widespread "knowledge" that the Muslim population was growing because of promiscuity and sexual excess. A clerk in a private company could not conceal a certain envy. "Laws for the Muslims are different and marriage laws are also not the same. Muslims have four or five wives and ten-twelve children. Only for Hindus the rule is that one should have two children. We want the same rules."

The myth of "pampering" and the many facilities allegedly given to Muslims were never specified, except for the Shah Bano case and the permission to have loudspeakers on mosques. The feeling of being dominated and displaced as Hindus was obviously, as in all true ideological causes, "undefinable." The Babri Masjid therefore served as an important example of the alleged denial of the right to be Hindu, for low and profane "political reasons," as a BJP supporter expressed it: "We feel bad because we in our country cannot build a temple for our God. We have to fight with our own people and the Congress is opposing us for political reasons—because they want the Muslim vote. . . . After the Ramjanmabhoomi issue we have to tell the people that they are Hindus. We have to tell the people that we who live in Hindustan are Hindus."

The local Muslim population was concentrated in a few areas, predominantly in Mumbra, a township adjacent to Kalwa but separated by a steep hill. In Kalwa there were only few dispersed Muslim families. A schoolteacher from Kalwa collapsed the categories of Muslims and dreaded "plebeians" in the following way:

> In Mumbra area their number is so high that it is as good as a mini-Pakistan. [In Kalwa] we are friendly to all, but only maintain relations for specific reasons. We do not interact with them on a daily basis and nor do we keep friendships with them. . . . [M]ost of the Muslims belong to the lower class and they stick to themselves. That is the reason why we don't have friendships with these people. When there was a riot last time in 1984, the Muslims were beaten up by the people very badly, and hence they did not make any moves this time [after the demolition of Babri Masjid].

It is evident that the widespread anti-Muslim sentiments and fears among many Hindus in Thane in general, and in the the BJP and Shiv Sena strongholds in particular, constitute important factors in the consolidation of a constituency for the BJP and the Sangh parivar. Communalism has effectively condensed the general feeling of loss and displacement in the middle class in the face of continued democratization and lower-caste assertion, and the frustration with politics and politicians, with a tangible and threatening Muslim enemy portrayed as the concentrated mark of impurity, the *objet petit à*, that refers to the larger chaos and "political" origin of every ostensibly stable social form.

After the Wave

In late 1993, elections were scheduled in the four states ruled by BJP governments prior to 6 December 1992. The party portrayed the election as a "referendum" on whether the Ram mandir should be built in Ayodhya, as a "mini-general election," with slogans like *Aaj panch pradesh, kal sara desh* (victory in five states today, the rest of the country tomorrow). Kalyan Singh was fielded as the "hero of Ayodhya," and he and other BJP leaders represented the demolition of Babri Masjid as the climax of the "largest national movement" in the history of India. The cost of the BJP's election campaign was estimated at approximately 250 million. rupees, much more than that of Congress.[59] The party fielded a large fleet of more than one hundred videoraths—vans and trucks carrying large video screens—a large number of video films, and advertising tailored and applied to various audiences: specific lyric versions to a rural audience, more violent and hard-hitting ones for urban youth, and even special video rickshaws that targeted housewives for special afternoon shows in residential areas. Interestingly, the BJP avoided direct references to religious or communal themes and concentrated on caricatures of a sleepy and inactive Congress prime minister, Narasimha Rao, as responsible for the general state of chaos, violence, and opening of the country to "foreigners," be they multinationals or illegal immigrants from Bangladesh. The VHP, now working at full steam under the name Virat Hindu Sangam, supported the election campaign by circulating audio and videotapes, and the RSS supported the campaign by staging thousands of meetings at which sadhus and sants asked to voters to vote for the Ram bhakts (devotees of Ram) in the BJP.

The dramatic loss of seats and of the majority in both Himachal Pradesh and Madhya Pradesh, however, marked an unexpected and unceremonial punishment of the ineffective, corrupt, and often highhanded style of administration on the part of the BJP cabinets in those two states. In Himachal Pradesh only four out of its forty-nine MLAs elected in 1990 were reelected.[60] In Madhya Pradesh the party lost more than one hundred seats and more than 5 percent of the popular vote, while Congress regained dominance in the state. There was a high degree of negative voting against the BJP administration, whose resistance to implementation of reservation policies, and whose drive against illegal encroachments on public land by slum dwellers, hawkers, and small workshops had generated enthusiasm in the urban middle class and deep resentment among urban and rural poor (Jaffrelot 1996). In Rajasthan, the BJP retained its position as the largest party in the state, and even expanded its network to the entire state (Jenkins 1994).

The most significant effect of the elections came from Uttar Pradesh, where the alliance between the Samajwadi party (SP) and the Bahujan Samaj party (BSP), drawing primarily on votes from minorities, OBCs, and scheduled castes won a slim victory over the BJP. As a succinct analysis of the electoral outcome has pointed out, however, both the major blocks enjoyed substantial support from OBC groups (while Dalits and Muslims rather massively voted for the SP-BSP combine), and a majority of voters actually favored construction of a Ram mandir in Ayodhya (Yadav 1993). Even though it lost power and seats in the state, the BJP nonetheless consolidated its position as the single largest party in the state and the heir to Congress's earlier constituencies there.

The election results demonstrated the complex stakes and expectations of voters in the fiercely competitive theater of electoral politics, and brought an end to the complacent hopes nurtured within the Sangh parivar of riding to political power on the Ayodhya issue. The "victory" in Ayodhya had, paradoxically, caused some confusion in the Hindu nationalist movement, which by then had experienced a certain "loss of the loss," that is, a "loss" of what previously had been made the condensed signifier of the Hindu "loss"—of unity, pride, political power, and so on. Although the ban on the RSS and VHP and other "injustices" done to the Hindu nationalist movement could provide, at least for a period, a new "loss," it could not rival the complexity of signification organized around the Babri Masjid. After a period of strategic reorientation, a new line of diversification of issues was adopted. Several branches of the Sangh parivar plunged jointly into a campaign against the new GATT agreement that was designed to boost international trade (the "Dunkel Draft"). Prompted by clear signals from the state elections in 1993, there was a concerted effort within the BJP to promote more OBCs, Dalits, and tribals as local leaders and contestants in elections.[61] This move caused apprehension among the more orthodox RSS leaders, but there were several signs that the RSS under the new leadership of Rajendra Singh, known as a keen observer of the complexities of the political field, began to take the rising assertiveness of OBC and Dalit groups very seriously.[62]

With the BJP scaling down its dependence on religious symbolism and steering toward a more diversified strategy in compliance with what had proved to be the rather resilient "rules of the game" in the political field, the VHP—largely unaffected by the "phony" ban imposed on the organization—emerged once again as the main carrier of the continued Hindutva movement. The more than 30,000 sadhus and religious heads organized in the Dharma Sansad emerged as an ever more active and somewhat "freebooting" organization, which on several occasions proved difficult to control for the deputed RSS pracharaks in charge of the organizational apparatus of the sansad. At a large gathering at Hardwar in April 1994, the VHP decided to step up the campaign to "liberate" the shrines in Mathura and Varanasi from "Muslim structures" allegedly imposed on them. The Dharma Sansad, however, also adopted resolutions against the Dunkel draft, against the "casteism" of OBCs(!), against "Bangladeshi infiltration," and so forth. The message was clearly that although the BJP tried to dissociate itself somewhat from the VHP and the direct involvement of sadhus in electoral politics, the VHP was not prepared to accept such a division of labor.

In the state elections in late 1994 in the southern states and in early 1995 in Maharashtra and Gujarat, the BJP seemed to recuperate at least part of its earlier electoral strength and political initiative. Given the changes that had taken place in the political field with the powerful assertion of the lower castes as a prospective and impatient constituency, and the new emphasis on social and economic issues and the liberalization of the economy, it was important for the BJP to demonstrate that it could win elections without resorting primarily to religious symbolism and the sustained power of communal antagonisms.

6

Communal Identities at the Heart of the Nation

The Normal and the Pathological

Canguilheim argued with respect to the human body that pathologies are known as deviations from notions of normality that in themselves are always/already products of contestation and historical change. Medical thought is marked by two alternating conceptions of the pathological—one locating the cause of pathology in disturbances caused by factors external to the healthy organism, another locating the cause in internal imbalances transforming an otherwise healthy function into a state of excess that damages the body. In the first case the "evil" is constructed as extrinsic, as something to be expunged, in the other case it is intrinsic, as an excess to be suppressed or controlled by other intrinsic forces (Canguilheim 1994, 321–25). Similar models of causality are at work within the social sciences, especially in debates on violence, civil strife, and xenophobias. In the classical modernization teleology of development, politics, and public life, postcolonial societies were often depicted as "incomplete." These realms were marked by traces of (abnormal) irrationality and incoherence because they were suffused with a "tradition" originating outside the edifice of the modern state and public sphere, and therefore unstable and prone to recurrent pathologies of violence and strife.

Within colonial epistemologies, communalism and sectarian violence were regarded as exaggerations of the "pathologies" of the East—the uncontrollable, deeply rooted religious sentiments that made the Orient oriental. However, communalism seemed to apply more to the "masses" than it did to the reasonable "educated sections." During the serious Hindu—Muslim riots in Bombay in August 1893, the *Times of India* observed "a disturbing and most dangerous element in the riots—that the millhands responded in large and apparently well organized gangs" (14 August 1893). On the same day the daily *Bombay Samachar* observed "the authorities will find it difficult to deal with the millhands now that they have learnt to act in concert with each other." (14 August 1893). The *Bombay Gazette* reported on the same day, however, "one gratifying circumstance in this outbreak of lawlessness is that amongst the hundreds that have been arrested, there is not a single respectable Hindu or Mahommedan." Press, police, and officials agreed that the cause of the riots was the inciting of the "lower classes" and the instigations by criminal elements, badmash, residing in the slums. Lord Harris wrote to the governor general, "It gives me pleasure to state that the rioters appeared to have included among their number only the lower classes and that the better educated sections of both communities did not take part in the disturbances" (Krishnaswamy 1966, 39). After administering a draconian and violent policing on the unruly mobs, the police commissioner decided, in keeping with the governmentality of the colonial state, to call a meeting of "representatives and respectable members of the communities" to discuss how normality could be restored and how these "respectable citizens" could control and influence "their" communities and thus limit the corrupting influence of the badmash on the lower classes (ibid., 39).

This construction of communalism as the irrational force of primitive and atavistic hatred emanating from the "masses" steeped in tradition and superstition, and easy targets for manipulators, has remained dominant within the "educated" middle classes and the political elite in India to this day, albeit in slightly changed forms.

With the advent of the sovereign nation-state born in streams of blood during Partition, communalism was constructed in similar ways as a "primitive" community feeling that now finally had been rendered obsolete and relegated to the past by the new "normality" of the Indian state, which belonged to a higher stage in history. Communal utterances and attempts to restage what now was constructed as "older forms" of communal politics were ideologically constructed as an absolute evil emerging from the "outside," that is, from the distortions inflicted by colonialism or "tradition." Communalism was now a "pathological" upsetting of the proper historical course of events, and by virtue of its divisive effects on the secular nation the issue of religious community had to be "depoliticized" and moved to the realm of culture and religion, beyond politics.

This signified not only the enactment of a new bureaucratic ethos of production of normalized citizens of the Indian state but also a strategy of national unification and political accommodation that yielded considerable dividends in the first three decades after Independence. At the political level, in the judiciary, the bureaucracy, and the new educational institutions, and in most of the national press, the new political episteme of "communal balancing" and equal respect for all religions was squarely linked to the discourse of national unity.

Communal violence did not vanish altogether, but until the late 1960s communal disturbances were so localized, scattered, and ostensibly depoliticized that they conformed with their categorization as "pathologies," that is, irrational eruptions of community enmities generated by extraordinary social tensions or by relative backwardness of an area or certain communities.[1]

The incidence of communal riots and tensions escalated throughout the 1970s, along with increasing fragmentation of the Congress party and sharpened competition in the political field. The role of warring local politicians from the ruling party and from communal organizations in organizing such riots, which often involved complicity from the lower rungs in the police and the administration, became still more evident. But in the public debate it was still possible, and plausible, to regard communal disturbances as pathologies generated by imbalances such as a distorted class formation in a backward economy, or as instigated by outsiders, such as, professional "troublemakers" in the recurrent wars between "slumlords," gangsters, and local economic interests.[2] In both constructions the body of "the people" remained an "empty signifier"—healthy, sane, and secular, provided that none of these external evils of politics, or the badmash, got access to and weakened the social fabric to the extent that "communal poison" could enter and pollute this (abstract) people.

This discourse of the intrinsic tolerance and goodness of the people was, nonetheless, founded on a basic suspicion regarding the communal consciousness and potential barbarism of the so-called "general people" not yet touched by the civilizing project of education and secular tolerance promoted by the Indian nation-state. Educated people were generally believed to possess a certain capacity for secular reasoning and tolerance, whereas this capacity was assumed to be weak or absent among uneducated people; hence the need for keeping the "venom" of communal ideology out of the body politic.

As we have seen, religious symbols and communal stereotypes began to circulate in the public realm in the 1980s. These events forced a rethinking of the entire problematic of communalism upon the political field and the academy, as it became clear that the problem of communalism could no longer be reduced to episodic pathologies. Communal riots on the scale experienced in the late 1980s and 1990s could not be viewed as occasional aberrations from an average of genuine tolerance and cohabitation of an essentially secular and tolerant people. Communal discourses obviously resonated with an array of mutual distrust and resentment between Muslims and Hindus, which continued to evolve, and were more widespread than had previously been acknowledged. The model of communalism as generated by external evils thus gave way to an understanding of communalism as an articulation of certain features within the historically produced sense of normality itself.

The most urgent questions raised by the cataclysmic events produced by the "saffron wave" was, in other words, how "communal consciousness" and the so-called "poisonous atmosphere" that precipitated riots were constructed and sustained. How "normal" was it, how was it mobilized in communal subjects capable of unspeakable and often ritualized violence, and how did it produce political subjects available for collective action and new patterns of voting?

Violence and Communal Consciousness

The key to an understanding of the complex links between communal violence and the discourses of militant nationalism lies, to my mind, in the production of nationalist and communal identities and subjectivities at the level of everyday life. We need, in other words, to analyze the identity effects engendered and shaped by everyday proximity and social relations between communities, by localized histories of violence and antagonism, and by the communal forms of "knowledge" naturalized and sedimented over longer stretches of time. One needs to recognize that communal identities are not just effects of poisoning of the people by manipulators or criminals. They are widely existing forms of subjectivity, based on broadly disseminated forms of knowledge of the other community, often originating in nationalist discourses of an earlier epoch, and amplified by the everyday forms of mutual misrecognition and suspicion that characterize the coexistence of Hindus and Muslims, as well as of caste groups, in so many places in contemporary India.

For the sake of clarity it may be useful to identify three processes that interact and overlap in complex ways in the perpetuated construction of communal identities. First, there are everyday practices of neighborliness, often marked by discrete separations and "back-to-back intimacy." The relatively limited interaction across community boundaries have historically been substantiated by patterns of settlement in separate parts of villages or urban neighborhoods; by a relative separation of economic activities that in many places has isolated Muslims in self-employed service functions, trade, and so on; and by relatively limited practices of friendship and extremely rare cases of intermarriage across the community boundaries. The limited social interaction has, as Kakar points out in an interesting study of communal violence and identities in Hyderabad, everything do with the widespread stereotypes among

Hindus concerning the "dirtiness" of Muslims. These stereotypes are intimately linked to food habits, that is, to the fact that Muslims eat beef, which Hindus believe contaminates both the body and the mind, and to the corresponding Hindu beliefs in purification through consumption of only the appropriate types of food (Kakar 1995, 138–39). An equally persistent stereotype entertained among Hindus is that of the lecherous Muslim always staring at Hindu women who, uncovered by purdah, are exposed to Muslim youths, who only await the right moment to abuse and rape them, while Muslim women are covered and inaccessible to the gaze of the Hindu man. Among Muslims, the mixed and ostensibly unorganized religious practices of Hindus and their liberal attitude to interactions among the sexes are interpreted as lack of control and unpredictability, as if Hindus are slaves of their impulses, people without moral rules and fiber, cruel and pitiless—in brief as people to be neither respected nor trusted. Another stereotype flows from the same source, namely, that of Hindu cowardice and lack of organization and firmness (contrasted to the self-images of discipline and "hardness" entertained among Muslim men). Hindus only dare to fight in groups and mobs, the myth goes among Muslims; on their own they are weak and afraid, whereas Muslims are brave, know how to fight, and never give up even when outnumbered.[3]

Second, the narratives, rumors, and sometimes experiences of riots establish the other community as the source of absolute evil and brutality. To the vast majority, such "facts" of brutality and atrocities are encountered through circulation of rumors and "wandering stories" recycled again and again (gang rape, decapitations, and Muslim poisoning of food and water), especially during times of riots, when conventional criteria of credibility and judgment seems suspended. The climate of fear during riots also engenders a paradoxical sense of fearful fascination with detailed accounts of excesses of rape and brutality committed by both sides. The proliferation of this narrative genre further demonizes the other community and further suspends the "normal" parameters of honor and humanity, thus allowing for excesses that almost match those of the rumors. Tambiah emphasizes the coexistence and paradoxical reinforcement of fear and anger during riots, which leads to mounting tension and explodes in violent excesses because this brutality is driven by a mortal fear of reprisal. As Tambiah aptly puts the frightening and immensely energizing mood of crowds: "the reverse of their sense of power is their sense of vulnerability. . . . Panic frequently leads to the disintegration of the crowd and the evaporation of the emotional ties that hold it together. . . . They go on the attack again, feeling euphoric and omnipotent, but retreat is not far behind." (Tambiah 1996, 285).

In his study, Kakar provides unique accounts of the moral economy among communal warriors in Hyderabad, the *pehlwans*—the professional wrestlers-cum-strongmen who play pivotal roles among both Muslims and Hindus in organizing attacks on the neighborhoods of the other community. The pehlwans involved in communal rioting are projected as heroes and icons who condense the martial power and prowess of the communities, while they try to uphold an older code of martial honor and conduct that forbids rape or assault on women and children. At the same time, their often deep involvement in criminalized activities and local politics undermine their elevated moral stature.[4] Kakar shows that whereas warriors and rioters on both sides take pride in being part of a straight fight against the men from the other community, and everybody uniformly condemns the killing of children and the rape of women, these actions have, nonetheless, become still more routinized parts of riots. This violence often takes ritualized forms, but the ritualization cannot completely "purify" the violent acts or neutralize the transgression, as Girard suggests (Girard 1977, 36). Although such transgressions committed by the other community serve as important reasons for retaliation, they also seem to justify similar atrocities and transgressions committed in the course of these retaliations. This, in turn perpetuates the conflict and consolidates the myths on both sides concerning the other community's cruelty and cowardly attacks on women and children.[5] These transgressions, these unspeakable and morally indefensible acts—also indefensible in the world of their perpetrators—thus remain the kernel resisting symbolization, that which is done but cannot be talked about, that kernel around which fear as well as retribution is organized.

Many of the communal riots in contemporary India, especially those occurring in what police records often term "trouble spots" with a long record of such ritualized violent encounters with the other community, do not appear as pathological parentheses in a sea of normality. They are, rather, points of condensation where the everyday knowledge, events, and interactions that may take the form of "joking relationships" or minor irritants which in themselves cannot constitute a major insult, suddenly coalesce with older myths and narratives of enmity and violence into chains of equivalence, (re-)constructing the perennial enmity and antagonism between the groups. The provoking event is often teasing girls, fighting among youths, or police brutality that in combination with a communally charged atmosphere built up over some time may ignite large-scale violence. In such areas, communal violence and enmities are regular features of their social and political organization, with local strongmen and political activists maintaining systems of organization and vigilance with predesigned roles and choreography, ready for the next confrontation, or what Brass has termed "riot systems." (Brass 1996, 12–15).

Recent experiments by police authorities with the so-called mohalla (neighborhood) committees in the western parts of India are designed in ways that strikingly resemble strategies of policing deployed a century ago in Bombay: bodies of concerned and "respectable" citizens from all communities in a neighborhood are called upon to take responsibility, to calm down sentiments, and to assist the police in taking preventive action. When the mohalla committees were initiated in Bombay in 1994, mainly individuals with education and status from the Muslim community were recruited. Among police officers it was assumed that the Muslims constituted the problem and cause of the riots—in spite of the fact that radical Hindu nationalists were instrumental in organizing the anti-Muslim pogrom in January 1993. A police officer stated frankly: "We want to generate a new leadership among the Muslims." However, as political attention faded, the committees were subtly transformed into occasional "summits" between the police and their networks of informers and friends in the localities, who now were recruited in large numbers as committee members. These were individuals involved in a variety of semilegal activities, often known as small-time "fixers" and brokers in the neighborhood, and often seeking to be recognized as prominent men in the locality.

The committees were explicitly set up in this way in order to contain communal violence, that is, to reduce it to occasional outbursts of irrational social behavior and to reduce the element of "political manipulation" that standard common sense among police officers (and many social scientists) in India hold to be the main reason behind riots. Members of political parties or local politicians were not admitted into the committees, in order to retain these committees as instruments in the hands of the police, and as police officers put it "to curb the divisive effects of partisan interests." These measures have indeed reduced the incidence of violence, but they have neither removed the mechanisms producing communal enmity nor removed the organizations and networks perpetrating this violence. On the contrary, the mohalla committees have in many ways only provided an instrument through which the police may keep order in what is known in the public as "notorious trouble spots" though a network of underworld operators. Needless to say, this well-known nexus between police and underworld is also perpetuated by the enormous flow of black money and other assets it channels and protects.[6]

The example of the mohalla committees sheds some light on how the dominant governmentality of the postcolonial state in India has in multiple ways reproduced the position of the colonial state as a "neutral arbiter" between warring communities among the "lower classes," that is, positing itself as a locus of a higher rationality outside the complexities and irrationalities of the lives of the "masses." As in the colonial period, the state seeks today to govern by authorizing and producing self-styled representatives of these communities as governable representations of "the people."[7]

This brings us to the third dimension of the complex reproduction of communal violence: the formation, organization, and dissemination of political identities around discourses on the other. One may somewhat conventionally distinguish between one form of identification of the self and the community that is derived primarily from experiences of riot situations, rumors, and daily practices, and the form of identification of the community and the nation that derives its principles of intelligibility from larger ideological constructions and political problematics of a more general nature. To understand communalism, it is crucial to scrutinize the interface between these two modes of identification, their imbrication, and especially how the generalized discourses disseminate knowledge and modes of reasoning that structure everyday practices. There are obvious differences and discrepancies between the more generalized communal and majoritarian discourse of, say, the Hindu nation and localized expressions of Hindu community and communal enmities, always circumscribed and conditioned by local circumstances. As Kakar shows in his study of the lower-caste Pardis in Hyderabad, the question of honor and the reputation of fighting skills within this community in repetitive confrontations with Muslims was inextricably linked to a long-standing strategy of earning recognition from the higher castes through a gradual sanskritization of habits and practices.

It is, however, equally clear in Kakar's study, as well as in my own material and other accounts of recent riots, that the high-profile communal discourse of the Sangh parivar has left a large number of traces in everyday discourse—new slogans, mythologies, and other discursive fragments—that have contributed in crucial ways to exacerbate tensions between Hindus and Muslims all over India. The waves of rioting between 1990 and 1992–1993 were in most parts of India rarely triggered by local circumstances but rather by the ideological fantasies and Hindu communal discourse systematically circulated and organized in the public in the preceding years.

Among Muslims the modes of identification of self and community seem in many cases to be organized around a sense of fatalistic acceptance of being caught in a marginalized position in Indian society because of an excessive obedience to religion and religious community. Social conservatism and lack of integration into the modern economy are widely recognized as important reasons for the loss of *hukumat* (ability to rule). A somewhat melancholic myth of the fall of Muslims from power and civilization is probably most pronounced in the former strongholds of Muslim rulers, as in Hyderabad, analyzed by Kakar, and Aurangabad (see Hansen 1996c, 199–202). It is probably also indicative of the frame of mind engendered by minority status that this sense of loss often is turned inward, as a punishment for not being observant enough in one's religious practices, for not having attended enough to the inner bonds that tie the community together.[8]

As in the case of Hindu communalism, Muslim communal organizations have also actively contributed to strengthen the isolationist and communalist tendencies in the Muslim community by pointing to Islamic culture and the Middle East as primary loci of identification. To many conservative Muslim leaders, integration into the economy, the educational system, and the labor market was often secondary to the attention paid to maintenance of personal law and administration of religious institutions.[9]

The question is, how can one make sense of the processes that make communal identities attractive and at times make communal violence the most plausible, and even necessary, line of action? Can one find a way between, on the one hand, a simplistic reduction that attributes the conversion of misrecognition into violence to mere manipulation, and, on the other hand, an essentialization of the divided and separate Hindu and Muslim social worlds and imaginaries?

Communal identities can obviously provide strong loci of group formation due to their radical message of a deadly threat from the other, given the generally high demand for secure and stable identities in a society marked by multiple social dislocations. Communal identities are built around a clear, strong, and threatening other whose size and might in itself bestows a sense of urgency on the communal venture and is also driven by what Girard has called "mimetic desire" (Girard 1977, 18–30).

Kakar has argued in his latest work that the particular fervor that characterizes communal identities stems from the vital religious connotations invoked by symbols that refer to "truths" and imperatives of a higher moral order, and thus allow and justify extraordinary acts of violence. The specific intensity of immersion of the individual in a collective body, a larger whole of sounds and sensory experiences, that characterizes religious processions and communal riots may also account for the extraordinary moral transgressions committed by rampaging mobs that in some cases develop from such processions (Kakar 1995, 245–49). Here, Kakar moves very close to an endorsement of the classical model of communalism as a premodern pathology, as excessive religious fervor on the part of groups and individuals exposed to "abnormal" stages in a larger societal (mal-)development; pathologies that would seem inescapable in "deeply religious" as well as developing societies like the Indian.

I would suggest instead that we regard communal violence as integral to the specific struggle for constitution of national and ethnic communities within the historically produced political field in India. The historical evolution of this field was, as I have argued, marked by mobilization around a communal antagonism so deep that one may argue that the majority of Indians who came to know themselves as political subjects did so through categories, knowledge, and stereotypes that, one way or the other and not always explicitly, were woven around communitarian symbols and related to this communal antagonism. In fact, Kakar has himself produced an indication of the extent to which the Hindu-Muslim antagonism has been naturalized and has struck deep roots in unconscious layers of the mind. In his study of spirit possession in rural north India, Kakar found that in fifteen out of twenty-eight cases the malignant spirit possessing Hindu men and women was identified as Muslim. According to the cured persons, these evil spirits had attempted to make the possessed persons eat beef, kill family members, and commit other unspeakable acts (Kakar 1990, 136–37).

The structure and psychic economy of this "communal unconscious" should, I believe, be regarded as an ideological construction similar to that of anti-Semitism and racism, and thus not strictly dependent on exposure to certain social experiences or certain specific social milieus. Among people or families who were exposed to the horrors and displacements of Partition, the communal disposition is naturally sedimented in family narratives and is often, but far from always, readily available for open enunciation. On the whole, however, the "communal unconscious" is shaped by exposure to ideological/mythical knowledge of the other rendered in tales, myths, and narratives. Like racism, it works as "ideological fantasies structuring reality," a form of disposition that shapes actions and "gut reactions," not easily susceptible to modification by arguments and evidence, and often invisible in more consciously held beliefs of an individual. The sense of fear and fascination that the display of discipline and power at Friday namaz in India or anywhere in the Muslim world evokes in many Hindus, as well as others, may be an example of how a single symbolic formation (*objet petit à*) can open an entire field of "knowledge" of Muslims and concomitant connotations that the spectator may not even not recognize as "knowing" or possessing.

Second, I would propose that communal violence be seen as a specific historical articulation of a broader logic of formation and stabilization of identities through a constitutive attempt to exorcise the other, attempts to expunge the *objet petit à*, the sign of the "lack," to expunge that "impurity" which produces subjects as "subjects of lack," organized around the ultimate impossibility of producing positive and "full" identities.[10]

As Žižek argues, the national or ethnic community is ultimately undefinable and only manifest through symbolic re-presentation.

> National identification is by definition sustained by a relationship towards the Nation qua Thing. . . . It appears to us as "our Thing" as something only accessible to us, as something "they," the others, cannot grasp, but that is nonetheless constantly menaced by "them." It appears as what gives plenitude and vivacity to our life, and yet the only way we can determine it is by resorting to different versions of an empty tautology: all we can say about it is, ultimately, that the Thing is "itself," "the real Thing," "what it really is about" and so on. . . . All we can do is to enumerate disconnected fragments of the way our community organizes its feasts, its rituals of mating, its initiation ceremonies—in short all the details by which is made visible the unique way a community *organizes its enjoyment* (Žižek 1992a, 196; italics as in original).

A nation, like other objects of ideology, is an imaginary "cause"—paradoxically produced by its effects. It only exists as long its subjects believe in it. Yet the nation can only proliferate as a mass phenomenon if crystallized around a nondiscursive kernel of social practices, such as rituals and festivals, that is, enjoyment both as fun and as pain, in brief as *jouissance*. But the nation is not identical to enjoyment as such. The nation is this "Thing" that endows this enjoyment with its meaning, its significance and its sense of purpose.

Žižek argues that the essence of the nation-community qua enjoyment can ultimately only be expressed through the narrative of its loss and impossibility, ascribing to the "other" (nation, group, community) an excessive enjoyment, which "steals our enjoyment" and prevents a community from fully enjoying its particular way of life. What is concealed by this construction of a "theft of enjoyment" is the fundamental "lack," namely, that the community never possessed what is allegedly stolen from it. Or to put it in the terms referred to above, the only "secret" of the community is that there is no substantial secret to protect, but that "it," nonetheless, belonged to us.

Hindu nationalist discourse reflects, as we saw, this paradoxical ideological structure by posing the other as Muslim or Christian—as extraterritorial by origin and loyalty. Golwalkar referred to the Hindu as "undefinable" and identified the Hindu nation only as the feeling of presence, of being one with the world, while serving the nation. The coherence and unity of the Muslim community was, on the contrary, assumed without hesitation and exaggerated into myths of "excessive enjoyment." The search for fullness as Hindus, the overcoming of the "lack" of being a full community, constitutes the national cause to Golwalkar. It was precisely only through striving, "service to the motherland," that the recuperation of the not yet fully fledged national spirit at all became possible—and hence ultimately impossible ever to realize as a self-evident positivity.

The fundamental reason behind the capacity for ethnic hatred and violence appears thus to be lack of self-esteem, lack of self-respect in a community because of its perceived lack of self-discipline and strength. The image of the strong and lustful "other" is always characterized by fascination with his excessive enjoyment. Communities always fantasize about the special and inaccessible ways in which the other enjoys life—how others have more fun—ultimately revealing to themselves ways in which they also could enjoy themselves, and their ambivalence toward these forbidden enjoyments. The inability to control the self, to discipline one's enjoyment and fantasies, and to unfold fully one's own enjoyment as part of a nation or community, institute self-hatred and a sense of castration. The community is weak, sinful, and unfulfilled. The only way to remedy this is by destroying the other, whose very presence (as threat qua temptation and fascination) weakens and prevents the inherent discipline, strength, and manliness in the community from blossoming (Žižek 1992a, 200).

Again, this seems to illuminate the ideological fantasies at the heart of Hindu nationalism. The myths of the lustful, wily, and over-enjoying Muslim with many wives and secret links to rich Arabs are widespread in India. Not that such persons actually exist out there, or are known to anyone—it is an entirely "abstract" or phantasmagoric Muslim existing as an ideological fantasy in the popular imagination among many Hindus. It is this "abstract Muslim" rather than actual physical Muslim cohabitants in a slum who is the object of intense communal hatred. Similarly, imaginings of the hedonistic Westerner—the excessive, intoxicated, and immoral consumer—is an established and fascinating other, not hated intensely, but rather somehow ambivalently admired for technical capability, while ridiculed for lack of self-control. Both represent "excess" in various forms, an excess that has to be controlled and mastered in the Hindu in order for Hindu culture to become strong, pure, and full. This is the point at which communal ideology has an elementary appeal as an ideology of control, promising to discipline the weak and undisciplined Hindu. Since excess is tantamount to fascination with the other, which causes cultural displacement and imbalance, only purification of the self can deliver the ultimate national fullness.

One finds a similar logic at play among radical Muslims, although here the "structure of othering" privileges the western other above that of the Hindu other. The West and especially practices of promiscuity and nudity among western women are often depicted as signs of moral decay, of the lack of self-respect among westerners, and a sign of the weakness of the western male and his inability "to protect his women." At the same time, these features of western culture are objects of intense fascination and preoccupation, especially as they appear through satellite TV, music, films, and advertising, and thus threaten to weaken the Muslim community by "diverting and perverting the minds of our young men," as an elderly Muslim in Bombay put it to me recently. The Muslim construction of the Hindu other often revolves around a similar contempt for, and fascination with, the more overt display of eroticism in religious art, in dress, and in contemporary Hindi movies.[11] This excessive eroticism is sometimes used to account for what is seen as the treacherous and morally degenerate status of Hindus. Every act of violence, the recurrent evidence of pro-Hindu sympathies and complicity with Hindu communal forces within the police force, and the dominance of the political realm by Hindus seem only to reinforce and add new layers to the stereotyped knowledge of the Hindus as weak and unworthy people only protected by the powers of the state.

These processes of attaining self-respect, of overcoming the fundamental "lack," are general in nature, but become problematic and antagonistic—and thus potentially violent—in situations of continuous social dislocation. To human beings experiencing social mobility, or a loss of socioeconomic and cultural status produced by urbanization or "minoritization," the issue of identity—the urge to eradicate the doubt that splits the subjects—becomes more acute than in situations of relative social stability. The receptivity to discourses of cultural purification and social harmony as enunciated by Hindu nationalism and Muslim fundamentalism are thus in a general sense made possible by the larger processes of urbanization and capitalist development. The logics of "theft of enjoyment" and recuperation of discipline and self-restraint appear as particularly relevant in periods of rapid political and cultural change, when authority and certitudes are undermined, and when enjoyment (as practices of identification, for example through public rituals) may be in short supply as well as unstable and indeterminate in their meanings and forms.

Religious festivals in urban India have become condensed displays of the problematic of the community-as-enjoyment, and of enjoyment as the expression of the national/communal "thing" that can never be fully possessed or grasped. During religious festivals, thousands of frustrated young men seek to organize their enjoyment in a literal sense and to manifest themselves momentarily, that is, to sense and enact their own communitas. This is done by noisily occupying and domesticating public spaces that are normally seen as neutral ground between the more permanently domesticated community spaces in and around streets, houses, temples, and mosques belonging to one or the other community. Religious festivals also display the co-articulation and imbrication of religious and nationalist rituals in public spaces, which has a long and specific history in the Indian subcontinent (van der Veer 1996).

It is no mere coincidence that violence so often occurs at these junctures. The frustration of being neither "full", and strong nor sufficiently manly; and the experience of the festivals as not really being the "real thing" anyway, because of lack of money, cultural restrictions on conduct, and sublimated sexual desires sometimes explodes in collective rage that is let loose on the neighborhoods of the others, as "thieves of enjoyment."

The discourse of the expunction of the Muslim other is ceaselessly circulated by Hindu nationalism. So are the myths of the excessive sexual desire of Muslims in popular discourses (four wives, too many children, easy divorces by a threefold declaration). The myths of Hindu weakness, effeminacy, and lack of discipline correspond neatly to myths of the manliness, secret organization, and corporate strength of the Muslims. To young Hindu men without steady jobs, deprived of a chance to support a family and thus deprived of essential prerequisites for proving their manliness, the Muslim other can easily become an object of intense hatred: stealing his job, stealing his pride as a man, his enjoyment of community, and his sense of the self.

Conversely, the myths among equally displaced and deprived Muslims of the inert strength, discipline, cultural superiority, and former *hukumat*—capacity for rule—in India, now suppressed and threatened by arrogant and complacent "Hindu idolators" protected by a partial state and police, provide a corresponding sense of humiliation and sense of "theft" and weakening.

To join the communal bandwagon, to attack homes and shops, to burn, kill, rape, and loot becomes a way of shedding this perceived humiliation, and a way of restoring masculinity. The well-known practices of women who distribute bangles to men who do not participate in the fighting, ridiculing them for their effeminacy, indicates that the theme of restoring masculinity through communal violence has been a central component in the communal common sense for a long time. In "popular" neighborhoods, this theme of proving ones masculinity is not necessarily couched in the oedipal metaphors that abound in more elaborate forms of Hindu nationalist discourse, but is often more directly linked to fascination with the assumed sexual power, physical strength, and martial prowess of the pehlwan warrior icons. When violence is perpetrated within such ideological registers, bodies of the enemy as well those of the perpetrators are constructed as "historical bodies," that is, condensations of the history and destiny of the community ("defense for survival") or as condensations of the spatial history of the ethnic community (when an other is caught in "our territory" this body is an alien substance "out of place"). The individual body becomes a metonymical representation of the community (Feldman 1991, 78–81).

In contemporary India, communal discourses such as those espoused by the Sangh parivar have clearly not created communal stereotypes ex nihilo, but have worked upon existing ideological fantasies and fears that they have condensed and organized into ever-new localized dyadic forms. In most cases, they have derived their energy from their often tacit promise to control the erosion and contamination of cultural values and communities in the face of capitalist development and democratic assertions, and to deliver a "modernity minus excess of enjoyment."

Communal Subjects and Political Action

Communal riots tend to harden communal antagonisms, myths, and separations, and tend to diminish the everyday interactions between the affected and adjacent communities. Riots tend, in other words, to (re-)produce their own cause and to spread varieties of rumors and narratives widely beyond affected localities and communities. In ensuing periods of relative stability and nonviolent interactions, these narratives either settle in the "communal unconscious" or are converted into important motivations for political action and mobilization. As mentioned above, rather clear correlations can be established between the occurrence of riots after 1989 and the pattern of BJP voting in many places in northern and western India. There seems, on the whole, to be strong evidence for the conclusion that the BJP's electoral fortunes remained vitally dependent on reaping the votes that grew out of the seeds of communal propaganda and campaigns sown by other agencies of the Sangh parivar.

This smooth-running argument must, however, be somewhat qualified. Evidence presented by studies over the years suggests that communal stereotypes and attitudes are widely dispersed across regions, communities, and classes; that they, indeed, vary in intensity with outbreaks of riots or public staging of communal antagonisms, but also that they are as strong or stronger in groups and sections not directly affected by riots (such as the urban middle-class groups in Pune and Thane analysed in the previous chapters), than among those directly affected. There is also persuasive evidence which suggests that communal consciousness does not always spill over into voting for parties with communal programs.[12]

The process through which communal mythologies are abstracted from their context, generalized, and hence sedimented in localized forms far beyond their place of origin is captured well by what Tambiah terms the process of nationalization and parochialization. Tambiah cites Ayodhya as the prime example of a process whereby a national issue (carefully constructed through what Tambiah would call "localization" of a conflict) "explodes like a cluster bomb in multiple context-bound ways" (Tambiah 1996, 257).

The appropriate conclusion seems to be that the Hindu nationalist movement, with innovative technologies and on a scale unprecedented in independent India, has brought communal discourses and attitudes to the fore in public arenas and in electoral politics. This has contributed to ignite an unprecedented number of communal riots, but the ideological fantasies feeding into the communal antagonism, the rising levels of public assertiveness, and the fierce competition over jobs and education have not been created by the Hindu nationalists, and certainly the more general dislocations of urbanization and modernity conditioning this entire process are not their doing. The heightened communal tension could, during certain conjunctures, help the BJP secure electoral gains or political power, which was often lost again due to administrative incompetence and the inability to convert the logic of militant agitations into credible forms of governance.

By way of returning to the starting point, I will argue that if communal consciousness and stereotypes are not a normal state, they are at least integrated parts of the social and political imaginary in many parts of India. It is only when this consciousness is articulated in communal riots, or in clear-cut communal agitations, that it appears as "pathological." The communal violence in western India in 1992–1993 betrayed not only signs of new levels of brutalization but also wider dispersion of rioting in many types of neighborhoods without any tangible local rivalry going on, and far beyond the areas marked by established "riot systems."

This development, and the reports of systematic and growing participation of women from various classes in both looting and atrocities, have in public debates been taken as a sign of the gradual "normalization" of communalism—or, in the words of Sudhir Chandra, as "an ominous portent . . . of a general lowering of the middle-class Hindu's resistance to communal violence" (Chandra 1993, 1884). To my mind, there is an element of hypocrisy in this discomfort with the ostensible "normalization" of communalism. It indicates a discomfort with the dismantling of the classical colonial and postcolonial image of communalism as pathological irrational violence between bands of (primitive) uneducated and manipulated men from the lower castes and classes.

The discomfort arises because the Hindu nationalist movement has been able to create a discourse capable of activating the "communal unconscious" among individuals who may not otherwise subscribe to its political program. This reactivation has revealed that communal consciousness is enormously widespread and exists and thrives in the middle-class society at the core of the nation, to the extent that educated men and women, believed to be good-hearted and susceptible to reason and secular practices have shown their capacity for hatred and violence. The hypocrisy, to my mind, lies in the fact that the "pathologization" of communalism into a matter for primitive, criminalized lower-caste males "outside" normal social life conceals the historical origins of communal myths and stereotypes in educated groups, always more anxious to protect status and purity.

As the Hindu nationalist mobilization in India has demonstrated, education was historically never the road to eradication of communal stereotypes and promotion of secular values, as the Nehruvian creed went, but rather the site of their production and perpetuation. A similar hypocrisy has been involved in the idealization of women as inertly peaceful and forgiving, as unilaterally victimized by riots, and never communal subjects themselves. This mythical construction has been undermined by the successful mobilization of women by the Sangh parivar and the new visibility of women during communal conflict.

If nothing else, the "saffron wave" and the widespread violence it engendered have demonstrated that the "massification" of national identities in the last decades in India has produced public enunciation of communal myths and enmities, not least within the upper-caste Hindu middle class as a reaction against the sustained political mobilization of cultural communities and cultural differences from the lower and hitherto marginalized rungs of Indian society and polity. The anger vis-à-vis the Muslims might be seen in this context as the rage against the Muslims as an *objet petit à*, the symbol that condenses a larger and more fuzzy anxiety engendered by the rising plebeian assertiveness in the postcolonial democracy in India.

An older "truth" of Indian politics and society has thus been returned to the forefront of contemporary debates, namely, that communitarian identities remain crucial and constitutive substrata of the national identity. Communalism and the violence it engenders is thus neither a "pathology" nor the antithesis of nationalism, but merely its dark underside that refuses to go away.

7

Hindu Nationalism, Democracy, and Globalization

IN THE GENERAL elections in 1996, the BJP emerged for the first time as the largest political party in India. Atal Bihari Vajpayee was given two weeks to explore the BJP's possibilities of forming a government, but the party's systematic use of communal rhetoric had antagonized both Congress and left-of-center political forces to the extent that no coalition was possible. The BJP had won the election but not power, and was soon returned to a position of "mighty marginality." Once again, the party could portray itself as the unjustly neglected voice of the true majority of Hindus. In the following months, however, the BJP leadership embarked more fully on a strategy aimed at creating alliances with a host of "regional interpreters" in a range of states where the BJP's own potential for further electoral consolidation was circumscribed by language, caste, and by the fact that the Hindu nationalist movement in the eastern and southern parts of India is strongly associated with the Hindi-speaking "cow belt." The first result of this strategy appeared in March 1997, when the alliance between the premier Sikh party, Akali Dal, and the BJP in the state of Punjab won a resounding victory in the polls for the state legislative assembly. In the following months the BJP continued this strategy, and as general elections were held in early 1998, the BJP had made electoral alliances and adjustments with a range of smaller political formations in different states—formations with constituencies based on regional sentiments or caste communities to which the BJP had no access on its own. These maneuvers enabled the BJP to strengthen its popular mandate once again, but the political price of this pragmatism was considerable. In the difficult and protracted negotiations in March 1998 leading up to the formation of a multiparty government headed by the BJP, the party had to compromise on most of the issues that had been at the heart of its campaigns for more than a decade: the imposition of a uniform civil code, the scrapping of Kashmir's special constitutional status, the construction of a Ram temple in Ayodhya, and so on. Of the BJPs high-profile themes, the only ones remaining were the tougher line toward Pakistan, the decision to set up a National Security Council, and the decision "to re-evaluate the nuclear policy and exercise the nuclear option," as was written in the "National Agenda for Governance" agreed upon by all the coalition partners in late March 1998. The decision to start the nuclear test program was taken immediately thereafter, ostensibly in an attempt by the BJP to demonstrate political will and determination on an issue that was bound to generate national enthusiasm. Given the considerable consensus on foreign policy matters, and in particular on the relations with Pakistan, from left to right in India, it was a low-risk decision in terms of its domestic political repercussions, especially as the critical reactions from western opinion and the sanctions imposed by western donors almost inevitably turned out to benefit the BJP.[1]

To conclude the arguments developed in this book, I briefly discuss here the future of Hindu nationalism from three distinct perspectives. First, I discuss how the Hindu nationalists look at the structure and practices of the Indian state, on the basis of statements, programs, and the emerging evidence of the BJP's practices of governance in Delhi as well as in certain states in India. Second, I take stock of the gradual transformation of the Hindu nationalist movement from a strictly disciplined cadre movement to a more amorphous mass movement ever more deeply entangled in the logics of the political field, and ever more confronted by the compulsions of democratic politics in India. Third, I take stock of the ambiguous but to my mind crucial desire driving the Hindu nationalists for cultural and political recognition of India and Hindu culture, and of the Hindu nationalists as the appropriate representatives of both, from powerful nations in the world.

Hindu Nationalism and Governance

Can one identify a distinctly Hindu nationalist practice of governance, or even a distinct vision of the appropriate relationship between the state and its subjects and citizens? Do this vision and these practices depart from dominant forms in contemporary India to the extent that we have reason to believe that the coming to power of the BJP will entail a restructuring of the Indian state and a curb on democracy in India? Bearing in mind the overall ideological construction of the RSS, one could expect the contours of a somewhat more centralized, authoritarian kind of relationship between state and citizens. One could expect that the RSS would mold itself as a "moral force" outside politics, while the BJP and other Hindu nationalist organizations would intervene ever more deeply into social life, seeking to impose a sense of loyalty and commitment of citizens and communities vis-à-vis the state and the cultural practices of the Hindu middle classes. As I have argued, the ideological frame of the Hindu nationalists points, at one level, toward a virtually nineteenth-century vision of the Hindu nation as a cultural-civilizational unit expressed in a centralized, uniform, and culturally homogenous nation-state with a self-reliant economy and technology and defended by a strong military force.

Many of the points of the BJP's 1996 election manifesto, and its only slightly revised manifesto in the 1998 elections—where many of the Hindutva themes were downplayed—certainly point in that direction.[2] The long-standing quest for a uniform civil code and a national register with ID cards for all Indian citizens (to detect illegal immigrants, as it is said) suggests a desire for a state with stronger capacity for surveillance.[3] The ethnic-majoritarian subtext of these proposals was clear when BJP leaders suggested in 1996 that ID cards would make it possible to differentiate between non-Hindu and Hindu immigrants. Just as Israel is the homeland for Jews all over the world, it was suggested, India should be made the "natural" homeland for Hindus, where any Hindu could freely come and settle. The implication that non-Hindu Indians did not have this "natural" entitlement to citizenship was evident, though unstated.

The demand for assertion of Indian sovereignty in Kashmir, the suggestions of barbed wire and heavy vigilance along the borders, and the quest for speeding up indigenous production of missiles and a full-fledged nuclear program indicate a desire to make India more heavily armed and, it is hoped, respected for its strength. After the nuclear tests in May 1998 and the Pakistani response, the regional "cold war" between these two countries has indeed received more international attention, and has forced the American government to rethink its strategies and alliances in South Asia.[4]

The RSS's campaigns against foreign investments in the consumer goods sector and foreign fast-food chains which are "contaminating Indian culture and food habits," and the restrictions on foreign investment to high-technology sectors ("Potato chips, no; Computer chips, yes!" as the slogan went in 1996), all seem to point toward a notion of a "patriotic capitalism." BJP strategists are fascinated by the history of self-reliance, the high rate of domestic savings, and the ostensible commitment to domestic consumption in countries like Japan and Germany. But swadeshi should not be enforced through bureaucratic regulation, they believe, but, in line with the organicist discourse of the nation-as-community, should flow from the patriotic commitment of Indians.[5]

The ambiguities of the Sangh parivar's peculiar quest for a strong nation-state combined with a pronounced distaste for the rehearsal of social splits and contradictions in the sphere of politics also manifests itself in the recurrent suggestions for a "presidential system" that would produce strong governments instead of the "instability of parliamentary democracy," as Vajpayee put it prior to the election campaign.[6] Similar ambiguities apply to the BJP's and Jana Sangh's longstanding demand for subdividing the Indian states into smaller units and regions. Although this is represented as a policy to deepen and extend democracy, it is also informed by a desire to limit the considerable power of the states, the regional sentiments, and vernacular public arenas that since the 1950s have become ever more crucial units in governance, in forging political alliances, and so on. The demand for decentralization is undoubtedly linked to the underlying agenda of strengthening the Union government and the national state.

As I have tried to show in the preceding chapters, however, the organizational practices and the techniques of political mobilization employed by most of the Hindu nationalist organizations are deeply structured by the constitutive difference between middle-class "society" and the communities of "the masses," upon which the governmentalities of the modern Indian state are founded. Judging from their political practices, Hindu nationalists do not desire to transcend this bifurcation of Indian society. On the contrary, Hindu nationalism arguably represents an attempt to renew and reinvigorate the paternalist spirit of reform, enlightened and committed leadership, and "uplift" of the masses through their gradual incorporation into the national modernity of the middle classes—visions which, as we saw in Chapter One, had their heyday in the 1950s but in some ways were also renewed by the Gandhian wave in the 1970s, and even in strangely perverted ways served to justify the authoritarian policies of order and reform pursued during the Emergency period. But this is certainly also a construction of politics that would attempt to "stem the rot of politics in our society," as BJP activists sometimes put it, and to reconstruct politics as the "virtuous vocation" it was imagined to be prior to the "plebeianization" of Indian politics, at a time when democratic politics was the pursuit of "cultured individuals" from the middle-class core of the Indian nation.

But how have these high-minded visions fared when confronted with the complexities and stratagems of the populist governmentality refined by Congress for more than a decade? As has already become evident in the short life of the BJP-led government in Delhi, coalition politics with many different partners who have specific interests and less inclination for ideological elaboration than the BJP makes it difficult to implement the "principled" policies and the new "cleanliness" in politics promised by the BJP. The BJP's experiences of coalition

government with the otherwise "like-minded" regional party Shiv
Sena in Maharashtra since 1995 has demonstrated that handling the
process of economic liberalization, as well as the question of corruption, proved to be particularly difficult.

Soon after the new cabinet in the state had been sworn in, a critical
review of a disputed power station to be built in collaboration with the
American company Enron south of Mumbai was commenced. The RSS
had earlier set up a nationwide organization, Swadeshi Jagaran Manch
(SJM), to promote the notion of swadeshi and economic nationalism.
SJM was a prominent force in the anti-Enron campaign, involving local
protests and physical confrontations at the construction site, which BJP
leaders in Maharashtra made a big issue in the elections in early 1995.
The issue at stake was whether Enron would be allowed to charge what
was claimed to be excessive electricity tariffs, and whether the previous
Congress cabinet had been bribed into forging this deal with Enron.
The Shiv Sena leadership, which unlike the RSS had always been eager
consumers of the signifiers and products of modernity, felt uncomfortable with this result.[7] Pressed by Shiv Sena, the BJP finally agreed to
resume negotiations with Enron, and in January 1996 the redrafted
project was finally approved without major amendments.[8]

In this perspective, the unbridled technological fetishism of upcoming strata of new entrepreneurs and parties like the Shiv Sena—
however philistine they may be—seem nonetheless to mark a more
radical departure from the hitherto dominant political culture of the
Indian state than the "swadeshi alternative." The mixture of a Gandhian-inspired swadeshi rhetoric thundering against "consumerism"
and a quest for a disciplining state seems to be informed by a paradoxical yearning back to the heyday of the Nehruvian state (minus socialist
rhetoric), a state that was able to assert itself in an international context
and yet protect the national culture of India because it was held together by a single party, and not constantly weakened by compromises
and the incoherence of policies that characterize competitive democratic politics.

The handling of the Enron affair seemed to indicate that the new
cabinet, like Congress governments before them, governed through
high-profile symbolic "raids," token actions and decisions—often supported by a press willing to quote ministers and officials at length—
rather than through administrative reform. On many of the vital issues
of economic policies and of the intensity and form of state regulation in
all spheres, the cabinet seems, so far, to deviate only marginally from
the practices of the preceding Congress administration. BJP ministers,
and even more so their Shiv Sena colleagues, operate largely according
to the established modalities of administration and what one may call

an "economy of loot": the channeling of resources to one's constituencies and networks of patronage, involvement in the real estate market, appropriation of government funds for private and semi-private purposes, and so on. Corruption had been one of the main targets of the campaign conducted by the BJP in Maharashtra in 1995. One of its unexpected allies became the Gandhian reformer Anna Hazare, who ran a successful, almost classical "antipolitical" campaign for austerity and moral integrity in public office. After the formation of the BJP-Shiv Sena cabinet, Hazare was invited to be a member of a high-powered committee encouraging responsible citizens to report examples of corruption. After a year, the evidence of large-scale involvement of both BJP and Shiv Sena leaders in massive corruption was overwhelming. Hazare left the committee, and the ensuing inquiry did substantial damage to the BJPs carefully built image of providing "clean government."[9]

Recent evidence from other states such as Gujarat and Rajasthan seems to indicate that the concrete "economy of politics" intrinsic to many practices of government in contemporary India is not easily controlled by the ideological edifice of the RSS, or by the "men of character" deputed to act and live in this profane world of money and power. Older RSS men attribute this to the declining quality of BJP activists, who in Maharashtra and states like Gujarat are increasingly individuals drawn from peasant and lower-caste communities and therefore, according to conservative but powerful forces in the RSS, lack the intrinsic moral and cultural fiber that can enable them to withstand the temptations of power and money.

Hindu Nationalism and Democracy

The Sangh parivar had by 1996 successfully built a large constituency, but the price has been a certain social isolation in the middle-class world in India, and a pronounced political isolation from other national parties. This isolation stemmed in no small measure from a cultural narcissism and a "cocooned" worldview within the movement, which at times have tended to produce a condescending misreading of the popular mood, or clumsy and transparent attempts to manipulate symbols.

The RSS remains deeply committed to an overall vision of control—controlling its members, its organizational family, and ultimately the entire society. This is a vision nurtured in a limited political subculture, for decades working for a long-term gradual expansion toward becoming coextensive with the entire Hindu society. As the Sangh parivar has grown increasingly into a mass movement, this vision and method have been challenged.

The imperatives of large-scale agitational politics and the BJP's entrenchment into institutionalized politics of patronage seem to affect the authority of the RSS within the Sangh parivar. Within a political subculture one could uphold the idea of directing and shaping "the masses," because the ideology and organization of most of the Hindu nationalist movement protected it from the actual anarchy and disorder of mass politics. Once the Ramjanmabhoomi agitation became a mass movement, from the late 1980s onward, sustaining this immense source of power also became imperative. Two different strategies were deployed to consolidate and further widen the popular base of the various Sangh parivar organizations: on the one hand, the movement continuously staged and reinvented new techniques of mass mobilization—seen as "the unique selling point of the party"—usually on issues with a communal bent: Kashmir, the "liberation" of Hindu shrines in Varanasi and Mathura, and in 1995 and 1996 increasingly on socioeconomic issues, swadeshi, and anti-corruption issues. This methodology remained the same, while returns were diminishing.[10] On the other hand, the mass organizations in the Sangh parivar tried to popularize themselves in order to transgress the middle-class, higher-caste cocoon within which the political subculture had so far existed. Especially for the BJP, operating within the compulsions of a political field that forced it to construct itself as a genuinely popular alternative to Congress, this consolidation predominantly took the form of promotion of a lower-caste public face of the party.

The challenge before the RSS is, hence, to cope with a new role as arbiter among an expanding array of interests and compulsions inside the movement as well as outside its own ideological and social universe. I argue that the Hindu nationalist movement faces two major obstacles to its further expansion and consolidation in Indian society. The first and most important problem is the relative isolation of the movement in social and cultural terms, confined as it is mainly to Hindu upper-caste and middle-class milieus. However dominant these milieus may be, the compulsions of electoral politics compel the BJP to transgress these social groups one way or the other. The "anti-minority" image of the BJP is also not only damaging their prospects of ever attracting support from Muslims or Dalits, it has also jeopardized the BJP's room for maneuver in the political field and is likely to be a liability for the movement, given the current trend of lower-caste assertiveness in many fields of the public culture in India. The second obstacle is the questionable inner cohesion of the larger Hindu nationalist movement—especially the relation between the RSS and an ever more powerful BJP, plagued by mounting tensions between those valuing internal discipline and ideological purity, and those who favor a more pragmatic approach to political power.

As I have argued throughout this book, the decisive breakthrough of Hindu nationalism in Indian politics and public culture took place as a systematic and unfettered mobilization of existing anti-Muslim stereotypes into a widely disseminated and popularized set of "truths" about Muslims, as what I termed a "communal common sense." The BJP began in 1994 to play down this xenophobic side of its discourse, leaving the agitation around new claims to religious sites to the now fully legalized VHP.[11] The BJP has been lingering on the issues of the "liberation" of shrines in Varanasi and Mathura which have been on and off the party's agenda several times. The temptation to make the two shrines in Uttar Pradesh new targets, in a replay of the Ramjanmabhoomi agitation, has so far been resisted, though it was deliberated at length within the party and the RSS on several occasions.[12]

The unresolved contradictions between the communal "core" in the VHP and RSS, and the BJP's repeated attempts to parade a liberal face were displayed when in 1995 Advani promised that the BJP would do its best in the future to support "the integration of Muslims into the national mainstream." Advani launched the "three Ts"—*taleem* (education), *tanzeem* (organization—under the RSS?), and *tijarat* (employment)—as the slogan for improvement of the lot of the Muslims in India. These were largely symbolic measures, a rhetoric as superficial as that addressed to the lower castes. An example of this condescension occurred when the Minorities Cell in the BJP, led by what many Muslims sarcastically refer to as the "kept Muslim pets of BJP," Arif Beg and Sikander Bakht, announced that they would initiate a translation of the Koran to Sanskrit in a move to show respect and "to make a bridge to the Muslim masses," as party spokesmen said. Given that translations of the Koran already exist in many Indian vernaculars, the translation to Sanskrit would hardly have any political impact except as a remote symbolic gesture. Besides the obvious arrogance of the suggestion in light of the desperate social situation of Muslims, the whole idea of constructing the translation of the Koran into the "sacred language of Hindus" testified more to the degree of cultural narcissism in the Hindu nationalist movement than to any commitment to dialogue with Muslims.[13]

But according to the Muslim leader of the BJP's Minority Cell in Mumbai, the BJP is not anti-Muslim; it is only against the "anti-national Muslims who don't recognize India as their Motherland." After all, M. U. Khan said, religion is not the issue, culture and the way of life are what matters: "What is Hinduism? Hinduism means the culture of India and what is that? Joint family system, respect for elders, for mothers, fathers, sisters—so we want to maintain this culture against that of other countries where there is too much freedom, where the reputation of the ladies is spoilt because they have to show their body and all . . . we just want our freedom of religion and freedom of marriage, that is all. The BJP wants to protect all that, and I tell Muslims that they have more protection with the BJP than if they oppose them."[14] The Hindu nationalist strategy vis-à-vis lower-caste groups is not dissimilar from the strategy of "controlled emancipation" administered toward women inside and around the larger movement. The growing assertiveness of the lower castes and Dalit groups is approached with a mixture of paternalist condescension and promotion of the Hindu community as *the* encompassing national community. This strategy has, however, only yielded a certain, and often transient, popular constituency when articulated in situations of communal polarization.

The BJP administration in Uttar Pradesh tried between 1991 and 1993 to combine its commitment to the Ram temple with a promotion of OBCs in the state's administration. This caused frustration in the party apparatus, dominated by individuals from upper-caste milieus, and in turn it produced a factionalism that weakened Chief Minister Kalyan Singh's authority in the BJP organization in Uttar Pradesh. The ensuing caste polarization in the state only reinforced the BJP's image as a upper-caste, middle-class party (Hasan 1996).

However, the defeat of the BJP at the hands of political parties deriving their strength from a distinctly lower-caste profile made an impression on the Hindu nationalist movement. At the celebrations of the first anniversary of the demolition of the Babri Masjid in Ayodhya in 1993, the obligatory panel of RSS and VHP leaders was flanked by two equal-sized images of Ram and Dr. Ambedkar, the pioneer spokesman and organizer of Dalits in western India. The entire theme of Hindutva was significantly downplayed, and most of the leaders were instead busy showering praise on Dr. Ambedkar and condemning the practices of untouchability.[15]

The RSS seemed, however, to have precious little to offer besides cultural nationalism bent on anti-Muslim rhetoric. The attempts to portray Dr. Ambedkar, who publicly denounced Hinduism and embraced Buddhism, as a good patriot, that is, as anti-Muslim and by implication a good Hindu in a cultural sense, were, like the courting of Muslims on symbolic issues, marked by the cultural narcissism prevailing within the movement. In speeches in Ayodhya, Ashok Singhal and several prominent VHP sadhus praised Ambedkar for resisting the tempting offers from Jinnah and the nizam of Hyderabad to let all Dalits be converted to Islam: "Instead he let his people be converted to Buddhism—a religion grown in the soil of this country. That was the Hindu in him!"[16] VHP president Ashok Singhal expressed this view even more clearly in an interview a few weeks later: "For us Hindu means all those religions which have come up from this soil of Hindustan. Dr. Ambedkar upheld the spirit of this country when he stopped the flow of Dalits into foreign religions like Christianity and Islam by propagating the ideals of Buddhism. That way he contributed greatly to the Hindu Dharma. And that is why we consider him one of the pioneers of our ideology and our movement."[17]

The attempt to recruit Ambedkar on patriotic grounds was expanded upon by claiming, almost like the Arya Samaj, the possibility of a synthesis between the heritage of Ambedkar—a fierce critic of rigid brahminical Hinduism—and the *Manusmriti*, the ancient lawbook normally regarded as an authoritative legitimization and codification of caste hierarchies: "it is absolutely wrong to interpret Manu as a man who created differences in society. . . . Manu has to be studied deeply and the wisdom of this and other *Brahma Vidyas* have to be incorporated into a new smriti [scripture]. It is here we see the importance of Dr. Ambedkar's work. His preachings would become part of a new *Manusmriti* for a modern Hindu society. In this modern society there would be no place for untouchability. The beauty of Hindu society is its infinite capacity for change. . . . The next century will be a Vedic century. The wisdom of the Vedas will no more be hidden. And we hope that our movement will create a Vedic atmosphere the world over" (ibid.).

The mounting quest for recognition by the lower castes in several places in India has since 1993 been approached with a similar condescending, socially claustrophobic, and narcissist attitude. The RSS seems to suppose that the innermost desire of individuals of the lower-caste communities is to be allowed entrance to temples, and to be magnanimously helped and assisted by "cultured people" of the upper castes, or to be included in a large consensual community, defined and led by an upper-caste vision—however modernized—of authority, tradition, ritual order, and so on.

A clear example of this was the new Ekamata yatra campaign launched by the VHP in order to target and attract Dalits and tribals. In a replay of the earlier campaign in 1982–1983, the concept was to have ten yatras from different parts of India moving toward Nagpur and finally congregating at the large memorial constructed for Ambedkar, the Ambedkar Deeksha Bhoomi, in Nagpur. The yatras did not evoke much enthusiasm among Dalits, however, and even less enthusiasm among cadres who found it difficult to engage wholeheartedly in embracing and organizing people they detested and for long had branded as "antinational." The final congregation at the Ambedkar Deeksha Bhoomi in Nagpur, scheduled to be a mass rally with thousands of people and hundreds of sants and sadhus, turned out to be a small unenthusiastic crowd who met with hostility and apprehension from bystanders and officials looking after the monument.[18] This conclusion of a large and high-profile endeavor by the VHP and RSS expressed succinctly the persistent gap in idioms, approach, and understanding between Dalits and the Hindu nationalists.

The second problem facing the Hindu nationalist movement is its own internal cohesion and discipline, always an object of pride, and a model in miniature of the vision of the morally controlled nation. As the constituencies of the BJP have grown, it is, however, no longer self-evident that the RSS family will remain the primary reference point and constituency for the party. There have been inducted into the party a large number of activists and MLAs with more superficial commitments to— or no knowledge of—the "spirit of the Sangha," as old RSS men prefer to call the distinct atmosphere inside the Hindu nationalist movement. These "newcomers" have few apprehensions vis-à-vis the economic reforms and are in this respect anathema to the "purist" advocates of discipline and swadeshi. This is in many ways indicative of a conflict between two visions of politics and modernity—one a pragmatic, procapitalist outlook committed to an often philistine notion of a "clean society," the easy life with consumer durables, and modern living; the other being an austere, ideologically pure, more socially conscientious outlook, uncomfortable with what it interprets as the brutality, fragmentation, and hedonism of the modern world. These two tendencies—*car sevaks* versus *kar sevaks*—were for a long time united by a joint communalism and a joint commitment to asserting Hindu pride. As the symbolic issues of religion and nation became less prominent items on the party's agenda, and more "profane" policy issues have come to the fore, this long-standing difference has been rearticulated (see Hansen 1998c).

The increasingly public face and political involvement of the RSS after Rajendra Singh took over as sarsanghachalak has made the question of politics and electoral strategies of the BJP more important than ever. The transformation of the RSS's relation to the BJP from one of authority to one of competition has been compounded by the de facto move of the RSS headquarters to Delhi—the city of power—where Rajendra Singh spends most of his time and makes most of his many public statements. The long-standing representation of the RSS leadership as elderly, quasi-saintly authorities residing in Nagpur, in the center of India, representing the Sangha and "Hindu society" versus the impurities of politics in Delhi, has simply crumbled. The RSS's position on political issues, on party preferences, and on electoral strategies were not previously an object of public knowledge, but transpired in private consultations when the party's leadership collectively went to Nagpur to "seek guidance." This arrangement has now given way to Rajendra Singh's frequent press briefings on a host of issues. In March 1996, the RSS held a national convention in Lucknow, the All India Pratinidhi Sabha, where pracharaks from the entire country met to discuss political issues and the situation of the country. The event was widely covered by the press, and the convention requested Indian voters, through the press, to vote for parties supporting Hindutva and for those who wished to defend the country "against the plunder of multinational companies."[19] After the formation of the BJP-led government in 1998 and in connection with the nuclear tests, the RSS and its leadership have gone public in an unprecedented fashion with countless statements and interviews on global TV networks, and soon.

The hardened line of the RSS was provoked by the much-debated defection scandal in Gujarat, where the powerful president of the BJP in Gujarat, Shankersinh Waghela, staged an open rebellion against the party leadership. Waghela was all that the RSS would otherwise trust: a long-standing RSS man from a Rajput family, elected for the Jana Sangh and involved in the build-up of the BJP to its present position as the dominant party in Gujarat. Nevertheless, rivalries over the dramatically increased stakes after the party came to power in the state between the chief minister, Kesubhai Patel, and Waghela suddenly erupted. The central leadership tried to reduce the whole affair to a "personality clash," but the crucial issue at stake was whether the RSS should have a decisive say in nominations for posts and tickets within the BJP. The logics of competitive politics proved this time to be stronger than the "controls" of the RSS. Waghela left the BJP in August 1996, formed his own party, and succeeded shortly afterward, with generous help from Congress and other forces, in toppling the BJP government and acquiring the post of chief minister in the state.

Hindu Nationalism and Globalization

India's spiritual superiority and the universal mission of Hindu philosophy to be a "spiritual corrective" to a materialistic and overly rationalist western world remains a cornerstone in contemporary Hindu nationalism. Golwalkar portrayed Hindus as the "first thought-givers to the world ... long before the so-called modern age the seers and savants of this land had delved deeply into the vital questions. The ideal of human unity, of a world free from all traces of conflict and misery has stirred our hearts since times immemorial"(Golwalkar 1966, 2). Hindus posess the recipe for redemption and may provide what Golwalkar calls the "last refuge for mankind."

In a more recent RSS publication, H. V. Sheshadri, a high-ranking leader in the RSS, argues that true nationalism in India as elsewhere is "a stage for self-expansion of the human spirit ... it is a journey towards selflessness; towards sacrifice for the larger whole ... nationalism is a stage of human evolution" (Sheshadri 1991, 7) . Thus, the world mission of the Hindus—to save the world from military aggression, excessive consumerism, and exploitation of natural resources—can only be achieved through a proper development of Hindu nationalism in India itself.[20]

In another recent RSS publication, the assertion of the Hindu culture as a path beyond and ahead of capitalism and the collapsed communism, by virtue of its ancient wisdom, which always upheld the holism and ecological respect that scientists in the West are only now discovering, is taken further. The twenty-first century will be a "Hindu century" based on holism and integralism. The publication goes on to state, "The proclamation that the coming century will be the Hindu century is thus not a chimera, but based on hard facts, analysis and prospects."[21]

In 1995, a professor based in Canada, Arvind Sharma, drafted a "Hindu Declaration of Universal Human Rights" claimed to be derived from classical Sanskrit texts. This declaration was promoted and much praised in a number of RSS publications. Contrary to the "Western idea of rights" based on law and morality, Sharma argued that the Hindu Declaration is "identified with truth and provided with an ontological and therefore even more firm basis by being rooted in an *isness* rather than an *oughtness."* Interestingly, the Hindu Declaration arrives at virtually the same points as those enshrined, for instance, in the UN charter, pertaining to freedom of religion; rights to protection from state power, to pursuit of happiness, and to legal protection. But the Declaration also contains a right to "freedom from pollution"(!) and a freedom of unrestricted movement across all countries.[22]

Although ostensibly fashioned as proud assertions of a self-conscious Hindu creed challenging western universalism and positing an alternative to western thought, these formulations clearly express a quest for recognition in a public sphere dominated by secular and liberal discourses. This quest is posed in a somewhat paradoxical way. On the one hand, Hindu nationalist ideologues criticize "western philosophy" for producing inhuman, disharmonious societies. In so doing it reproduces critiques of rationality and exploitation that have accompanied modernity and organized capitalism from the outset. On the other hand, RSS publications are full of references to modern science ("based on hard facts and analysis"), and utterances of more or less famous western scientists, historians, and politicians, who either praise India or criticize certain features of western society. This almost constitutive sense of peripherality and concomitant desire to construct Hindu nationalism and its organizations as a pathbreaking and original, sincere, rational, and powerful force clearly articulate the Hindu nationalist movement's attempt to overcome the long-standing sense of alienation from the political and social establishment in Indian society.

An example of this craving for recognition that constitutes such a powerful force within the Hindu nationalist movement was the depiction in an RSS mouthpiece of how the BJP's 1996 election manifesto was received. Under the headline "The Critics are Left Gasping," it was said that the BJP's election manifesto had left all its critics "dazzled and stunned." The article emphasized that even the *Times of India*, often regarded as an epitome of the liberal establishment in India, was "full of admiration for the manifesto . . . that is modern, daring and forward looking—as no other manifesto in the past." It was also reported how the American ambassador had repeatedly invited BJP leaders for consultations, and how BJP leaders were constantly approached by "foreign countries." The report quotes a list of these, clearly compiled according to their relative importance—beginning with France and Germany, ending with Nepal and Uzbekistan.[23]

The Hindu nationalist claim of a universal mission of Hindu culture is not new to Indian nationalism, as we saw in Chapter 2. But in the Hindu nationalist appellation, this alternative universalism is no longer a critique of the West, but rather part of a strategy to invigorate and stabilize a modernizing national project through a disciplined and corporatist cultural nationalism that can earn India recognition and equality (with the West and other nations) through assertion of difference. The more the Hindus assert their deep and constitutive difference vis-à-vis the West, and the more Hindu civilization asserts the purity of its alternative universalism and its civilization, the more it will be respected and admired, the reasoning goes. However, in order to gain respect from the West and from its neighbors, India must be strong and powerful. The Hindu nationalists are not the only forces in India that wish to see India a well-armed major world power. Some of the largest and most decisive arms purchases and strategies of technological upgrading took place in India during the tenure of Rajiv Gandhi as prime minister. However, it is no coincidence that the most decisive steps toward going nuclear, and toward extracting the recognition from the West that the western world was unwilling to extend on its own, were taken by the Hindu nationalists.

The ambiguities in this quest for equality through difference vis-à-vis the "big" western others, and the quest for being integrated and respected within a globalized modernity have come out even more clearly in the writings of BJP ideologue Jay Dubashi. On one occasion Dubashi took issue with the charge that Hindu nationalists were fascists because they wanted to remove the Babri Masjid. The removal of the mosque only amounted to what every people does when shedding the chains of oppression, he argued, removing the monuments of their former colonizers or old regimes. He compared the Babri Masjid to a hypothetical monument built by a victorious Hitler in Trafalgar Square. In this regard there is no "oriental exception" at work: "Well, India is *not* different. Hindus are *not* different. If it is right to pull down Hitler columns in England, and Lenin Mausoleums in Russia, I see nothing wrong in pulling down a Babar monument in Ayodhya. He had no business to be in India just like Hitler would have no business to be in London."[24] The national rights of Indians were here asserted in unequivocally universalist terms, as the universal right of a sovereign people to determine its own future and to get rid of oppressors and their symbols. This, argued Dubashi, was nothing special to Hindus. It is a historical right of all people to get rid of rulers who do not belong to their land.

In an earlier piece, Dubashi went even further, and linked the surge of Hindu nationalism and the crumbling hegemony of the Nehruvian state to the transformations in Eastern Europe and epochal changes on a global scale: "On the very same day the first brick of the Ram Shila foundation was being laid at Ayodhya, the Berliners were removing bricks from the Berlin Wall. While a temple was going up in Ayodhya, a communist temple was being demolished five thousand miles away in Europe. If this is not history, I do not know what is. . . . [These events] mark the end of the post Nehru era and the beginning of a truly national era in India on the one hand, and the end of the post communist era and the beginning of a truly democratic era in Europe on the other. History has rejected Nehru in India and also overthrown communism in Europe."[25] The underlying point was obviously that India was neither different from other nations nor peripheral in the world. India partakes in the universal history on a par with other nations; the larger historical developments in the world unfold in India as elsewhere; and the Indian people contribute, as much as other peoples, to global transformations.

In 1995, the RSS sarsanghachalak Rajendra Singh went on a trip to the West (none of the former sarsanghachalaks had ever gone abroad) and returned disillusioned with the stagnation in India, lamenting the "lack of work culture" and the rampant corruption: "Why is this country lagging behind, this India which was once hailed as the Golden Bird before foreign invaders discovered her. . . . Beggars, that is what we have been reduced to, because we are going with begging bowls before the affluent nations and multinationals."[26]

The confluence of the broader stratagems of "patriotic consumption," national purity, and anti-Muslim stereotypes were condensed in a single incident in 1995, when the BJP government in Delhi decided to close down a Kentucky Fried Chicken outlet on the somewhat flimsy grounds that flies had been recovered inside the kitchen premises of the restaurant. This rather selective hygienic zeal on part of the BJP administration, which had previously led to closure of some abattoirs run owned by Muslims in Delhi, obviously employed, if only by implication, notions of impurity and amorality of "foreign" as well as Muslim food habits, and broader themes of erosion of the Hindu family and the Hindu home. The entire problematic of consumption of "western" products—food, styles of dress, electronic gadgets, music—is among Hindu nationalists (and others) linked to the contamination, exposure, and corruption of the body, especially the female body. Foreign food, and fast food, erode the Hindu family and the observance of ingredients and procedures of cooking food; western styles of dress—skirts, jeans, t-shirts, swimsuits, and so on—exposes the female body to the indecent gaze of the male, including the particularly obscene gaze of the Muslim and lower-caste male; western music and films incite indecent emotions and indecent patterns of intermingling between the sexes. The male body and the power assumed to derive from the control of desire and retention of semen are equally weakened by constant exposure to explicitly erotic imagery and narratives; and the access to electronic implements, motorized transport, and excessive watching of TV divert the attention away from healthier and more physically demanding pursuits, and so on.

The BJP and other parts of the Hindu nationalist movement do not, however, take any clear stand against foreign investments as such. Instead they seem to negotiate an ambivalent attitude through a peculiar double discourse that at one level expresses self-depreciation: "we are reduced to beggars," "we lack work culture," and simultaneously articulates a tough self-assertion: "India will not allow itself to be raped," "the West needs India." This discourse caters to the middle classes and upcoming social strata who are anxious not to loose self-respect in the maelstroms of modern urban culture while, at the same time, they are painfully aware of their own peripherality in the world.

Hindu nationalism desires, in the spirit of romantic orientalism, to be recognized through deep and constitutive differences while respected as the "civilizational other" of the West. Hindu nationalism of the 1980s and 1990s presented the Indian Muslims as embodying the undecidability and ambivalence which prevented the clarity of counterposition between a Hindu East and the (rational) West to become clear. With this blot of impurity, this undecidability, and, more importantly, this abyss of fear in its womb, the Hindu nation cannot emerge, the Hindu nationalists argued. As we saw, Muslims were constructed as a polyvalent signifier of premodernity, of the uncivilized but vigorous, of excessive sexuality, excessive patriarchy, and excessive population growth threatening to destroy the country. If the abstract notion of a "true Hindu culture" that cannot emerge is the "empty signifier," that undefinable and unreachable object of desire which keeps in place the entire Hindu nationalist construction of Hindus as a properly civilized people of the world on a par with the British or the Germans, then the complex signifier of the Muslim is certainly its most crucial precondition.

Hindu nationalism shares the worship of strength, masculinity, cultural purity, and radical difference from the West with many other forms of radical or religious nationalism in other parts of the world. One can argue that it grows out of the same unease with modernity, the same discrepancy between imaginings of the modern world and the sense in which it is experienced as that of the petty *bazaris* and schoolteachers supporting the Muslim Brotherhood in Egypt, the angry young men in Algeria, or the lower-middle-class clerks supporting the Refah party in Turkey.

However, the sheer size, breadth, and duration of the Hindu nationalist movement in India, and the multiple ways in which it has fused modern democratic discourse and liberal, middle-class values and horizons with violent xenophobic rhetoric and symbols, should remind us that Hindu nationalism, and other similar forces, are far from "abnormal," or the not yet modern, "outside" of a democratic and modern world order. On the contrary, these movements are driven by a desire to abandon the location assigned to them as exotic or irrational peripheries at the lower steps of the global evolutionary ladder. Through internal cultural purification and moral discipline and awakening, they want to arrive as national, sovereign modernities—as "lights onto themselves"—and thus be recognized as respected members of that elusive global "comity of nations" that remains the most sublime object of desire among even the most parochial nationalists anywhere.

Democracy and Xenophobias in India

Has the Indian democracy been weakened by the BJP's expansion over the last decade and its recent formation of the central government in New Delhi? Is this only the beginning of a gradual Hindu nationalist penetration of the public administration, the judiciary, the military, and the press that over time may constrict democratic procedures, and encourage a more heavy-handed line toward public protests, social movements, and others who are critical of the government or just oppose economic and social exploitation? These are the questions being asked by many citizens in India, concerned with what Congressmen and the substantial Left movement in India have for decades called the "fascism" of the RSS and the Hindu nationalist movement.[27] Throughout this work I have presented evidence and arguments that in many ways support the conclusion that the RSS represents a kind of "swadeshi fascism" decisively vernacularized and shaped by modern Indian colonial and postcolonial history. The political utility of this label notwithstanding, however, I feel, that such an analysis tends to isolate the evil and to simplify the matter too much, that is, to identify the Hindu nationalist movement as the culprit, the enemy of democracy, and so on, and hence to posit other political actors or social forces as truly "secular" or "democratic." To my mind, the advent of Hindu nationalism forces us to ask larger and more uncomfortable questions.

As I have shown throughout, there are indeed strong authoritarian tendencies in the RSS and its affiliates, and there is little doubt that the RSS is pressing for recruiting as many of the right "men of character" for key posts in the bureaucracy as possible. There is little doubt that the BJP's road to power has ridden over the dead bodies of thousands of innocent Muslims; and there is no doubt that strong forces within the movement and in the BJP's sizeable constituency among bureaucrats, commercial strata, and officers would like to see India as a much stronger, less democratic, and more repressive state that could provide security, labor, and the pleasant sides of modern life to the elite and the middle class.

But we need to realize that this authoritarian trend, this uneasiness with a democracy that creates disorder, is an uneasiness that has arisen historically whenever the "masses" have stepped out of their predesigned roles as recipients and consumers of government policies and political rhetoric. As I have argued, the bifurcation of public culture and the strictures on political practices have been evident in governance and political discourse throughout much of this century and is constitutive for both democracy and nationalism in India. Powerful planners and technocrats have for decades regarded democracy as a necessary evil, just as the commitment to democratic procedure, to encouragement of broader political participation, and to secular practices do not have any glorious history in the Congress party. There has been a constituency for Hindu majoritarianism and heavy-handed technocratic governance in Congress as well as in the urban middle class for decades. Mrs. Gandhi addressed this constituency when she promised to create order and deliver cleanliness and discipline during the Emergency between 1975 and 1977. Heavy-handed and brutal methods have continuously been deployed in dealing with "insurgencies" and "terrorism," and the mentality, organization, and daily practices of the police forces and other security forces in India constitute a real source of fear and worry among ordinary Indians, that is, those who do not belong to "respectable society." Anyone following letters to the editor in Indian newspapers will soon realize that a major part of them come from "respectable" citizens calling for more prompt and disciplined action from the authorities in order to deal with public hygiene, squatters, congestion, pollution, immorality, declining standards in education, and so on.

It has been central to the BJP's success that it has put itself in a position where it could credibly enunciate both a discourse of Hindu majoritarianism (which is older and wider than the RSS) and this broader constituency for "strong governance" and public order fed by the sense of decay and "plebeianization" of the public culture in India. We should not forget, however, that even the electoral constituency of Hindu nationalism is limited to 25 percent of the popular vote, which amounts to a mere 15 to 16 percent of the adult population in India. However influential and well-educated much of this constituency is, it still has to work within a democratic political system and a political culture it cannot control, but to whose compulsions and logics the Hindu nationalists have to adapt themselves in terms of discourse, electoral alliances, the framing of policies, and the ever more pronounced anti-incumbency tendency that makes most governments at state or central levels lose power during elections. The Hindu nationalists also have to consolidate themselves within contemporary Indian society, which is more pluralist than ever, where the right to stage a local protest, to vote, and to demand certain entitlements from those in power have become integral to popular cultures. Contemporary India is also more regionalized than ever; regional languages are important in the public culture, regional political parties grow in importance, and the state level has over the years become an ever more important arena for distribution of both financial and symbolic resources, now including the competition to attract foreign investments.

This increasing pluralization of Indian society testifies to the centrality of the political field and democratization in the Indian experience of modernity. And it testifies that even though democratic institutions may be feeble, endangered, and at times nonfunctional, the social effects of democracy and the democratic revolution form a much larger, more amorphous, and chaotic process beyond the control of political parties or the state. The Hindu nationalist movement, arguably the most authoritarian movement ever in power in the country, has come to power at a time when the prospects for actually imposing cultural homogeneity, political unity, and uniform governance on the country as a whole have never been bleaker. The fact that the Hindu nationalists are facing this paradoxical situation undoubtedly makes the future of democratic governance in India somewhat more certain than it would otherwise appear.

Notes

Introduction

1. *Asian Age*, 2 June 1998.
2. Interview with activists of the RSS-sponsored Swadeshi Jagaran Manch, an organization campaigning against multinational investments in India, in Mumbai, 15 February 1997.

Chapter 1

1. To Laclau, "the political" occupies "the role of what we can call an ontology of the social . . . [which] consist[s] only in the sedimented forms of a power that has blurred the traces of its own contingency" (Laclau 1996, 103).
2. The argument on the gap between power and legitimacy is in part inspired by Ernesto Laclau's argument on the "impossibility of society"; that is, the impossibility of society as an always/already integrated whole. The construction of society, Laclau argues, is an always existing political project that, due to the fundamentally conflictual constitution of the social, can never be fully achieved (Laclau 1990, 89–93). Societies are the fragmented and temporary effects of competing strategies of power and legitimacy (Laclau 1994, 17–23).
3. James Scott has argued that hegemonies are fundamentally illegitimate within the horizons of peasant consciousness because the subordinates live through different discourses and in different ontologies. Scott claims that peasants' everyday transgressions of rules are tantamount to a de facto and wholesale negation of the dominant discourse (Scott 1985). I find it more plausible to understand everyday forms of resistance and transgressions as "distributional fights" within the logic of the hegemonic discourse, or between competing patrons or dominant groups.
4. The notion of contingency in a philosophical sense does not mean that social forms are random products of pure accident. On the contrary, it presupposes constant attempts at creating and naturalizing an order. Contingency is that residue and inherent instability that threatens this endeavor: "Contingency is not the negative other side of necessity, but the element of impurity which deforms and hinders its full constitution" (Laclau 1990, 27).
5. See Foucault's remarks on "subjugated" and local knowledges in Foucault 1980a, and 1980b. See also John Ransom's recent attempt to systematize Foucault's rather scattered remarks on "resistance," protest, and the limits of discipline (Ransom 1997, 101–53).
6. Talking about genealogy as an analytical strategy, Foucault seems to imply the possibility of recuperating the self when he writes that the task of genealogy is to "separate out, from the contingency that has made us what we

are, the possibility of no longer being, doing or thinking what we are, do, or think" (Foucault 1984a, 46).

7. This is the apt phrase used by Sudipta Kaviraj about the over extension of what he calls the "Tocquevillean thesis," making democracy into the master logic of all societal tranformations of modernity (Kaviraj 1997b).

8. Discourses can be seen as linguistic and material practices that establish meaning through differential relations between their constitutive moments. These differential moments are always unstable because no single articulation of difference can exhaust the range of possible meanings of given a symbol or discursive construction.

9. The particular economy between metonymy and metaphor was outlined by Lacan in a lecture entitled "Metaphor and Metonymy II" (Lacan 1993, 222–31). Jacques-Alain Miller elaborated this into the "logic of the signifier" central to later elaborations of Lacanian thought by Zizek and Laclau. To Miller, the signifier is a symptom of the (constitutive) negativity of the "real," which has opened a space of representation of the real through signifiers that "stand in" and substitute for the real. This "original" metaphorical substitution, trying to bridge the gap between that which "is" and the names we give to it, opens to the logic of incessant sliding of signification—the endless play on meanings and words in order to say and grasp the real that we never can come to represent fully (Miller 1966, 39–51).

10. By political interest I mean the specific strategic imperatives and desires that flow from the location of a given political actor in the political field. To my mind, interests do exist, not as properties of the individual but as properties of historically specific social fields.

11. Mahmoud Mamdani makes a similar "anti-culturalist" argument concerning the colonial construction of modern forms of governance and, hence, structures of modern political identities (Mamdani 1996).

12. The centrality of colonial governmentality in shaping communalism and knowledge of communities was originally pointed out by Bernard S. Cohn (Cohn 1987, 224–55). Later the concept of enumeration was developed imaginatively by Sudipta Kaviraj in his account of the transformation of communities from "fuzzy" precolonial entities to "enumerated" entities with precise boundaries in the colonial period and after (Kaviraj 1992).

13. In a review of Gyanendra Pandey's book, *The Construction of Communalism in North India* (Pandey 1990), Dipankar Gupta points out that Pandey seems to infer that communities in the precolonial era lived in a state of more harmonious "fuzzy" boundaries. Gupta argues that religious identities probably were rather clear at that time, at supralocal levels as well, but were not at stake as crucial sources of legitimacy in the public realm (Gupta 1993). Community identities were in this period neither aggregated in larger abstract "cultures" (imbued with rights in the modern sense), nor were they a central stake in the political and public realm, where notions of legitimacy and representation (of people, communities, or cultures) had not yet been introduced in their modern form.

14. As early as the 1860s the Indian Muslim elite started a range of educational institutions and reform movements that sought to retrieve what they saw

as the lost unity among Indian Muslims, and to substitute for the lost aura of princely rule a new modern spirit of community. Aligarh College (1876); the reform madrasa in Deoband, U.P. (1867); the Nizamiya Madrasa at the old center of Islamic learning, Firangi Mahal, in Lucknow in 1906; and not least Aligarh Muslim University (1898) became important centers in the growing drive toward cultural reform and modern organization of the Indian Muslim community (see Robinson 1975; Brass 1975; Hasan 1991; Lelyveld 1978).

15. One of the many ironies in the meticulous enumeration of the colonial subjects arose in 1911, when the census director, E. A. Gait, decided to adopt a more rigorous method of determining the correct classification of persons: namely, to ask the local census supervisors to collect locally used criteria for who was considered a Hindu. The result was bewildering as "a quarter of the persons classed as Hindus deny the supremacy of Brahmans, a quarter do not worship the great Hindu gods, . . . a half do not regard cremation as obligatory, and two-fifths eat beef" (*Census of India 1911*, vol. 1, 116). The census findings caused a storm of protests from Hindu nationalists, and as the government found the results impractical(!) the effort was abandoned (Muralidharan 1994, 26).

16. Ordinary people encountered classifications and objectifications in, for example, recruitment for the colonial army, where certain communities were given preference, and even more significantly in encounters with the legal institutions. As pointed out in great detail by Marc Galanter, the notion of South Asian society as fundamentally compartmentalized into mutually exclusionary groups was a cornerstone in colonial legal conceptions and practices. Colonial subjects thus came to know themselves as equal before the law as communities rather than as individuals (Galanter 1989, 101–83).

17. In a study of the local incidents of Hindu-Muslim clashes during the cow protection movement in the Bhojpuri region, Pandey shows that the popular mobilization had a lot to do with upper castes trying to consolidate their position in a situation of unstable hierarchies, and lower caste communities trying to win recognition and higher status by demonstrating their commitment to "Hinduness" (Pandey 1990, 158–201). Though obviously pointing to local complexities in communal mobilization, Pandey's example also demonstrates that the very notion of a "Hindu community" had become a powerful signifier in local processes of identification.

18. It is my contention that local cultural horizons cannot always be regarded as the ultimate arbiters of meaning, as historicist reasoning will hold. Doxa and social practices are always incomplete and full of cracks and inconsistencies that render them, rather, open to modification and new strategies of domination. The market of ideological interpretations is, in other words, one of the least free markets in existence. Consumers of such interpretations choose among available options not of their own choice, rather than on the basis of what their social practices might render more logical or functional.

19. This discursive and political strategy was applied by a host of early Indian reformers and so-called moderates from Rammahoun Roy and Surendranath Bannerjea in Bengal, to Justice M. G. Ranade and Gopal Krishna Gokhale in western India.

20. Like most other nationalist leaders, Gandhi found any upsetting of the essentially paternalist relation between the middle-class world of the enlightened leadership and the masses objectionable. His unique position derived from straddling these two worlds, not from collapsing them, and from being ennobled, in the eyes of his middle-class constituency, by his voluntary and fearless immersion in the world of the masses. At a more pragmatic level, Gandhi also feared that landed interests would turn against the national movement if he supported rebellious peasants (see, for instance, Pandey 1988).

21. The eighteenth century saw in German-speaking areas the emergence of the so-called *Polizeiwissenschafft*, or Cameralism, in the meaning of "prudent governance" that enhanced the overall happiness of both ruler and subjects (see Pasquino 1991).

22. This basic text of nationalism was long regarded as a *kampfschrifft* (militant text) of German chauvinism (it was distributed in enormous quantities to German soldiers in the trenches in World War I), but may also, as Balibar has shown, be read as a universalization of the nation and nationalism to a transcendental principle of human life. Fichte had also developed some of his visions of a modern nation-state in his *Der geschlossene Handelsstaat* (The Closed Commercial State) from 1800 (Fichte 1977).

23. The popular franchise was at this point only extended to 2.7 percent of the population. The real breakthrough appeared with the Government of India Act of 1935 which, after years of deliberation in shifting franchise committees, allowed an expansion of the franchise for provincial elections on the basis of educational qualifications, to comprise 10 percent of the population (30.1 million). The franchise was in the following years further extended, and in 1946 was estimated to include 40 million voters. For an account of this development see Chiriyankandath 1992a.

24. The Khilafat movement was started in 1919 by Muslim leaders demanding the restitution of the caliphate of the Ottoman sultanate, which had been defeated by the allied forces in World War I and forced to make large concessions in the Middle East. Gandhi approved of the movement, and merged the large-scale Non-Cooperation movement from 1920 onward with the Khilafat mobilization. Combined, these two movements created an unprecedented level of political activity, mass mobilization, and unrest in the entire subcontinent from 1919 to 1922. In Punjab, the movement provoked another round of Hindu-Muslim competition as Hindu nationalist campaigns for conversions (*shuddhi*) and organization of Hindus (*sangathan*) provoked Muslim equivalents in the field of religious propagation and conversion (*tabligh*) and community organization (*tanzim*) (Minault 1982, 192–212).

25. The literature on Gandhi is vast and varied. Some of the best interpretations of Gandhi's political practice may be found in Judith Brown's work (1972 and 1977). Gandhi's philosophy is interpreted by Bhikhu Parekh (1989), and, from different viewpoints, by Partha Chatterjee (1986), and Ashis Nandy (1983).

26. See Mamdani 1996, 37–108. Potter reports that only a total of six hundred British officers worked in the Indian Civil Service, the apex administrative cadre, all over India in 1946. By 1952 the number was down to three. The pro-

portion of British personnel was negligible at the lower rungs of bureaucracy, though more concentrated in the military and the security forces (Potter 1987, 130–50).

27. The notion of "cunning" is taken from de Certeau's analysis of the tactics of ordinary people, or "everyman" in de Certeau's terms, against ostensibly unassailable powers; the use of *la perrugue*, that is, the use of tools and materials for other purposes than intended; and so on (de Certeau 1984, 24–28).

28. The Emergency period is for a variety of reasons still "a white spot" on the map of research on India. One of the few exceptions is Emma Tarlo's brilliant exploration of the "banality of evil" involved in the massive sterilization-cum-slum clearance programs in Delhi in this period (Tarlo 1998).

29. Nehru actually shared a good deal of Gandhi's belief in the village as the original unit of Indian history, and wrote that "the village [still] holds together by some invisible link and all memories revive. It should be possible to take advantage of these age-old traditions" (Nehru 1980, 536).

30. This banning of parties from the panchayat structure did not last. On the contrary, the local political arenas became ever more important, and from the 1970s on the panchayat structure became in many Indian states a crucial arena for the emergence of new strata of leaders and politicians from the large peasant communities.

31. Government prose such as the *Report of the Study Group on the Welfare of the Weaker Sections of the Village Community*, 1961, and writings of Gandhians such as J. P. Narayan, Vinoba Bhave, and academics involved in the community development schemes, abound with exhortations to their middle-class audience regarding the importance of "moral change," of "the obligations of the educated to set examples for the masses."

Chapter 2

1. See Laclau's excellent argument for revitalizing the theory of ideology (1996b, 201–20).

2. Lacan was deeply influenced by Alexander Kojéve's interpretation of Hegel's master-slave dialectic and the notion of desire as the need for *Annerkennung*, for self-realization, self-constitution, and fullness (see Lacan 1989, 308–13, and Kojéve 1969, 45–55).

3. Parrhesia is the term Foucault uses for the courageous act of disrupting dominant discourses, thereby opening a new space for another truth to emerge, not a discursive truth but rather a "truth of the self," an authenticity of the courageous performer of this "eruptive truth-speaking" (see Ransom 1997, 162–67).

4. Žižek extends this argument to the extreme ritualization, repetition, and celebration of form, characteristic of highly stylized and choreographed expressions of ideology found most extremely in fascism and various forms of Stalinism. The appeal of the "spirit of sacrifice" and the demands of unconditional obedience do not lie in the remote gratifications that are offered, but in the existential security bestowed by the rituals themselves, in the pleasure of being able "to continue to walk straight in one direction." Yet the emptiness

and lack of meaning of such a perverse and profane pleasure (what Lacan calls *jouissance*) must be concealed by loftier goals such as service of the people, the Divine, and so on (Žižek 1989, 81–84).

5. Enjoyment refers in Lacan's usage to a paradoxical pleasure, or fascination, derived from the encounter with something unknown, disturbing, or undefinable that generates curiosity and attraction. Enjoyment is, in other words, that which eludes reason and explanation, but which, nevertheless, is "in us more than ourselves," that is, the urge to posses a "wholeness." Enjoyment thus correlates with Lacan's notion of the desire to explore the boundaries of what we are, what we can know about our own constitutive impossibility (ibid., 87–120).

6. This line of reasoning is parallel to Zygmunt Bauman's idea of the stranger as the destabilizing element who reveals the fragility of the social order and of social identities constituted between friends and foes, and thus becomes the object of intense hatred (Bauman 1991, 53–75).

7. As Peter van der Veer argues, the notion of the ideal brahmin was born out of the long-standing orientalist/Indological textual classification of the brahmin as a "god on earth," an ascetic world renouncer with little resemblance of the actual complexities of the practices of brahminical priesthood in various parts of India (van der Veer 1989, 67–71).

8. As David Ludden has pointed out, orientalist knowledge was not just a body of knowledge making itself available to colonial rule but also provided data and knowledge employed in critiques of colonialism; it is also employed in contemporary strategies of governance in modern India (Ludden 1993).

9. Schlegel also produced the (in)famous distinction between "dead," that is, mimetic and mixed languages (such as French and English), and dynamic languages, the original, self-born languages that contained the real potential for authentic expression (such as Sanskrit and German). This thesis was central to German nationalism and the theory of Aryan languages as *Ursprache*, which engendered a considerable interest in indology in Germany in the nineteenth century. Twentieth-century German orientalism was also involved in the construction of the theories of the Aryan *Urheim* during the Nazi period (Pollock 1993).

10. See Kaviraj 1995b for a profound exploration of this tension.

11. In her new study of Vivekananda, Shamita Basu concludes: "Democratizing religion, distinguishing it from priestcraft and emphasizing the historicist character of religious ideas compatible with the contemporary spiritual culture, Vivekananda made religious discourse open to rational analysis, and spiritual realization an exclusively subjective affair. At the same time, it also became an important text on national history" (Basu 1997, 188).

12. I owe this point to Partha Chatterjee, who pointed out to me that praise of the purity of the people originates in the nineteenth-century Bengali Renaissance, and is to be found subsequently in pluralist as well as communal depictions of Indian culture, the national spirit, and so on (see also Chatterjee 1992).

13. In his historical treatise *Rise of Maratha Power* (Ranade 1961), Ranade developed the parallels between the European Reformation and the bhakti cults of Deccan. Ranade believed that the bhakti rebellion against brahminical domi-

nance, like the protestant rebellion against papism, had unleashed new energies and creativities (Kumar 1968, 289–93).

14. Swami Dayananda rejected the view that Europe had developed because of its egalitarianism. On the contrary, the strength of the West stemmed from "education of boys and girls, they educate themselves . . . and they devote their body, soul and wealth to the well-being of their country. . . . These Europeans are very dutiful and well disciplined" (Saraswati 1960, 550).

15. The nineteenth century saw a measure of "classicization" of South Asian Islam wherein the allegedly purer, scriptural Wahhabi reform movement sought to purge the widespread local syncretized modes of worship of Sufi saints (*pīrs*), with their emphasis on healing, the sanctity of the saint's body, and large festivals with orgiastic elements. However, these elements continued to play a prominent role in the practices of "popular" Islam. The reform wave of the twentieth century was, like the Wahhabi movement, anti-Sufi and "classicizing," but more political and nationalist (van der Veer 1994, 56–77).

16. The systematic use of Urdu written in Persian-Arabic script in schools for Muslim children and youth only commenced from the mid-nineteenth century, in an effort toward general education of Muslims jointly promoted by segments of the Muslim elite and the colonial administration. For the emerging nationalist elite among the Muslims, Urdu became a means of producing a single syndicated "Muslim community." Prior to this initiative, Muslim boys had been taught Arabic and Persian in the madrasas (Koran schools) for religious instruction, and the bulk of high literary works had for centuries been written in Persian (see Brass 1975; and 1979, and Robinson 1974). As David Lelyveld has pointed out, the notion of an original unified Hindi-Urdu language destroyed by communal bigotry is probably an invention of a certain slightly idealizing secular historiography. The linguistic diversity of north India prior to colonial rule was more complex, and the issues of script and writing were confined to the miniscule literate segment of precolonial societies (Lelyveld 1993).

17. Kenneth Jones notes that the nonbrahmin profile of the Arya Samaj helped the movement to win a considerable base in areas where brahmin literati were traditionally weakly represented, such as the urban Hindu merchant communities in Punjab, and the rural areas of Punjab and United Provinces, where the Jat peasantry was dominant (Jones 1976, 52–70).

18. For an argument along these lines, see Zavos 1996. See also Tucker 1970.

19. Lajpat Rai 1980, 2. Lajpat Rai argued that Shivaji was the ultimate emblem of the Hindu warrior, which has to be rediscovered by the weak and effeminized Hindus. "If our Muslim brethren call us cowards they are justified in taunting us," he wrote (ibid., 10).

20. This commitment was expressed in very clear terms by Bipin Chandra Pal in a speech to the Young Men's Mahomedan Association in Calcutta in 1907. Pal hailed the contributions of Islamic culture to India—jurisprudence, rationalism, equality—and called for India to become a "federated nation" (Pal 1958, 42–57).

21. The generally cooperative attitude of the Muslim elite vis-à-vis the colonial power began to erode as Britain turned against the Ottoman empire in the Balkan Wars and World War I. The more radical Muslims collected funds for

relief work among "Muslim brethren" affected by British imperialism, even as the growing popularity among Hindus of the movement for swaraj as well as the mushrooming Hindu movements and initiatives made it clear that continued cooperation with the British would isolate the Muslim elite and make it vulnerable to the rising Hindu assertiveness. The Lucknow Pact in 1916 must be seen in this light (Minault 1982, 45–64).

22. Pradeep Datta has discussed the impact on public opinion and "common sense" in Calcutta and parts of north India of a book entitled *Hindus—A Dying Race*, as well as some pamphlets, by a U. N. Mukherji, published in 1909–1911. Mukherji argued in a sharply communal vein that Muslims, with their multiple wives and "primitive" procreative capacity, would outnumber Hindus in a few decades. Mukherji was also active in the debate surrounding the Gait circular concerning the authorized definition of Hindus in 1911 (see Chapter 1), where he strongly opposed the proposition that Hindus could be seen as made up of multiple communities. Datta shows convincingly how most of the tropes, themes, and myths circulated in contemporary Hindu nationalist discourse were already active in Mukherji's work, and that the not always conspicuous circulation of such discursive structures reproduce a "communal common sense" through the decades (Datta 1993).

23. Mazzini was a "big hit" in India throughout the latter half of the nineteenth century. Translation of his writings into several Indian languages played a major role in the formation of nationalist ideology. Bipin Chandra Pal, Lala Lajpat Rai, and Bal Gargadhar Tilak, as well as Savarkar, were deeply influenced by Mazzini (for an analysis of Savarkar's praise of Mazzini and Garibaldi, and his suggestion that their relation as philosopher and revolutionary could be compared to that of the Maratha king Shivaji and his advisor Ramdas, see Fasana 1994). Apart from the colorful character of Mazzini's writings, a part of their attraction undoubtedly lay in the parallelism of the Italian and Indian situation, as the early nationalists saw it: a weak and divided nation, object of plunder, internal squabbles, weighed down under the rigidity of tradition and self-serving elites, but with a glorious past to be retrieved. In Italy there was the Renaissance and earlier, the Roman empire. In India there was the pre-Islamic sophistication of literature, philosophy, and art, the empire of Ashoka, and so on.

24. For a thorough discussion of the contested terrain of the origins of Aryan language and the status of Aryans as "invaders" or original inhabitants of the subcontinent, see Thapar 1996.

25. One of Golwalkar's references is the German scholar J. C. Bluntschli, who in 1875 wrote an influential book *Lehre vom Modernen Staat*, translated as *The Theory of the State*, published by Oxford University Press in 1885. Bluntschli promoted the German notion of a *Volks-nation* as the true expression of a nation, a view supported by most of the other (British) scholars quoted by Golwalkar, as Jaffrelot has shown (Jaffrelot 1995, 50–52). Golwalkar's reasoning was, in other words, not drawing on some marginal view, as the "German theory" of nation has been made out to be in the aftermath of Nazism, but on a broadly accepted view in the scholarly and political environment at the time regarding the "natural" congruence between culture and territory.

26. In his most recent work, Jaffrelot argues that Golwalkar's ideology may be called "virtually totalitarian," but neither fascist nor Nazi due to the lack of worship of the leader, of the strong state, or of a racial doctrine. I find it difficult to talk about "fascism as such." Any ideological articulation emerges as a specific combination of elements and received conceptual grammars—fascist, nationalist, socialist, idealist, and so on—borrowed and hence vernacularized within an historically produced connotative domain. It is, therefore, obvious that Golwalkar was never a fascist in the European sense. The RSS represents, nonetheless, the most significant import into and domestication within India of vital elements of the incoherent mélange of ideological fragments that made up various forms of fascism in Europe.

27. A somewhat similar attempt to establish continuities and trace the journey of notions and concepts from Bankim to Golwalkar and the influence of orientalism (but without linking these concepts to Herder, Fichte, and so on), can be found in Klimkeit 1981. In spite of the assertion by contemporary nationalist ideologues of fundamental differences between the Indian concept of nationalism and that of Europe, the European experience remains, nevertheless, the central reference point when the concept of the pure Hindu nation is defined.

28. Gandhian and Hindu nationalist discourse have come close to one another in later years, not only in the political field. A publication from the Ramakrishna Mission, *Hindu Thought and World Harmony*, written in 1989 by a disciple of Vinoba Bhave who is now a sarvodya worker, testifies that the argumentative structure, the thematic, and the style of modern Gandhian discourse and of Hindu nationalism resemble one another in striking ways. One finds the same massive presence of positive statements from more or less well-known personalities about the deeds and virtues of Hinduism. In this discourse, Arnold Toynbee provides scientific credibility to the eulogy of Hindu history. Vedanta contains the ultimate truth, superior to that of modern physics (verified by quotes from western scientists), and it contains the answer to the challenges of modern man, promotes humanism and an "integral approach," cares more for women, and the family, is inherently tolerant and peaceful, and is more emotionally alert to fellow beings. "Hinduism is the culmination of the cultural evolution of mankind," the author concludes.

Chapter 3

1. The history of revolutionary and messianic movements is also the history of self-proclaimed chosen peoples, of groups whose special insight, predicaments, or fate elevate them above ordinary standards of humanity, and who have a sublime duty beyond moral concerns. If the Nazi leadership was the most robust and barbaric in this respect, the Stalinist celebration of communists as people of a special mold, of iron wills and determination, or the hysteria of the Chinese Red Guard "with their hearts full of devotion to Chairman Mao," were more persistent, enduring, and mass-produced examples of totalitarian subjects. The Sendero Luminoso, the Khmer Rouge, and the Tamil Tigers are more recent examples of the same type of dual teleology, determined to extract

the "true" History from the rubble of the actual history they seek to destroy, and to extract a purified "true People" from the piles of corpses of the actual people they kill. More generally, they enact the (futile) attempt to give the "empty signifier" (of the people or the nation) a concrete content.

2. The Hindu Mahasabha functioned as a broad platform and caucus for divergent groups and ideological tendencies that shared the fear of Muslim assertiveness and a commitment to a sangathan strategy of organizing and constructing a national Hindu community. Opinions ranged from political organizers such as B. S. Moonje, a Hindu Sabha leader in Nagpur who was instrumental in the creation of the RSS; to Swami Shraddhananda from Punjab, who advocated the construction of large Rashtra mandirs (national temples) that would be meeting places for a national, catholic Hinduism transcending older sects and boundaries of caste; or Dr. Kurtkoti, a religious leader from Maharashtra who, in the image of the ulama institution in Islam, tried to establish the political-legal authority of Hindu religious leaders (Jaffrelot 1996, 14–17).

3. The akhara institution has been analyzed in great detail by Joseph Alter (1992). Sandria Freitag, in her work on communalism in north India, has pointed to the multiple meanings and functions of the akharas—from defenders of the community to martial brotherhoods with criminal connotations—which from the turn of the century on were used by both Congress and Hindu nationalist forces as vehicles for political and communal mobilization (Freitag 1990, 122, 225).

4. Like all effective ideological strategies, the RSS's strategy and ideology condense a large number of references in the connotative domain created by nationalism and cultural revival in India, in a polyvalent practice that seeks to make itself intelligible to both popular cultural idioms (such as that of the akhara) and to elite and higher-caste cultural idioms. The idiom of spiritual perfection and renunciation in the service of the nation—the "political monk" or karma yogin—had already been developed by Vivekananda. The RSS tried to embody this notion, and the representation of the RSS as an independent authority, like monks ennobled and elevated above everyday petty squabbles by its renunciation and dedication, remains a powerful discursive stream in the movement. It is interesting that RSS men always refer to the movement as "Sangha—the term used for Buddhist communities of monks—and refer to the authority of the RSS in ways similar to those of Buddhist monastic orders in Thailand, Burma, and elsewhere that have assumed the role of spiritual corrective to the powers that be.

5. Craig Baxter quotes the program adopted by the Hindu Mahasabha in 1925 under the leadership of Lala Lajpat Rai as the single document that had the most enduring influence on subsequent programs and strategies of the RSS and later the Jana Sangh. Among many things, the program contained these points: "(1) To organize Hindu Sabhas throughout the length and breadth of the country. (2) To provide relief to such Hindus, men and women, who need help on account of communal disturbances. (3) Reconversion of Hindus who have been forcibly converted to Islam. (4) To organize gymnasiums for the use of Hindu young men and women. (5) To organize seva samitis [volunteer corps]. (6) To popularize Hindi . . . in cooperation with the Hindi Sahyita Sam-

melan. (7) To open Hindu temples as halls where people may gather. (8) To celebrate Hindu festivals. (9) To promote good feelings with Mohammedans and Christians. (10) To represent communal interests of Hindus in all political controversies" (quoted from Baxter 1969, 15).

6. Lise McKean gives a good account of the popularity Savarkar achieved during his extensive tours all over the country in the late 1930s and the 1940s. He was honored by religious institutions, by Sanatana dharma sabhas and militant organizations, and often welcomed and celebrated by large crowds as the "sangathanacharya"—the supreme head and "dictator" of militant Hinduism (McKean 1996, 91–96).

7. Savarkar propagated this line under the slogan "Militarize Hindusthan." The objective was to enroll as many Hindus as possible in the British Army in order to reverse the "effeminization" of the Hindus which, according to Savarkar, had been going on during British rule due to the recruitment of soldiers along the colonial theory of martial races. Recruitment of Hindus would tilt the Muslim-Hindu ratio in the armed forces in favor of the Hindus, a ratio Savarkar believed would be crucial for the loyalty and orientation of the forces out of which a new national army would be molded (Phadke 1989; see also Sumante 1991).

8. Interview with S. H. Deshpande, economist, Marathi author, and swayamsevak in the 1930s and early 1940s, in Pune, 12 August 1992.

9. Gandhi's assassin Naturam Godse, a Chitpavan brahmin from Pune, had been a member of the RSS for some years, as well as a member of the Hindu Mahasabha. In the early 1940s Godse left the RSS to form a militant organization, Hindu Rashtra Dal, aimed at militarizing the mind and conduct of Hindus, to make them "more assertive and aggressive" (interview with Naturam Godse's brother Gopal Godse, still a member of the Hindu Mahasabha, in Pune, 3 February 1993).

10. Maureen Patterson gives an account of the attacks on Chitpavan homes and institutions in western Maharashtra in the weeks following the assassination. Attributing it to long-standing resentment of Marathas against the Chitpavans and to the machinations of local Congress leaders, she displays her own deeply biased position quite openly when writing: "It was an unsavory episode that brought out the worst passions of Maharashtra's dominant, and now ruling caste, the Marathas. They fell back on their age old methods of problem solving: on violence and retribution" (Patterson 1988, 36). See also Nandy's far more insightful analysis of the Chitpavans and their links to Hindu nationalism, (Nandy 1980, 70–96).

11. For a comprehensive account of the historical development of these affiliates see Andersen and Damle 1987, 108–37.

12. Interview with Mrs. Saraswatibai Apte, in Pune, 4 September 1993.

13. The recruitment of motherhood in the nationalist discourse developed from around the turn of the century, as a response to the question of women's emancipation. Patriotic motherhood elevated the conventional strictures on the women's movement and women's virtues to a sublime expression of the very core of the cultural nation. As has been shown recently, the question of emancipation of women presented a difficult issue for nationalist leaders such as

Lajpat Rai, who oscillated between a liberal emancipatory attitude and a more conservative celebration of the traditional virtues and purity of motherhood (Malhotra 1994). In more liberal Bengal, the educated middle classes produced a discourse of the modern, Indian woman as an educated mother guarding the "inner domain" of the nation (the family), who also moved freely and competently in the colonized "outer domain," the public sphere, protected by her supreme virtues of chastity, purity, and moderation (Chatterjee 1993, 127–31).

14. I have developed this argument in more detail in Hansen 1994). See also Tanika Sarkar's pioneering study (Sarkar 1991), various contributions in Sarkar and Butalia 1995, and Mazumdar 1992, 1–24.

15. Group interview with sevikas at the Jijamata Trust in Thane, 28 January 1993.

16. Interview with Durga Vahini activists in Thane, 18 January 1993.

17. *VHP: Messages and Activities* (New Delhi, 1981).

18. The most prominent of this category of modern gurus is Swami Chinmayananda, whose fashionable Sandyapani Academy in Bombay has for decades attracted well-to-do segments of the metropolitan middle classes. See also van der Veer 1994, 136–37.

19. McKean presents a highly interesting analysis of several of these gurus and sadhus, some of them associated with or running reputed ashrams such as the Bharat Mata temple in Hardwar (McKean 1996, 124–63).

20. Interview with Balasaheb Naik, VHP organizing secretary for the western zone (Gujarat, Maharashtra, and Goa), in Pune, 16 September 1992.

21. In 1979, the VHP held its second International Hindu Conference with high-profile representation of Sikhs, Jains, and numerous sects, and the VHP has in the 1980s held several large world conferences in Europe and North America, where the VHP presents itself to the political and cultural establishment in the concerned countries as representatives of "Hinduism" as such, and systematically seeks to generate goodwill and recognition. Another vital part of the VHP's work in Europe, North America, East Africa, and Southeast Asia has been very successful fundraising and extension of cultural activities among expatriate Indians, seeking to turn them into truly diasporic communities tied to India though the VHP. See McKean, 1995.

22. Pamphlet from Vanvasi Kalyan Kendra in Talasari, Thane district.

23. See the RSS publication edited by Seshadri 1988, 234–36.

24. A revelation, or literalization, of the secret would amount to the dissolution of the group, as it would become apparent that the secret is that there is no secret—and that the leaders are rather ordinary people indulging in profane tussles over power, money, and recognition.

25. This "mirror effect" means that tightly knit political groups/sects/organizations organized with authoritarian structures, clandestine organization, and multiple layers of secrecy, all portray their enemy—the state, the capitalist class, the Muslim conspiracy, the Jewish conspiracy, and so on—as extremely powerful, operating through similar clandestine networks and conspiracies. Opposing such a powerful other bestows, in turn, a particular grandeur on the organization or sect and its cause, which ethically neutralizes any crime or abuse committed in the name of this cause.

26. The festivals are, first, Varsh Pratipad, the Hindu New Year, but also "Founder's Day" (Hedgewar's birthday), when the memory of Hedgewar is celebrated. The next is Hindu Samrajya Divotsav, the coronation day of Shivaji. Here the historical victories over Muslim conquerors are celebrated. Third comes Raksha Bandhan, a ceremony normally performed in the family, in which the sister in a family will tie a thread around her brother's wrist and apply a tika (dots of red paste) on his forehead, in order to show symbolically her respect for her brother and ask for his protection in the future. This ceremony was transferred to the RSS and is now performed among the swayamsevaks in order to affirm their mutual loyalty. Fourth comes Guru Dakshina, when the swayamsevaks offer money to their "teacher and guide"—the RSS—and revere a still-expanding galaxy of national heroes, including Shivaji, Ramdas, Rana Pratap, and other martial figures; the galaxy centers around the projection of Hedgewar and Golwalkar as supreme national heroes. Fifth comes Dassera, a large festival celebrated all over India by most Hindus. In the RSS version, it commemorates the victory of Lord Ram over the demon Ravana in the epic *Ramayana*. On this occasion swayamsevaks march through the cities in uniforms with music. One of the highlights of the RSS version of Dassera is the worship of weapons (swords, daggers, and so on)—associated with Shivaji and kshatriya values. Finally, the year ends with celebration of the winter solstice, the Makar Sakrant, which emphasizes selflessness and service to the nation.

27. Interview with Professor S. Shastri, RSS pracharak for western Maharashtra, in Pune on 5 August 1992.

28. Recent research on nascent nationalism in Bengal in the nineteenth century has demonstrated the centrality of the mother as a nationalist icon rendered in a deplorable and fragile state—due to the lack of protection by emasculated Bengali men—hence to be protected and rescued by nationalist sons (see Bagchi 1990). The proto-nationalist reverence of the mother icon also led to what in historical hindsight might appear as a paradoxical interpretation among the middle-class audiences in Calcutta of Queen Victoria as representing a sort of benevolent, fulfilled motherhood, whose supposed elevated justice Indians could appeal to, like the image of the "good Tsar" (Chowdhury-Sengupta 1992).

29. I perceive, in the spirit of Lacan, the Oedipus complex as a structure not confined to Western societies, which in any case are heterogeneous. To my mind, the power of the oedipal structure derives from the ambiguities it ascribes to female sexuality as both destructive/demonic and protective/nurturing. The whole point is that Oedipus's mother was simultaneously sexually attractive and a protecting mother, and, hence, that an oedipal discourse is articulated around metaphors bent on this ambiguous tension between desire and devotion vis-à-vis the mother symbol. The distinction in traditional Hindu worship between unmarried, sexually frustrated, "hot" and destructive goddesses, and the serene, fertile, "cold" and yet powerful position of married mother goddesses (see Fuller 1992, 29–56), testifies that goddesses need marriage to control their demonic side. Further, at the level of family practices, the relations between sons and mothers are in most Hindu families close and not without sexual ambiguities. Finally, I believe that the sublimation of mother-

hood in what Chatterjee calls "the dominant middle-class culture coeval with the era of nationalism" (Chatterjee 1993, 131), that is, a middle-class culture wherein gender and sexuality were constructed around nationalist appropriations of Victorian ideals of purity and chastity and the mother/whore dichotomy, has over the last century modified the construction of femininity and masculinity so much that derivation of their cultural meanings from religious traditions and practices provides at best only a part of the framework of their articulation. This dominant culture, communicated for decades through educational systems and official discourse, and the contested representations of gender in the public sphere—not least in Hindi films—provides images and archives of gender constructions that are at least as powerful as those flowing from religious narratives.

30. As in the communist movements, the supreme leader is a "secretary," that is, literally the keeper of the secret of the organization. This ostensibly administrative denomination also refers to this "secretary" as an executor and administrator of the larger movement of history, in which radically teleological movements like the RSS view themselves as instruments furthering an already irresistible logic.

31. Baxter 1969, Appendices 2–3; Graham 1990, 259–65.

32. The Hindu Mahasabha resumed political activity in 1949 after having been inactive for almost a year after the assassination of Gandhi. The party was, however, seriously weakened and did poorly in the first general elections in 1951–1952, where it secured only four seats in the Lok Sabha. The party's share of the popular vote further declined in the following years, and it was reduced to only two Lok Sabha seats in 1957, and only one in 1962. The Hindu Mahasabha retained some local strength in Uttar Pradesh and in Madhya Pradesh, but at the state level as well as the national level the party was overshadowed and marginalized by the Jana Sangh's gradual but steady growth (Smith 1963, 473–79).

33. A prospective ban on cow slaughter had, after sustained pressure from conservative elements within Congress, been included in the directive principles of state policy in the Indian Constitution. Throughout the 1950s there were protracted debates on the issue. The expert committee appointed in 1955 to probe into the issue recommended a total ban. In 1958, the Supreme Court ruled in favor of such a total ban after sustained pressure from Congress legislators and public support gathered on the issue. The RSS, the Jana Sangh, and the Hindu Mahasabha succeeded in generating considerable goodwill in central and northern India on this issue; see ibid., 483–89.

34. The party was able to win four seats in the state legislative assembly in Maharashtra, as well as four in Mysore and three in Andhra Pradesh, and therefore did, in a limited way, break out of its northern confines (Graham 1990, 261). These electoral gains occurred in constituencies with a significant presence of RSS networks. This correlation between RSS presence and electoral strength remained pertinent even in the unprecedented wave of Hindu nationalism in the late 1980s.

35. An analysis by D. L. Sheth of the voter profile of various Indian parties in 1967 revealed that the Jana Sangh had a fairly broad following in both cities and rural areas, but that the urban middle-class groups belonging to higher

castes in north India were significantly overrepresented among Jana Sangh's voters (Sheth 1976, 281, and Jaffrelot 1993, 278).

36. According to Richard Fox, the alliance between J. P. Narayan and the RSS testified that J. P.'s Sarvodhya as well as Gandhian philosophy in a broader sense lacked any real radicalism or perspective of social reform (Fox 1987, 233–47). The entire process of alignment between the J. P. movement and the RSS/Jana Sangh is discussed and well documented by Jaffrelot 1993, 300–19.

Chapter 4

1. As Paul Brass has shown, central intervention in the affairs of the states grew dramatically during Mrs. Gandhi's period. Chief ministers were routinely replaced and President's Rule was imposed frequently in the course of internal tussles between state and central leaderships within Congress (Brass 1982).

2. The changing electoral basis of Congress is documented in detail in the state-by-state analyses in Sisson and Roy 1990. The changing strategies of recruitment of activists and the management of large unaccountable funds within political parties are shown in various ways in the study by Malik and Marquette 1990.

3. This is the argument presented by Atul Kohli (Kohli 1990, 387–400). In a slightly different vein, Paul Brass has argued that the populist strategies of Mrs. Gandhi and her new lieutenants in the 1970s sought to bypass and undermine existing clientelistic networks and address poor farmers or slum dwellers directly, just as they sought to disentangle the bread-and-butter issues of local-level politics from the national elections hereafter fought predominantly on large, fuzzy, and emotional issues, fit for populist engineering rather than aggregation of power through complex clientelist networks (Brass 1990, 82–98).

4. Robert Wade notes, in a preliminary study of the economy of clientelism and corruption in the state bureaucracy in a south Indian state, that the most profitable revenue sources for the clientelist networks operating within the state administration are bribes paid in connection with public works, and "transfer sums" in connection with transfer of administrative cadres to higher offices or to so-called "wet" areas where many bribes are available. These offices are literally sold at fixed prices (Wade 1989). Similar practices of circulating black money in and out of the bureaucracy does not seem, however, to be clearly linked to the proliferation of populist politics. In 1964, the *Report of the Committee on Prevention of Corruption* from the so-called Santhanam Committee identified "the transfer system" and many other corrupt practices in the early 1960s (Myrdal 1968, 937–60).

5. Rajiv Gandhi, in an interview with a BBC journalist, had commented that if elections actually were held at the local level, not only Congress but all the politicians at that level would have been "cleaned out." That was, apparently, too much of a risk to run (Nugent 1992, 48–49).

6. The impact of the serials made it apparent to politicians, intellectuals, and journalists that audio-visual representation, films, and cultural products had important bearings on the dynamics of the political field. The serialized epics were presented as a legitimate representation of an important religious narra-

tive, and were widely accepted as such when they were broadcast. See also Farmer 1996.

7. Official figures from the Ministry for Information and Broadcasting estimates a viewership of 250 million for the Doordarshan channel, and a surprisingly high 42 million viewers of cable and satellite TV in 1991. The growth rate of cable and satellite TV viewers was steep in all urban areas. A Bombay marketing firm estimated in 1992 that 200 to 250 households were linked up to cable and satellite TV every day in the Bombay region (Sethi 1992). Today, in 1998, the ownership of cable and sattelite TV in India undoubtedly runs to several hundred million people.

8. These technological innovations also provided new possibilities for the mass production and widespread dissemination of various cultural forms—images, music, and so on. See for instance Peter Manuel's pathbreaking study of cassette culture in northern India (Manuel 1993).

9. For various aspects of the financial and fiscal squeezes that compelled the Government of India to implement rather far-reaching reforms, see Jalan 1992, 141–251. For a recent evaluation of the impact of the economic reforms, see Vaidyanathan 1995. For a more critical assessment of the social interests and assumptions behind the liberalization policy, see Bagchi 1994, 18–27.

10. "The 'lower castes' form an economic and social stratum that is sandwiched between the middle castes above them and the scheduled castes below. It is composed of marginal farmers, sharecroppers, and landless laborers from low-status agricultural castes together with the traditional service and artisan castes—barbers, boatmen, blacksmiths, carpenters, fishermen, grain parchers, oilpressers, and so on. The proportion of this stratum of the population varies from region to region, but it is usually about a third of the population. Because individual castes are usually small and widely dispersed, as well as poor, the lower castes find it difficult to develop a common sense of identity or to assert much political power on their own." (Church 1984, 231). For evidence of the growing political mobilization of hitherto passive groups and the emergence of local political elites within these groups, see Mitra 1991.

11. The actual category was called Social and Educational Backward Classes (SEBC). A large number of such groups were identified in the 1950s, and it was decided to grant them substantial educational and occupational quotas in government service—reservation of up to 40 percent of all Class III jobs (lower clerks, and so on), 30 percent of Class II (qualified middle positions), and 25 percent of Class I jobs (leading positions) in the public administration. These recommendations remained unimplemented, and the Mandal Commission formed in 1979 by the Janata cabinet under Charan Singh found that the OBC groups, constituting 52 percent of the population, held only 4.69 percent of Class I jobs, 10.63 percent in Class II, and 24.40 percent in Class III (Choudhary 1991: 111).

12. See Mitra 1987 and; Woods 1987. See also Baxi 1990, 219–39.

13. Statistics presented by the Scheduled Tribe and Scheduled Castes Commission in 1986–1987 demonstrated that all the southern states had more than a 30 percent reservation for OBC groups (44 percent in Andhra Pradesh), and that states like Uttar Pradesh and Bihar at that time already had between 15 and

20 percent of all educational seats and government jobs, respectively, reserved for OBCs (Engineer 1991a, 290).

14. There are three groups of criteria. Social (4×3 points), educational (4×2 points) and economic (4×1 point). To qualify as backward one needed 12 points, which meant that a prosperous but socially and culturally conservative group easily could qualify as "backward," while a poorer and less educated group living along more "modern" or urban norms would hardly qualify (Engineer 1991a, 294).

15. "Recommendations of the Mandal Commission" reproduced in Engineer, ibid., 281–89.

16. The OBC categories defined by the commission also included significant Muslim communities, and thus marked a departure from the practice sanctioned by the Supreme Court of granting reservations only to depressed Hindu castes, and not allotting reservations to confessional communities. This practice was challenged when the Neo-Buddhist Mahars in 1969, after years of contention, were granted some of the vital benefits extended to scheduled castes in the state of Maharashtra, after being excluded from this category since their conversion in 1956 (Galanter 1984, 319–24). The inclusion of Muslims in the OBC category still awaits legal adjudication.

17. For an account of the anti-Sikh riots in Delhi in 1984, see van Dyke 1996, 201–21. It is common knowledge that in her last period as prime minister Mrs. Gandhi increasingly employed religious symbols and majoritarian rhetoric, openly appealing to Hindu sentiments in north India, where Congress had been seriously challenged since the 1967 elections. The discourse of national unity (against "anti-nationals" such as separatists or "illoyal" minorities aided by a "foreign hand") during the 1984 electoral campaign was in the same way premised on a strong undercurrent of Hindu majoritarianism.

18. This act came into being in 1937 after long-standing pressure from members of the ulama who urged legal authorization of certain practices and exclusion of "un-Islamic" practices. As Michael Anderson has pointed out, the act reflected a view of the shari'a (Islamic law) molded by a century's evolution of Anglo-Mohammedan law (Anderson 1990).

19. This opportunistic strengthening of the most conservative forces among Muslims generated widespread frustration among liberal and progressive Muslim leaders and intellectuals. Union minister Arif Mohammad Khan resigned from the Congress cabinet as a protest against this maneuver. In the face of massive protests, Congress leaders tried to wash their hands by portraying the bill as a necessary concession that the Government had to make in the face of unified Muslim pressure. False as this was, it nevertheless helped to harden the myth of Muslims as intransigent fanatics (see Hasan 1990b, 27–37). For a compilation of diverse views in the debate as well as pertinent documents, see Engineer 1987.

20. In 1988, communal tension had been built up, especially in Uttar Pradesh, to the extent that several of the major Hindu celebrations in the month of October had to be held under curfew in many districts in the state. In spite of this, the then Congress chief minister of Uttar Pradesh allowed Syed Shahabuddhin and the Babri Masjid Movement Coordination Committee (BMMCC) to

lead a march of thousands of Muslims to Ayodhya to offer a namaz (prayer) at the holy site. At the same time, the VHP was permitted to carry out a huge Shri Rama Maha Yagna in Ayodhya, a five-day congregation at which 1–200,000 people turned up, many armed with "traditional" or "ritual" weapons, explicitly determined to "defend" the site against the Muslim worshipers. Shahabuddhin canceled the march, but the incident revealed how the Congress administration consciously let the communal escalation between the Hindus, led by the RSS, and the Muslims, led by a combination of Janata Dal populists and religious conservatives, go on unhindered. See reports in *India Today*, 30 November 1991.

21. An ominous indication of the rising level of tension and animosity between Hindu and Muslim communities in various parts of the country in this period was the growing number of riots and the rising number of casualties—mostly Muslims—in these riots. This trend and its intimate connections with the complicity of local political leaders with the (Hindu) instigators of riots, and the brutality and involvement of police forces—especially the Provincial Armed Constabulary (PAC) of Uttar Pradesh—has been well documented by Engineer in various works (Engineer 1991b) and analyzed by Ashish Bannerjee (1990).

22. The general standard of living and literacy—particularly among women—are markedly lower in the Muslim community than in the Hindu community. This may go a long way to explain the higher fertility rates, as documented for instance by the report *Levels, Trends and Differentials in Fertility*, Office of the Registrar General, New Delhi, 1979, or in the *Sarvekshana*, National Sample Survey, 43rd Round, Delhi 1990.

23. For an overview of the economic significance of remittances from the Gulf in Kerala, see Saith 1992.

24. Quite a few of the Indian Muslims I met who had working experience in the Gulf confided to me, strictly off the record, that they had lost their faith in Muslim solidarity after having been bullied by their Arab employers, who hold the often dark-skinned Indian Muslims in very low esteem. Interestingly, this obvious contradiction—in Lacanian terms the "lack" in the construction of a Muslim identity—was clearly tabooed in public discourse, or glossed over with phrases like "there are bad people everywhere." The imperative of keeping a unified Muslim identity in the face of Hindu assertion was particularly strong in communally charged places like Mumbai. I have explored aspects of the Muslim identity economy in conjunction with migration in Hansen 1997a, and Muslim livelihood strategies in central Mumbai in Hansen 1997b.

25. Asghar Ali Engineer is one of the best-known critics of fundamentalism and conservatism in the Muslim establishment, but many younger intellectuals have lately emerged as very articulate voices in the debate. Sadjid Rashid, editor of the *Urdu Times*, Mumbai: argued that the "fundamentalist leaders have successfully installed our Muslim identity as the prime concern—as far more important than the deplorable social situation of the Muslim community. . . . Personally I am for a Common Civil Code if all special rules for the other communities (for instance the Hindu Marriage Act) was scrapped as well. But I cannot write it in the newspaper. My readership would kill me" (Interview in Bombay, 22 October 1992).

26. Editorial signed by Syed Shahabuddin in *Muslim India* (New Delhi) no. 108 (December 1991).

27. Radical Islamic groups in India such as the Jamaat-i-Islami, the Students Islamic Movement (SIM) and in Kerala the Islamic Sevak Sangh (ISS) have experienced a growing popularity in the last decade. The attack of the international coalition against Iraq in 1991, and the Government of India's permission to American military aircraft to land in Bombay, for instance, provoked demonstrations and protests in several major cities in India. The office of the *Urdu Times* in Bombay was attacked by young Muslims after the editor, on a cautious note, had questioned Saddam Hussein's Islamic credentials.

Chapter 5

1. As pointed out in the previous chapter, Bharat Mata emerged as a representation of the more general figure of the mother goddess, worshiped in innumerable forms and incarnations all over India—not least in Bengal, where the nationalist appropriation of the mother goddess first took place. One of the most popular incarnations of the mother goddess has in recent times been Santoshi Ma, a minor goddess whose shrine is in Jammu, but who is now popularized all over the India through a popular Hindi film released in 1975 (see Kurtz 1992, 1–28).

2. One yatra went from Kathmandu to Rameshwaram in Tamil Nadu, another from Bengal to the Somnath temple in Gujarat, a third from Hardwar to Kanya Kumari. All the yatras were joined by numerous minor processions on the way, and were headed by chariots—decorated trucks—carrying huge pots (*kalashas*) with water from the Ganga sold to devotees en route. The yatras converged at the same time in Nagpur, the center of India and the headquarters of the RSS, to symbolize the essential unity of India, and the centrality of the RSS in upholding this unity. See, for example, van der Veer 1994, 122–26, for a discussion of the design of this campaign.

3. Reports in *India Today*, 30 November 1983, seems to confirm the massive popular response to this huge enterprise, which with the 50,000 swayamsevaks involved, also demonstrated the organizational capacity and discipline of the Sangh parivar. See also McKean 1996, 115–22.

4. This endeavor was obviously most successful in areas where the Sangh parivar had a strong network among influential people, as in Madhya Pradesh (see Jaffrelot 1994, 206–7), in Delhi and U.P., and in parts of Maharashtra. For a condensed overview over the development of the VHP into a mass organization, see Basu et al. 1993, 56–70)

5. For a detailed account of these processes and events see Jaffrelot 1993, 413–28. Jaffrelot characterizes these syncretic endeavors of the VHP as an attempt to construct itself as "une église hindoue." In 1984 the first Dharma Sansad was held to discuss religious matters, and it unanimously demanded liberatation of Lord Ram's alleged birthplace in Ayodhya from its "occupation" and desecration by the Babri Masjid.

6. At the Second World Hindu Conference organized in 1979 in Prayag (Allahabad) in U.P., a special session was devoted to representatives from VHP units from all over the world (*Hindu Vishwa*, Special Number, March-April

1979). In 1985 a large European Hindu Conference was organized by the VHP in Copenhagen, and in 1989 the VHP stood as the main organizer of the hitherto largest VHP conference outside India, the Virat Hindu Sammelan in Milton Keynes in the U.K., presented as an almost ecumenical congregation of 350 Hindu organizations, but in reality totally dominated by the VHP and the RSS, which in Britain is organized as Vishwa Swayamsevak Sangh. In both cases large numbers of prominent citizens, ministers, and MPs were invited as honorary guests and speakers.

7. Van der Veer argues that "the VHP's ideas are directly derived from the discourse of modern spiritual Hinduism. In other words, the VHP takes a kind of 'oriental spiritualism' that was offered as a package to Western audiences and brings it back to India" (van der Veer 1994, 136). See also McKean's interesting discussion of the "commodification" of spirituality in contemporary India (1996, 6–17).

8. See, for example, Thapar 1989, and Lutgendorf 1990. Lutgendorf estimates that about 100 million people followed the serial on TV, and an unknown number have viewed the widely circulated video version. See also van der Veer (1994, 172–78) for a brief discussion of the importance of the Ramayana, both as a widely disseminated text and as a TV serial.

9. In the RSS mouthpiece *Organiser* (19 January 1986) a leading pracharak, H. V. Sheshadri, depicted the new assertiveness of Muslims as a "New Khilafat movement," and thus alluded to the massacres of Hindu landlords and proprietors during the Moplah revolt in northern Kerala which followed the Khilafat movement from 1919 onward.

10. The RSS also approved of Congress's pro-Hindu line in Jammu as opposed to the BJP's more cautious and accommodating line in the state assembly election campaign in the state in 1983. According to Malkani, a RSS pracharak deputed to the BJP, it was more important that the Hindu nationalist line be successful than that the BJP candidates be elected (see Jaffrelot 1993, 392–96).

11. Vajpayee 1980, 1–5.

12. *Our Five Commitments*, Bharatiya Janata Party Publications, New Delhi, 1980.

13. In Bihar the party got 8.4 percent of the votes and won 21 seats, whereas in U.P. it drew 10.8 percent of the vote but gained only 11 seats. In spite of 14 percent of the popular vote in Gujarat, the party could only win 9 seats. In Maharashtra the party fared better (9.4 percent of the vote and 14 seats), and was able to attract several Janata constituencies outside the traditional strongholds of the Jana Sangh (Graham 1987a, 11; Malik and Singh 1995, 182–84).

14. "As the president of the party I take full moral responsibility on myself for the failure of our party in the Assembly and Lok Sabha elections, and I shall be gladly willing to undergo any punishment that the party decides" (Vajpayee 1985, 3).

15. *Working Group Report*, Bharatiya Janata Party, 20 July 1985.

16. *Resolutions* (3–5 January 1986, 5).

17. *Resolutions* (1 January 1987, 17). In this resolution heavy military vigilance along the borders, a national register of citizens, revision of electoral rolls, and introduction of photo identity cards in border areas were proposed.

18. One of the architects behind this was Jay Dubashi, former economic journalist and editor. Dubashi, who belongs to the small group of party leaders without an RSS background, was one of the first leading BJP figures to formulate the "Hindu cause" as a political cause, and thus gradually disentangle the Ayodhya issue from the VHP's more religious idiom. As early as in 1987, Dubashi wrote the much-quoted piece "Angry Hindus are Political Hindus": "This new breed of political Hindus do not go to temples, have not perhaps even seen a Shankaracharya in person, could not recite the Gayatri mantra even if they tried, but nonetheless, are Hindus who believe that India is a Hindu nation that must be a home to every Hindu anywhere and where Hindus must be respected, just as Christians are respected in Europe and the Jews in Israel" (Dubashi, November 1987, in *Probe India*).

19. *Resolutions* (9–11 July 1989, 17). In this National Executive meeting the Ramjanmabhoomi issue figured for the first time in a BJP resolution, by and large repeating the position of the VHP on the so-called disputed area on which the Babri Masjid is located: "The BJP holds that the nature of this controversy is such that it cannot be sorted out by a court of law. . . . [The court] cannot adjudicate as to whether Babar did actually invade Ayodhya, destroy a temple and build a mosque in its place. [A court] cannot suggest remedies to undo the vandalism of history."

20. *Chunav Ghosua-patra: Loksabha Chunav, 1989* (Hindi), BJP Election Manifesto, Lok Sabha elections, 1989.

21. *Times of India*, 11 November 1989.

22. *India Today*, 31 March 1990. The BJP was now shedding earlier cautiousness, and the party's status as the political wing of the RSS now became a central part of the BJPs self-description. Only one year earlier, RSS chief Deoras had cautiously told a journalist that his sympathies "primarily were with the BJP" (*Telegraph*, 25 February 1989).

23. The theme of this propaganda was that Hindus had for centuries fought against Muslims to gain control over Ram's birth place in Ayodhya, and that the sacrifice in lives on the side of the Hindus had been enormous. Youths were urged to join the final and glorious battle and thus save the honor of the Hindu nation. See reports in *Indian Express*, 11 October 1990, and 2 November 1989; *Tribune*, 12 October 1989.

24. *Hindu Vishwa* 12r, no. 25 (Silver Jubilee Issue) (1990), quoted from the compiled figures in Jaffrelot 1993, 458. See also *Indian Express*, 11 October 1989. Though obviously an exaggerated figure, there is no doubt that this campaign was one of the most effective and conspicuous political/religious campaigns ever in independent India.

25. I have analyzed aspects of the BJP's and Shiv Sena's rural expansion in Maharashtra in the 1980s in Hansen 1996c.

26. The protracted judicial inquiry into the riot resulted in 1995 in a report putting the blame for the riot on the "unholy alliance between the police and the BJP," and on what it calls the "puerile nonchalance" of the district administration. *Indian Express*, 20 March 1995.

27. L. K. Advani, *Presidential Address, National Council Meeting*, Bombay, 25 September 1989.

28. This general correlation has since been corroborated by a growing number of studies of the communalization of various cities and localities, and ensuing riots and killings, in the wake of the campaigns of the Sangh parivar. For Maharashtra, see Hansen 1996c. For a study of the communalization of the town of Bijnor in western Uttar Pradesh, known for its almost mythical communal amity and peace, see Jeffrey and Jeffrey 1994. For the development in Gujarat, particularly Surat, see Engineer 1994 and Breman 1993. For a study of a similar process of communalization in Jaipur in Rajasthan, see Mayaram 1993.

29. The organizer of the yatra was the young BJP chief in Maharashtra, Pramod Mahajan, who also was the architect behind the alliance with Shiv Sena in Maharashtra. Shiv Sena had for years used the bow and arrow (the god Ram's emblem) as a party symbol, and with the Rath yatra this symbol became a regular part of the BJP and RSS symbolic inventory. See Davis 1996, for a detailed discussion of the iconograhies and representational techniques involved in the campaign.

30. For an overview of the symbolic strategies employed by the Sangh parivar in 1989–1990 as well as the communal violence this engendered, see Pannikar 1993 and Datta 1993b.

31. Compared to the reach and local intensity of the Ram shila puja and the earlier Ekamata yatra, Advani's Rath yatra, due to its sheer speed (300 kilometers per day and five to six public meetings each day), was in many ways designed more as a theatrical performance for national representation via press reports and TV than for intense mass contact at the local level. Due to the superb press management of the BJP, which conveniently lead journalists and TV crews to selected spots according to the schedule of the yatra, the event received an overwhelming and effective publicity far exceeding anything the Sangh parivar could have organized on its own.

32. The martyrdom of the kar sevaks killed in Ayodhya on this occasion was systematically utilized by the VHP and BJP. Small booklets and videos with the gory details of mutilated bodies, broken skulls, bodies recovered from the nearby river (some of them primitive frauds arranged with decomposed bodies) were widely circulated all over the country as proof of the brutality of the "pseudo secularist" anti-Hindu forces. As the booklets circulated, the myth of the police killings multiplied, and it was claimed—and believed—by local VHP workers I met in Maharashtrian villages and urban areas that the real death toll was several thousand. Urns with the ashes of the "martyrs of Ayodhya" were also circulated as objects of worship and reverence in various parts of the country.

33. Engineer 1991c.

34. See the MARG analysis in *India Today*, 15 July 1991.

35. *Independent*, 21 September 1991. During my field work in Pune, numerous conversations with officers, active and retired, confirmed this impression, although very few officers wished to state anything regarding their political preferences in the presence of a tape recorder. See also Jaffrelot 1996, 424–31.

36. The BJP won 34 percent of the popular vote and secured 223 seats (Malik and Singh 1995, 187). Immediately after the electoral victory, the BJP's chief

minister Kalyan Singh, went to Ayodhya in a pompous symbolic gesture to thank Lord Ram for his good fortune and "to seek guidance and inspiration" (*Independent*, 5 July 1991).

37. A detailed account of the three-month campaign as presented by ABVP can be found in the booklet *In Defence of Nations Sovereignty*, Akhil Bharatiya Vidyarti Parishad (Central Office), Bombay 26 January 1991.

38. The party fortnightly magazine *BJP Today* expressed the thinking and strategy underlying the yatra when calling it "A Balm to the Nation's Wounded Pride" (*BJP Today* nos. 1–2, January 1992).

39. On this occasion the air was full of anti-Pakistani and jingoist slogans like "this yatra is only a rehearsal, now we will go to Srinagar, later to Kabul." There were fears, after the appeals from the home minister to discontinue the yatra (*Times of India*, 21 January 1992), that the government would ban the yatra from proceeding northward from Delhi. Thousands of activists and vehicles therefore diffused quietly out of Delhi in the following days to reassemble in a yatra that now swelled to 40–50,000 people.

40. The conclusion of the yatra was full of almost surrealist incidents. The yatra had, for instance, carried and worshiped the flagpole and the flag supposed to be hoisted at Lal Chowk. In the confusion this was forgotten at the Jammu border, and the Indian army had to provide flag and flagpole to an obviously frightened Joshi performing the ceremony.

41. *India Today*, 29 February 1992. The yatra was also driven by another compulsion, namely, an attempt by Murli Manohar Joshi—more of an orthodox RSS man than Vajpayee and Advani—to assert his own position within the party leadership by emulating Advani's recipe. Like Advani he picked a noble cause, a large scheme, and just as Advani had used Pramod Mahajan to execute the entire operation, Joshi picked another young energetic BJP organizer, Narendra Modi from Gujarat, to do the same in the case of the Ekta yatra.

42. *Swadeshi Andolan: Struggle for Economic Freedom* (Bangalore: Sahitya Samgama, 1991).

43. Interview, *Organiser*, 26 January 1992.

44. In an interview in February 1992, Advani said that it was Congress which in its liberalization program had taken over the BJPs line, and that the party welcomed that. According to Advani, multinationals should play a role only in high-tech sectors. For the BJP, Advani said, the "RSS corrective" to the party program of 1991 was "in a way necessary" (*Sunday*, 16–22 February 1992). The quotation is from *Humanistic Approach to Economic Development (A Swadeshi Alternative)* 1992, 8.

45. Drawing on Derrida's notion of the "crypt" as the place wherein "a dead object remains like a living dead abscessed in a specific spot in the ego" (Derrida 1985, 57), Don Miller suggests that to the Hindu nationalist movement "the Babri Masjid was the crypt which had to be ripped open to expose its otherness, to reveal the true temple beneath—a crypt being always cryptic: hiding and concealing something beneath" (Miller 1996, 199).

46. I have elsewhere developed the argument of Hindutva as a bid for recognition from "significant others"—major powers in the world—through

exorcising of the "lack" inflicted upon India by the Muslim impurity. See Hansen 1996a.

47. Swapan Das Gupta, "Ayodhya—Road to Nationalism," *Times of India*, 15 April 1991. In Das Gupta's steady stream of articles, the perspective remained that of a totally bifurcated political space wherein any opposition to the Ramjanmabhoomi agitation became an opportunistic and mindless "pampering of Muslims" violating the majoritarian logic of civilizations Das Gupta referred to when asking, "Would anyone deny Catholics the right to build a church in Rome?" (ibid.).

48. See, for instance, the interview with L. K. Advani in the *Times of India*, 25 December 1991. "I am not a religious person," Advani states emphatically in the course of the interview.

49. Evidence excavated by the Archaeological Survey of India under B. B. Lal in the 1950s and 1960s showed evidence of many earlier layers of civilization at the site but did not lend any evidence supporting the VHP's claim that a Muslim general, Mir Baq, destroyed a Ram temple at the site and subsequently had the Babri Masjid constructed. On several occasions the VHP presented various types of evidence—archaeological, written sources, and so on (see Vishwa Hindu Parishad 1991, and the account by Koenraad Elst, a Belgian Catholic of a radical anti-Muslim persuasion who tries to make himself useful as a "fellow traveler" of the Hindu nationalist movement; Elst 1990). In all cases this evidence has been refuted and contested by most of the serious authorities of archaeology and medieval Indian history (see Panikkar 1991b, 22–36; Thapar 1991). For a succinct discussion of the more recent archaeological findings, see Mandal 1993. In his analysis, Mandal stresses that no evidence of large-scale destruction of elaborate structures such as a temple has been found at the site, even after the demolition.

50. For an account of the changing interpretations of the legend of Ram and of historically diverse interpretations of Ram rajya as the reign of justice and truth, from Tulsidas's bhakti interpretation to nationalist appropriations of Ram up to the present day, see Lutgendorf 1995.

51. As van der Veer has pointed out, competing interpretations of devotion to Ram, and its bhakti incarnations in the Ramahandi sect, have played a part in the production of modern Hinduism. Both the interpretation of Ramahandis as basically egalitarian and the communal interpretation of the sect as martial defenders of Hinduism against Muslim onslaught are without foundation in fact. The Ramahandis were an internally differentiated and highly mobile community of traders and soldiers engaged in multiple ways in the politics and economy over the centuries. See van der Veer 1988 and 1995.

52. For a superb account of the transformation of representations of Ram from a sweet and peaceful child to a warrior, see Kapur 1993.

53. Quoted from *Times of India*, 19 July 1992.

54. I attended a number of public functions in connection with this campaign in various places in rural and urban Maharashtra. The lack of enthusiasm among activists and the lukewarm public response to the concept was openly admitted by activists and local leaders. The campaign was run almost exclusively by the VHP and not backed with manpower and logistics by the BJP, as

in the case of previous campaigns. Local VHP leaders assured me, however, that the response in north India was much better because "people there are far more religious than here" (interview, VHP activists, Thane city, 22 October 1992).

55. Although BJP and RSS leaders, immediately after the demolition, blamed "irresponsible elements" for the demolition and thus implicitly admitted that planning probably had been involved, the BJP's White Paper, published months after the events, depicts the demolition as an "unexpected" and "spontaneous" response of Hindus to the manipulative and contemptuous tactics of the government (Bharatiya Janata Party 1993, 131–32). Although no one with insight into the workings of the Sangh parivar doubted that planning had taken place, the government also denied this energetically (see, for example, *Pioneer* 3 January 1993), presumably to conceal its own pathetic lack of intelligence reports or systematic surveillance of the agitation.

56. On the evening of 10 December 1992, I went to the RSS headquarters in Delhi, which was almost closed down in anticipation of the coming ban. In one of the rooms was Rajendra Singh, then powerful coordinator of the RSS in the entire north India, now sarsanghachalak, waiting patiently for the police to arrive. While he was waiting I interviewed him, and a few hours later he was arrested and an official ban imposed on the RSS on 11 December 1992.

57. I attended Kalyan Singh's address at a BJP rally in Pune in mid-February 1993. Singh gave a long account of the entire process preceding the demolition of Babri Masjid, and claimed that the demolition was a spontaneous revolt against the lingering and betrayal of the central government on the issue. Occasionally, Singh interrupted this narrative and yelled a few slogans, as if to respond to the upbeat atmosphere, only to resume his account immediately.

58. Although the mandal is in a formal sense apolitical, its celebration of the 1992 centenary of the Ganpatiutsav [Ganesh celebration], which I attended in September 1992, was a conspicuous display of political symbolism, whose mandap (staged) tableaux demonstrated an elaborate narrative of the Indian freedom struggle with animated life-sized dolls, sound, light, and decorations. The much-attended play, which received an award, celebrated Tilak as the founder of the national liberation struggle, which still is unfinished and is today carried on by the Sangh parivar, with the BJP as the torch bearer of democracy, national freedom, and cultural dignity. For an analysis of how the Ganpatiutsav is traversed by political and commercial discourses in contemporary Mumbai, see Kaur 1998.

59. For a report on the campaign spending of the various parties, see *India Today*, 15 November 1993.

60. Ibid., 36.

61. The BJP in Madhya Pradesh had especially suffered setbacks due to its continued upper-caste bias, and the new policy created a protracted debate in the party that compounded the already rampant factionalism in the state unit (Jaffrelot 1995).

62. See, for instance, the article "The Demonization of the Upper Castes" in *Organiser*, 30 October 1994.

Chapter 6

1. Bipin Chandra has argued that relative backwardness in education and economic status, and blocked social mobility of lower-middle-class groups, have historically provided conditions hospitable to the growth of communal sentiments and antagonisms (Chandra 1984, 180–207).

2. This is the recurrent conclusion emerging from the many studies of communal riots undertaken by Ashgar Ali Engineer since the 1970s.

3. See Kakar 1995, 160–65. The Muslim sense of martial/masculine superiority was expressed by several of my informants, among them a young Muslim living in central Mumbai. He explained that the only reason why Shiv Sena and the RSS had been able to gain ground in Mumbai was support from the police: "Let the police come here as neutral bystanders and let them keep order. Then let the Shiv Sainiks come, unarmed, and let us fight man to man, Hindu against Muslim. Then you'll see that these Hindu college boys are no good and you'll see what fighters the Muslims are."

4. Some of the elderly pehlwans expressed a curious sense of decline in the quality of riots and fighting because opponents had turned into "soft" men who were too easy to kill! The involvement of fighters and wrestlers from akharas is widespread during riots in north India, where branches of the Sangh parivar such as Bajrang Dal run their own akharas and gymnasiums. For an example from Jaipur, see Mayaram 1993, 2,529. But as Joseph Alter has pointed out, the communal ethos promoted by the Sangh parivar is in many ways different from and at odds with the classical ethos of bodily discipline and austerity nurtured in the akharas (Alter 1994).

5. Kakar 1995, 66–109. A similar set of rules of conduct pertaining to the permissible and nonpermissible were also expressed by ordinary residents in both Hindu and Muslim neighborhoods affected by riots. As if to protect the notion of honor and to be able to live on somehow, the transgressions were ascribed to people from "outside" (ibid., 125–33 and 157–60).

6. The information on the mohalla committees was gathered during fieldwork in Mumbai in 1996, where I met members of mohalla committees and police officers in predominantly Muslim areas in central Bombay. One of the areas most affected by violence was a blue-collar-worker neighborhood of chawls (huts) with both Hindus and Muslims, popularly known as "the Jammu and Kashmir ward." I have in a recent paper explored the relations between the police and the local Muslim population here, as well as the proceedings of the Srikrishna Commission inquiring into the riots in Bombay in December 1992 and January 1993 (Hansen 1998a).

7. For a somewhat similar critique of the widespread acceptance of the externality of the Indian state vis-à-vis society, communalism, and communal violence, see van der Veer 1997: 261–63).

8. Kakar refers to what has been called the "Andalusian syndrome," the melancholy and feeling of loss inflicted on the Muslim world after the loss of the culture blossoming in Andalusia until the Castilian reconquista in the sixteenth century (Kakar 1995, 164–67). I experienced a similar sense of silent but proud

desperation and sense of loss among elderly Muslims in the Marathwada region, which until 1953 was ruled by the nizam of Hyderabad and a Muslim administrative cadre.

9. See for instance Javeed Alam's analysis of Muslim communalism in Hyderabad (Alam 1993).

10. I realize that this imposition of Lacanian reasoning upon the cultural and historical field of India may not escape charges of unwarranted universalism. I will argue, nonetheless, that Lacanian theory, in its insistence on the three psychic orders of the Imaginary, the Symbolic, and the Real as a structural logic of subjectivation, remains relatively immune to the critique of the eurocentricity of psychoanalytical reasoning that has been leveled against Kakar's egopsychology by Stanley Kurtz (Kurtz 1992). According to Kurtz, the oedipal structure does not apply in India because the family structure is that of joint families where the place of the mother is held by a plurality of women, and where the father is relatively absent. Instead, he proposes to see the crucial process of ego formation as that of the "Durga complex," wherein the child learns to discern and stabilize the "motherly" forces into the good and protective on the one hand and the demonic and punishing forces (symbolised in Durga's incarnation as the goddess Kali) on the other. I fail, however, to recognize the joint family as a specifically Indian phenomenon, just as I find Kurtz's interpretation of the mother figure in psychoanalysis as a single biological individual a rather facile target of criticism. To my mind the pertinence and power of the oedipal structure derives exactly from the ambivalence of the mother figure as both a caring and a sexual/demonic force, which represents a place in the psychic structure, not a particular person.

11. As a young Muslim in Bombay put it to me, "How can you have half-naked women as gods? Everything Hindu is obsessed with this. All is sexy, sexy. And how can you respect people who worship images of an elephant or a monkey?"

12. An attitudinal survey conducted by Ghanshyam Shah in Surat, with more than 700 respondents, revealed that communal consciousness was at a rather high level, fairly evenly distributed across age, class, gender, and profession, but higher among educated professionals than among illiterates and manual labourers, and not correlated in any way with economic status. The survey also revealed that there were no clear correlations between a high level of religiosity, communal attitudes, and support for the BJP. Further, it revealed that the BJP and Congress had an equal share of voters with high levels of communal consciousness (Shah 1994).

Chapter 7

1. The strategic and tactical challenges and complexities facing the BJP after the 1996 elections are analyzed in some detail in the "Introduction" by Hansen and Jaffrelot in Hansen and Jaffrelot 1998. The 1998 elections and the formation of the BJP-led cabinet in March 1998 are briefly analyzed in the "Afterword" by Hansen, Hasan, and Jaffrelot, in the same volume.

2. For a full list of election commitments of the BJP, see *Organiser* (special edition), April 1996, and the party's 80-page election manifesto, *For a Strong and Prosperous India*, 1996.

3. See Advani's suggestion of "multipurpose identity cards which serve the purpose of voter identity cards, give citizenship details, and stand as testimony of other minor details needed by the administration" (*Observer*, 18 March 1996). This somewhat enigmatic formulation indicates the desire among BJP leaders to have a more systematic knowledge and to classify properly (and prioritize?) citizens.

4. Debates in the Indian press and my impressions from conversations with Indians since the nuclear tests seem to confirm that the tests have corrected the unjust neglect of India in the world, and has forced particularly western media and decision makers to recognize India as a major power. As an Indian citizen settled in a European country told me recently, "Look at all the attention given to India by the press now. In all my years here I have never seen anything like it. . . . That is, at least, a good thing in itself."

5. Interview with Jay Dubashi, leader of the BJP's Economic Policy Cell, at the BJP main office in New Delhi, 13 November 1996.

6. See *Pioneer* 2 February 1996.

7. Shiv Sena's embrace of the signifiers of modernity was amply demonstrated when a business organization floated by the party took charge of a huge Michael Jackson show in Mumbai in October 1996. In a move designed to consolidate its hold on the youth in the state and to establish the liberal credentials of the party, the party *supremo* Bal Thackeray invited Jackson to his house and ordered the entire party leadership to sit through the concert (many wearing earplugs).

8. For a more detailed analysis see Hansen 1998c.

9. The trajectory of the BJP in Maharashtra is analyzed in more detail in Hansen 1998b.

10. Almost as an act of catharsis, L. K. Advani , who was indicted in a massive corruption scandal in 1996, launched during the 1996 election campaign a Suraj (good government) yatra from south India to Delhi. The popular response was at best lukewarm and in many cases virtually absent, and the yatra was terminated before it reached Delhi.

11. The ban on the VHP was lifted in a controversial verdict by the Delhi High Court. In an open critique of ruling politicians, the judge stated that the ban only served to "prolong the disharmony among citizens" and ascribed the ills of the country to the "insatiable desire for power which makes persons loose balance" (quoted from *Frontline* 28 July 1995).

12. RSS chief Rajendra Singh reiterated in May 1995 the demand that the two shrines "should be handed over to Hindus—but the sants and sadhus have also resolved that this cannot be done except if the present government is defeated in the elections" (interview, *Asian Age*, 1 May 1995). This was a clear challenge to the BJP, reluctant to take up this religious issue and again expose itself to charges of illegal election practices, as in the cases pending against several MPs and MLAs accused of using religious propaganda in their election campaign.

Regarding the debates in the party, see reports in *Indian Express*, 21 August 1995; *Economic Times*, 16 August 1995; and *India Today*, 15 October 1995.

13. See reports in *Indian Express*, 21 April 1995. There was a profound irony in the fact that a few weeks after this announcement Arif Beg quit the BJP and denounced it as essentially anti-Muslim. Persisting in its strategy of token symbolism vis-à-vis the Muslim minority, Sikander Bakht was given the portfolio for urban affairs and employment in the interim cabinet formed by BJP in late May 1996. Like all other measures taken by the BJP in this regard, these were also symbolic gestures devoid of any content or seriousness.

14. M. U. Khan, leader of the BJP minority cell in Mumbai, interview in Byculla, Mumbai, 14 February 1997.

15. *Sunday*, 19–25 December 1993.

16. VHP speaker in Ayodhya on 6 December 1993 (*Sunday*, 19–25 December 1993).

17. Ashok Singhal, interview in *Frontline*, 31 December 1993.

18. See reports in *Frontline*, 17 November 1995. On the evening before the event in Nagpur, the yatras had congregated in Ramtek, fifty kilometers outside Nagpur. Here the conventional anti-Muslim and Hindu communal agenda had prevailed in speeches by Singhal, Sadvi Ritambra, and others.

19. *The Hindu*, 10 March 1996; *Pioneer*, 9 March 1996. The full text of the pledge was printed in *Organiser* (special edition), March 1996.

20. Sheshadri 1991. This figure of thought reflected, almost to the word, the Fichtean notion of nationalism as a stage in the realization of the universal spirit.

21. *RSS: Widening Horizons* (Bangalore: Sahitya Sangama, 1992), 30.

22. The Hindu Declaration is drafted in Sanskrit and not yet available in English. The excerpts are from an article referring to its contents (*Pioneer*, 17 June 1995). According to this account, the preamble to the declaration goes: "A Hindu is like any other human being, only more so, wherefore all human beings possess the following rights as they are all the children of the Earth and descended from Manu and possess rationality and morality in common."

23. *Organiser*, 5 May 1996.

24. *Organiser*, 16 December 1990.

25. *Organiser*, 26 November 1989.

26. Rajendra Singh in *Telegraph*, 4 May 1995.

27. For a recent restatement of this analysis, see Vanaik 1996.

Glossary

Akhanda Bharat — Undivided India
akhara — wrestling ground
badmash — hooligans
bania — merchant, businessman
baudhik — ideological training
bhadralok — lit. "big people"; Bengali term for the educated elite
bhagwa dhwaj — the saffron flag
bhajans — devotional songs
bhakti — devotional form of Hinduism
Bharat Mata — Mother India
dada — strongman
dalal — brokerage
Dalit — "untouchable"
dharma — religion; spiritual matters
dharma yuddha — holy war
Ganpati — name of the god Ganesh in Maharashtra
garib hatao — "remove poverty" (slogan of Indira Gandhi)
gau mata — mother cow
goonda — muscleman
guru — religious teacher, advisor
Hindu rashtra — the Hindu nation
Hindutva — Hinduness
hukumut — ability to rule
jati — caste group
jawan — ordinary soldier
jouissance — enjoyment, especially of something unknown or disturbing
kar sevak — temple construction volunteer at Ram mandir, Ayodhya
kirtan — chanted prayer
mandal — council
mandir — Hindu temple
Manusmriti — ancient Hindu lawbook
Marwari — trading community of north India, originally from the state of
    Mewar in Rajasthan
masjid — mosque
mohalla — neighborhood, locality
moksha — state reached after deliverance from the cycle of births and rebirths
namaz — Muslim prayer
objet petit à — alien element, impurity
panchayat — local governing and adjudicating council
parrhesia — heroic defiance of power
pehlwan — professional wrestler/strongman

pir — Muslim saint in the Sufi tradition

pitrubhoomi — Savarkar's term for "holy land"

pracharak — full-time RSS organizer

puja — Hindu worship

pundit — learned Hindu scholar

purdah — veil, curtain; seclusion of women

Ram Rajya — the rule of Ram

Ramjanmabhoomi — movement to build a Ram mandir to replace the Babri Masjid at the reputed site of Ram's birth in Ayodhya

rashtrasevika — female equivalent of swayamsevak

rashtra mandir — national, nonsectarian Hindu temple

sadhu — renunciant, holy man

sadhvi — female sadhu

sammelan — congregation

samskar — virtuous behavior, moral teaching

sanatana dharma — Hindu traditionalism, orthodoxy

sanatani — member of or believer in sanatana dharma

sangathan — organization of Hindus

sangathanist — supporter of the sangathan

sangathan sangathanacharya — supreme head and "dictator" of militant Hinduism

Sangh parivar — the RSS "family" of organizations

sangha — "organization," term used for the RSS by its members

sannyasa — renunciation of worldy things in the Hindu tradition

sannyasi — Hindu renunciant

sant — saint; holy man

sarpanch — head of village panchayat

sarsanghachalak — president of an organization

sarvodaya — welfare for all

sati — immolation of widows

satyagraha — truth force

seva samiti — volunteer corps

sevika — rashtrasevika

shakha — in the RSS, daily meeting of young men or women for exercise, drill, and ideological training; in Shiv Sena, neighborhood headquarters building

shakti — creative force, power

shuddhi — "purification" and (re-)conversion to Hinduism

swadeshi — Indian manufacture and consumption

swayamsevak — RSS volunteer

swaraj — self-rule, independence

tabligh — propaganda for conversion to Islam

tanzim — Islamic community organization

tilak — mark placed on the forehead

trishul — trident, emblem of the god Shiva

ulama — Muslim men of religious learning

upayatra — subsidiary yatra

varna — Vedic fourfold social ranking

yatra — pilgrimage, religious procession
zamindar — big landlord entrusted with tax collection
zamindari — zamindar's land
zopadpatti — slum

Bibliography

Government of India Publications

Government of India. 1951. *First Five Year Plan: A Draft Outline*. New Delhi.
————. 1952. *First Five Year Plan*. New Delhi.
————. 1961. *Report of the Study Group on the Welfare of the Weaker Sections in the Village Community*. 2 vols. New Delhi.
————. 1964. *Report of the Committee on Prevention of Corruption*. New Delhi.
————. 1979. *Levels, Trends and Differentials in Fertility*. New Delhi: Office of the Registrar General and Census Commissioner.
————. 1986. *India 1985*. New Delhi: Ministry of Information and Broadcasting.
————. 1990. *National Survey Sample, 43rd Round*. New Delhi: Office of the Registrar General and Census Commissioner.
————. 1993. *White Paper on Ayodhya*. New Delhi.

Other Sources

Alam, Javeed. 1993. "The Changing Grounds of Communal Mobilization: The Majlis-e-Ittehad-ul-Muslimeen and the Muslims in Hyderabad." In *Hindus and Others*, edited by Gyanendra Pandey, 146–76. New Delhi: Viking.
Alberoni, Francesco. 1984. *Movement and Institution*. New York: Columbia University Press.
Alter, Joseph. 1992. *The Wrestler's Body: Identity and Ideology in North India*. Berkeley and Los Angeles: University of California Press.
————. 1994. "Somatic Nationalism: Indian Wrestling and Militant Hinduism." *Modern Asian Studies* 28, no. 3: 557–88).
Andersen, W., and S. Damle. 1987. *Brotherhood in Saffron*. Boulder, Colo.: Westview Press.
Anderson, Benedict. 1991. *Imagined Communities*. 2d rev. version. London: Verso.
————.1994. "Exodus." *Critical Inquiry* 20 (Winter): 314–27.
Anderson, Michael. 1990. "Islamic Law and the Colonial Encounter in British India." In *Islamic Family Law*, edited by Chibli Mallat and Jane Connors, 205–23. London: Graham.
Appadurai, Arjun. 1981. *Worship and Conflict under Colonial Rule: A South Indian Case*. Cambridge: Cambridge University Press.
Bachetta, Paola. 1996. "Hindu Nationalist Women as Ideologues." In *Embodied Violence: Communalising Women's Sexuality in South Asia*, edited by K. Jayawardena and M. de Alwis, 126–67. New Delhi: Kali for Women.
Bagchi, Amiya K. 1994. "Globalising India: The Fantasy and the Reality." *Social Scientist* 22, nos. 7–8 (July-August): 18–27.
————, ed. 1995. *Democracy and Development*. London: Macmillan.

Bagchi, Jasodara. 1990. "Representing Nationalism: Ideology of Motherhood in Colonial Bengal." *Economic and Political Weekly* 25 (20 October): 65–68.

Balibar, Etienne. 1991. "The Nation Form: History and Ideology." In *Race, Nation, Class: Ambiguous Identities*, edited by Etienne Balibar and Immanuel Wallerstein, 86–107. London: Verso.

————. 1993. *Classes, Masses and Ideas*. London: Routledge.

Bannerjee, Ashish. 1990. "Comparative Curfew: Changing Dimensions of Communal Politics in India." In *Mirrors of Violence: Communities, Riots and Survivors in South Asia*, edited by Veena Das, 37–68. Delhi: Oxford University Press.

Bardhan, Pranab. 1985. *The Political Economy of Development in India*. Oxford: Blackwell.

Basu, Shamita. 1997. "Religious Revivalism as Nationalist Discourse. Swami Vivekananda and the Nineteenth-Century Neo-Hindu Movement in Bengal."Ph.D. dissertation, International Development Studies, Roskilde University.

Basu, T., et al. 1993. *Khaki Shorts and Saffron Flags*. Hyderabad and Delhi: Orient Longman.

Bauman, Zygmunt. 1991. *Modernity and Ambivalence*. Cambridge: Polity Press.

Baxi, Upendra. 1990. "Reflections on the Reservation Crisis in Gujarat." In *Mirrors of Violence*, edited by Veena Das, 215–39. Delhi: Oxford University Press.

Baxter, Craig. 1969. *The Jana Sangh: Biography of an Indian Political Party*. Philadelphia: Pennsylvania University Press.

Bayart, Jean François. 1989. *The State in Africa: The Politics of the Belly*. London: Longman.

————. 1991. "Finishing with the Idea of the Third World: The Concept of the Political Trajectory." In *Rethinking Third World Politics*, edited by James Manor, 51–71. London: Longman.

Berlin, Isaiah. 1976. *Vico and Herder: Two Studies in the History of Ideas*. London: Hogarth Press.

Bharatiya Janata Party. 1993. *White Paper on Ayodhya and the Rama Temple Movement*. New Delhi.

Blumenberg, Hans. 1983. *The Legitimacy of the Modern Age*. Cambridge: MIT Press.

Bobbio, Noberto. 1996. *The Age of Rights*. Cambridge: Polity Press.

Bogey of Dual Membership. 1979. Bangalore: Jagarana Prakashana.

Bokhare, M. G. 1993. *Hindu Economics*. Swadeshi Jagaran Manch. New Delhi: Janaki Prakashan.

Bourdieu, Pierre. 1990a. *In Other Words*. Cambridge: Polity Press.

————. 1990b. *The Logic of Practice*. Cambridge: Harvard University Press.

————. 1991. *Language and Symbolic Power*. Cambridge: Harvard University Press.

Bourdieu, Pierre, and Terry Eagleton. 1992. "Doxa and Common Life." *New Left Review* no. 191 (January-February): 111–20.

Brass, Paul R. 1975. *Language, Religion and Politics in North India*. Cambridge: Cambridge University Press.

———. 1979. "Elite Groups, Symbol Manipulation and Ethnic Identity among the Muslims of South Asia." In *Political Identities in South Asia*, edited by David Taylor and Malcolm Yapp, 35–77. London: Curzon Press.

———. 1982. "Pluralism, Regionalism and Decentralizing Tendencies in Contemporary Indian Politics." In *The States of South Asia: Problems of National Integration*, edited by A. J. Wilson and Dennis Dalton, 223–64. London: C. Hurst.

———. 1990. *The Politics of India since Independence*. Vol. 4 of *The New Cambridge History of India*. Cambridge: Cambridge University Press.

———. 1991. *Ethnicity and Nationalism. Theory and Comparison*. New Delhi: Sage Publications.

———, ed. 1996. *Riots and Pogroms*. London: Macmillan.

Breckenridge, Carol, and Peter van der Veer, eds. 1993. *Orientalism and the Postcolonial Predicament*. Philadelphia: University of Pennsylvania Press.

Breman, Jan. 1993. "Anti-Muslim Pogrom in Surat." *Economic and Political Weekly* 28 (17 April): 737–41.

Brown, Judith. 1972. *Gandhi's Rise to Power: Indian Politics 1915–22*. Cambridge: Cambridge University Press.

———. 1977. *Gandhi and Civil Disobedience: The Mahatma in Indian Politics 1928–34*. Cambridge: Cambridge University Press.

Burchell, Graham, Colin Gordon, and Peter Miller, eds. 1991. *The Foucault Effect: Studies in Governmentality*. London: Harvester Wheatsheaf.

Canguilheim, Georges. 1994. *A Vital Rationalist: Selected Writings from Georges Canguilheim*. Translated by Francois Delaporte. New York: Zone Books.

Cashman, Richard. 1975. *The Myth of the Lokamanya: Tilak and Mass Politics in Maharashtra*. Berkeley and Los Angeles: University of California Press.

Chandra, Bipan. 1984. *Communalism in Modern India*. New Delhi: Vikas.

Chandra, Sudhir. 1993. "Of Communal Consciousness and Communal Violence." *Economic and Political Weekly* 28 (4 September): 1883–87.

Chatterjee, Partha. 1986. *Nationalist Discourse and the Colonial World: A Derivative Discourse*. London and Delhi: Zed Press.

———. 1992. "The Nationalization of Hinduism." *Social Research* 59, no. 1 (Spring): 111–49.

———. 1993. *The Nation and Its Fragments*. Princeton: Princeton University Press.

———. 1995. "Religious Minorities and the Secular State: Notes on an Indian Impasse." *Public Culture* no. 8: 11–39.

Chiriyankandath, James. 1992a. "Democracy under the Raj: Elections and Separate Representation in British India." *Journal of Commonwealth and Comparative Politics*, 30, no. 1 (March): 39–64.

———. 1992b. "Tricolour and Saffron: Congress and the Neo-Hindu Challenge." In *Electoral Politics in India: A Changing Landscape*, edited by Subrata Mitra and James Chiriyankandath, 55–80. New Delhi: Segment Books.

Choudhary, Kameshwar. 1991. "Reservation for OBCs: Hardly an Abrupt Decision." In *The Mandal Commission Controversy*, edited by Ashgar Ali Engineer, 105–24. Delhi: Ajanta Publications.

Chowdhury-Sengupta, Indira. 1992. "Mother India and Mother Victoria: Motherhood and Nationalism in Nineteenth Century Bengal." *South Asia Research* 12, no. 1: 20–37.

Chunav Ghosua-patra: Loksabha Chunav (Hindi). Election Manifesto 1989. New Delhi: Bharatiya Janata Party.

Church, Roderick. 1984. "The Patterns of State Politics in Indira Gandhi's India." In *State Politics in Contemporary India*, edited by John R. Woods, 226–52, Boulder, Colo.: Westview Press.

Cohn, Bernard S. 1987. *An Anthropologist among the Historians*. Delhi: Oxford University Press.

Curran, J. A. 1951. *Militant Hinduism in Indian Politics: A Study of RSS*. New York: Institute of Pacific Affairs.

Das, Veena, ed. 1990. *Mirrors of Violence: Communities, Riots and Survivors in South Asia*. Delhi: Oxford University Press.

Datta, Pradip Kumar. 1993a. "Dying Hindus: Production of Hindu Communal Common Sense in Early 20th Century Bengal." *Economic and Political Weekly* 28 (19 June): 1305–19.

———. 1993b. "VHPs Ram: The Hindutva Movement in Ayodhya." In *Hindus and Others: Questions of Identity in India Today*, edited by Gyanendra Pandey, 46–73. New Delhi: Viking.

Davis, Richard H. 1996. "The Iconography of Rama's Chariot." In *Making India Hindu*, edited by David Ludden, 27–54. Delhi: Oxford University Press.

de Certeau, Michel. 1984. *The Practice of Everyday Life*. Berkeley and Los Angeles: University of California Press.

Derrida, Jacques. 1985. *The Ear of the Other*. New York: Schocken Books.

Deshpande, G. P. 1985. "The Plural Tradition." *Seminar* no. 313 (September): 18–25.

de Tocqueville, Alexis. 1966. *Democracy in America*, Translated by J. P. Mayer and Max Lerner. London: Harper & Row.

Deutsch, Kenneth, and Thomas Pantham, eds. 1986. *Political Thought in Modern India*. New Delhi: Sage Publications.

Dhanagare, D. N. 1988. "An Apoliticist Populism." *Seminar* no. 352 (December): 24–31.

Dirks, Nicholas B. 1992. "Castes of Mind." *Representations* 37 (Winter): 56–78.

Dixit, Prabha. 1986. "The Ideology of Hindu Nationalism." In *Political Thought in Modern India*, edited by Kenneth L. Deutsch and Thomas Pantham, 122–41. New Delhi: Sage Publications.

Dubashi, Jay. 1992. *The Road to Ayodhya*. Delhi: Voice of India.

Dumont, Louis. 1983. *Essays on Individualism*. Chicago: University of Chicago Press.

———. 1994. *German Ideology*. Chicago: University of Chicago Press.

Elst, Koenraad. 1990. *Ramjanmabhoomi vs. Babri Masjid*. Delhi: Voice of India.

Engineer, Asghar A., ed. 1987. *The Shah Bano Controversy*. New Delhi: Sangam Books.

———, ed. 1991a. *Mandal Commission Controversy*. Delhi: Ajanta Publications.

———, ed. 1991b. *Communal Riots in Post-Independence India*. New Delhi: Sangam Books.

―――. 1991c. "Communal Riots before, during and after Lok Sabha Elections." *Economic and Political Weekly* 24 (14 September): 2135–38.

Engineer, Irfan. 1994. "Backward Communities and Migrant Workers in Surat Riots." *Economic and Political Weekly* 29 (28 May): 1348–60.

Ergang, Reinhold. 1931. *Herder and German Nationalism*. New York: Columbia University Press.

Farmer, Victoria. 1996. "Mass Media: Images, Mobilization and Communalism." In *Making India Hindu*, edited by David Ludden, 98–115. Delhi: Oxford University Press.

Fasana, E. 1994. "From Hindutva to Hindu Rashtra: The Social and Political Thought of Vinayak Damodar Savarkar." Paper presented at the 13th European Conference of Modern South Asian Studies, Toulouse (30 August–3 September).

Feldman, Allen. 1991. *Formations of Violence*. Chicago: University of Chicago Press.

Fichte, Johann Gottlieb. 1955. *Reden an die Deutsche Nation*. Hamburg: Felix Meiner Verlag. English version: J. G. Fichte. 1922. *Addresses to the German Nation*. Translated by R. F. Jones and G. H. Turnbull. Chicago: Open Court Publications.

―――. 1977 [1800]. "Der geschlossene Handelsstaat." In *Ausgewählte Politische Schrifften*, edited by Zwi Batscha and Richard Saage, 59–167. Frankfurt a. M.: Suhrkampf.

For a Strong and Prosperous India. Election Manifesto 1996. New Delhi: Bharatiya Janata Party.

Foucault, Michel. 1980a. "Two Lectures." In *Power/Knowledge*, edited by Colin Gordon, 78–108. New York: Pantheon.

―――. 1980b. "Power and Strategies." In *Power/Knowledge*, edited by Colin Gordon, 134–45. New York: Pantheon.

―――. 1984. "What is Enlightenment?" In *The Foucault Reader*, edited by Paul Rabinow, 32–70. Harmondsworth: Penguin.

―――. 1984. "Nietzsche, Genealogy, History." In *The Foucault Reader*, edited by Paul Rabinow, 76–100. Harmondsworth: Penguin.

―――. 1991. "Governmentality." In *The Foucault Effect: Studies in Governmentality*, edited by Graham Burchell, Colin Gordon, and Peter Miller, 87–103. London: Harvester Wheatsheaf.

Fox, Richard. 1985. *The Lions of Punjab*. Berkeley and Los Angeles: University of California Press.

―――. 1987. "Gandhian Socialism and Hindu Nationalism: Cultural Domination in the World System." *Journal of Commonwealth and Comparative Politics* 25, no. 3 (November): 233–47.

―――. 1990. "Hindu Nationalism in the Making, or the Rise of the Hindian." *Monograph Series* no. 2: 63–81. Washington, D.C.: American Ethnological Society.

Frankel, Francine R. 1978. *India's Political Economy 1947–77: The Gradual Revolution*. Princeton: Princeton University Press.

Frankel, Francine, and M.S.S. Rao, eds. 1990. *Dominance and State Power in Modern India*. 2 vols. Delhi: Oxford University Press.

Freitag, Sandria B. 1990. *Collective Action and Community: Public Arenas and the Emergence of Communalism in North India*. Delhi: Oxford University Press.

Freud, Sigmund. 1967. *Group Psychology and the Analysis of the Ego*. Translated by James Strachey. London: Hogarth Press.

Frykenberg, Robert E. 1989. "The Emergence of Modern 'Hinduism' as a Concept and as an Institution: A Reappraisal with Special Reference to South India." In *Hinduism Reconsidered*, edited by G. D. Sontheimer and H. Kulke, 29–70. Delhi: Manohar.

Fuller, C. J. 1992. *The Camphor Flame*. Princeton: Princeton University Press.

Galanter, Marc. 1984. *Competing Equalities: Law and the Backward Classes in India*. Delhi: Oxford University Press.

———. 1989. *Law and Society in Modern India*. Delhi: Oxford University Press.

Gellner, Ernest. 1983. *Nations and Nationalism*. Oxford: Blackwell.

Ghai, R. K. 1990. *Shuddi Movement in India*. New Delhi: Commonwealth Publishers.

Girard, René. 1977. *Violence and the Sacred*. Translated by P. Gregory. Baltimore: Johns Hopkins University Press.

Golwalkar, M. S. 1947. *WE, or, Our Nationhood Defined*. Nagpur: Bharat Prakashan.

———. 1966. *Bunch of Thoughts*. Bangalore: Jagarana Prakashana.

Gopal, Sarvepalli, ed. 1990. *Anatomy of a Confrontation: The Babri Masjid-Ramjanmabhumi Issue*. New Delhi and Harmondsworth: Penguin.

Gordon, Richard. 1975. "The Hindu Mahasabha and the Indian National Congress 1916–26." *Modern Asian Studies* 9, no. 2: 143–208.

Graf, Violetta. 1992. "The Muslim Vote." In *Electoral Politics in India*, edited by Subrata Mitra and J. Chiriyankandath, 213–40. New Delhi: Segment Books.

Graham, Bruce D. 1987a. *The Challenge of Hindu Nationalism: The Bharatiya Janata Party in Contemporary Indian Politics*. Hull Papers in Indian Politics, no. 40. Hull, Eng.

———. 1987b. "The Jana Sangh and Bloc Politics, 1967–80." *Journal of Commonwealth and Comparative Politics* 25, no. 3: 248–65.

———. 1990. *Hindu Nationalism and Indian Politics*. Cambridge: Cambridge University Press.

Guha, Ranajit. 1989. "Domination without Hegemony." In *Subaltern Studies VI*, edited by Ranajit Guha, 210–310. Delhi: Oxford University Press.

Gupta, Dipankar. 1991. "Continuous Hierarchies and Discrete Castes." In *Social Stratification*, edited by Dipankar Gupta, 110–41. Delhi: Oxford University Press.

———. 1993. "Nationalism and Communalism in North India." *Economic and Political Weekly* 28 (20 February): 339–41.

Hansen, Thomas Blom. 1993. "RSS and the Popularization of Hindutva." *Economic and Political Weekly* 28 (16 October): 2270–72.

———. 1994. "Controlled Emancipation: Women and Hindu Nationalism." *European Journal of Development Research* 6, no. 2: 82–94.

———. 1996a. "Globalisation and Nationalist Imaginations." *Economic and Political Weekly* 31 (9 March): 603–15.

———. 1996b. "Recuperating Masculinity: Hindu Nationalism, Violence and the Exorcism of the Muslim 'Other.'" *Critique of Anthropology* 16, no. 2: 137–72.

———. 1996c. "The Vernacularisation of Hindutva: BJP and Shiv Sena in Rural Maharashtra." *Contributions to Indian Sociology* 30, no. 2: 177–214.

———. 1997a. "Bridging the Gulf: Migration, Modernity and Identity among Muslims in Mumbai." Paper presented at the seminar "Narratives, Mobility and Boundaries," Copenhagen (30 August–1 September).

———. 1997b. "Segmented Worlds. Livelihoods and Identities in Central Mumbai." Paper presented at the conference "Workers in Mumbai," Mumbai (20–23 November).

———. 1998a. "Governance and State Mythologies in Mumbai." Paper presented at the workshop "The Anthropology of the Indian State." London School of Economics and Political Science (9 May).

———. 1998b. "BJP and the Politics of Hindutva in Maharashtra." In *The Compulsions of Politics: BJP and Competitive Politics in India*, edited by Thomas Blom Hansen and Christophe Jaffrelot. Delhi: Oxford University Press.

———. 1998c. "The Ethics of Hinduva and the Spirit of Capitalism." In *The Compulsions of Politics: BJP and Competitive Politics in India*, edited by Thomas Blom Hansen and Christophe Jaffrelot. Delhi: Oxford University Press.

Hansen, Thomas Blom, and Christophe Jaffrelot. 1998. "Introduction." In *The Compulsions of Politics: BJP and Competitive Politics in India*, edited by Thomas Blom Hansen and Christophe Jaffrelot. Delhi: Oxford University Press.

Hansen, Thomas Blom, Zoya Hasan, and Christophe Jaffrelot. 1998. "Afterword." In *The Compulsions of Politics: BJP and Competitive Politics in India*, edited by Thomas Blom Hansen and Christophe Jaffrelot. Delhi: Oxford University Press.

Hasan, Mushirul. 1991. *Nationalism and Communal Politics in India 1916–1928*. Delhi: Manohar.

Hasan, Zoya. 1990a. "Power and Mobilization: Patterns of Resilience and Change in Uttar Pradesh Politics." In *Dominance and State Power in Modern India: Decline of a Social Order*, edited by Francine Frankel and M.S.S. Rao, 133–203. Delhi: Oxford University Press.

———. 1990b. "Changing Orientation of the State and the Emergence of Majoritarianism in the 1980s." *Social Scientist* 18, nos. 8–9 (August-September): 27–39.

———. 1996. "Communal Mobilization and Changing Majority in Uttar Pradesh." In *Making India Hindu*, edited by David Ludden, 81–97. Delhi: Oxford University Press.

Hegel, J.W.F. 1956. *The Philosophy of History*. Translated by J. Sibree. New York: Dover.

Heimsath, Charles H. 1964. *Indian Nationalism and Hindu Social Reform*. Princeton: Princeton University Press.

Herder, J. G. 1964. *Reflections on the Philosophy of the History of Humankind*. Translated by Frank E. Manuel. Chicago: Phoenix Books.

———. 1965. *Über der Ursprung der Sprachen*. Berlin: Freies Geist Leben.

Hindu Vishwa. 1979. Special Number (March-April). New Delhi: Vishwa Hindu Parishad.

Hobsbawm, Eric. 1990. *Nations and Nationalism since 1780: Programme, Myth, Reality*. Cambridge: Cambridge University Press.

Humanistic Approach to Economic Development (A Swadeshi Alternative). 1992. New Delhi: Bharatiya Janata Party.

Inamdar, N. R. 1986. "The Political Ideas of Lokmanya Tilak." In *Political Thought in Modern India*, edited by Kenneth Deutsch and Thomas Pantham, 110–21. New Delhi: Sage Publications.

Inden, Ronald. 1990. *Imagining India*. Oxford: Blackwell.

———. 1995. "Embodying God: From Imperial Progress to Progress in India." *Economy and Society* 24, no. 4: 245–78.

In Defence of Nations Sovereignty. 1991. Bombay: Akhil Bharatiya Vidyarti Parishad, Central Office.

India at the Crossroads. 1980. Presidential address. First National Convention of the Bharatiya Janata Party. New Delhi: Bharatiya Janata Party.

Jaffrelot, Christophe. 1993. *Les nationalistes hindous*. Paris: Presses de la Fondation Nationale des Sciences Politiques.

———. 1994. "Les (re)conversions a l'hindouisme (1885–1990): Politisation et diffusion d'une 'invention de la tradition.'" *Archives des Sciences Sociales des Religions* 87 (July-September): 73–98.

———. 1995. "The BJP in Madhya Pradesh: The Challenge of the OBCs and the Tribals." Paper presented at the conference "Political Violence in India: The State and Community Conflicts," Amherst (September 23–24).

———. 1996. *The Hindu Nationalist Movement in Indian Politics*. New York: Columbia University Press.

Jalan, Bimal, ed. 1992. *India's Economy*. New Delhi: Viking.

Jeffery, Roger, and Patricia Jeffery. 1994. "The Bijnor Riots, October 1990." *Economic and Political Weekly* 28 (5 March): 551–58.

Jenkins, Rob. 1994. "Where the BJP Survived: Rajasthan Assembly Elections, 1993." *Economic and Political Weekly* 29 (12 March): 635–41.

Jessop, Bob. 1990. *State Theory: Putting the Capitalist State in Its Place*. Cambridge: Polity Press.

Jones, Kenneth W. 1976. *Arya Dharm: Hindu Consciousness in Nineteenth-Century Punjab*. Berkeley and Los Angeles: University of California Press.

Juergensmeyer, Mark. 1993. *Religious Nationalism Confronts the Secular State*. Berkeley and Los Angeles: University of California Press.

Kakar, Sudhir. 1989. *Intimate Relations*. New Delhi: Penguin.

———. 1990. "Some Unconscious Aspects of Ethnic Violence in India." In *Mirrors of Violence*, edited by Veena Das, 135–45. Delhi: Oxford University Press.

———. 1993. "Reflections on Religious Group Identity." *Seminar* no. 402 (February): 50–56.

———. 1995. *The Colours of Violence*. New Delhi: Viking and Penguin.

Kapur, Anuradha. 1993. "Deity to Crusader: The Changing Iconography of Ram." In *Hindus and Others*, edited by Gyanendra Pandey, 74–109. New Delhi: Viking.

Kaur, Raminder. 1998. "Performative Politics: Artworks, Festival Praxis and Nationalism with Special Reference to the Ganpati Utsava in Western India."

Ph.D. dissertation, Department of Anthropology, School of Oriental and African Studies, London.

Kaviraj, Sudipta. 1991. "State, Society and Discourse in India." In *Rethinking Third World Politics*, edited by James Manor, 72–99. London: Orient Longman.

———. 1992. "The Imaginary Institution of India." In *Subaltern Studies VII*, edited by Partha Chatterjee and Gyanendra Pandey, 1–40. Delhi: Oxford University Press.

———. 1995a. "Development and Democracy in India." In *Development and Democracy*, edited by Amiya K. Bagchi, 92–130. London: Macmillan.

———. 1995b. *The Unhappy Consciousness*. Delhi: Oxford University Press.

———. 1997a. "The Modern State in India." In *Dynamics of State Formation: India and Europe Compared*, edited by Martin Dornboos and Sudipta Kaviraj, 225–50. New Delhi: Sage Publications.

———. 1997b. "Democracy and Social Inequality." Unpublished manuscript. School of Oriental and African Studies, London.

Klimkeit, Hans Joachim. 1981. *Der politische Hinduismus*. Wiesbaden: Otto Harrassowitz.

Kohli, Atul. 1987. *State and Poverty in India*. Cambridge: Cambridge University Press.

———. 1990. *Democracy and Discontent*. Cambridge: Cambridge University Press.

Kojéve, Alexander. 1969. *Introduction to the Reading of Hegel*. New York: Basic Books.

Kooiman, Dick. 1996. "The Strength of Numbers. Enumerating Communities in India's Princely States." Paper presented at the 14th European Conference of Modern South Asian Studies, Copenhagen.

Kothari, Rajni. 1970. *Politics in India*. Boston: Little Brown.

Krishnaswamy, S. 1966. "A Riot in Bombay, August 11, 1893. A Study of Hindu-Muslim Relations in Western India in the Nineteenth Century." Ph.D. dissertation, Department of History, University of Chicago.

Kumar, Krishna. 1990. "Hindu Revivalism and Education in North-Central India." *Social Scientist* 18, no. 10: 4–26.

Kumar, Nita. 1992. *The Artisans of Banaras: Popular Culture and Identity 1880–1986*. Princeton: Princeton University Press.

Kumar, Ravinder. 1968. *Western India in the Ninetenth Century*. London: Routledge and Kegan Paul.

Kurtz, Stanley N. 1992. *All Mothers Are One: Hindu India and the Cultural Reshaping of Psychoanalysis*. New York: Columbia University Press.

Lacan, Jacques. 1989 [1971]. *Ecrits*. Translated by Alan Sheridan. London: Routledge.

———. 1992. *The Ethics of Psychoanalysis, 1959–1960: The Seminar of Jacques Lacan. Book VII*. Translated by Dennis Porter. London: Routledge.

———. 1993. *The Psychoses: The Seminar of Jacques Lacan. Book III, 1955–56*. Translated by Russell Grigg. London: Routledge.

———. 1994. "The Mirror-phase as Formative of the Function of the I." In *Mapping Ideology*, edited by Slavoj Žižek, 93–100. London: Verso.

Laclau, Ernesto. 1990. *Reflections on the Revolutions of Our Time*. London: Verso.
———. 1994. "Minding the Gap. The Subject of Politics." In *The Making of Political Identities*, edited by Ernesto Laclau, 11–39. London: Verso.
———. 1996. *Emancipation(s)*. London: Verso.
———. 1996b. "The Death and Resurrection of the Theory of Ideology." *Journal of Political Ideologies* 1, no. 3: 201–20.
Laclau, Ernesto, and Chantal Mouffe. 1985. *Hegemony and Socialist Strategy*. London: Verso.
Lajpat Rai, Lala. 1980. *Shivaji, the Great Patriot*. Delhi: Metropolitan Publishers. Original published in Urdu in 1896.
Lefort, Claude 1988. *Democracy and Political Theory*. Cambridge: Polity Press.
Lelyveld, David. 1978. *Aligarh's First Generation: Muslim Solidarity in British India*. Princeton: Princeton University Press.
———. 1993. "The Fate of Hindustani: Colonial Knowledge and the Project of a National Language." In *Orientalism and the Postcolonial Predicament*, edited by Carol Breckenridge and Peter van der Veer, 189–214. Philadelphia: University of Pennsylvania Press.
Lenneberg, Cornelia. 1988. "Sharad Joshi and the Farmers: The Middle Peasant Lives!" *Pacific Affairs* 61, no. 3 (Fall): 446–66.
Lorenzen, David, ed. 1995. *Bhakti Religion in North India*. Albany: State University of New York Press.
Ludden, David. 1993. "Orientalist Empiricism: Transformations of Colonial Knowledge." In *Orientalism and the Postcolonial Predicament*, edited by Carol Breckenridge and Peter van der Veer, 250–78. Philadelphia: University of Pennsylvania Press.
———. ed. 1996. *Making India Hindu*. Delhi: Oxford University Press.
Lutgendorf, Philip. 1990. "The Ramayan: The Video." *Drama Review* 4, no. 2: 127–76.
———. 1995. "Interpreting *Ramraj*: Reflections on the *Ramayana*, Bhakti and Hindu Nationalism." In *Bhakti Religion in North India*, edited by David Lorenzen, 253–87. Delhi: Manohar.
Madhok, Balraj. 1986. *RSS and Politics*. New Delhi: Hindu World Publications.
Malhotra, Anshu. 1994. "Every Woman Is a Mother in Embryo: Lala Lajpat Rai and Indian Womanhood." *Social Scientist* 22, nos. 1–2 (January-February): 40–63.
Malik, Yogendra, and Jesse F. Marquette. 1990. *Political Mercenaries and Citizen Soldiers*. Delhi: Chanakya Publications.
Malik, Yogendra, and V. B. Singh. 1995. *Hindu Nationalists in India. The Rise of the Bharatiya Janata Party*. New Delhi: Vistaar Publications.
Malkani, K. R. 1980. *The RSS Story*. New Delhi: Impex.
———, ed. 1992. *How Others Look at RSS*. New Delhi: Impex.
Mamdani, Mahmoud. 1996. *Citizen and Subject*. Princeton: Princeton University Press.
Mandal, D. 1993. *Ayodhya: Archaeology after Demolition. A Critique of the "New" and the "Fresh" Discoveries*. Tracts for the Times 5. Hyderabad: Orient Longman.
Manthan. 1991. Periodical published by the Deendayal Research Institute, Delhi (July-September).

Manuel, Peter. 1993. *Cassette Culture: Popular Culture and Technology in North India*. Chicago: University of Chicago Press.

Mayaram, Shail. 1993. "Communal Violence in Jaipur." *Economic and Political Weekly* 27 (20 November): 2524–41.

Mazumdar, Sucheta. 1992. "Women, Culture and Politics: Engendering the Hindu Nation." *South Asia Bulletin* 12, no. 2 (Fall): 1–24.

McKean, Lise. 1995. "The Transnational Context of Communalism: The 1993 Chicago's Parliament of the World's Religions and Hindu Nationalism." Paper presented to seminar on "Communalism in South Asia," University of Pennsylvania.

———. 1996. *Divine Enterprises. Gurus and the Hindu Nationalist Movement*. Chicago: University of Chicago Press.

Miller, Don. 1996. "Mosque, Temple and Crypt." In *Politics of Violence: From Ayodhya to Behrampada*, edited by John Mcquire, Peter Reeves, and Howard Brasted, 193–206. New Delhi: Sage Publications.

Miller, Jacques-Alain. 1966. *Cahiers pour l'analyse*. Paris: Seuil.

Minault, Gail. 1982. *The Khilafat Movement: Religious Symbolism and Political Mobilization in India*. New York: Columbia University Press.

Mitra, Subrata. 1987. "The Perils of Promoting Equality." *Journal of Commonwealth and Comparative Politics* 25, no. 3: 292–312.

———. 1991. "Room to Maneuver in the Middle: Local Elites, Political Action and the State in India." *World Politics* 43 (April): 390–413.

———. 1992. "Democracy and Political Change in India." *Journal of Commonwealth and Comparative Politics* 30, no. 1 (March): 9–39.

Mitra, Subrata K., and James Chiriyankandath, eds. 1992. *Electoral Politics in India: A Changing Landscape*. New Delhi: Segment Books.

Muralidharan, Sukumar. 1994. "Patriotism without People." *Social Scientist* 22, nos. 5–6 (May–June): 3–38.

Myrdal, Gunnar. 1968. *Asian Drama: An Inquiry into the Poverty of Nations*. New York: Twentieth Century Fund.

Nandy, Ashis. 1980. *At the Edge of Psychology*. Delhi: Oxford University Press.

———. 1983. *The Intimate Enemy*. Delhi: Oxford University Press.

Navya Rajyatantrakade: Loksabha Niradnuk Jahirnama (Toward a New Polity: Election Manifesto) (Hindi). 1984. New Delhi: Bharatiya Janata Party.

Nehru, Jawaharlal. 1980 [1946]. *The Discovery of India*. Delhi: Oxford University Press.

Noorani, A. G. 1991. "Legal Aspects to the Issue." In *Anatomy of a Confrontation*, edited by S. Gopal, 58–98. New Delhi: Penguin.

Nugent, Nicholas. 1992. "Rajiv Gandhi and the Congress Party: The Road to Defeat." In *Electoral Politics in India*, edited by Subrata Mitra and James Chiriyankandath, 43–53. New Delhi: Segment Books.

Omvedt, Gail. 1988. "The New Peasants Movement in India." *Bulletin of Concerned Asian Scholars* 20, no. 2 (April–June): 14–24.

———. 1991. "Twice-born Riot against Democracy." In *The Mandal Commission Controversy*, edited by Ashgar Ali Engineer, 6–24. Delhi: Ajanta Publications.

———. 1995. *Dalit Visions*. Tracts for the Times 8. Hyderabad: Orient Longman.

"Opening Remarks." *National Executive Meeting*. December 1–2, 1990. New Delhi: Bharatiya Janata Party.

Pal, Bipinchandra. 1910. *The Spirit of Indian Nationalism*. London: Macmillan.
———. 1958. *Writings and Speeches*. 3 vols. Calcutta: Yugayatri Prakashak.
Pandey, Dhanpati. 1972. *The Arya Samaj and Indian Nationalism*. New Delhi: S. Chand.
Pandey, Gyanendra. 1988. "Congress and the Nation 1917–47." In *Congress and Indian Nationalism. The Pre-Independence Phase*, edited by Richard Sisson and Stanley Wolpert, 121–33. Delhi: Oxford University Press.
———. 1990. *The Construction of Communalism in North India*. Delhi: Oxford University Press.
———. 1991a. "In Defence of the Fragment: Writing about Hindu-Muslim Riots in India Today." *Economic and Political Weekly*, 26 (annual number), nos. 11–12 (March): 559–72.
———. 1991b. "Hindus and Others: The Militant Hindu Construction." *Economic and Political Weekly* 26 (28 December): 2297–3009.
———, ed. 1993. *Hindus and Others. Questions of Identity in India Today*. New Delhi: Viking.
Pannikar, K. N., ed. 1991a. *Communalism in India: History, Politics and Culture*. Delhi: Manohar.
———. 1991b. "A Historical Overview." In *Anatomy of a Confrontation*, edited by S. Gopal, 22–36. New Delhi: Penguin.
———. 1993. "Religious Symbols and Political Mobilisation." *Social Scientist* 21, nos 7–8 (July-August): 63–77.
Pantham, Thomas, and Kenneth Deutsch, eds. 1986. *Political Thought in Modern India*. New Delhi: Sage Publications.
Parekh, Bhikhu. 1989. *Colonialism, Tradition and Reform: An Analysis of Gandhi's Political Discourse*. New Delhi: Sage Publications.
Pasquino, Pasquale. 1991. "Theatrum Politicum: The Genealogy of Capital—Police and the State of Prosperity." In *The Foucault Effect: Studies in Governmentality*, edited by Graham Burchell, Colin Gordon, and Peter Miller, 105–18. London: Harvester Wheatsheaf.
Patterson, Maureen L. P. 1988. "The Shifting Fortunes of Chitpavan Brahmins: Focus on 1948." In *City, Countryside and Society in Maharashtra*, edited by Donald Attwood, Milton Israel, and N. K. Wagle, 35–58. Toronto: Centre for South Asian Studies, University of Toronto Press.
Phadke, Y. D. 1989. "Swatantraveer Sarvarkaranchi Shastrastranchta Vaparabadalchi Bhumika" (Savarkar's Views Regarding the Use of Arms) (Marathi). Working paper, Department of Political Science, Pune University.
Pollock, Sheldon. 1993. "Deep Orientalism? Notes on Sanskrit and Power beyond the Raj." In *Orientalism and the Postcolonial Predicament*, edited by Carol Breckenridge and Peter van der Veer, 76–133. Philadelphia: University of Pennsylvania Press.
Potter, D. 1987. *India's Political Administrators*. Oxford: Clarendon Press.
"Presidential Address." *National Council Meeting*, Bombay, September 25 1989. New Delhi: Bharatiya Janata Party.
Purohit, B. R. 1986. "The Social and Political Thought of Swami Dayananda Saraswati." In *Political Thought in Modern India*, edited by Kenneth Deutsch and Thomas Pantham, 53–66. New Delhi: Sage Publications.

Putnam, Robert, D. 1993. *Making Democracy Work. Civic Traditions in Modern Italy*. Princeton: Princeton University Press.

Raje, Sudhakar, ed. 1972. *Pundit Deendayal Upadhyaya: A Profile*. New Delhi; Deendayal Research Institute.

Ranade, M. G. 1961. *The Rise of Maratha Power*. Bombay: Bombay University.

Ransom, John S. 1997. *Foucault's Discipline*. Durham: Duke University Press.

Resolutions. National Executive Meeting, January 3–5, 1986. New Delhi: Bharatiya Janata Party.

Resolutions. National Executive Meeting, January 1, 1987. New Delhi: Bharatiya Janata Party.

Resolutions, National Executive Meeting, July 9–11, 1989. New Delhi: Bharatiya Janata Party.

Robinson, Francis. 1974. *Separatism among Indian Muslims: The Politics of the United Provinces' Muslims*. Cambridge: Cambridge University Press.

RSS Resolves. Full Texts of Resolutions from 1950 to 1983. 1988. Bangalore: Prakashan Vibhag.

RSS: Widening Horizons. 1992. Bangalore: Sahitya Sangama.

Rudolph, Lloyd, ed. 1984. *Cultural Policy in India*. Delhi: Chanakya Publications.

———. 1992. "The Media and Cultural Politics." In *Electoral Politics in India*, edited by Subrata Mitra and James Chiriyankandath, 81–98. New Delhi: Segment Books.

Rudolph, Lloyd, and Susanne H. Rudolph. 1967. *The Modernity of Tradition*. Chicago: University of Chicago Press.

———. 1987. *In Pursuit of Lakshmi*. Hyderabad: Orient Longman.

Said, Edward W. 1978. *Orientalism*. New York: Vintage.

Saith, Ashwani. 1992. "Absorbing External Shocks: The Gulf Crisis, International Migration Linkages and the Indian Economy, 1990 (with Special Reference to the Impact on Kerala)." *Development and Change* 23, no. 1: 101–46.

Saraswati, Dayananda. 1960. *The Light of Truth*. Translated by G. P. Upadhyaya. Allahabad: Kala Press.

Sarkar, Tanika. 1991. "The Woman as Communal Subject: Rastrasevika Samiti and Ram Janmabhoomi Movement." *Economic and Political Weekly* 26 (31 August): 2057–62.

———. 1993. "Women's Agency within Authoritarian Communalism: Rastrasevika Samiti and Ramjanmabhoomi." In *Hindus and Others*, edited by Gyanendra Pandey, 24–44. New Delhi: Viking.

———. 1994. "Educating the Children of the Hindu Rashtra: Notes on RSS Schools." *South Asia Bulletin* 14, no. 2: 10–15.

———. 1996. "Imagining Hindurashtra: The Hindu and the Muslim in Bankim Chandra's Writings." In *Making India Hindu*, edited by David Ludden, 162–84. Delhi: Oxford University Press.

Sarkar, Tanika, and Urvashi Butalia, eds. 1995. *Women and Right-Wing Movements: Indian Experiences*. London: Zed Books.

Savarkar, V. D. 1925. *Hindu Pad Padashi—or a Review of the Hindu Empire of Maharashtra*. Madras: B. G. Paul.

———. 1969. *Hindutva*. Bombay: Veer Savarkar Prakashan.

Scott, James. 1985. *Weapons of the Weak: Everyday Forms of Peasant Resistance.* New Haven: Yale University Press.

———. 1990. *Domination and the Art of Resistance.* New Haven: Yale University Press.

Seal, Anil. 1968. *The Emergence of Indian Nationalism: Competition and Collaboration in the Late Nineteenth Century.* Cambridge: Cambridge University Press.

Seshadri, H. V. 1981. *Dr. Hedgewar: The Epoch-maker.* Bangalore: Jagarana Prakashana.

———. 1988. *RSS—A Vision in Action.* Bangalore: Jagarana Prakashana.

———. 1991. *Universal Spirit of Hindu Nationalism.* Madras: VIGIL Publications.

Seth, Sanjay. 1992. "Nationalism, National Identity and 'History': Nehru's Search for India." *Thesis Eleven* no. 32: 37–53.

Sethi, Sunil. 1992. "Making Waves: The Problem." *Seminar* no. 390 (February): 12–15.

Shah, Ghanshyam. 1994. "Identity, Communal Consciousness and Politics." *Economic and Political Weekly* 29 (7 May): 1133–40.

———. 1996. "BJP's Rise to Power." *Economic and Political Weekly* 31 (13 January): 165–71.

Sheth, D. L. 1976. "Profiles of Party Support." *Economic and Political Weekly* 6 (5 January): 278–85.

Singhal, Arvind. 1989. *India's Information Revolution.* New Delhi: Sage Publications.

Sisson, Richard, and Ramashray Roy, eds. 1990. *Diversity and Dominance: Changing Bases of Congress Support.* New Delhi: Sage Publications.

Smith, Donald E. 1963. *India as a Secular State.* Princeton: Princeton University Press.

Speeches Delivered at the National Integration Council. 1992. Bangalore: Jagrita Bharati Prakashana.

Sontheimer, Günther D., and Hermann Kulke, eds. 1989. *Hinduism Reconsidered.* Delhi: Manohar.

Sumante, Yaswant. 1991. "V. D. Savarkar. A Maharashtrian Revolutionary." Ph.D. dissertation, Department of Political Science, Pune University.

Swadeshi Andolan: Struggle for Economic Freedom. 1992. Bangalore: Sahitya Sangama.

Tambiah, Stanley J. 1996. *Levelling Crowds.* Berkeley and Los Angeles: University of California Press.

Tarlo, Emma. 1998. "Paper Truths: Anthropology in the Records Room of the Slum Department of the Municipal Corporation of Delhi." Unpublished paper. London School of Economics.

Taylor, Charles. 1992. *Sources of the Self.* Cambridge: Cambridge University Press.

Taylor, David, and Malcolm Yapp, eds. 1979. *Political Identity in South Asia.* London: Curzon Press.

Thapar, Romila. 1989. "The Ramayana Syndrome." *Seminar* no. 353 (January): 71–75.

———. 1991. "A Historical Perspective on the Story of Rama." In *Anatomy of a Confrontation,* edited by S. Gopal, 141–63. New Delhi: Viking.

———. 1996. "The Theory of Aryan Race and India: History and Politics." *Social Scientist* 24, nos. 272–74: 3–29.

Towards Ram Rajya: Election Manifesto—Our Commitments. 1991. New Delhi: Bharatiya Janata Party.

Tucker, Richard P. 1970. "From Dharmashastra to Politics." *Indian Economic and Social History Review* 7, no. 3: 325–45.

Tuteja, K. L., and O. P. Grewal. 1992. "Emergence of Hindu Communal Ideology in Early Twentieth Century Punjab." *Social Scientist* 20, nos. 7–8 (July-August): 3–27.

Upadhyaya, Deendayal. 1991. *Integral Humanism.* Special Issue of *Manthan.* Delhi: Deendayal Research Institute.

Vaidyanathan, A. 1995. *The Indian Economy: Crisis, Response and Prospects.* Hyderabad: Orient Longman.

Vajpayee, A. B. 1985. *Opening Remarks at the National Executive Meeting.* March 1985. New Delhi: Bharatiya Janata Party.

Vanaik, Achin. 1996. *The Furies of Indian Communalism.* London: Verso.

van der Veer, Peter. 1988. *Gods on Earth: The Management of Religious Experience and Identity in a North Indian Pilgrimage Centre.* London: Athlone.

———. 1989. "The Concept of the Ideal Brahman as an Indological Construct." In *Hinduism Reconsidered,* edited by Günther Sontheimer and Hermann Kulke, 67–80. Delhi: Manohar.

———. 1994. *Religious Nationalism: Hindus and Muslims in India.* Berkeley and Los Angeles: University of California Press.

———. 1995. "The Politics of Devotion to Rama." In *Bhakti Religion in North India: Community, Identity and Political Action,* edited by David N. Lorenzen, 288–305. Albany: State University of New York Press.

———. 1996. "Riots and Rituals: The Construction of Violence and Public Space in Hindu Nationalism." In *Riots and Pogroms,* edited by Paul R. Brass, 154–76. London: Macmillan.

———. 1997. "The Victim's Tale: Memory and Forgetting in the Story of Violence." In *Violence, Identity and Self-Determination,* edited by Hent de Vries and Samuel Weber, 186–200. Stanford: Stanford University Press.

van Dyke, Virginia. 1996. "The Anti-Sikh Riots of 1984 in Delhi: Politicians, Criminals and the Discourse of Communalism." In *Riots and Pogroms,* edited by Paul R. Brass, 201–20. London: Macmillan.

Vishwa Hindu Parishad. 1981. *VHP: Messages and Activities.* New Delhi.

———. 1991. *History versus Casuistry: Evidence of the Ramjanmabhoomi Mandir Presented by the Vishwa Hindu Parishad to the Government of India in December-January 1990–91.* Delhi: Voice of India.

Vivekananda, Swami. 1960. *Complete Works.* 7 vols. Calcutta: Advaita Ashrama.

Wade, Robert. 1989. "Politics and Graft: Recruitment, Appointment and Promotions to Public Office in India." In *Corruption, Inequality and Development,* edited by Peter M. Ward, 73–109. London: Routledge.

Washbrook, David. 1981. "Law, State and Agrarian Society in Colonial India." *Modern Asian Studies* 22: 649–721.

Weiner, Myron. 1967. *Party Building in a New Nation: The Indian National Congress.* Chicago: University of Chicago Press.

Wolpert, Stanley. 1961. *Tilak and Gokhale*. Berkeley and Los Angeles: University of California Press.

Woods, John R., ed. 1984. *State Politics in Contemporary India: Crisis or Continuity?* Boulder, Col: Westview Press.

———. 1987. "Reservations in Doubt: The Backlash against Affirmative Action in Gujarat." *Pacific Affairs* 60, no. 3 (Fall): 408–30.

Working Group Report. 1985. New Delhi: Bharatiya Janata Party.

Yadav, Yogendra. 1993. "Political Change in North India. Interpreting Assembly Election Results." *Economic and Political Weekly* 28 (18 December): 2767–74.

Zavos, John. 1996. "Defending Hindu Tradition: Sanatana Dharma as a Symbol of Orthodoxy in Colonial India." Unpublished paper. Bristol University.

Žižek, Slavoj. 1989. *The Sublime Object of Ideology*. London: Verso.

———. 1992a. "Eastern Europe's Republics of Gilead." In *Dimensions of Radical Democracy*, edited by Chantal Mouffe, 193–207. London: Verso.

———. 1992b. *For They Know Not What They Do*. London: Verso.

———. 1993. *Tarrying with the Negative*. Durham: Duke University Press.

Index

Advani, L. K., 114, 129, 132, 184, 225. *See also* Bharatiya Janata Party

akhara, 93, 248n.3; and wrestlers, 205, 214

Akhil Bharatiya Vidyarti Parishad (ABVP), 99, 130, 168, 261n.37. *See also* Rashtriya Swayamsevak Sangh

Aligarh Muslim University, 73, 240n.14

All India Babri Masjid Action Committee, 175. *See also* Babri Masjid

Ambedkar, Babasaheb, Dr., 226

Arya Samaj, 71–75, 92–93, 127, 227, 245n.17

Aurangabad, 161–62, 169–70

Ayodhya, 125, 150, 155, 157, 164. *See also* Babri Masjid

Babri Masjid, 5, 149–50, 155, 160, 196, 232, 255n.20, 259nn. 19, 22, 23, and 24, 261n.45; and archeology, 175, 262n.49; demolition of, 182–85, 263nn. 55 and 56. *See also* Ramjanmabhoomi

Babri Masjid Action Committee, 163

Bajrang Dal, 100, 154, 163. *See also* Vishwa Hindu Parishad

Benares Hindu University, 73, 74

Bengal, 69–70, 71

Bhagalpur, 162. *See also* communalism

Bhagwa Dhwaj, 98, 108, 110

Bharat Mata, 83, 94, 112, 154, 257n.1

Bharati, Uma, 166, 180. *See also* Vishwa Hindu Parishad

Bharatiya Janata Party (BJP), 3, 98, 133, 157–59; and communal tension, 160–64, 186–87, 225, 256n.21, 259n.18, 260n.28; economic policy of, 172, 261n.44; and electoral performance, 158, 163, 166–67, 198–99, 221–23, 258n.13, 260nn. 34 and 36; and governance, 197, 219–23; and minorities, 158, 225–26; national executive of, 159; and regional allies, 218; strategies of, 157–72, 186, 197, 220–21, 258nn. 10, 11, 12, and 14

Bharatiya Janata Sangh (BJS), 84–85, 105, 115, 126–33, 158, 248n.5, 252nn. 33, 34, 35, and 36; and RSS, 128–29; constituen-cies of, 120, 127–29; and Janata Party, 131–33

Bihar, 158, 163, 165

Bombay Presidency, 75; and policing, 201–2

Brahminical culture, 107–8, 110–11, 113–15, 227; and democracy, 145–48; in Pune, 116–19; in Thane, 99–101, 192; and tribals, 103–7

Bukhari, Imam, 151

caste, 17; adjudication of, 34–36; associations, 35; and democracy, 147–48; reform of, 74; and RSS, 121–26. *See also* community

Chattopadhyaya, Bankimchandra, 68–69, 112

Chinmayananda, Swami, 156, 250n.18

Chitpavan brahmins, 96, 115, 119, 126, 249nn. 9 and 10. *See also* Pune

civilization, 11; Aryan/Vedic, 65–67, 75, 227, 246n.24; Hindu, 76, 77, 231

clientelism; 135–36; and populism, 137, 142. *See also* corruption

communalism, 55–56, 125; and colonial-ism, 200–202, 240n.13, 241n.17; Hindu, 159–60; and identity, 192–96, 202–9; and mythical knowledge, 195–96, 203–5, 264nn. 11 and 12; in north India, 37, 165–66; and violence, 200, 204–7

communitas, 37–38, 184; and ritual, 213

community: enumeration of, 36–37; Hindu, 13, 36, 38; objectification of, 65–67; religious, 34; representation of, 40; rights of, 35; village, 51–52

Congress Party, 5, 37, 40, 44, 48, 57, 76, 92, 94, 118, 128; and Ayodhya, 182–85; constituencies of, 166–67, 253n.2; crisis of, 152–53; hegemony of, 134–40; and Indira Gandhi, 129–30, 131–32, 141, 148, 253n.1, 255n.17; and Rajiv Gandhi, 138–40, 148–49, 160, 166, 231, 253n.5; and religious symbolism, 148–50

corruption, 16, 50, 222–23, 253n.4; and dalal, 136–37

Cow Protection Movement, 38, 112